CORNELL STUDIES IN CLASSICAL PHILOLOGY

EDITED BY

W. R. JOHNSON * G. M. KIRKWOOD
GORDON M. MESSING * PIERO PUCCI

VOLUME XXXIX

Lucan: An Introduction

Poetry and Poetics from
Ancient Greece to the Renaissance
Studies in Honor of James Hutton

Early Greek Monody
by G. M. Kirkwood

The Attalids of Pergamon
by Esther V. Hansen

Sophrosyne
by Helen North

St. Jerome as a Satirist
by David S. Wiesen

LUCAN

AN INTRODUCTION

FREDERICK M. AHL

CORNELL UNIVERSITY PRESS

ITHACA AND LONDON

1976

Cornell University Press gratefully acknowledges
a grant from the Andrew J. Mellon Foundation
that aided in bringing this book to publication.

First published 1976 by Cornell University Press.
Published in the United Kingdom by Cornell University Press Ltd.,
2-4 Brook Street, London W1Y 1AA.

International Standard Book Number 0-8014-0837-7
Library of Congress Catalog Card Number 75-16926
Printed in the United States of America by Vail-Ballou Press, Inc.
*Librarians: Library of Congress cataloging information
appears on the last page of the book.*

For Mary, Sid, and Kathleen

Preface

This book examines the meaning of the *Pharsalia* and, so far as can be determined, Lucan's purpose in writing it the way he did. I hope to provide some fresh perspectives on the poet and his work and to present them in a form accessible to the Latinless reader as well as to the classicist.

The poet, his subject matter, and his historical and political views are highly controversial. It is, therefore, all too easy for the critic of the *Pharsalia* to find himself disputing Lucan's ideas rather than describing them. Since my chief concern is to establish what Lucan's vision is, not to quarrel with it, I have tried to represent his perspectives as accurately and objectively as I can. The "facts" that I am concerned with are what Lucan has to say in his epic, and it is to these "facts" that I attempt to remain faithful.

To achieve a measure of critical objectivity, I have based my treatment of the *Pharsalia* throughout on a close reading of the original. Above all, I have avoided attributing to Lucan ideas he himself does not actually express. One of the greatest obstacles to our understanding of Lucan (and of other Latin poets) has been that curious mode of argument which runs: Lucan is a Stoic, therefore he must hold such and such to be true. Indeed, Lucan makes prolific use of Stoic thought and diction. But Roman Stoicism is far from monolithic, and Lucan does not always use in the *Pharsalia* some of the most widespread Stoic notions, such as that of a beneficent providence. Lucan's divergences from mainstream Stoicism may be as important as—if not more important than—his areas of conformity. In them we discern that vital individuality which marks him off from Seneca and Cornutus.

Similarly, though it is obvious that Lucan is much influenced by Vergil, scant justice is done either poet by setting up a straw Vergil to simplify the discussion of Lucan. Vergil's poetry, particularly the *Aeneid,* is remarkably elusive, susceptible of various interpretations, yet ultimately defying them all. To understand the relationship of the *Pharsalia* to the *Aeneid* we must somehow come to terms not just with what Vergil means but with what Lucan takes him to mean. I have therefore kept general assumptions about Lucan's attitudes toward philosophy and the poetic tradition to a minimum; these are issues to be explored, not presupposed.

In organizing my material into chapters I have generally concentrated the treatment of the themes and motifs of the *Pharsalia* around Lucan's characters—as Lucan himself does. The first two chapters, however, are intended as a preamble to the discussion of the *Pharsalia* itself. Chapter 1 explores the political and literary milieu in which Lucan lived and wrote, discusses such details of his biography as seem reasonably sure, and examines the question as to whether the invocation of Nero in *Pharsalia* 1 or the criticism of imperial power elsewhere in the epic sets the political tone of the *Pharsalia.* Chapter 2 assesses Lucan's reasons for approaching heroic epic in an unconventional way and gives some account of the reaction to the *Pharsalia* in antiquity. Chapters 3 and 4 explore some of Lucan's themes as evidenced in his treatment of minor characters, and set the backdrop for the discussion of the protagonists. Chapters 5, 6, and 7 are studies of Pompey, Caesar, and Cato. I have reserved my discussion of them until the middle chapters because it is not until *Pharsalia* 7 that Lucan allows them to dominate his narrative; they share the earlier books with a variety of lesser characters. Chapter 8 discusses Lucan's use of the divine and his substitutes for the traditional Olympians. Chapter 9 synthesizes the ideas and motifs mentioned in the earlier chapters and brings them to bear on the problem of the scope Lucan envisaged for his completed work. Finally, there is the Appendix. To it I have relegated questions pertaining to Lucan's biography that are susceptible of only the most speculative answers.

I have not devoted separate chapters to Lucan's treatment of history and philosophy. Rather, I have discussed the major historical and philosophical issues in the contexts where they arise, for I believe that it is better not to isolate the historical and philosophical elements from one another and from the events and characters of the epic.

The Latin text of Lucan used (unless otherwise noted) is that of A. E. Housman, though I have not always followed his spelling and punctuation. Citations from Vergil are from Mynors' Oxford Classical Text. All quotations from Latin and Greek authors are either translated or paraphrased throughout the main body of the book. This practice is not extended to the footnotes, however, since the result would have been an unconscionable increase in the size of this volume. Occasionally translations of passages cited more than once may vary, to permit emphasis on a particular point that may be more important in the context of one discussion than of another. Unless otherwise noted, all translations are my own.

I should like to express my sincere thanks to the many scholars who have helped me in the preparation of this study. My greatest debts are to Gordon Kirkwood, Susan Nugent, John Garthwaite, Frederick Williams, M. Gwyn Morgan, and the anonymous reader for Cornell University Press. They saved me from many errors—factual, stylistic, judgmental—and offered invaluable suggestions. I owe much also to Piero Pucci, James Hutton, Ralph Johnson, Douglass Parker, John Fitch, Al Shoaf, John Sullivan, and David Armstrong. A special word of thanks is due to James Bishop and Leoda Anderson, whose friendship and advice helped me over many difficulties. I am much indebted to Cornell University for research grants in 1971 and 1972 that enabled me to prepare the groundwork for this study and to the editors of *Hermes, Latomus, TAPA,* and *Classica et Mediaevalia* for allowing me to re-use portions of the following articles: "The Pivot of the *Pharsalia*," and "The Shadows of a Divine Presence in the *Pharsalia*," *Hermes* 102 (1974), 305–320 and 566–590; "Hercules and Curio: Some Comments on *Pharsalia* IV, 581–824," *Latomus* 31 (1972), 997–1009; "Lucan's *De Incendio Urbis, Epistulae ex Campania,* and Nero's Ban," *TAPA* 102 (1971), 1–27; "Pharsalus and the *Pharsalia*," *CM* 29 (1968), 124–161; "Appius Claudius and Sextus Pompey in Lucan," *CM* 30 (1969), 331–346. But above all, it has been the help, guidance, and tolerance of my wife, Mary, that has made the toil of writing and rewriting the numerous drafts bearable.

FREDERICK M. AHL

Ithaca, New York

Contents

Abbreviations

Abbreviated titles of ancient works are those used in the *Oxford Classical Dictionary*.

ABSA   *Annals of the British School at Athens*
AeR   *Atene e Roma*
AIV   *Atti dell' Instituto Veneto di Scienze, Lettere ed Arti, Classe di Scienze morali e Lettere*
AJP   *American Journal of Philology*
Ant. Class.   *L'Antiquité Classique*
CAH   *Cambridge Ancient History*
CHJ   *Cambridge Historical Journal*
CIL   *Corpus Inscriptionum Latinarum*
CM   *Classica et Mediaevalia*
CP   *Classical Philology*
CQ   *Classical Quarterly*
CR   *Classical Review*
CW   *Classical World*
FH 15   *Fondation Hardt, Entretiens* vol. 15, *Lucain*, ed. F. Durry. Vandoeuvres-Genève, 1970.
FHG   *Fragmenta Historicorum Graecorum*, ed. Müller. Paris, 1841–1870.
GRBS   *Greek, Roman, and Byzantine Studies*
HSCP   *Harvard Studies in Classical Philology*
HThR   *Harvard Theological Review*
IL   *L'Information Littéraire*
JHP   *Journal of the History of Philosophy*
JRS   *Journal of Roman Studies*
Klass. Phil. Stud.   *Klassisch-Philologische Studien*
MH   *Museum Helveticum*
PBSR   *Papers of the British School at Rome*
PQ   *Philological Quarterly*
RE   *Realencyclopädie der Classischen Altertumswissenschaft*, ed. A. Pauly, G. Wissowa, W. Kroll, and Karl Mittelhaus. Stuttgart, 1894–.
REA   *Revue des Etudes Anciennes*
REL   *Revue des Etudes Latines*

RFC *Rivista di Filologia Classica*
RFIC *Rivista di Filologia e di Istruzione Classica*
RhM *Rheinisches Museum für Philologie*
RIGI *Rivista Indo-Greca-Italica di Filologia, Lingua, Antichità*
RSC *Rivista di Studi Classici*
RSI *Rivista Storica Italiana*
SIFC *Studi Italiani di Filologia Classica*
SO *Symbolae Osloenses*
SP *Studies in Philology*
SR *Studi Romani*
SVF *Stoicorum Veterum Fragmenta*, ed. J. von Arnim. 4 vols., Leipzig, 1903.
TAPA *Transactions of the American Philological Association*
TRSC *Transactions of the Royal Society of Canada*
WS *Wiener Studien*
YClS *Yale Classical Studies*

LUCAN

An Introduction

CHAPTER 1

Introduction to the Poet
and His Age

I. The Poet and the Principate

The majority of Roman writers of the first and early second centuries A.D. take a cynical view of the world in which they live. The attacks on the abuse of power, wealth, and human life in Petronius, Persius, Martial, Tacitus, Juvenal, and Suetonius are familiar enough to even the casual reader of the classics. Often neglected, however, is the degree to which this cynicism is found, in one form or another, in writers less frequently read by the modern reader. Valerius Flaccus informs us in the first book of his *Argonautica* that people of his day have little use for the delights of Elysium.[1] Silius Italicus wishes that Carthage were still standing—better this than that Rome should be what it is in his age.[2] Lucan's disgust at contemporary decadence as well as Seneca's —and indeed Statius'—vivid portraits of tyrannical savagery and callousness show the same urge to describe a world poised on the brink of spiritual bankruptcy.

There are, of course, exceptions to this widespread disenchantment, but they are few. We may adduce the rather hollow flattery rendered to Domitian by Statius in the *Silvae* and by Martial in the *Epigrams,* or the relief expressed by Pliny and Tacitus at the improved atmosphere in the reigns of Nerva and Trajan.[3] The

---

1. *Argon.* 1.833–846.   2. *Pun.* 10.658.

3. On the flattery of Domitian see O. Weinreich, *Studien zu Martial,* Stuttgart, 1928, particularly 155–170; K. Scott, "Statius' Adulation of Domitian," *AJP* 54 (1933), 247–259; G. Lugli, "La Roma di Domiziano nei Versi di Marziale e di Stazio," *SR* 9 (1961), 1–17; P. Ercole, "Stazio e Giovenale," *RIGI* 25 (1931), 43–50; D. Nisard, *Études sur les poètes latines de la décadence²,* Paris, 1849, 262 ff.; David Vessey, *Statius and the Thebaid,* Cambridge, 1973, 1–7,

only clearly enthusiastic view of the post-Augustan world is that of Velleius Paterculus, but then he knew only the first of Augustus' successors.

Even if the accounts of Tacitus, Suetonius, and others often do less than justice to the positive achievements of the Caesars, there is little reason to doubt that vexation and despondency at the political situation in the Roman world lay at the roots of Silver Age cynicism. Life under Tiberius, Claudius, Nero, and Domitian could hardly merit expressions of enthusiasm from the literate upper and middle classes. The abuse of power by the Caesars might seem, in itself, sufficient grounds for hostility. But what made things worse was the feeling that the Caesars had no right to exercise power at all. For Tacitus, as R. Syme observes, "the essential falsity of the principate lay in the fiction that the supreme authority in the Roman state was voluntarily offered [sc., to the *princeps*] and legally conveyed, or at least ratified." [4] But the principate was not, in either theory or practice, a magistracy. Unlike the dictator of republican times, the *princeps* had no constitutional right to exercise executive power. While it is true that none of the powers Augustus held was without precedent of some sort, and that these powers were generally both magisterial and constitutional, the mere agglomeration of magisterial powers by Augustus did not convert his position as *princeps* into a magistracy per se.

The Julio-Claudians usually sought confirmation of their powers by the army, senate, and people, but this approval, except in the case of the army, was a formality. Only the army held the raw power to make or dispose of emperors. But the army's power in politics was hardly constitutional. It was not legally entitled to

---

and the sources cited there. For the reaction of Tacitus to the principates of Nerva and Trajan, see *Hist.* 1.1. In general, I disagree with the conclusion of these scholars that Statius intended his flattery of Domitian sincerely, for reasons discussed in Section II of this Chapter.

4. *Tacitus*, Oxford, 1963, 1.412. If we remember, however, that some scholars have argued a rather different view of the principate, we can see the importance of establishing this point. B. Henderson, for example, in *The Life and Principate of the Emperor Nero*, London, 1903, offers the following definition: the *princeps* was "but a magistrate endowed, *ad hoc*, with powers extraordinary alike in content, combination and duration, but always conferred and approved by Army, by Senate and by People" (p. 10).

bestow any kind of public office on anyone. When Tacitus refers, in *Annales* 1.7, to the *senatus milesque et populus* he is commenting ironically on the de facto not on the de jure situation. Even if we are not prepared to go as far as Syme, who, in the opening sentence of his *Tacitus*, observes: "the principate arose through usurpation," we must concede that it resulted from the *breakdown* of constitutional government.[5]

It is quite understandable, then, that elements within the senate should have balked at recognizing the principate as a duly constituted magistracy, since it was, indeed, nothing of the sort. Tacitus saw the title *princeps* as the veil with which Augustus masked his power.[6] And here, perhaps, lay the most irritating facet of the principate. Augustus took some pains to maintain the fiction that the new government was essentially a continuation of the republic, that no fundamental change had taken place. Tiberius, on his accession, followed suit. As a result there was no attempt to define, in constitutional terms, what the *princeps* was. Theoretically the senate and people still controlled the state, but clearly they did not really do so. Popular elections were either done away with or rendered meaningless by the practice of *destinatio;* imperial nomination became the pathway to high public office.[7] The reduction of the consuls' tenure to six months by using *consules suffecti* combined with the growth of an imperial—and often non-Latin—bureaucracy responsible only to the *princeps* threatened to reduce the senate to a position of inferior administrative and even more inferior legislative status.[8] Senators resented not only the curtailing of their prerogatives but also the galling fabrication that they could still act independently of the palace.

There would probably have been less friction between senate and Caesars if the Caesars had defined their powers more clearly.

5. *Ibid.,* ix.
6. *Ann.* 1.1: "nomine principis sub imperium accepit." Also *ibid.,* 1.9: "non regno tamen neque dictatura sed principis nomine constitutam rem publicam." See also Syme, *Tacitus,* 1.408: "Between the formula and the realities a wide gap yawned. The main elements in the supremacy of Augustus derive from sources outside the Roman constitution."
7. H. H. Scullard, *From the Gracchi to Nero*[2], London, 1963, 231–235, 283; 433, note 6, and the sources cited there.
8. For the freedmen, particularly in Claudius' reign, see Suetonius *Claud.* 28–29 and P. R. C. Weaver, *Familia Caesaris,* Cambridge, 1972, 199–296.

No doubt the fate of Julius Caesar proved to be a deterrent to Augustus and Tiberius, who probably felt it safer to leave matters judiciously undefined. It was left to Domitian to adopt the title *Dominus et Deus* (Lord and God) and to put an end, once and for all, to the Augustan myth of the division of power.[9] After Domitian there was no question of the emperor being merely *primus inter pares*. Hateful though Domitian's action seemed, it served as a constitutional landmark, finally delineating the emperor's relationship to the state as both its secular and religious leader.

Because the Julio-Claudians were less bold than Domitian, they encouraged, albeit unintentionally, the *stasis* between curia and palace. Their lip service to the division of power kept republican dreams alive in the opposition. By refusing to define their own position in terms of the constitution they made it easy for their foes to characterize them as usurpers of power. Their attempts to "load" the senate with their own nominees often strengthened rather than weakened the opposition. The new senators were absorbed by the old traditions; they, rather than the senate, changed. The careers of the elder Cato and of Cicero should have served as warnings that *novi homines* could demonstrate surprising vigor. The Caesars learned by painful experience that the new nobility, such as the Annaei, Thrasea Paetus, and Helvidius Priscus, could prove more troublesome than the often decadent last scions of the great families of the republic.

Yet if the position of the *principes* themselves was somewhat ambiguous, so were the attitudes of senatorial writers. Seneca, in the *De Clementia*, asks Nero to consider himself and his powers in the following way:

Have I of all mortals found favour with heaven and been chosen to serve on earth as vicar of the gods? I am the arbiter of life and death for the nations; it rests in my power what each man's lot and state shall be; by my lips Fortune proclaims what gifts she would bestow on each human being; from my utterances people and cities gather reasons

9. On the title *Dominus et Deus* see K. Scott, *The Imperial Cult under the Flavians*, Stuttgart, 1936, 61–188; also F. Sauter, *Der Römische Kaiserkult bei Martial und Statius*, Stuttgart, 1934, 36–40.

for rejoicing; without my favour and grace no part of the wide world can prosper; all those many thousands of swords which my peace restrains will be drawn at my nod; what nations shall be utterly destroyed, which banished, which shall receive the gift of liberty, which shall have it taken from them, what kings shall become slaves, and whose heads shall be crowned with royal honour, what cities shall fall and which shall rise—this it is mine to decree.[10]

There is nothing here to suggest a magistracy; rather we see a power almost godlike or, at the very least, divinely sanctioned. It is bewildering that a man like Seneca should have filled the head of his young charge with such notions. Perhaps his purpose was to mold Nero into a Just King; perhaps it was a ploy to lure Nero away from Agrippina's influence by fantasies of independent power. Even if Seneca is being ironic, he must bear the responsibility for encouraging megalomania in Nero. It is indeed curious that the author of the *Thyestes* and the *Trojan Women,* who knew so well the corruption that absolute power works in its holders, should offer such advice.

At the same time, Seneca's words to Nero underscore the paradoxical situation of the Roman at the hub of power during the first century A.D. Although Seneca may have resented the power of emperors as much as Tacitus did, there was not much he or anyone else among the aristocracy could do to check it. One could, of course, play Cato in the senate, as Thrasea Paetus did, reminding one's listeners of the illegality of imperial power. The alternatives were to cooperate silently or to accept the power for what it had come to be, regardless of legalities, and attempt to shape it into something noble and good. But very few senators ever had the sort of influence that Seneca exercised at Nero's court. By and large they cooperated silently and resentfully, saving their wrath for their histories, letters, and poetry. Their bitterness was doubtless accentuated by the fact that they too shared some burden of guilt by their political passivity.

II. The Roman Microcosm

In most countries and in most ages, an oppressive political cli-

10. *Clem.* 1.1.2; trans. by J. W. Basore in the Loeb Seneca, *Moral Essays,* 1, London, 1928.

mate might induce one to pack his bags and leave the country. But the Roman world, unlike some modern nations, needed no walls and guards to prevent that. By the time of Augustus, the whole of the Mediterranean was under Roman control either directly or indirectly. Outside this Roman enclave, only the Parthians among all nations west of the Indus could make any pretence to an advanced culture. No matter how much someone wanted to escape, there was nowhere to go. No province was strong enough to shelter a writer or political figure who had angered the emperor. The Arsacid monarchy in Parthia was not an attractive alternative. One would merely change a familiar tyranny for an unfamiliar one, while sacrificing one's whole cultural and linguistic identity.

Even in desperation, Romans were unwilling to turn to Parthia for help. Their reasons are sketched by Lucan in the *Pharsalia*. When Pompey suggests that the defeated republicans turn to Parthia for aid against Caesar, he is overruled by the angry Lentulus who declares that this is the one nation in the world he would rejoice to see conquered by Caesar himself. Every imaginable prejudice Lentulus can find is hurled against the Parthians. He conjures up allegations of everything from sexual profligacy to racial inferiority to defeat Pompey's arguments. The only possible door to the world outside is slammed shut; the Roman is trapped by his own Romanness.[11]

Vast though the Roman empire was, it was also paradoxically small. Its largeness made it a prison in times of political oppression; nothing was beyond the emperor's reach. Outside, there was no acceptable refuge. The senatorial opposition may be forgiven for taking a somewhat jaded view of Roman greatness; they had conquered the world only to lose their freedom to the Caesars. As Lucan's Curio declares to Julius Caesar in *Pharsalia* 1.285: "tibi Roma subegerit orbem" (Rome will have conquered the world for you). When Silius Italicus exclaims "potius Carthago maneres" (Carthage, better you were still standing), we should not view his words as utterly hyperbolic.[12] Though the destruction of Carthage had eliminated the greatest obstacle to Roman expansion, it also

11. *Pharsalia* 8.325–455; see also M. P. Charlesworth, "The Fear of the Orient in the Roman Empire," *CHJ* 2 (1926), 1–16.
12. *Pun.* 10.658.

removed the last major force in the Mediterranean that kept Roman swords from Roman throats.

The disintegration and collapse of the republic at Rome must have affected the intelligent Roman much as the aftermath of the Macedonian conquest of Greece had affected his Athenian predecessor. The focus of his political life had shifted dramatically; he had lost something of his political identity. Even the professional writers of Augustus' literary circles who were largely men of bourgeois status show, to varying degrees, ambivalence about the new political order. Doubts about the Caesars and about the blessings of the *Pax Augusta* were by no means confined to the aristocratic circles of later generations. In fact, our general assessment of Augustan literature might be considerably modified if we had more senatorial writing of that period, if we had Asinius Pollio as well as Livy, or Gallus in addition to Tibullus and Propertius. As we shall see in Chapter 3, there are striking similarities between the tone of Horace, *Odes* 2.1 (which may well reflect Asinius Pollio's view of the civil war) and the theme of Lucan's *Pharsalia*.[13]

Offsetting the advantages of imperial prosperity, at least to the educated, was the fact that a monarchical government, however benevolent, ran counter to the basic ideology of the Greco-Roman world. Athenian and Roman alike found it difficult to reconcile the ideals of *eleutheria* and *libertas* with an absolute ruler.[14] Thus, no matter how happy the Augustan may have been to see the restoration of peace and order, the Caesars posed an ideological dilemma. And one element in the Roman experience made it even more sour than that of the Greeks under Philip and Alexander. The Roman could not claim that he had lost his freedom because of some powerful, *external* foe. Rome had collapsed of her own strength, as Horace suggests in *Odes* 2.1 and *Epodes* 7 and 16.[15]

13. For Lucan's sources see R. Pichon, *Les Sources de Lucain*, Paris, 1912, 51 ff., and particularly 51–105; also P. Grimal, "Le Poète et l'histoire," in *FH* 15.69; H.-P. Syndikus, "Lucans Gedicht vom Bürgerkrieg," Diss. Munich, 1958, chap. 1; C. Hosius, "Lucan und seine Quellen," *RhM*, N.F. 48 (1893), 380–397.

14. For a full discussion of the notion of *libertas* at Rome see C. Wirszubski, *Libertas as a Political Idea at Rome during the Late Republic and Early Empire*, Cambridge, 1950.

15. Cf. R. Syme, *The Roman Revolution*, Oxford, 1939, 1–9, and Chapter 3 below.

We should not be unduly perplexed, then, by the fact that Roman writers are possessed of a remarkable urge to self-scrutiny. Obviously their strength of hand had not failed them, as it had failed the Athenians; something must have gone wrong inside the Roman spirit. There must have been a moral breakdown within the state and within the individual. Given this perspective, a man like Julius Caesar could easily come to represent the invincible yet amoral might of the Roman genius, capable of turning the sword of victory into the very vitals of the state. Such raw expertise in power became less attractive than a stubborn, if politically impotent, display of dedication to principle. Lost political freedom led to a quest for the freedom that the Stoic sage could enjoy within the realm of his own soul, a freedom that could not be affected by tyranny or physical suffering. Man struggled to retain a sense of his own dignity and autonomy by denying that events outside his immediate control could affect him detrimentally. This thinking was not restricted to the Stoics; it can be found in many Greek and Roman writers of both the Alexandrian and early imperial periods. A typical instance occurs in this passage from Plutarch:

> καὶ ὁ Ζήνων ἐπανορθούμενος τὸ τοῦ Σοφοκλέους·
> "ὅστις δὲ πρὸς τύραννον ἐμπορεύεται,
> κείνου 'στι δοῦλος, κἂν ἐλεύθερος μόλῃ"
> μετέγραφεν
> "οὐκ ἔστι δοῦλος, ἢν ἐλεύθερος μόλῃ."
> [Plutarch *Quomodo adulescens poetas audire debeat* 33 D]

(And Zeno *corrected* Sophocles' remark: "Whoever engages in dealings with a tyrant becomes his slave, even if he acted of his own free will." Zeno wrote in reply: "He is not a slave, if he acted of his own free will.")

That Plutarch believes Sophocles was in error shows that he agrees with the Stoic Zeno at least on this point. The absolute distinction drawn by Sophocles is typical of an age and society accustomed to freedom, where tyranny is usually a threat, not a permanent reality. Zeno's reply reflects an age when there was no means to avoid some kind of transaction with a tyrant, short of total withdrawal from social life. What matters to Zeno, and to most Roman moralists, is the frame of mind in which one approaches such transactions.

Ultimately, however, withdrawal into a search for philosophical virtue was not enough, particularly for the more fiery soul. Even the Stoic could not entirely resign his concern for the external world so readily. He found that he, like the Aristotelian great-souled man, needed something of the external to actualize his potential. Further, the Stoic doctrine of the interrelationship of all matter in a totally material universe still left him indissolubly bound within the causal nexus.[16] His philosophy proved, in the long run, a rather limited consolation. Seneca's life and works show this all too clearly. The composed facade of the philosopher is but one of his three masks.[17] It is offset by the callous pragmatism of Seneca the statesman, and the anguished gloom and despair of Seneca the tragedian. It is pointless to argue which mask shows us the real Seneca. Probably they all do, for the Roman identity was split, each element at war with the others.

III. The Man of Letters in a Totalitarian Society

A writer, regardless of his social status, has good reason to feel oppressed in a totalitarian society, whether it be military dictatorship or Platonic Utopia. The more broadly educated the individual, the more difficult to ensure his absolute conformity to anything. Further, if he is also a prominent public figure, he is an even greater potential threat to ruling powers or ideologies. If he is not carefully checked by bribery, censorship, or threats to his personal safety, his ideas may corrupt and subvert others. A dicta-

16. For a good assessment of the atmosphere, see C. J. Herington, "Senecan Tragedy," *Arion* 5, 4 (1966), 422–471. For a discussion of Stoic notions of the physical nature of the universe, see S. Sambursky, *The Physics of the Stoics*, London, 1959; H.-A. Schotes, *Stoische Physik, Psychologie und Theologie bei Lucan*, Bonn 1969, 14–46; also Chapter 3 below.

17. Herington, 422 ff., thinks of Seneca as a man of two rather than three masks. But it would be wrong to consider any one of his "personalities" more real than the others. It is not so much that the "real" Seneca assumes two alien guises in addition to his true personality, but that all three of his guises are no less real or unreal than the others. In fact, we could make a case for distinguishing between the Seneca of the *Epistles to Lucilius* and the Seneca of the *Moral Essays*, for even in his philosophical works, Seneca's pose varies.

torship or doctrinaire ideology cannot ignore the intellectual if its rule is to be secure.

At the beginning of the principate at Rome, many writers felt, no doubt, that the advantages of the new administration were no less evident than its drawbacks. But as years passed and the situation that gave rise to the change of government lost its immediacy, a more critical awareness of the new system's flaws emerged. Further, as the principate became thoroughly entrenched and began to flex its muscles, the need for placatory offerings to the literati declined. Tiberius, Caligula, and Claudius were far less concerned than Augustus with establishing a good press for themselves, and thus far less tolerant of opposition. They committed the error to which autocracies are prone: giving little encouragement to writers who might praise them, discouraging the able but faint-hearted, and offering martyrdom to anyone who sought to oppose them. They drew attention to the ideas of their foes by persecuting them and thus exaggerated the dimensions of the causes they were trying to suppress.

During this period the writer's position became increasingly un-comfortable and dangerous. Lack of imperial patronage was in it-self a damaging blow to literature; these must have been lean years for the professional writer. In fact, the only notable names of Latin writers whose productive years lay in the reigns of Tiberius and Caligula are Cremutius Cordus, Velleius Paterculus, Manilius, Phaedrus, and Valerius Maximus. Cremutius' works were burned, as those of Labienus had been burned by Augustus.[18] Other writers of the period are known by their fates rather than their works: Aelius Saturninus and Sextus Paconianus were put to death by Tiberius on the grounds that they had attacked him in their verse; Mamercus Aemilius Scaurus felt obliged to commit suicide after being accused of maligning Tiberius in a tragedy; an un-known writer of farce was burned alive by Caligula.[19]

Total silence is the writer's last resort; it is the ultimate paralysis occurring only in the most extreme situations of terror and repression. But there are varying degrees of silence. The writer ignores certain subjects or approaches them with great caution: forth-

18. Tacitus *Ann.* 4.34–35; see also Dio 57.24.2–3; Suetonius *Tib.* 61. For Labienus, see Seneca *Controv.* 10, preface 4–8.
19. Suetonius *Calig.* 27.

rightness is replaced by a studied obliqueness. Cicero, in *Ad Atticum* 2.20, observes:

De re publica breviter ad te scribam; iam enim charta ipsa ne nos prodat pertimesco. itaque posthac, si erunt mihi plura ad te scribenda, ἀλληγορίαις obscurabo.

(I shall now write you a few words about the political situation: I'm beginning to fear that the very paper I use will betray us. If I have anything else to write you about in future, I'll veil it in allegory.)

Cicero wishes to continue communication, but feels he can do so with impunity only if he disguises his steps. An adverse political climate forces the writer to adopt allegory, double entendre, and innuendo as part of his rhetorical armory.

The writer at Rome in the Silver Age was quite prepared both to communicate and to detect such literary undercurrents. Seneca, for example, in *De Ira* 1.20.4, takes the oft-quoted line from Accius' tragedy, *Atreus*, "oderint dum metuant" (let them hate, provided that they fear), and comments thus on the play: "Sullano scias saeculo scriptam" (You would know that it was written in the time of Sulla). Caligula had given new life to Accius' words; so had Tiberius. In fact, Tiberius added a personal twist to the quotation: "oderint dum probent" (let them hate provided that they go along with what I want).[20] Men of letters and *principes* alike were well aware that Accius' drama was not merely a reworking of the tale of the house of Atreus; it bore the mark of the terror under Sulla and continued to be recognized as a comment on the tyrannical mind for years to come.

In making his observation about this remark in Accius' play, Seneca invites us to look at his own tragedies in a similar light. Can we not detect from this passage that Seneca himself is affected with a little of the atmosphere of his own age?

Eteocles: . . . Pro regno velim . . .
Iocasta: Patriam, penates, coniugem flammis dare?
Eteocles: Imperia pretio quolibet constant bene.

[*Phoenissae* 662–664]

20. O. Ribbeck, *Tragicorum Romanorum Fragmenta*, Leipzig, 1887, 1.187; Suetonius *Calig.* 30; *Tib.* 59.

Eteocles: To be a king I would willingly . . .
Jocasta: Destroy your native land and gods and wife with fire?
Eteocles: Power is a bargain no matter what the price you pay.)

The later years of the reign of Claudius and the early years of Nero provided a somewhat improved atmosphere for writers.[21] With this came the burgeoning of literature which continued into the second century A.D. Nero, in particular, was a generous patron of the arts. There is little evidence that prior to A.D. 65 his principate was notable for the repression of free thought and expression, even though most historical sources are extremely hostile to Nero. Yet we should not conclude that openness and frankness were common among writers of the Neronian age. Persius notes in his first satire how impossible it is to be a Lucilius any more:

> Sed quid opus teneras mordaci radere vero
> auriculas? vide sis ne maiorum tibi forte
> limina frigescant: sonat hic de nare canina
> littera.   [*Satire* 1.107–109]

(But what's the point of nagging sensitive ears with biting truth? Be careful that the doors of the mighty do not freeze you out! They don't snarl with written words, but straight through the nose.)

Persius warns himself and others of the dangers of yapping at the heels of powerful men, biting their sensitive ears with the truth. For when they bite back, it is not with words; their fangs are real. The prudent course, the poet concludes, is to confine oneself to literary topics. The mythological bombast of the age, however wretched, has the merit of being safe. As Juvenal was to observe in a later generation, one had better forget the real criminals unless one desired to conclude one's life as a torch in the arena (*Satire* 1.155–157).

These observations on the impossibility of writing true satire, however, constitute a form of direct criticism. Even to remind one's readers of the inadvisability of free speech in view of the potential reprisals is a slashing political comment. And, curiously enough, there were factors at work during the last half of the first

21. See G. Charles-Picard, *Augustus and Nero*, trans. Len Ortzen, New York, 1968, 85 ff. For a somewhat different view, see M. A. Levi, *Nerone e i suoi Tempi*, Milan, 1949, 84–112.

century A.D. that made critical comment somewhat easier than it had been under the earlier *principes*.

Emperors like Nero and Domitian, who demanded divine honors from the Romans and encouraged poets to compare them to the gods, opened up new avenues for satire.[22] Domitian, who assumed the title of Lord and God, could hardly take exception to a poem in which he was compared to Jupiter, even though such an analogy might be somewhat double-edged. In *Silvae* 3.4, for instance, Statius compares the relationship of Domitian and his eunuch favorite Earinus to that of Jupiter and Ganymede. What sours the ostensibly flattering analogy is, of course, the tradition that Jupiter's rape of Ganymede was prompted by homosexual passion. "The paths of flattery are ever fraught with hidden dangers," David Vessey comments cryptically on this passage.[23] Must we really presume that Statius had not realized the less savory implications of his analogy, even when he assures us in his preface to *Silvae* 3 that he had hesitated long in preparing and presenting this poem? Vessey himself seems to appreciate that his explanation is not really adequate, so he takes another tack a few lines later: "But Statius does not want any unfortunate conclusions to be drawn from too close an interpretation of this analogy." [24] How, one wonders, does Vessey know this? Even if he were right, however, the fundamental question has eluded him. If, as Quintilian notes (*Inst.* 8.3. 47), readers of the first century A.D. were not likely to bypass the opportunity to adduce the worst meaning, "occasionem turpitudinis rapere," how could Statius be fairly sure that *Domitian* would not draw unfortunate conclusions? The protest, "Sire, you read it too closely; I did not want unfortunate conclusions drawn," would have been to no avail. Suetonius tells us of the fate of a writer whose tale of Paris and Oenone was thought by Domitian to be a satire on his divorce from Domitia.[25]

We surely cannot rule out the possibility that a poet might be

22. For Nero, see Charles-Picard, 101–108; 133–137. For Domitian, see Scott, *Imperial Cult*, 61–188.

23. P. 32. Curiously Vessey does a very good job of adducing all the elements of *Silvae* 3.4, that might be construed as critical of Domitian (pp. 28–36) but cannot bring himself to the logical conclusion. See my review of Vessey in *PQ* 53, 1 (1974), 141–144.

24. Vessey, p. 32.   25. *Dom.* 10.

intending to offend the emperor in his poetry by means of some ambiguous reference. Let us take as an instance the conventional attribution of great weight and stature to the gods, a notion as old as Homer.[26] By rhetorical *reductio ad absurdum*, a limit can be reached where the analogy between weight and divinity becomes ludicrous, as it does in Lucan's apotheosis of Nero in *Pharsalia* 1 or in Statius' *Silvae* 1.1.[27] Lucan suggests that Nero should not sit to one side of the heavenly dome, for fear of disrupting the equipoise of heaven; Statius describes the gigantic equestrian statue of Domitian as causing the forum to groan beneath his *genius*.[28] These remarks can be construed literally as well as in a purely figurative manner. Traditional mass of divine genius or no, Nero *was* corpulent, and Domitian conducted a reign of terror which made the forum utter groans all too real. To argue that one meaning precludes the other is to beg the question; both are there, and by design rather than by accident. The poet is addressing himself to both the "literal" and the prudent "official" truth.

What protects the poet from adverse imperial reaction is much the same as what has so often protected the dissident writer in modern Eastern Europe and in Cuba. Provided that the criticism is not direct and outspoken, but follows, at least superficially, the official ideology and propaganda of the regime, the writer has a good chance of emerging unscathed. This enabled the director of the Cuban film *Ustedes Tienen La Palabra* to receive plaudits while the poet Padilla was sent to jail. Both criticized the regime. The former did so by attacking not the revolution itself but the chaos and naiveté involved in the implementation of its ideas. The latter's bitterness clearly marked him as counterrevolutionary. At the same time, however, Castro would rather win a Padilla to his side (or at least to neutrality) than simply dispose of him. The ruler who wants a good press has to compromise with the talented writer no less than the writer has to compromise with the regime.

26. *Iliad* 5.837 ff., for example. It is surprising how willing scholars are to assume that poets were really serious when they referred to the emperor in such exaggerated terms. In addition to Vessey, see also Scott, *Imperial Cult,* and H. Cancik, *Untersuchungen zur Lyrischen Kunst des P. Papinius Statius (Spudasmata* 13), Hildesheim, 1965, 93–100.

27. For a discussion of Lucan's apotheosis of Nero, see Section V, below.

28. *Pharsalia* 1.56–58; Silvae 1.1.1–21; 56–58.

Ultimately the ruler in search of a poet who will glorify his deeds has more need of the poet than the poet has of him. And lukewarm, even half-hearted, praise from a talented poet is more valuable than enthusiastic endorsement from a third-rate hack. Domitian could not afford to react violently against Statius or Martial. It is better to be praised ambiguously than not to be praised at all. Indeed, if it were not for Statius and Martial, there would hardly be a good word about Domitian in ancient literature.

If the emperor's desire for praise protected the poet, so too did the very absurdity of imperial pretensions. If Nero and Domitian insisted on masquerading as gods and eliciting, even demanding, divine honors, they could not very well take umbrage when they received them.[29] At least they could not do so openly. The emperors created and maintained the "Big Lie"; they, like the discreet poet, had to give at least lip service to it. Statius can argue quite logically, then, that if Domitian is Jupiter in *Silvae* 3.4, Earinus can be no one else but Ganymede. Mythology provides no other parallel. Similarly, Lucan and Statius, if pressed on their attribution of great weight to their emperors, can fall back on the argument that godlike beings are traditionally large and heavy, and they can quote Homer in their defense. The only weapons left to the emperors against such literary ambiguity were those they were, in general, unprepared to use. They could kill, exile, or otherwise silence the poet on some trumped-up charge. But then they would lose the only writers who were prepared to offer them flattery, or, in Domitian's case, say anything at all. Alternatively they could accuse the poets of violating the literal truth in order to attack them. But to do this, they would have to shed the trappings of their own divine pretentions and serve the literal truth themselves. In short, they were ensnared in their own nets.

There must have existed, then, between poet and emperor, an uneasy truce. The emperor realized the ambivalence of the poet, and the poet was careful not to go so far as to reveal his antipathy openly. Literary ambiguity was the poet's means of achieving a

29. C. Milosz's study, *The Captive Mind* (New York, 1953), shows how similar techniques of using the "Big Lie" against its perpetrators have been employed by modern Polish poets.

kind of freedom of speech, despite all obstacles. Quintilian was well aware of this technique. In rhetorical terminology it is *emphasis,* intentional double entendre. Quintilian describes *emphasis* as the process whereby the writer leaves something beneath the surface of his words for the reader to "discover": "aliud latens et auditori quasi inveniendum" (*Inst.* 9.2.65). Its principal use occurs when it is not very safe to speak openly: "si dicere palam parum tutum est" (*ibid.,* 66). There is almost a note of contempt in Quintilian's guidelines as to how double entendre may be employed by the orator:

Quamlibet enim apertum, quod modo et aliter intellegi possit, in illos tyrannos bene dixeris, quia periculum tantum, non etiam offensa vitatur. Quod si ambiguitate sententiae possit eludi, nemo non illi furto favet. [*ibid.,* 67]

(You can speak as openly as you like against those tyrants I was talking about, and to good effect, as long as your words can be taken in a different way. You're trying to avoid personal danger, that's all. You're not trying to avoid giving offense. If the danger can be dodged by some ambiguity of expression, everyone will admire the cunning with which it is done.)

From a rhetorical point of view, Quintilian observes, *how* one offends makes no difference. "nihil interest quomodo offendas"; but one must be circumspect and cautious, since this *figura* is no longer a *figura* if it becomes obvious (*ibid.,* 69). Surely Statius and Lucan were no less aware than Quintilian of the advantages of double entendre:

Haeret enim nonnumquam telum illud occultum, et hoc ipso, quod non apparet, eximi non potest; at si idem dicas palam, et defenditur et probandum est. [*ibid.,* 75]

(Sometimes the hidden shaft sticks, and because it cannot be seen on the surface it cannot be taken out. But if you were to say the same thing openly, it can be warded off and its existence demonstrated.)

For all this, the strain of writing under such conditions must have been immense. It is natural that writers under the principate looked back on the late republic with envy and nostalgia. The very factionalism of the republic provided some measure of protection. If all else failed, a man could align himself with some faction whose views resembled his own. The greater diversity of interests allowed a greater diversity of opinion. Even at the height of the chaos prior to the civil war, Cicero still felt that he had at least two sides to choose between and freely expressed reservations about both.[30]

Once the principate was established, the degree of free expression tolerated depended largely on the disposition of an individual *princeps* at a given time. The dissenter had neither legal protection nor the shelter that diversity of opinion among aristocratic cliques could afford. Even Nero, who was remarkably tolerant of criticism for much of his reign, had a breaking point. In short, the fact that imperial censorship was possible made its use almost inevitable. Sooner or later someone would go too far and bring down the full force of imperial wrath upon himself and others.

In Nero's reign, the results of an early tolerance of dissent were almost more catastrophic than total repression of free speech would have been. Younger writers, especially those who enjoyed a position of privilege, were probably lured into the open by Nero's patronage of the arts. Unlike Seneca, whose experience with Caligula and Claudius had taught him something of the anger and power of princes, they knew the potential range of imperial wrath and censorship only by what they had been told of previous reigns. They could see the senate restored to some of its earlier prerogatives; senators spoke more freely.[31] Although, as Persius notes, undue license was still to be avoided, there was a degree of freedom, particularly during the so-called *quinquennium Neronis,* which has no parallel until the time of Nerva and Trajan.

But this relative freedom was deceptive. It encouraged writers to be more frank and open in their opinions than they would have dared under Caligula or Claudius. There was a very real danger of

---

30. For Cicero's conflicting feelings on the outbreak of civil war in 49 B.C., see *Att.* 7.11; 8.3; 7.22; 10.8; and *Fam.* 16.12.

31. See above, note 21. In support of Levi's view we may adduce L. A. MacKay, "The Vocabulary of Fear in Latin Epic Poetry," *TAPA* 92 (1961), 308 ff. MacKay notes that words indicating fear occur more frequently in Lucan and Statius than they do in Ovid and Vergil. His figures are based on 59 words which he recognizes as evoking the idea of fear, and exclude words such as *tremo* and *horreo* which do not always imply fear.

underestimating Nero's ability to retaliate if pushed too far. If Lucan had heeded the advice which his Cotta gives Metellus in *Pharsalia* 3.145–146, he might have lived longer: "libertas" inquit "populi quem regna coercent / libertate perit" ("The freedom of a people that is controlled by kings," he said, "perishes if you attempt to assert it").

In the aftermath of the Pisonian conspiracy in A.D. 65, the frightened Nero initiated a massive purge. The earlier freedom made dissenters readily identifiable. There was little the victims could do but wait for the inevitable death sentence. The grimmest testimony to the paradoxical smallness of the Roman world is that the emperor needed but to pronounce sentence, or simply accuse, in full confidence that the condemned would commit suicide. In these circumstances suicide was not motivated solely by the desire to preserve one's dignity and retain property for one's heirs. There simply was no practical alternative. The Roman could do no more than turn in upon himself, following the example of Cato, transforming the act of self-destruction into a symbolic defiance of temporal authority. It is little wonder that the appeal of Stoicism was so great in this age and that its patron saint was Cato. Regardless of the individual's philosophical school, he could find some consolation in the example of Cato, just as Cato had found similar consolation, on the eve of his suicide, in the example of Socrates.[32]

Surely the generally negative reaction to the principate found in so many writers of the Silver Age has some historical justification. Not that we should see the values of the senatorial opposition as absolutely correct; of course they were not. They were narrow, and they were hardly impartial or objective. We might admire the efficient administration of a *princeps* such as Claudius; Seneca could not. The crucial difference is that Seneca, because of his proximity to the hub of power, had to live with *all* the aspects of imperial rule, and his experience taught him something modern scholarship too often forgets. He knew that the only real controls upon the emperor's powers were those that he imposed upon himself. The sanity of his rule could rarely transcend his personal sanity. Unlike other people, he had the power to transform his

32. Plutarch *Cato* 67–70.

most hideous wish into an even more hideous reality. Once aroused, he could be stopped only by assassination.

IV. Lucan and Nero

The general observations about the principate offered here are crucial to an understanding of Lucan. For even the most casual reading of the *Pharsalia* reveals a poet implacably hostile to tyranny in general and to the Caesars in particular. Yet there is a persistent strain in the criticism of Lucan that denies him to be as hostile to the principate as he appears. Such misapprehensions arise from a misconstruction not only of the *Pharsalia* but also of the age in which it was written. Jacqueline Brisset, for example, argues that Lucan regarded the principate and liberty as reconcilable, despite the fact that Lucan assures us they were not.[33] The basis of this argument, such as it is, can be sketched as follows: Lucan flatters Nero in *Pharsalia* 1.33–66, and presents us with an extremely favorable portrait of the emperor's ancestor, Lucius Domitius Ahenobarbus; further, Lucan was educated as a Stoic and much influenced by his uncle Seneca, who seems to be developing the notion of the philosophical Just King. Therefore Lucan must somehow envisage Nero as a Just King.

If we are to make any reasonable sense of the *Pharsalia,* these notions must be dispelled. Let us first look at what can be pieced together about Lucan's life from our principal ancient

33. *Les Idées politiques de Lucain*, Paris, 1964, p. 221. Also, for a similar view, see M. Pavan, *L'Ideale politico di Lucano*, *AIV* 113 (1954–1955), 209–222. For the notion that Lucan began with high hopes for Nero but then became disillusioned, see R. Castresana Udaeta, *Historia y Política en la Farsalia de Marco Anneo Lucano*, Madrid, 1956, and W. Wünsch, "Das Bild des Cato von Utica in der Literatur der Neronischen Zeit," Diss. Marburg, 1949, 78 ff. and 272. For views closer to my own, see O. Schönberger, "Zu Lucan, Ein Nachtrag," *Hermes* 86 (1958), 230–239; G. Pfligersdorffer, "Lucan als Dichter des geistigen Widerstandes," *Hermes* 87 (1959), 344–377; A. W. Lintott, "Lucan and the History of the Civil War," *CQ* 21 (1971), 488–505; D. Gagliardi, *Lucano Poeta della Libertà*, Naples, 1958. See also, however, W. Rutz, "Studien zur Kompositionskunst und zur epischen Technik Lucans," Diss. Kiel, 1950, 189 ff. and "Lucan 1943–1963," *Lustrum* 9 (1965), 243–340, especially 298. For a further bibliography and discussion, see O. Schönberger, *Untersuchungen zur Wiederholungstechnik Lucans*, Munich 1968, 2–5 and 123–124.

sources, Statius, Tacitus, Suetonius, Dio, and Vacca, to see if anything in Lucan's biography might offer some evidence as to his
relationship with Nero.[34] Since our sources are scant and often
contradictory, the more controversial issues will be avoided here
and discussed more fully in the Appendix.

Marcus Annaeus Lucanus was born at Corduba in Spain on No-
vember 3, A.D. 39. His father, Marcus Annaeus Mela, was the
brother of Lucius Annaeus Seneca (the philosopher, poet, and
statesman) and the son of Seneca the Elder.[35] By right of birth,
then, Lucan belonged to one of Spain's most distinguished families, whose talents had secured wide recognition—and considerable wealth—at Rome. Lucan was brought to Rome at an early
age, where he enjoyed all the wealth and prestige that the Annaei
could provide, particularly after A.D. 49, when Seneca was recalled
from exile to become the tutor to Nero, the heir apparent to the
throne. After formal training at the school of a grammarian,
Lucan became the pupil of the Stoic philosopher Annaeus
Cornutus, whose name suggests that he may have been a freedman
of Lucan's own family.[36]

Considering Seneca's position in public affairs at Rome, which
grew ever stronger between A.D. 49 and A.D. 60, it is hardly surprising that Lucan was quickly drawn into the very heart of
Roman social and political life. He probably spent a good deal of
time with Nero himself. After all, Lucan and Nero were only two
years apart in age, and both manifested an avid interest in literature. When Lucan left Rome for Athens to pursue his studies,

34. The principal sources are: Statius *Silvae* 2.7; Suetonius *Lucan;* Vacca
Life of Lucan; Tacitus *Ann.* 15.49; Dio 62.29.4; Suetonius *Life of Persius* 5.
Of dubious value is the life in the codex Vossianus II. The *Lives* of Suetonius,
Vacca, and the codex Vossianus may be found, most conveniently, in Hosius'
edition of the *Pharsalia*[3], Leipzig, 1913. (Citations from Vacca and Suetonius'
Lucan are noted by page and line of Hosius' edition). For a fuller discussion
of the sources and secondary literature, see the Appendix.

35. The source for these details is the Vacca *Life.*

36. The exact relationship of Cornutus to the Annaei is not at all clear.
Perhaps it would be better to err on the conservative side and observe, with
H. J. Rose, *A Handbook of Latin Literature,* New York, 1960, 379, that
"among his [sc., Lucan's] acquaintance were Cornutus and Persius." Given
the lack of evidence on the matter, I find Berthe Marti's observation in "The
Meaning of the *Pharsalia,*" *AJP* 66 (1945), 354, too categorical: "L. Annaeus
Cornutus, one of Lucan's Stoic teachers and a freedman of the Annaei. . . ."

Nero soon recalled him to become part of the imperial *cohors amicorum*.[37]

While we have no positive evidence of the degree of personal friendship, as opposed to social convenience, involved in the relationship between Lucan and Nero, there is no particular reason to suppose any lack of cordiality on either side until after A.D. 62. In fact, at the *Neronia* of A.D. 60, Lucan sang Nero's praises publicly, and Nero appears to have reciprocated by advancing him to senatorial rank. On December 5, A.D. 62 (or possibly a year later) Lucan was appointed quaestor and, about the same time, made a member of the college of augurs.[38] Preferment to the quaestorship before one's twenty-fifth year was remarkable even for the most privileged men during the principate. Only princes of the blood could normally anticipate such distinction.[39]

To this point, everything was going well. But when Lucan entered upon his quaestorship—perhaps even a little earlier—the shadows of impending trouble began to appear. Nero seems to have been growing more and more restless, irked by his role as a puppet prince whose actions were controlled first by his mother, then, after her death, by Seneca and the praetorian, Burrus. When Burrus died in A.D. 62, only Seneca was left to restrain Nero. Shortly thereafter, Seneca himself gave up much of his estate and decided to retire from public life, possibly at Nero's insistence. By some time late in 63 or early in 64, the friendship between Lucan and Nero had begun to sour. The reasons are not at all clear, and the details in our ancient sources are scant and confused. I shall advance only a sketch here, and treat the problem more fully in the Appendix. For a mixture of literary and political reasons, Nero imposed a ban on Lucan in the later months of A.D. 64, forbidding him to engage in either poetic recitations or advocacy in the law courts.[40] This ban spelled an end to Lucan's career. Soon afterwards, in the early days of 65, Lucan joined Calpurnius Piso's

37. Suetonius *Lucan* 332.9–10: "revocatus Athenis a Nerone, cohortique amicorum additus."

38. Vacca *Life* 335.13–17: "gessit autem quaesturam . . . sacerdotium etiam accepit auguratus."

39. For a fuller discussion of this, see the Appendix, note 24.

40. The sources for information on the ban are the Vacca *Life*, Tacitus *Ann.* 15.49, and Dio 62.29.4. See the Appendix for a more detailed discussion.

plot to assassinate Nero. According to one account, he was virtually its symbol.[41] Unfortunately for Lucan, the plot was discovered, and, after intensive enquiry and interrogations, Nero ordered the conspirators to take their own lives or be put to death. On April 15, A.D. 65, Lucan committed suicide. He was not yet twenty-six years old. Before the end of 66, Nero disposed of Lucan's father, Lucius Annaeus Mela, and his uncle Seneca. The distinguished house of the Annaei was, to all intents and purposes, obliterated.

Lucan would merit a footnote in any account of Nero's reign, even if we knew no more about him than what is outlined above. As it is, Lucan's role in the political turmoil of Neronian Rome is dwarfed by his literary achievements. But we should not forget that political role. For it is one of the many respects in which Lucan is an unusual figure in Roman literature.

A survey of Roman literary activity from the late republic to the middle of the second century A.D. shows that more than half of all the surviving prose writers are men of senatorial rank. Poetry, by way of contrast, is dominated by writers of lower social and economic standing who relied on their pens for a living. Such, at least, is the pattern of extant literature, and even if extant literature is not typical of general literary tendencies, our observations do hold true of those regarded by the ancients as the major Roman writers. Success in poetry rarely accompanied an active political career. The senatorial muse was more at home with history, epistolography, natural sciences, and philosophy than with lyric or epic. Lucan is one of the few exceptions. Along with his uncle Seneca and his older contemporary Silius Italicus, Lucan is one of a small elite that succeeded in producing major works of poetry while pursuing an active career in public life.

Lucan's poetry covered a considerable variety of genres. Though only his incomplete epic, the *Pharsalia* (also known as the *De Bello Civili*), has survived, we have the titles of numerous other works, which range from an unfinished tragedy, *Medea,* to satirical and occasional poetry.[42] There is no way of assessing either the

41. Suetonius *Lucan:* "paene signifer Pisonianae coniurationis extitit."
42. A list is given in the Appendix. A few fragments of Lucan's other works survive and are listed in the Hosius edition of the *Pharsalia,* 328–331. There

quality or length of these nonextant works—except his ten books of *Silvae* which, perhaps, were each about the same length as an average book of Statius' *Silvae*. Lucan's biographer Vacca tells us that not all of his works were worth reading with care, but we do not know which works Vacca had in mind.[43] When one considers, however, that the bulk of Lucan's poetry, including the ten books of the *Pharsalia*, was probably produced in about five years, between A.D. 60 and the early months of 65, his output must be described as prodigious. Most remarkable of all is that he composed so much of his verse at the same time as he was engaged in his political career. Silius Italicus, by way of contrast, wrote his *Punica*, or at least substantial parts of it, after his retirement. He reserved his poetry, as Sallust had reserved his history, or Cicero his philosophical works, for a period of withdrawal from affairs of state.

Lucan, then, enjoyed neither the *otium* of the retired senator nor the professional poet's singleness of occupation. Vergil was able to spend eleven years of his mature, creative life working almost exclusively on the *Aeneid*. The *Thebaid* occupied Statius for twelve years. Lucan worked on the *Pharsalia* for no more than five years, and possibly less than three, when he was still in his early twenties. And while he worked, he held an augurate and a quaestorship and joined a conspiracy to kill the emperor. A final tribute to his impetuous genius is that his *Pharsalia* exercised a considerable influence on the next generation of epic poets, which included, among others, Silius Italicus, who was fourteen years Lucan's senior.

The intensity, compactness, and brevity of Lucan's experience make nonsense of attempts to isolate Lucan the politician from Lucan the poet. Unlike Vergil, he did not watch contemporary political struggles from the sidelines; he was very much a part of what was going on in the senate and palace. Yet, if we may venture a guess, the poet in Lucan was there before the politician. The

---

are no serious doubts as to the incomplete state of the *Pharsalia*. See Chapter 9, Section II and note 3.

43. Probably he is referring to most of the minor works mentioned in the last sentence of his *Life* when he notes: "non fastidiendi quidem omnes, tales tamen" (336.21–22).

key to Lucan's somewhat peculiar career lies in the equally peculiar career of Nero. If Lucan's mixing of politics and poetry is atypical, Nero's chosen role as the great artist-emperor is practically unique in Western history. Certainly Rome cannot provide any comparable phenomenon. Given Nero's obsession with poetry and the arts, it is not surprising that he gathered around him those who showed some promise as men of letters. If the atmosphere of Nero's court kindled Lucan's passion for poetry, Lucan's success as a poet must have fascinated Nero, who doubtless saw in him a kindred spirit. Here was a good opportunity for Nero to let his own enthusiasm for the arts be communicated to the senate. Lucan's aristocratic birthright and obvious poetic talents must have made him seem an ideal ambassador for Nero's purposes. But there were some attendant dangers.

Although Lucan's advancement to senatorial rank probably owes much to Nero's recognition of his artistic abilities and to Nero's friendship, Lucan had every reason to expect an active career in public life even without the emperor's special favor. He was, after all, Seneca's nephew. He moved among the senatorial elite as a social equal. There was a strong possibility that senatorial rank might arouse the political yearnings of the young aristocrat. And this possibility was realized. Lucan did not convert the senate to art; the senate converted him to politics. In less than two years Nero had to muzzle Lucan's poetic and political activities. The experiment was a failure.

Almost inevitably Lucan was caught in the snare of divided loyalties. Like Calpurnius Piso, whose conspiracy against Nero he ultimately joined, Lucan enjoyed the emperor's trust. Yet, as a senator, he felt the pull of the republican past. Many factors contributed, no doubt, to Lucan's final decision to identify himself with the senatorial opposition. Seneca's fall from favor must have cooled the friendship between poet and emperor somewhat. Mutual jealousy and artistic rivalry probably played their part. The process was, I suspect, one of steadily increasing, mutual disenchantment. Lucan's biographer Vacca even goes so far as to assign Lucan's quaestorship to the happy days of his career.[44] This could suggest that Lucan was a senator for at least a year before

44. Vacca *Life:* "equidem hactenus tempora habuit secunda."

things went sour. More likely, however, Vacca means that Lucan did not lose Nero's favor completely until the end of his quaestorial year. It may have taken the emperor some time to realize what was happening in the mind of his protégé.

Personal jealousy or literary and philosophical rivalry are not enough to account for the devastating ban that Nero imposed on Lucan in the latter part of A.D. 64. The catalyst was almost certainly something Lucan wrote and presented publicly, or Nero would not have banned him from reciting his poetry. And Lucan's political views must have entered the picture somewhere, or Nero would not have banned him from activity in the law courts. Most likely it was some political statement in Lucan's poetry that angered Nero.

In A.D. 63–64 Lucan produced two works which might have provoked such a response from the emperor. The poet, who heretofore had treated such standard set pieces as the ransoming of Hector's body, a descent into the underworld, and the tale of Orpheus, wrote a work on the great fire at Rome in A.D. 64, the *De Incendio Urbis*. Though it is no longer extant, we may divine something of its content (see the Appendix). He also published part of his historical epic on the Roman civil war, the *Pharsalia*.

The *Pharsalia* is Lucan's only surviving work, and it is unfinished. Its date is uncertain, though it seems likely that it belongs between the years A.D. 61 and 65.[45] Since, so far as we can tell, only three books of it were published during Lucan's lifetime, we may infer that the publication of the remaining seven was prevented by Nero's ban. This further suggests that a substantial part of the epic was being composed and revised during those years when Lucan's relationship with Nero was deteriorating. Some scholars would argue that the whole of the *Pharsalia* was written in 64 and 65; others maintain that the epic was begun as early as 58.[46] Al-

45. The various arguments are discussed in K. F. C. Rose, "Problems in the Chronology of Lucan's Career," *TAPA* 97 (1966), 379–396, and in my own article, "Lucan's *De Incendio Urbis, Epistulae ex Campania* and Nero's Ban," *TAPA* 102 (1971), 1–27, of which the Appendix to this book is a modification.

46. The extreme positions are those of G. Bagnani, *Arbiter of Elegance,* Toronto, 1954, 8, who argues for 58; and C. Vitelli, "Sulla Composizione e Pubblicazione della Farsaglia," *SIFC* 8 (1900), 33, and K. F. C. Rose, who argue for composition in 64 and 65. Bagnani's argument is colored by his desire to find a suitable date for the *Satyricon*.

though neither of these arguments convinces me, they cannot be dismissed entirely since there is simply no conclusive evidence. Discussion of the order of books is no less risky. It may seem logical that the *Pharsalia* was written in more or less chronological sequence, but this cannot be proved.[47]

On the other hand, Lucan's biography provides some grounds for suspecting that the poet's attitude toward the principate and toward Nero was not necessarily static throughout the last five years of his life. And since the *Pharsalia* is a historical and political epic, covering the civil wars from Caesar's crossing of the Rubicon to the events in Alexandria in the fall of 48 B.C., it is quite possible that there are traces of a more outspoken antipathy toward the Caesars in those books which were composed last. The most obviously explosive book of the *Pharsalia* is 7, and here are two of the most torrid passages:

> . . . fugiens civile nefas redituraque numquam
> libertas ultra Tigrim Rhenumque recessit
> ac, totiens nobis iugulo quaesita, vagatur
> Germanum Scythicumque bonum, nec respicit ultra
> Ausoniam, vellem populis incognita nostris.
> volturis ut primum laevo fundata volatu
> Romulus infami conplevit moenia luco,
> usque ad Thessalicas servisses, Roma, ruinas.
> de Brutis, Fortuna, queror. quid tempora legum
> egimus aut annos a consule nomen habentis?
> felices Arabes Medique Eoaque tellus,
> quam sub perpetuis tenuerunt fata tyrannis.
> ex populis qui regna ferunt sors ultima nostra est,
> quos servire pudet. sunt nobis nulla profecto
> numina: cum caeco rapiantur saecula casu,
> mentimur regnare Iovem. spectabit ab alto
> aethere Thessalicas, teneat cum fulmina, caedes?   [7.432–448]

(Liberty has fled beyond the Tigris and the Rhine to escape civil war, and she will never return. Although we have sought

47. Pichon, 270–271, argues that the three published books of the *Pharsalia* Vacca mentions must be other than *Pharsalia* 1–3. But K. F. C. Rose's rebuttal, 384, is unconvincing, even though, I suspect, he comes nearer the truth. His argument that "no-one would publish individual books of a historical epic out of chronological sequence" is weak. Cf. Brisset, 181–182.

her so often with unprotected throat, she strays from us,
blessing the Germans and the Scythians, but never glancing back
on Italy. How I wish our people had never known her! From
the day the ill-omened vulture's flight marked your foundation,
Rome, and Romulus filled your walls with criminals, until
the day of doom in Thessaly you should have stayed in bond-
age. Fortune, I regret you gave us the Bruti. What use is it that
once we had the rule of law and years named for elected magis-
trates? How blessed are the Arabs, Medes and all the peoples
of the East; the fates kept them under tyranny perpetually. Of
all the peoples who endure the rule of kings, ours is the grimmest lot; for we are ashamed to be slaves. Surely there are no
gods watching over us. The centuries are hurried on their way
by blind chance, and so it is a lie to say that Jupiter rules the
universe. Will he just watch the slaughter on the field at Pharsalia from heaven on high, although he holds the thunderbolt
in his hand?)

maius ab hac acie quam quod sua saecula ferrent
volnus habent populi; plus est quam vita salusque
quod perit: in totum mundi prosternimur aevum.
vincitur his gladiis omnis quae serviet aetas.
proxima quid suboles aut quid meruere nepotes
in regnum nasci? pavide num gessimus arma
teximus aut iugulos? alieni poena timoris
in nostra cervice sedet. post proelia natis
si dominum, Fortuna, dabas, et bella dedisses.   [*ibid.*, 638–646]

(The wound the people suffered from that battle [i.e., Pharsalia]
was too great to heal in one generation. Much more was lost
than life and a chance for safety. We are cast down until the
end of time. Each new generation which will be slaves lost its
freedom when the swords clashed at Pharsalia. What did the
sons of the vanquished, or their grandsons, do to deserve that
they be born into the rule of kings? Did we fight like cowards
or protect our throats from the sword? The punishment for
others' cowardice is chained upon our necks. O Fortune, if you
had to give a tyrant to rule those born after the battle, you
should have given us a chance to fight!)

Nothing in the remainder of the *Pharsalia* rivals these passages
in intensity. In fact, there is no comparable outburst in Latin

literature, from the time of Cicero onwards, that so clearly and savagely indicts the oppressiveness of the writer's own day. To suggest that these lines were not the product of a mind obsessed with hatred for the principate is ridiculous. They encapsulate almost all the antipathy toward the Caesars we have noted in the preceding sections and have that touch of desperate atheism which suggests, even if it does not actually demonstrate, that Lucan was, as O. S. Due notes, a "Stoic who has lost his faith." [48] The anger, frustration, and hopelessness of Lucan in these passages make it very tempting to conclude that they were written after the ban but before he joined the conspiracy of Piso.

The sentiments expressed in these passages are not unique or even atypical of the *Pharsalia* as a whole. They stand out because of their length and directness. If we compare what Lucan says in 7 with the words he puts in the mouth of Nigidius Figulus in 1, we will see that they share a common message: the civil war brings despotism to Rome.

This madness [i.e., the civil war] will go on for many years. And what use is it to ask the gods to bring it to an end? When peace comes, a tyrant comes with it (*cum domino pax ista venit*). Rome, maintain a continual series of disasters (*duc, Roma, malorum continuam seriem*) —drag on the catastrophe for many years. You are free now only so long as civil war lasts (*civili tantum iam libera bello*). [1.668–672] [49]

In book 1, then, Lucan has taken some pains to make his criticism oblique by attributing these words to one of his characters. In a similar vein, he suggests (1.303–305) a comparison between Caesar and Hannibal but carefully attributes the words to Caesar; in 7, however, Lucan shows no hesitation in making such a comparison directly.[50]

Passages like these are highly inconvenient to those who would

48. "Lucain et la philosophie," *FH* 15.214. Due rejects the notion that Lucan occasionally veers toward Epicureanism. Such "atheistic" passages are not uncommon in Senecan tragedy. Perhaps the classic example is *Trojan Women* 371–408.

49. On the similarity of this passage to *Pharsalia* 4.822–823, see G. Pfligersdorffer, 347; cf. R. T. Bruère, "The Scope of Lucan's Historical Epic," *CP* 45 (1950), 227.

50. Most notably at 794–803.

maintain, as Brisset does, that Lucan thought that principate and *libertas* were reconcilable. It is pointless to argue that Nigidius' comments in 1 are the expression of a certain point of view with which Lucan himself does not necessarily "agree" and rank them with Iarbas' uncharitable comments about Aeneas in *Aeneid* 4.215–218. Lucan's remarks in 7 make it perfectly clear that he does agree. W. E. Heitland explored one possible approach to the matter by dividing the whole epic into narrative and "padding." [51] The outbursts in 7 are included in the approximately 30 percent of the *Pharsalia* that Heitland dismisses as "padding." R. T. Bruère adopts a somewhat similar approach, when he characterizes the passages as a "striving for bravura effect" which defies "logic, precision and restraint." [52] Having so judged them, Bruère feels free to continue his argument as if they did not exist.

Both Heitland and Bruère imply that these expressions of anger and disgust on Lucan's part are either irrelevant or nonsensical. If they are right, then Lucan is hardly worth reading. If about a third of the *Pharsalia* is, as Heitland suggests, mere stuffing to fill out the rest, Lucan is clearly incompetent. It is surely more reasonable to suggest that Nero's ban and Lucan's subsequent association with the Pisonian conspiracy add credibility to his outbursts in 7. Besides, if Lucan really believed that Nero and the principate were good for Rome, why should he make these comments *at all?* There was good reason to veil one's criticism during the principate, but none, so far as I can see, to veil one's flattery.

The fury of *Pharsalia* 7 abates considerably in 8 through 10, yielding to what is best described as secretive confidence. Two references to the assassination of Julius Caesar highlight this change. The first, in 7, describes Brutus' efforts to kill Caesar at Pharsalia:

> nil proficis istic
> Caesaris intentus iugulo; nondum attigit arcem,
> iuris et humani columen, quo cuncta premuntur,
> egressus meruit fatis tam nobile letum.
> vivat et, ut Bruti procumbat victima, regnet.   [7.592–596]

51. *M. Annaei Lucani Pharsalia*, ed. C. E. Haskins, with an introduction by W. E. Heitland, London, 1887, xxxii–xxxiv.
52. Bruère, "Scope of Lucan's Historical Epic," 230.

(You will achieve nothing on this occasion though you are aiming for the throat of Caesar. For he has not yet attained the pinnacle, the height of human power when everything is crushed beneath him. He has not yet gone beyond the bounds of fate and earned a death so noble. So let him live and—so that he may fall as sacrificial victim to the sword of Brutus—let him reign.)

A rather new and different note is struck in 10:

> procul hoc avertite, fata,
> crimen, ut haec Bruto cervix absente secetur.
> in scelus it Pharium Romani poena tyranni,
> *exemplumque perit.*   [10.341–344]

(Fates, avert this crime—and it would be a crime if Caesar's throat were slit when Brutus is not present. For then the punishment of a Roman tyrant becomes an Egyptian atrocity, *and the precedent is lost.*)

Although Lucan clearly relishes the thought of tyrannicide in both 7 and 10, it is not until 10 that he sees Brutus' killing of Caesar as an example for others to follow. There is a recovery of poise in the later book, bolstered, perhaps, by Lucan's own participation in the Pisonian conspiracy which offered him a chance to be set down in history as Brutus' successor. The same may be true of Lucan's comment in 9 that he and Julius Caesar will not be condemned to the shadows by any age, "nullo tenebris damnabimur aevo" (9.986). Here, perhaps, we see a defiant reaction to Nero's ban. They are certainly bold words if written after Nero's edict.

What matters more than the chronology of the *Pharsalia,* however, is the relative uniformity of attitude toward the principate found throughout the epic. Unless we dismiss all the adverse allusions to Caesarism as mere nonsense, and thus dismiss Lucan as an irrational and incompetent poet, we must surely concede that the *Pharsalia* is hostile to Caesarism.

But is it also hostile to Nero? Even in the later stages of the epic, Lucan is very careful to avoid any specific attack on Nero himself. Although there are many passages where references to the Caesars in general must clearly include Nero, even the wrath of 7 does not spill over into an overt denunciation of the emperor. If we add to this the apotheosis of Nero in 1 and the heroism of Domitius Ahenobarbus in 2 and 7 does it not contradict our arguments thus far?

V. Nero and Domitius Ahenobarbus

The invocation of Nero in 1.33–66 is the *only* passage in the entire epic where Nero is even mentioned by Lucan. Logically, therefore, it should attract the scholar's attention. But it would be well to bear in mind that it stands alone. Aside from the references to Domitius, it is the only passage in the whole poem that can be construed as favorable to Nero and Caesarism. Even if we add the Domitius scenes in 2 and 7, the sum total of "pro-Caesarian" passages constitutes around a hundred lines of the *Pharsalia*.[53] This is a very slender basis on which to build an interpretation of the epic. Although the denunciations of the Caesarism do not admit of an alternative explanation, the apotheosis of Nero does. The alternative was recognized as early as the commentary in the *Adnotationes super Lucanum* and the *Commenta Bernensia*.[54]

53. Nero: 1.33–66; Domitius: 2.478–525; 7.220 and 597–616.

54. Here are the notes of the *Adnotationes* scholiast on lines 55 and 57: "OBLIQUO SIDERE ROMAM adlusit; strabus enim Nero fuit, ideo 'obliquo sidere.' SENTIET AXIS O. et hic adlusit; fuit enim corporis pinguis." The *Commenta Bernensia* are almost exactly identical. Modern scholars are divided on the subject. A. D. Nock, "The Proem of Lucan," *CR* 40 (1926), 17–18, feels that the eulogy of Nero is no more than conventional language of the age and is not intended as extravagant flattery. Pfligersdorffer, 368 ff.; Brisset, 196 ff.; M. Levi, "Il Prologo della 'Pharsalia'," *RFC*, N.S. 27 (1949), 71–78; P. Grimal, "L'Eloge de Néron au début de la Pharsale, est-il ironique?" *REL* 38 (1960), 296–305, among others, argue that the prologue is not satirical. One of Brisset's arguments is indeed odd. She attempts to discredit the comments on Nero's physical peculiarities by suggesting that most appear "n'avoir jamais existé chez Néron" (197, note 3). In support of this contention she adduces Suetonius *Nero* 51. But Suetonius tells us that Nero had bad eyesight: "oculis caesis et hebetioribus"; that he was fat: "cervice obesa, ventre proiecto." And these are the *only* physical deformities that the *Adnotationes* mention as part of Lucan's satire in the apotheosis. The *Commenta Bernensia* clearly go too far, presuming, that is, that Suetonius' description is accurate, mentioning "hernia eius" (not noted by Suetonius) and, tentatively, a "pes grandis" (not noted by Suetonius; probably contradicted by Suetonius' observation that Nero had very slender legs: "gracillimis cruribus"); finally "calvities," flatly contradicted by Suetonius' "subflavo capillo." The scholiast's statement here may result from a misunderstanding of Juvenal's description

Both scholiasts understood the passage as satire. As we have noted, although weight is a traditional attribute of the divine, it is also an attribute of the historical Nero. Much the same can be said about the remainder of the apotheosis; every element admits of double entendre. Take, for example, the concluding lines in which Lucan dismisses Apollo and Bacchus and takes Nero as the only muse for his epic: "If I receive you within my breast, I would have no wish to trouble the god who stirs the secrets of Delphi, or to draw Bacchus away from Nysa. You are enough to give strength to a Roman song (*tu satis ad vires Romana in carmina dandas*)" (1.63–66). At first glance this may well seem to be pure flattery. But as one reads further it becomes apparent that Lucan's *Romanum carmen* deals with the imposition of slavery upon the Roman world, not Rome's rise to glory. Further, the deification of an emperor in an epic where the gods exercise no power, where the elevation of humans to divine estate will be man's *vengeance* on the gods for their indifference to human affairs, is at best a token honor.[55] In fact the soldier resurrected by Erichtho in book 6 vows that the ghosts of the republicans will trample these Roman gods under their heels.[56] Prima facie it is no small honor to substitute Nero for Apollo as muse of the epic. But in book 5 we learn that Apollo's inspiration and prophetic utterances are no longer of any interest to man.[57] His oracle is defunct, to all intents and purposes, revived briefly and disastrously by the only man who has any interest in the god—Appius Claudius Pulcher, the expert on religious antiquities.[58]

Were the *Pharsalia* a conventional epic with conventional gods we might pause before dismissing the possibility that Lucan is sincere in his praise of Nero. But it is not. How then, did Lucan

---

of Domitian as "calvo . . . Neroni" (*Satire* 4.38). In short, the *Commenta* want to see more than there is; Brisset, less than there is. In defense of the satirical nature of the apotheosis, see Berthe Marti, "Meaning of the *Pharsalia*," especially 374–376, and Schönberger, "Zu Lucan," 232; E. Griset, "Lucanea," *RSC* 3 (1955), 134–138, and Rutz, "Lucan 1943–1963," 296–302, and the articles discussed there, especially G.-B. Conte "Il Proemio della Pharsalia," *Maia* 18 (1966), 42–53.

55. See Chapters 4, 7, and 8.   56. 6.809; see Chapter 4.
57. See Chapter 4.
58. Chapter 4, notes 3 and 4, lists the sources for Appius' biography.

expect this satire to escape Nero's eyes, or *did* he expect it to? At the opening of the epic, the work's final nature is not manifest; the reader does not yet know that this is to be an epic without gods, in defiance of tradition. Thus only the more playful aspects of the satire would be noticeable: the double entendre about divine as opposed to human weight—a touch of the amusingly grotesque. Only as the epic continues do the really savage elements involved in the dedication to Nero become apparent.

This naturally raises the question as to why Lucan does not attack Nero openly and directly. Most obviously, of course, Lucan might not have been prepared to risk an outright attack at this point. After all, even without naming Nero, he goes farther than any Silver Age writer in condemning the contemporary political scene. But more important: his *Pharsalia* is not about Nero himself. It is an ideological onslaught on Caesarism rather than a personal attack on the latest of the Caesars. Clearly generalized attacks on Julius Caesar and the Caesars can hardly avoid encompassing Nero. And if Lucan had been intent on pleasing Nero he would surely have made a point of distinguishing him from the other Caesars, to obviate the possibility that some misunderstanding might arise. When Lucan suggests that the plight of contemporary Rome is one of slavery to a tyrant he is damning Nero. But to venture into a tirade against the emperor himself would add little to the force of his criticism. It might even be misleading to the reader, creating the illusion that the awesome, if cold-blooded, brilliance of Julius Caesar was shared by his dilettante successor. Not only would this weaken the effect produced by Lucan's Caesar; it would cause the poet to cross irrevocably the delicate boundary between epic and satire.

But what of Domitius Ahenobarbus? There is no trace, nor as far as I can see any possibility, of satire in Lucan's treatment of Nero's ancestor. Domitius appears twice in the epic, in 2 and 7, and in both instances is portrayed in high heroic style. Of all the other characters, only Cato and Brutus are so consistently well treated by Lucan. This alone might induce the belief that Lucan is flattering Nero through his ancestor, even though he never actually describes Domitius as Nero's ancestor. Indeed, the Domitius presented here is at odds with almost every other portrait of him that we have, and it is hard to avoid the conclusion that the poet is whitewashing a character who was as unpopular with the Pompeians as with the Caesarians. Clearly Lucan is battling tradition in thus restoring Domitius. Why, if not to please Nero?

We find the glimmerings of a solution to the dilemma in book 7. Domitius is given a very prominent role by Lucan in his account of the battle of Pharsalia. He dies valiantly, hurling words of defiance against the conquering Caesar.[59] Further, his is the *only* death that Lucan records during this battle. Although he assures us that heaps of Metelli were strewn over the plain in the great catastrophe of the republic, there is not one other identifiable corpse to be found in his account. As we search all other sources on the battle of Pharsalia, a curious and puzzling fact emerges. Although we are told of the many deaths of notable republicans in the battle, only one is mentioned by name in any of them: Domitius Ahenobarbus.[60] There must, of course, have been other prominent casualties in Pompey's army. But is there anyone famous enough in the republican cause that we notice his absence in subsequent campaigns? All of the principal republican worthies

59. 7.597–616.

60. Appian *BCiv.* 2.82 tells us that ten senators died on the republican side, but, like Caesar, *BCiv.* 3.99, names only Domitius. None of our other sources contributes any further names. Cicero *Phil.* 2.71 tells us that Mark Antony killed Domitius as he fled from battle: "L. Domitium . . . occideras multosque praeterea alios qui e proelio effugerant, quos Caesar, ut nonnullos, fortasse servasset, crudelissime persecutus trucidaras." Caesar himself is rather more charitable in *BCiv.* 3.99. Domitius died, he says, "cum vires eum lassitudine defecissent." It is well to note that Cicero, who has little patience elsewhere either with Domitius or with Caesar's *insidiosa clementia*, would find it, rhetorically at least, to his advantage to present Domitius here as the helpless refugee cut down by Antony's cavalry. For thus he underscores Antony's *saevitia*. By much the same reasoning, Caesar's affirmation of a heroic last stand by Domitius might be designed to obviate accusations that a massacre of survivors was perpetrated after the battle by his cavalry. F. E. Adcock, *Caesar as a Man of Letters,* Cambridge, 1956, notes that Caesar is not entirely dispassionate or scrupulous in his *Civil Wars* (46–48). And Adcock is never one of Caesar's harsh critics. Both Caesar and Cicero had taken the opportunity to exploit Domitius' death for rhetorical purposes; Lucan is hardly doing more than that. A final point: if Cicero had known the identity of the *multos alios,* especially if some of them had been prominent, he would hardly have resisted the temptation to mention them in the *Philippics* to blacken Antony's character even further. Cicero, like Lucan, was left with Domitius.

are found fighting again on other occasions; nor are any of the familiar faces and voices missing, apart from Domitius.

Pharsalia, unlike Philippi, Munda, or Thapsus, was not notable for the deaths of famous men. The only genuine and significant republican death that Lucan had at his disposal was that of Domitius. Since Lucan declares that the battle of Pharsalia is the supreme catastrophe of the republic, this lack of noble dead must have proved embarrassing. To talk, in glowing terms, of the demise of several senatorial backbenchers, or to concoct a fictitious Metellus or two, would make mockery of Lucan's entire thesis. Since Lucan is working with history, not myth, he must stay within the bounds of historical plausibility. He thus needs Domitius Ahenobarbus for the battle of Pharsalia.

Obviously it would be thematically disastrous to depict the sole representative of the republicans who died at Pharsalia in anything less than heroic style. But in order to do this convincingly, Lucan must remove the slur against Domitius' character that had been occasioned by his actions at Corfinium some time earlier. According to Caesar, Domitius betrayed the republican garrison at Corfinium: when he discovered that Pompey would not relieve him, he tried to escape, abandoning his legions.[61] Lucan does not deny that Domitius' legions went over to Caesar's side, but he tells us that this action resulted from their own treachery, not that of Domitius.[62] This change is important; it even has a certain ring of historical plausibility. After all, it was to Caesar's advantage, in terms of propaganda, to show Domitius as a traitor and to vindicate the legions that came over to his side at Corfinium. Further, if Domitius had actually betrayed the cause, it is odd that the Pompeians should have appointed him commander-in-chief at Massilia shortly thereafter.[63] If we follow R. Pichon and assume

61. *BCiv.* 1.15–23. As Pompey's letter to Domitius (Cicero *Att.* 8.12 D) shows, however, Domitius was in a very awkward predicament. Since Pompey did not trust his own raw recruits at this stage, he warned Domitius not to expect help but to escape Caesar's encirclement by any means possible. If knowledge of this message reached the troops, it is just as likely that they betrayed Domitius as it is that he betrayed them; see Seneca's account of Domitius' attempted suicide in *Ben.* 3.24.

62. 2.507–510.

63. Caesar *BCiv.* 1.34–36; 56–58; 2.3, 18, 22, 28, 32. Too little has been made of Lucan's omission of Domitius at Massilia. See I. Opelt, "Die See-

that Livy was one of Lucan's principal sources, it is quite possible
that Lucan took this nobler Domitius to be the historical one.
Livy's sympathies, after all, veered to the republican side.[64]

A further problem remains. In the whole account of the heroic
resistance of the Massiliotes in *Pharsalia* 3, there is no mention of
Domitius, despite the fact that he was commander-in-chief of the
republican forces in that city.[65] In fact, the only Roman, apart
from Caesar himself, who is mentioned in the battle for Massilia
is Caesar's admiral, Decimus Brutus.[66] If Lucan had wanted to pay
Nero a compliment by means of his ancestor, this would have been
a splendid moment to do so, since the defense of Massilia was well-
organized and staunchly fought. Instead, Lucan passes all the glory
to the Massiliotes themselves. They are displayed as fighting with
great valor for ideals that the Romans were supposed to cherish.

There was nothing shameful about Domitius' conduct at Massilia. On the contrary, Julius Caesar makes it clear that the speedy
and efficient organization of Massilia's defenses was almost entirely

---

schlacht von Massilia bei Lucan," *Hermes* 85 (1957), 435 ff., and R. Rowland, "The Significance of Massilia in Lucan," *Hermes* 97 (1969), 204–208.
O. A. W. Dilke, *Lucan, De Bello Civili VII*, Cambridge, 1960, 5, note 3, declares that he is puzzled by the omission, but pursues the matter no further.

64. See above, note 13. On Livy's republican views, see Tacitus *Ann.* 4.34.
Tacitus observes that Livy extolled Pompey to such an extent that "Pom-
peianum eum Augustus appellaret"; cf. Seneca *Controv.* 10, preface 5, and
R. M. Ogilvie, *A Commentary on Livy, Books I–V*, Oxford, 1965, 2 ff. It
should, perhaps, be added that Domitius' behavior was not very endearing to
either Pompey or Caesar. His epithet, "King of Kings," applied to Pompey,
is but one instance of his stinging tactlessness (Appian *BCiv.* 2.67; Plutarch
Pomp. 67; *Caes.* 41.2). Possibly Domitius' outspoken criticism of both Caesar
and Pompey is what made him particularly attractive to a republican sym-
pathizer of a later generation.

65. Caesar's own description of Domitius' arrival in Massilia (*BCiv.* 1.34–
36) says a great deal for Domitius' initiative in the matter. He set out for the
city with seven ships, manned by his own slaves and other dependents, and
was received as commander by the Massiliotes. It is curious, however, that
Caesar does not explain whether Domitius came to Massilia of his own accord or under orders from Pompey. He implies the former (*BCiv.* 1.34), but
the latter is equally likely. If Pompey sent Vibullius Rufus to Spain (*ibid.*),
even though he too had been captured at Corfinium, it is possible that he
asked Domitius to organize the defense of Massilia as part of a delaying action. But, given the private nature of Domitius' crews for the seven ships,
Domitius may have acted on his own initiative, in which case the defense of
Massilia falls even more to his credit.

66. 3.514, 535, 559, 563, and 761.

to Domitius' credit (BCiv. 1.34–36). On purely literary grounds, however, Lucan's decision not to use Domitius as the focal center of the Massilian resistance is understandable. Another heroic but unsuccessful action by Domitius would be repetitive so soon after the Corfinium episode. Lucan's studied emphasis on the Massiliotes' heroism allows him to explore new thematic and narrative textures. Such emphasis would be spoiled if Domitius were given the dominant role in the city's defense. But this is hardly an adequate reason for excluding him altogether. A few lines telling us how he aided the Massiliotes in their struggle for freedom would not have destroyed the rhetorical and artistic balance of the book or of the epic and would have established some good will with Nero.

Lucan's failure to mention Domitius at Massilia was hardly calculated to win Nero's favor. Any hopes Nero had as to his ancestor's potential role in the Pharsalia after Lucan's restored picture of Domitius' behavior at Corfinium must have been rudely shattered by the poet's total silence about Domitius at Massilia. For as surely as Lucan strips away Domitius' shame at Corfinium, he strips away his claim to glory at Massilia. He has no intention of making him a major character in the Pharsalia just to please Nero. He wants a respectable, republican Domitius, not a great one. He cannot deny that Domitius was Nero's ancestor, but he does not have to draw our attention to the fact either. It is surely no accident that Lucan is as silent on the subject of Nero's family connections with Domitius as he is on Domitius' role at Massilia. He wants to keep ancestor and descendant distinct and apart.

If Lucan recited Pharsalia 2 and 3 publicly and in Nero's presence, the emperor had good reason to be deeply offended by Lucan's silence on these matters. Sometimes the failure to provide the appropriate compliment is the most devastating form of humiliation.[67] Surely Lucan knew this.

67. Something of the sort could, in fact, have occasioned Nero's sudden departure from one of Lucan's recitations. Suetonius in his Lucan 332.12–13 declares that Nero left "nulla nisi refrigerandi sui causa" while Lucan was reciting and called a meeting of the senate. Since Suetonius cannot, or will not, state the cause of Nero's anger, suggesting rather that it was no more than spiteful whimsy, it may be that Nero was irked by something Lucan had not said rather than anything he did say. See my discussion in the Appendix.

In conclusion: there is no compelling reason to assume that the treatment of Domitius is intended as flattery of Nero or that the *Pharsalia* is favorable to *princeps* and principate. But there is much to suggest the opposite. Even if one does not concede the satirical nature of the apotheosis in book 1, we ought to bear in mind that dedications to kings and emperors are part and parcel not only of Roman, but of Elizabethan and Jacobean poetry. To denounce one's emperor in the opening book of an epic would be ill-advised, possibly even fatal to both poet and poem. We must not distort the remainder of the epic which is manifestly hostile to the Caesars in order to assert the sincerity of a few lines which are not necessarily favorable.

As we shall see in Chapter 9, those who have claimed that Lucan is favorably disposed to Caesarism and to Nero have usually had difficulty bringing the unfinished epic to a suitable, hypothetical conclusion. Bruère, for example, believes the *Pharsalia* would have ended with Octavian's return to Rome in 29 B.C., arguing that the defeat of Antony and Cleopatra would be the obvious highlight of an epic praising the establishment of the principate.[68] Here is the ultimate, bizarre consequence of seeing the *Pharsalia* as a eulogy of the principate. We must dismiss as nonsense a great deal of what Lucan says in the ten books we have and then postulate an enormous planned continuation. For if it takes Lucan ten books to get from the Rubicon to Alexandria— a time span of less than two years—how many books would it take him to cover the *nineteen* years between Alexandria and Octavian's triumphal entry into Rome?

VI. Problems of Republicanism

If our arguments thus far come close to the truth, we may suggest that Lucan's *Pharsalia* is a fair indicator of the poet's increasing alienation from Nero. The dangerously forthright nature of parts of book 7 are probably explained by the fact that they were composed after the ban, when further caution seemed unnecessary. For, so long as Nero lived and the ban was enforced, recitation and publication were out of the question. But, as we have noted, the difference between Lucan's attitude toward the Caesars in the

68. Bruère, "Scope of Lucan's Historical Epic," 217–245.

early books and in the later books is one of degree rather than kind. There is little doubt that he espoused the republican point of view in the civil wars.

Throughout the *Pharsalia*, Lucan avoids the word *princeps* when referring to Julius Caesar and his successors. Instead, he calls them Caesars.[69] He thus rejects the Augustan fiction that liberty and traditional government had been restored after the battle of Actium. If Brisset had noted this, she would have been less inclined to declare that, when Lucan uses the word *libertas*, he does not mean "republican *libertas*," but the freedom enjoyed by the citizen under the rule of the Just King.[70] To argue, as she does, that the identification of the theoretical *rex iustus* with the *princeps* allowed the reconciliation of principate and *libertas*, is to use terms in a manner utterly alien to Lucan's usage and perspectives.

Lucan's failure to supply an adjective such as "republican" to qualify *libertas* does not indicate that he did not mean freedom in the republican sense of the word. Classical Latin has no such word as republican. What we call a republican was, to the Romans, a *Pompeianus*—and even *Pompeianus* was a term more favored by the Caesars than by the opposition.[71] For *Pompeianus* implies a

69. In 4.823, he refers to them collectively much as we would refer to a monarchical dynasty: "Caesareaeque domus series" (the succession of the house of Caesar). I doubt that Nero is being alluded to in the description of Ptolemy, however, as P. McCloskey and E. Phinney suggest, "Ptolemaeus Tyrannus: The Typification of Nero in the *Pharsalia*," *Hermes* 96 (1968), 80–87.

70. J. Brisset. Here is her statement: "Le Principat était, selon lui [sc., Lucain] un régime fondamentalement différent d'une tyrannie: il n'excluait pas l'existence de la liberté. Par ce mot, Lucain, comme tous les Stoïciens de cette époque, entendait, non plus évidemment la liberté républicaine, mais la liberté dont jouit le citoyen sous l'empire du *rex iustus*. . . . L'identification du *rex iustus* et du *princeps* permettait de concilier Principat et *libertas*." She adduces, to support this contention, two passages from Pliny's *Panegyric* (45.3; 55.7). But (a) the nature of the principate was radically changed after Domitian's assumption of the title of *Dominus et Deus*; (b) Pliny's remark in 55.7 that the title of *princeps* is enough and that there's no place now for a *dominus* is a thinly disguised hope that Trajan would drop the title *dominus*, in comparison with which *princeps* seems almost republican. Trajan did not oblige. For Seneca and the concept of the *rex iustus* see A. Kopp, "Staatsdenken und politisches Handeln bei Seneca und Lucan," Diss. Heidelberg 1969, 139–164.

71. See above, note 64.

dedication to Pompey rather than to the republic. Lucan carefully points out in 7.696–697 that when the battle of Pharsalia continued after Pompey's departure, it proved that the senate was fighting for itself, not for Pompey. In 9.257–258, in fact, Cato uses the adjective *Pompeianus* as a term of contempt for those who think the struggle is over once Pompey is dead: "Pompeiana fuisti, non Romana manus." The fight is for *libertas,* and to Cato and Caesar's other opponents, *libertas* is the republic. Cato's mission is to die fighting for freedom and for Rome "whose name is *libertas,*" and whose empty shadow he will follow to the end (2.301–303).[72] Indeed, as Cato points out, *libertas* as a political reality is dead; even under Pompey, there is only the fiction of freedom. Its existence is now confined to the hearts of those individuals in whom the ideal of dying free remains.[73]

Just as Cato opposes Caesar, so too is the ideal of *libertas* opposed to Caesarism. Lucan, employing the gladiatorial imagery of which he is fond, informs us that *libertas* and Caesar are the new contestants matched against each other once Pompey withdraws from the field at Pharsalia: "par quod semper habemus, / libertas et Caesar, erit . . ." (7.695–696).[74] In short, even if Lucan supported the notion of a Just King, he hardly saw Caesar and his successors as potential candidates for such an honor. They belong, rather, to the ranks of the villains of the past.[75]

But is Cato, perhaps, Lucan's exemplar of the *rex iustus?* Certainly the Cato of the *Pharsalia* does not see himself that way. The kind of kingship Lucan has in mind for Cato is the self-sufficiency of the wise man in the domain of his own soul, the ideal found in the Stoic maxims: μόνος ὁ σοφὸς ἐλεύθερος and μόνος ὁ σοφὸς βασιλεύς (only the wise man is free, only the wise man is king).[76] We must

72. For a fuller discussion, see Chapters 7 and 8.
73. 9.204–206, 379–381; see also Chapter 7.
74. On Lucan's gladiatorial imagery, see Chapter 3, especially Sections I and II.
75. 4.821–824. Cf. below, Chapter 3, Section V.
76. The most sensible discussion of Lucan's philosophy is that of Due, "Lucain et la philosophie," 203–224, and the discussion that follows on 225–232). Due, like Herington, does not lose sight of the Roman tendency to eclecticism and thus does not fall into the trap that ensnared Brisset and Pichon, who view Lucan's relationship to Stoicism as that of the total devotee. Yet even Due does not make enough allowance for the possibility that

be careful in criticism of the *Pharsalia,* as in criticism of other Silver Age poetry, that we do not presume too much about the nature and influence of Stoicism. It is ill-advised to enter into the sweeping generalizations Brisset makes and argue that Lucan, "like all the Stoics of his age" believed in the idea of a *rex iustus.*[77] For we run the risk of creating a hypothetical Stoicism into which we squeeze all Silver Age writers. How unfortunate this can be is all too clear in David Vessey's recent book on Statius.[78] If we overplay the philosophical aspects of *libertas,* there is the danger we may forget its markedly political associations.

When Lucan assures us that the battle of Pharsalia is the great catastrophe of the republic, he is telling us that this is the moment when constitutional government, or what was left of it, fell. From Pharsalia onwards, *libertas,* the republic, no longer exists at Rome, though it continues as an ideal, enshrined in men like Cato. In this sense the battle of Pharsalia marks the day that the Roman state died, when crime became law. This, surely, is why the focus of the epic's ten books is on the struggle involving Caesar, Cato, and Pompey. For Pompey is the representative of the last moments of the republic itself, Cato the man who keeps the disembodied ideal alive, and Caesar the evil genius who brings an end to the republic as a political reality, but who, one suspects, will not be so successful in destroying the ideal.[79] Lucan's new Rome begins, not with the first of the *principes,* but with the first of the Caesars,

---

Lucan's philosophy, like his history, is tailored to the rhetorical needs of his theme.

77. See note 70 above.

78. Vessey not only concludes that Statius was a Stoic (58–60), without a single reference to a passage in Statius, but even explains the curious structure of the *Thebaid* in Stoic terms. "The *Thebaid,*" he notes on 328, "is a picture of the [sc., Stoic] cosmos, and so is arranged like it." In Lucan the danger of reading too much Seneca into the narrative is even greater. Although Due is probably right that "en parlant de la *Pharsale:* philosophie veut dire stoïcisme" ("Lucain et la philosophie," 204), we must not forget that Stoicism was, as Due points out, "formulé dans les deux derniers siècles de la République" (208) and, despite Seneca, remained the philosophy of the resistance. If Syndikus errs—which I doubt—in making Lucan first and foremost a Roman, as Marti suggests in her review (*AJP* 82 (1961), 329), his error is a useful corrective to the overly Stoical views of Brisset and indeed to those of Marti herself in "Meaning of the *Pharsalia.*"

79. See below, Chapter 7, Sections V and IX.

as Suetonius' *Lives* do. And this new Rome is much worse than the old. Not only does it rise from the ashes of the old; its founder, Julius Caesar, brought the old Rome to ruin.[80]

Lucan's republicanism has proved attractive to many over the centuries, but it has also earned him many foes. The Romantics, who shared much of the fervor of the new republicanism in France and North America, regarded him as a poet of the highest order. The youthful Shelley, writing to a friend in 1815, describes him as a poet of great genius and transcending Vergil.[81] For to Shelley, as to many of his contemporaries, Lucan was the great voice of protest against tyranny and oppression. The Marchese di San Tommaso, whose book *Considerazioni intorno alla Farsaglia* is an apology for republicanism that would make Cato blush, declares that Lucan is better than Vergil because he is full of "robust concepts, not the empty flowers of poesy." [82] Clearly the preference for Lucan shown by the writers of this period is motivated by the political aspects of the *Pharsalia* and the *Aeneid* rather than by their respective poetic merits. Vergil, who, superficially at least, endorses the Caesars, was hardly likely to have greater appeal than Lucan to thinkers who were opposed to any form of monarchy.

But as the excitement of the revolutionary spirit of the early nineteenth century lost some of its charms in the wake of the changing social and political patterns produced by the advancing stages of the industrial revolution, so did Lucan. The gradual emergence of the new socialism made the bourgeois ideal of republicanism less attractive, especially in England and Germany. England had progressed and prospered during the nineteenth century while other European countries found themselves plunged into internal conflict and revolution. For all this, the specter of civil war and its consequences haunted the English, who, despite

80. See below, Chapter 6, Section III.
81. *P. B. Shelley, Letters*, ed. F. L. Jones, Oxford, 1964, 1.432; also *ibid.*, 429–430. For more on Lucan and Shelley, see R. Ackermann, *Lucans Pharsalia in den Dichtungen Shelleys*, Zweibrucken, 1896.
82. Turin, 1837, 12. See also R. Tucker's two interesting articles: "Lucan and the Baroque: A Revival of Interest," *CW* 62 (1969), 295–297; and "Lucan and the French Revolution: The *Bellum Civile* as a Political Mirror," *CP* 66 (1971), 6–16.

the comfortable facade of Victorianism, found the growing discontent among the working class a contagion which threatened to debilitate the entire social order of the state. To many scholars of that period, a revolutionary poet was not appealing. And those who did favor a revolution had little use for Lucan's bourgeois ideal.

German scholarship had its own peculiar rationale for disliking Lucan. In the middle of the nineteenth century there emerged from the warring principalities of Germany a new nation, whose rapid growth stunned the older powers of Europe with its brilliant successes. Germany was at last united under a Teutonic Caesar. Understandably, national pride spilled over into the historical perspectives of the German scholar no less than it did in the case of his English contemporary. It is hard to share Lucan's hostility to Caesarism when a new Caesarism has elevated your nation to the forefront of European powers.

The judgment of the later years of the last century, however, proved fatal to Lucan in the English-speaking world. Widespread admiration for the achievements of Caesar and Augustus led to vicious and personal attacks on Lucan. Even Macaulay, who thought highly of Lucan, expostulated angrily that he had portrayed the "most humane conqueror the world has ever known" as "a bloodthirsty ogre." [83] Almost every charge that could be made against Lucan was brought during those years: his political ideals were irrelevant, his dedication to those ideals hypocritical. Lucan's alleged incrimination of his mother in the aftermath of the Pisonian conspiracy was used as ammunition against the poet's credibility. Thus B. Henderson could conclude that the poet died young "but hardly prematurely"; that he had ended his life "tangled on the briars of treachery and cold dishonour." As for the *Pharsalia*, "the world could spare another." [84]

In short then, Victorian and Edwardian hostility to Lucan was quite as political in nature as was the Romantic tendency to under-

83. Macaulay's note at the end of his copy of Shelley's *Adonais;* quoted by J. D. Duff at the end of his introduction to the Loeb *Lucan,* London, 1962, xiv–xv.
84. Henderson, 264–265.

rate Vergil. It resulted not so much from any poetical considerations but from a clash of ideals, perspectives, and personalities.
Scholars like Jacqueline Brisset perceived this but approached the
dilemma in the wrong way. They tried to redress the balance in
twentieth-century scholarship not by denying the premises on
which the charges were made, but by denying the charges themselves. Instead of conceding that Lucan was a republican in spirit,
but arguing that he had every right to be, they argued that their
predecessors were wrong in thinking Lucan a republican. Thus,
although they intended to render him a service, they ended up
doing precisely the opposite.

Underlying this approach is the assumption that the apparent
world view of Lucan is incredible: we all know Actium was the
key battle of the Roman civil wars, not Pharsalia, and republican
ideals in the age of Nero were anachronistic. Whether or not we
agree with Lucan in his reading of Roman history, however, it is
surely unreasonable to rehabilitate him by denying the very essence of what he wrote. Brisset senses Lucan's greatness but will
not admit that it lies, at least partially, in those areas where Lucan
is most vulnerable to attack by the historical critic. We should take
warning from Wilamowitz's efforts to make Sappho acceptable to
sensitive souls by denying that she was a lesbian.

A final thought. We have already noted that Heitland and
Bruère dismiss large segments of the *Pharsalia* as essentially meaningless: "padding" or "striving for bravura effect." Such criticisms
bear out the validity of C. S. Lewis' observation that "Silver" and
"rhetoric" are fatal words, "to which modern ears are deaf." [85]
"Rhetorical" became synonymous with "bad," at least when applied to poetry. More important, it was commonly thought that
passages which are "extravagantly" rhetorical are also meaningless.
And it was precisely such thinking that caused Lucan to slip from
the canon of commonly read Latin poets. The hostility of nine-
teenth-century critics relegated Lucan to the handbooks. For their
attacks coincided with that point in the history of education when
classical studies began to lose their central position in the educational curriculum. As a result, Lucan has no place in the newer
and narrower reading list of the modern classicist. He lies in what

85. "Dante's Statius," *Medium Aevum* 25 (1957), 133 ff.

P. Friedländer once called "the graveyard of literary history": extant, but unread.[86] If there is to be any hope of restoring him to life, we must confront the major task of restoring a proper perspective not only on his political views but on the most fundamental issue of all: his poetry.

86. "Das Gedicht des Statius an den Schlaf," *Antike* 8 (1932), 215; cf. W. Schetter, *Untersuchungen zur Epischen Kunst des Statius (Klass. Phil. Stud.* 20), Wiesbaden, 1960, 1.

CHAPTER 2

The Necessary Revolution

Plato's decision to banish poetry from his ideal city is, as he himself admits, a chapter in an "old antagonism between philosophy and poetry" (*Republic* 607B). The claim that "poets understand all the arts, and everything human that pertains to virtue and vice—not to mention the divine" (*ibid.* 598E) is not just extravagant, but fundamentally and inexcusably wrong. Poetry, he argues, is so far removed from reality that it is capable of dealing only with illusions. It subverts the intellect by bewitching the senses and is, consequently, an obstacle to understanding and virtue. Love of poetry, however, is so inbred in the Greeks by their educational system that even the philosopher must be ever on his guard against being drawn back into the childish ways of the unthinking multitude. The city of his soul is under constant siege (607E–608E). To protect everyone, then, poetry must be expelled from the state until such time as a plausible case is made in its defense.

Plato's objections to poetry are hardly unique in antiquity, nor are they confined to philosophers and Christian fathers. A number of poets found themselves at odds with poetic tradition. Both Lucretius and Lucan were aware that poetry in general, and epic in particular, was a major vehicle for the perpetuation of ideas they wished to refute. Poets had sanctified and regenerated the traditions of religious superstition which Lucretius so strongly detested.[1] But this did not force Lucretius to abandon epic and

1. As they continued to do for centuries. In fact, as traditional paganism revamped itself under the onslaughts of Christian polemicists during the third and fourth centuries, we find the Neo-Platonist Sallustius arguing that the myths are divine because of the men who used them: "Among poets, those who were divinely inspired, and among philosophers, the best made use of

launch into a prose treatise on the follies of religion, nor did it oblige him to disguise his antipathy to superstition and use the gods anyway simply because epic had always used gods. Lucretius asserted his prerogative to shape epic to ends which were in accord with his own vision of the world, to enrich poetry by change and by reaching out into the contemporary intellectual milieu. His reaction to tradition is not altogether different from that of Wordsworth, who felt that he must free poetry from its traditional vocabulary, its fictional deities and mythic men sketched against an idealized Arcadian landscape.

Lucretius realized that the most effective means of dislodging "wrong thinking," short of massive censorship and the restructuring of Roman education, was to subvert it on its own ground and with its own devices. The very roots of paganism were poetic; and the only way to displace one poetic vision is to supplant it with another. Lucretius' skill with the Latin hexameter so far surpassed that of his predecessors that he had some reason to anticipate success. More important still, his philosophical views would carry not only the intellectual appeal of reasoned exposition but the sense-bewitching magic of poetry. Thus, in *De Rerum Natura* 3 he relies heavily on the typical language of the Homeric vision to substitute a philosophical heaven for the Homeric Olympus.[2] In verse reminiscent of the unveiling of Olympian vistas, he displays not a banquet of the gods with nectar and ambrosia but a panorama of the atomist's eternity in which all thinking men may share, and where the food of eternal truth is the *aurea dicta*, the golden words of Epicurus. The echoes of Homer are used to enhance the beauty of his own vision. As a result, philosophical truth becomes more than a stimulus to the intellect and a means of achieving the good life; it is the nectar and ambrosia of the soul.

Myth; add to these the founders of rites and even the gods themselves in their oracles" (*On the Gods and the Universe*, 3). As H. J. Rose (*The Roman Questions of Plutarch*, Oxford, 1924, 53) and A. D. Nock (*Sallustius: Concerning the Gods and the Universe*, Cambridge, 1926, xliii) point out, the attribution of authority to divinely inspired poets along with lawgivers and philosophers was a standard defense of the value and truth of myth even in its dying days.

2. Lucretius 3.1–30. Cf. M. von Albrecht, "Der Dichter Lucan und die Epische Tradition," *FH* 15.269–301. For Euripides' similar use of Aeschylus see P. Pucci, "Euripides Heautontimoroumenos," *TAPA* 98(1967), 365–371.

I. The Vergilian *Donnée*

One of the most attractive features of Lucretius and Lucan is their obvious belief in the visions they are depicting. It is, of course, virtually impossible to produce a durable vision of something that neither you nor your world can readily accept as credible. But Lucan's task was made infinitely more difficult because Lucretius' greatest successor achieved the virtually impossible. Vergil took the damaged bastions of tradition and the Lucretian hexameter which had undermined them, and with them built a poem which has been described, not unjustly, as the cornerstone of subsequent Western poetry.

If the gods Lucretius expelled in favor of philosophy were utterly at odds with the enlightened world view of the Roman intellectual, they were far from dead politically. Their names and cults were deeply rooted in large areas of the Roman national identity. As such they were splendid tools in the hands of politicians, as Sulla, Pompey, and, to a far greater extent, Caesar and Augustus show.[3] Although many Roman families claimed the special patronage of one god or another, the Caesars went much further. Tradition associated them with direct descent from Venus, through Aeneas, the son of Anchises and the cousin of Hector. With the ascendancy of Caesar and Augustus, the whole myth of the Trojan War leaped back to life with a vengeance. Even Lucretius, though he has little use for the Olympians, begins his epic with *Aeneadum Genetrix* in reference to Venus. And let us not forget that *Venus Genetrix* was the patron goddess of the Julian clan.[4]

The religious revival under Augustus placed the intelligentsia in a rather embarrassing position. One could not very well denounce Venus without appearing to denounce Augustus and the Caesars. And this association of *princeps* with Olympus led to the long succession of imperial masquerades where the emperor not only claimed the patronage of the gods, but even pretended to be

3. For a discussion of the gods of the *Pharsalia* and the political uses of divinities by Pompey and, more particularly, Caesar, see Chapters 6 and 8. Cf. L. R. Taylor, *Party Politics in the Age of Caesar*, Berkeley, 1949, 76–97.
4. See Chapter 3, Section III; also Chapter 8, Section I, and note 24 for a fuller discussion.

one of their number.[5] With the deification of Julius Caesar, a whole new epoch in Roman religion began. With it came a new epoch in literature.

In this sense the *Aeneid* is the greatest exemplar of the curious change that came over the Roman world, not just the greatest product of that change. Throughout, it shows many uneasy sutures suggesting that Vergil was all too conscious that his gods were the product of political astuteness rather than renewed and deep-seated belief. For all the magnificence of the *Aeneid,* one senses an enormous moral vacuum in the poem. Men do what they do because they are told that this is right or necessary, not because they believe in it. Thus it is hard to tell whether Vergil is praising Aeneas and Augustus or criticizing them.

An assessment of Vergil's politics is not the aim here; this calls for a separate and detailed treatment in its own right. What matters is that Vergil creates a vision of Rome by interweaving myth and history. His hero, Aeneas, is the man chosen by fate to link myth, history, and the contemporary world. But Aeneas is not merely the founder of the Roman race. Vergil specifically identifies him as the ancestor of the *gens Iulia,* the forebear of Caesar and Augustus. Thus Vergil not only gives canonical form to the legendary connections between Aeneas and Rome, but also to those between Rome and the Caesars. In doing so, Vergil is treading sensitive ground. Brutus and Cassius had struck down Julius Caesar to demonstrate the incompatibility of Caesar and the Roman ideal. Vergil's epic not only suggests that they are compatible, but associates them together in the person of Aeneas— from the very moment, that is, of the nation's birth.[6]

Even if, as I believe, Vergil's vision of Rome, Aeneas, and Augustus is highly ambivalent, the fact remains that those hostile to the Caesars might well be angered at even the remotest suggestion that Rome and the Caesars could be reconciled. For the *Aeneid* was no mere political pamphlet, but a work bearing the stamp of greatness, claiming that peculiar sanctity reserved for the muses of poetry. To denounce it was not enough. It could

5. See Chapter 1 and the sources cited there in notes 3 and 9.
6. Especially in *Aeneid* 8. See Chapter 3, Section III.

only be invalidated by another *poet*. The facts of history were not enough of themselves to demolish the Vergilian vision.[7]

But as a beginning they were indispensable; for Vergil's vision of Rome is achieved by a combination of carefully edited myth and history, dovetailed to create the illusion of a continuum. An obviously assailable flaw in the *Aeneid*, from the viewpoint of a hostile critic, is the studious avoidance of the grim years of the first century B.C. Vergil dwells on the Fabii, the Scipios, and Lucius Brutus, but shuns Marcus Brutus, Sulla, Marius, and other controversial figures in his parade of Roman heroes in *Aeneid* 6. In 8 the struggle between Octavian and Antony is treated as a war between Rome and Egypt, an external war against Cleopatra.[8] The only stage of the civil wars at Rome which Vergil concedes to be civil in nature comes in Anchises' oblique reference to Caesar and Pompey in book 6.[9] And even then, he does not actually name the combatants. The only really menacing figure of civil discord in the first century who appears in the *Aeneid* is Catiline—a safely uncontroversial figure for whom neither the Caesars nor their opponents had any use.[10]

This is not to say that the specter of civil war is absent from the *Aeneid*. On the contrary it stalks almost every book, particularly the last six, as a delicate undercurrent. *Aeneid* 7 through 12 resembles a kind of civil war in retrospect, pitting Italian against Roman-to-be. The Fury Allecto is immediately responsible for stinging Turnus into a mad passion for war.[11] In Latin literature,

7. See Pfligersdorffer and the other works cited there for the idea of the *Pharsalia* as an anti-*Aeneid*, especially Syndikus; A. Guillemin, "L'Inspiration virgilienne dans la *Pharsale*," REL 29 (1951), 214–227; A. Thierfelder, "Der Dichter Lucan," *Archiv für Kulturgeschichte* 25 (1935), 1–20 (p. 14 for the anti-Vergilian approach of Lucan); F. Caspari, "De Ratione quae inter Lucanum et Vergilium Intercedat," Diss. Leipzig, 1908–1909.

8. 8.671–716 (especially 685–691); cf. I. Becher, *Das Bild der Kleopatra in der Griechischen und Lateinischen Literatur*, Berlin, 1966, 47–52; P. Jal, "Bellum civile . . . bellum externum dans la Rome de la fin de la République," LEC 30 (1962), 257–267 and his *La Guerre civile à Rome*, Paris, 1963, 19–42. For Lucan's attitude to the east and to Cleopatra, see E. M. Sanford, "The Eastern Question in Lucan's *Bellum Civile*," *Studies in Honor of E. K. Rand*, New York, 1938, 255–264; also Becher, 117–122 and the sources cited there; also Chapter 1, Section II and note 11.

9. 6.826–835; they are described simply as *socer* and *gener*.

10. *Aeneid* 8.668; Lucan consigns Catiline to Tartarus in *Pharsalia* 6.793.

11. 7.435–470; cf. *ibid.*, 323–405.

even more than in Greek, the Furies are the demons presiding over the shedding of kindred blood.[12] Vergil himself tells us in book 1 that the creature enchained within the temple of Janus is *Furor impius,* the demon of civil war.[13] Is there not a hint, then, that by opening the temple of Janus, as she does in 7, Juno is unleashing the same demon? [14] Further, and more disquietingly, the doors are opened against Aeneas, reminding us that he rather than Turnus is the intruder upon the peace of the Latin world.

Part of Vergil's caution and ambivalence can be ascribed to the nature of his times. Beneath the facade of Augustus there lurked the bloodied Octavian. Only time would tell which side of that enigmatic personality would emerge supreme—presuming, that is, that Augustus lived. The Roman of 20 B.C. could not have grasped, even in his wildest dreams, that he was witnessing the prelude to a half-millennium of Caesars. The memory of Caesar's murder, Augustus' uncertain health, and the lack of an heir apparent with sufficient *auctoritas* to assure stability at Rome must have left doubts in most minds about the durability of the new Golden Age. Yet peace was not to be despised, even if the price was high and the long-term prospects unsure.

By Lucan's time, hindsight allowed a rather different perspective. The time had come to assess not the value of the peace, but what had been sacrificed to gain it. Vergil might hope that Octavian's sword could cut the way for a new and better Rome, but Lucan could cherish no such illusions. The Caesars came not in the noblest traditions of the Roman past, but in the basest. Civil war, the darker side of Roman history, which is a plaintive undertone in the *Aeneid,* holds center stage in the *Pharsalia.* Lucan would replace the *Aeneid* with his own view of the Roman past. He wanted to match words and ideas with Vergil as Lucretius did with Homer and early Latin epic. To do so, he had to write a historical epic. And in this lie his greatness and his vulnerability.

II. The Illusion of Realism

Once Lucan had decided to write an epic about the Roman civil wars his approach was largely dictated by the nature of his

12. See W. Hübner, *Dirae im Römischen Epos,* Hildesheim, 1970, 34–42 and *passim.*

13. 1.293–296.   14. 7.601–619.

subject matter and his attitude toward the outcome of the conflict. The advice Eumolpus offers in *Satyricon* 118 was, I believe,
something Lucan could not possibly have followed if he was to
achieve his goals:

For example, if someone undertakes the massive subject of the civil
war, he will be crushed beneath the weight of his theme, unless he is
steeped in literature and learning. Further, one should not attempt to
use poetry as a medium for setting forth the facts of history. The historian does a far better job of this than the poet could. One should
approach a historical subject with a delicately mystical touch; one
should make use of the gods as agents in the process; the ideas should
be carefully intertwined with the fabric of myth. Inspiration will thus
have free rein, and the result will take on the appearance of divine
and prophetic genius pouring forth from a blazing soul. Better this
than the cold religion of corroborated fact.

A conventional epic, such as Eumolpus suggests, complete with
the usual divine apparatus, may serve the purpose of a writer
whose aim is to justify the Caesars or to subvert them by innuendo
rather than frontal onslaught. But if one's sympathies lie with the
losing side in a war, the divine apparatus is worse than useless.
The traditional epic mode invites us to accept what happens in
myth or history as justifiable merely because it happens, because
such is the will of the Olympians or of fate. Cities and men are
destroyed either because they have committed (or will commit)
actions which offend heaven, or because their removal is necessary
for the furtherance of the divine will and the process of destiny.
In short, defeat, even if it does not always imply guilt, implies a
cessation of usefulness. The victorious cause is bound to appear
justified, to some degree, simply because it wins, and the vanquished cause tarnished, if not discredited, simply because it loses.
The conventional divine machinery stands firmly in the way of
any examination of absolute good and evil.

The writer who wishes to damn the winner and glorify the
loser has to take refuge in issues of morality. The only way a
losing cause can be represented as better than a victorious one is
in terms of right and wrong on a moral scale. The winner must
be stripped of moral justification, and the loser must be shown as
virtuous. Caesar must seem desirous of asserting himself at the

expense of the Roman world and of humanity in general; Cato, desirous of ennobling mankind by his own example of virtuous conduct. If Caesar is shown as acting under the guidance of Venus, his behavior becomes explicable in terms of obedience to the gods. He is thus less "responsible" for any crimes he perpetrates. Similarly Cato, if sponsored by Hercules, would necessarily assume a lesser stature than his divine (and not always virtuous) patron. Finally, Caesarian propaganda had so cunningly exploited the Olympians that Caesar would have been at an impossibly large advantage over Cato in a conventional epic format, since Cato had made little use of divine propaganda during the war.[15]

In short, Lucan *had to* expel the Olympians from the *Pharsalia* to achieve the picture he desired, to bring the moral issues into the foreground, and to avoid conceding a distinct rhetorical advantage to the thoroughly mythologized Julian clan. Similarly he had to use Cato, rather than Pompey or Brutus, as the antithetical figure to Caesar. In order to underscore Caesar's badness, he needed an opponent of unimpeachable morality.

If Lucan's political views demanded the removal of the gods, they also demanded a more "realistic" approach to history than that recommended by Eumolpus. In order to eliminate Caesar's unassailable advantage in mythical propaganda, Lucan had to demythologize Caesar, and to do this, he had to demythologize his epic in the interests of rhetorical consistency. One can adduce many good reasons for Lucan's decision to pursue this plan. The civil wars were, after all, only three or four generations removed from Lucan's own day. The facts, even the details, of what happened would have been well known to his readers. The literary and intellectual infancy of the Roman world was long past, and with its passing, the possibility of representing familiar, historical events in the extravagant manner of traditional epic faded. As Seneca points out, only hunters and peasants fight wild beasts, and no one would now believe that the world could be lifted on the shoulders of one man.[16] Mythical creatures and miraculous

---

15. See Chapter 7, Sections V and VIII, for Lucan's similar problem in comparing Cato with Hercules and Alexander. Cf. Rutz, "Lucan und die Rhetorik," *FH* 15.233–257.

16. *Constant.* 2.2; see also Chapter 7, Section VIII.

happenings could be used freely only when treating those subjects already the province of folklore or shrouded with mystery: the tales of Aeneas or the Argonauts, even the Punic Wars. But Caesar, Pompey, and Cato could not readily be portrayed as fighting Hydras and Cyclopes, or hurling boulders which not six men of the present day could even lift.

Since good and evil are absolutes unaffected by history, Lucan need not meddle much with historical facts in order to achieve his purposes in the *Pharsalia*. Although epic gods and myth can get in the way, facts rarely do. While events and their results may be immovably fixed in tradition, history is rarely definitive in the details of what motivates an individual. Lucan does not have to deny Caesar's military achievements and thus ruin his own credibility. All he has to do is suggest that they were motivated by a depraved megalomania. One cannot *prove* this true, nor can one prove it false. But, from a rhetorical point of view, Lucan's general allegiance to historical fact gives a certain plausibility to the motives he attributes to his characters. His prosy language reinforces the effect.

Lucan is factual enough that it has taken the practised eye of the Renaissance and modern scholar to detect the few modifications he makes for rhetorical purposes or in the interests of poetic form. Indeed, as history, the *Pharsalia* compares surprisingly well with the works of most medieval and several ancient historians.[17] Lucan was thought by some critics to be, *in primis*, a historian rather than a poet. As Servius comments: "ideo Lucanus in numero poetarum esse non meruit, quia videtur historiam composuisse, non poema" (thus Lucan did not deserve to be reckoned among the poets, for he seems to have written a history, not a poem).[18] Such comments as these, or Eumolpus' suggestion that he was "a devotee of the cold religion of corroborated fact," would surely have amused rather than irritated Lucan. For his apparently

---

17. Several modern historians, though not necessarily sympathetic with Lucan's historical methodology, share something of his view, notably Lily Ross Taylor. Her comment (167) that "Cato had chosen to die with the republic" is virtually a paraphrase of *Pharsalia* 2.301–303. See her entire discussion of Cato and the republic on 162–182. Compare also Syme's approach in *Roman Revolution*.

18. Servius on *Aeneid* 1.382.

"realistic" approach to history is his means of attacking, rather than confirming, history's verdict. Occasionally Lucan's rhetorical stance even suggests that what happens in history is irrelevant. And it is here that Lucan's most hostile critics have usually grasped the wrong end of the stick. One cannot invalidate Lucan's vision by picking at his historical errors. In fact, many of his most noted blunders are not really blunders at all. The persistent identification of the sites of Pharsalia and Philippi, also found in Vergil's *Georgics,* is surely his way of noting the similar nature and outcome of both battles, not the result of ignorance.[19] Lentulus Crus and Lentulus Spinther are figures of small importance in the *Pharsalia,* so Lucan combines them into one composite Lentulus, leaving the reader to supply the appropriate *cognomen* in the appropriate context, if he wishes.[20] Even the necromancy of Sextus Pompey in *Pharsalia* 6 is probably no more than the relocation of an episode associated with Sextus during the Sicilian wars, not a gratuitous invention.[21] As noted in Chapter 1, the refurbishing of Domitius Abenobarbus is probably undertaken for reasons of dramatic effect. And it is worth noting that Lucan does not change the major fact of what happened at Corfinium, but rather alters the motivation of Domitius to suit his purposes.[22] Lucan's modifications of history in all these instances are undertaken because the work he has in view is an epic, not a history text. A consultation of the dead would be out of place in a history, but perfectly at home in epic. Yet in order to maintain the illusion of historicity, the incident must have some historical basis, even if this entails moving it from one point of time to another.

History, then, is the raw material of the *Pharsalia,* not its purpose. It is as much a means to an end as is Vergil's use of myth. It allows Lucan to give the semblance of reality to what he describes, a factual underpinning for his vision which makes the vision itself

19. *G.* 1.490. For a fuller discussion of this identification, see Chapter 9, Section II. For a discussion of Lucan's errors (both real and imagined) see R. Graves' translation of the *Pharsalia* (Baltimore, 1957) both in his introduction and footnotes; also Heitland's introduction to Haskins' edition of the *Pharsalia,* li ff., and Dilke, *Lucan,* 30–33.

20. Graves erroneously assumes that the Lentulus of the *Pharsalia* is always Lentulus Spinther. In general, Graves is often wrong in "correcting" what he takes to be Lucan's errors.

21. See Chapter 4, Sections III and IV.   22. Chapter 1, Section V.

very hard to refute. Thus Lucan's rejection of certain epic conventions both enhances the illusion of fidelity to fact and at the same time allows the poet to manipulate fact to his own ends. More important still, it blinds the critics.

The reader of the *Pharsalia* is so taken aback by Lucan's rejection of the mythic and divine that he can easily fail to perceive that what the poet has ostenstatiously thrown out the front door is often surreptitiously reintroduced through the back. Lucan's avowed antimythological, anti-Olympian stance enables him to expose Caesar's use of myth as shallow propaganda, but it does not prevent him from using careful mythical allusion to suggest that Cato is more Herculean than Hercules and more divine than any oracle, as we shall see in Chapters 7 and 8.

There is no doubt, however, that Lucan's approach creates numerous problems, which are not always satisfactorily resolved. It is all very well to remove the gods from epic to stress the importance of human morality and behavior, but when they are removed, with them goes the traditional poetic explanation of natural phenomena. The poet is forced to substitute meteorological and climatological explanations for conventional gods gathering clouds or unleashing winds. Unfortunately, the knowledge of man's environment was still at a rudimentary level in Lucan's day, and Lucan's grasp of such scientific learning as was available is occasionally none too sure.[23] Further, such naturalistic explanations are frequently less compact and to the point than traditional epic phenomenology.

A classic example of Lucan's dilemma is to be found in Cato's encounter with the Libyan serpents in *Pharsalia* 9.[24] Struggles with serpents are very popular throughout ancient myth and epic, whether Greek, Roman, Aztec, or any other tradition. But in a historical epic, such as the *Pharsalia*, the usual dragon had to be

23. Lucan's critics have a field day on this score. Heitland (lii–liii) observes: "Learning overpowered imagination in Lucan. . . . I propose to give a few instances of blunders, inconsistencies and laxity, chiefly in geography, which will suffice to prove how shallow was the erudition so ostentatiously displayed." Similarly Housman, on the subject of Lucan's astrology, in his edition of Lucan (Oxford, 1927), 325–337. It is typical of many misconceptions of the *Pharsalia* to assume that Lucan was attempting to use fact for the sake of fact rather than as a means to a poetic end.

24. 9.619–949.

avoided. There was no tradition that Cato had fought such a monster, and Lucan seems to know enough about snakes to realize that traditional stories about their origin and dimensions are nonsensical.[25] Had Lucan's purpose been merely to write history, Cato's encounter with the snakes could have been passed off lightly, with general references to the sufferings of his troops, or even omitted altogether. But since Lucan wants Cato to surpass the heroes of antiquity, the episode had to be included, to rival, perhaps, the story of Regulus' battle with the African serpent during the Punic Wars.[26] The similarity of historical locations and characters involved was too much for Lucan to resist. Thus, for all his stated embarrassment that he can offer no better explanation of the origin of the Libyan snakes than the Ovidian tale of Perseus and Medusa, one senses that he is quite happy that no more realistic account is actually available.

Instead of the vast monster which Regulus fought, Lucan provides us with a large number of smaller, if no less ferocious, creatures. There is no special reason to believe they would have impressed Lucan's contemporary reader as gross distortions and travesties of known fact. Lucan's descriptions are probably no more hyperbolic than those of his sources, and he obviously considers the snakes real enough to merit zoological names. But to the modern reader the serpents of *Pharsalia* 9 are hardly more probable than the literary monsters of Apollonius, Statius, and Vergil. Lucan has fallen between two extremes. While the critic can tolerate the snakes which swim from Tenedos to kill Laocoon and his sons in *Aeneid* 2.199–233, Cato's march across snaky Libya is too much to endure. Vergil is protected by the literary framework within which he is working; the reader is prepared to suspend his disbelief. Even though neither poet nor reader accepts the plausibility of such creatures, both understand the underlying symbolism in tradition which transcends questions of factual cor-

25. *Pharsalia* 9.619–623. In connection with the origin of the African snakes, see P. Grimal, "L'Episode d'Antée dans la Pharsale," *Latomus* 8 (1949), 55–61. For further discussion of Cato and the snakes, see Chapter 7, Section VII.

26. Livy, *Per.* 18; Silius, *Pun.* 6.140–260 give an account of Regulus' victory over the serpent. See also Chapter 7, Section VII, and E. Bassett's excellent article "Regulus and the Serpent in the *Punica*," *CP* 50 (1955), 1–20.

rectness. But Lucan, in his attempts to suggest the veracity of what he describes, gets, and to some degree deserves, criticism for lack of poetic common sense. His snakes are neither traditional literary serpents, nor the recognizable cobras and pit vipers of the modern herpetologist, but something in between: real enough to have zoological names, fanciful enough to be preposterous. More important still, from both an ancient and modern point of view, Lucan's attempt to give Cato an *aristeia* against "realistic" beasts instead of the conventional epic dragon leads him to substitute number for size. Even the largest dragon can be detailed in less than a third of the verses Lucan uses for his multitude of snakes.

The techniques, then, Lucan uses to annihilate Caesar's divine and heroic pretensions run him into trouble when he really wants to add a mythical aura to Cato. He is forced to circumvent his own ground rules. But the failure of the snake episode should remind us that Lucan's ultimate goal is a poetic rather than a purely historical vision. And his successes far outnumber his failures. Although Lucan's realism is forced upon him by the nature of, and his attitude toward, the events and people he is describing, it can result in passages of bewildering poetic grandeur, moving beyond the real into the surrealistic.

To complete his illusion of realism, Lucan has to adjust his language and style to suit his historical and unconventional treatment of subject matter. Here he has earned his severest criticism. In *Epigrams* 14.194, Martial attributes the following couplet to Lucan, as an apologia for his poetry:

> Sūnt quīdām quī mē dīcānt nōn ĕssĕ pŏētam;
> sĕd quī mē vēndīt bўblĭŏpōlă pŭtat.

> (There are certain people who would say I am not a poet; but the bookseller who sells my work thinks I am.)

I have marked the length of the syllables to emphasize a point I am sure Martial is intending us to catch: the epigram itself is only barely poetry—little more than a ponderous concatenation of words squeezed into elegiac form. Dactyls are included only where they are metrically indispensable. To put these verses into the mouth of one who is defending his claim to be considered a poet is most unflattering. So is the argument Martial attributes to Lucan. The suggestion that sales, rather than any inherent poetic virtues, define what is good poetry is an even nastier dig at Lucan. In a mere two lines, Martial caricatures Lucan as a lame poetic hack, whose popularity is his only poetic defense.[27]

Other ancient critics find Lucan's style something less than poetic. Quintilian comments that Lucan is a better model for orators than for poets: "magis oratoribus quam poetis imitandus" (*Inst. Or.* 10.1.90). Even Statius, who, in *Silvae* 2.7 offers the highest praise for Lucan's work, cannot resist a hint at the grandiose and emotional style of the *Pharsalia:* "Pharsalica bella detonabis" (66) (you will *thunder forth* the Pharsalian wars); "Pelusiaci scelus Canopi deflebis pius" (70–71) (you will nobly *weep* over the crime committed by the Egyptians). Fronto, in a clever critique of the *Pharsalia*'s opening, does much the same thing as Statius, though in a more elaborate manner.[28]

To a degree, the criticisms of Lucan's penchant for high rhetoric are justified. After all, the *Pharsalia* is intended to convince its reader rather than to suggest the labyrinthine possibilities of thought and reflection found in the *Aeneid*. Lucan's epic is highly emotional in both content and style, but this is not necessarily a vice. It is indeed one of the facets of the *Pharsalia* that make the poem exciting to read, adding more than an occasional touch of Juvenalian *saeva indignatio* laced with a sardonic wit.

27. Cf. A. Rostagni, *Svetonio De Poetis e Biografi Minori*, Turin, 1944, 149 (note on line 35).

28. Fronto, Ad M. Antoninum de Orationibus 7(A344). For a fuller discussion of Statius' *Silvae* 2.7, see the Appendix. Martial, of course, expresses a more favorable view of Lucan in *Epigrams* 7.21–23. But these poems were probably written at the request of Lucan's widow, Polla, possibly even as a commission at her expense, as Statius' *Genethliacon* appears to have been (to judge by the remarks addressed to Polla in lines 120–132). Although the date of these poems is uncertain, they appear to have been composed between 88 and 94, most probably in 89, the fiftieth anniversary of Lucan's birth. An outright attack on Lucan's poetry would have been singularly inappropriate on such an occasion. For further discussion of ancient attitudes to Lucan, see E. M. Sanford, "Lucan and His Roman Critics," *CP* 26 (1931), 233–257; H. J. Thompson, "Lucan, Statius and Juvenal in the Early Centuries," *CQ* 22 (1928), 24–27; P. Grimal, "Le Poète et l'histoire," *FH* 15.53–117; and von Albrecht, "Der Dichter Lucan."

III. Brundisium

The backdrop of the *Pharsalia* consists of settings as real as are
the historical motifs. In place of the idealized landscapes of Vergil
we find real towns and countryside, even real ruins. It is precisely
in such details that we can see the kind of skill that marks Lucan
as a poet.

For this reason it is worth examining one of the less famous narrative passages of the *Pharsalia*. It deals with a subject which, unlike much else in the epic, is not a matter of controversy: Pompey's arrival in Brundisium in 2.607 ff. I do not offer this as an
example of Lucan's descriptive powers at their best, but rather at
their most typical: a real town, a genuine historical event, and a
precise geographical location are treated in a highly impressionistic
manner, with, perhaps, even a touch of surrealism, yet faithful to
almost every detail of history and geography:

>   sic viribus impar
> tradidit Hesperiam profugusque per Apula rura
> Brundisii tutas concessit Magnus in arces.
>   Urbs est Dictaeis olim possessa colonis,
> quos Creta profugos vexere per aequora puppes
> Cecropiae victum mentitis Thesea velis.
> hinc latus angustum iam se cogentis in arcum
> Hesperiae tenuem producit in aequora linguam,
> Hadriacas flexis claudit quae cornibus undas.
> nec tamen hoc artis inmissum faucibus aequor
> portus erat, si non violentos insula Coros
> exciperet saxis lassasque refunderet undas.
> hinc illinc montes scopulosae rupis aperto
> opposuit natura mari flatusque removit,
> ut tremulo starent contentae fune carinae.
> hinc late patet omne fretum, seu vela ferantur
> in portus, Corcyra, tuos, seu laeva petatur
> Illyris Ionias vergens Epidamnos in undas.
> huc fuga nautarum, cum totas Hadria vires
> movit et in nubes abiere Ceraunia cumque
> spumoso Calaber perfunditur aequore Sason.
>   [2.607–627] [613: *artum,* Housman; 625: *hoc,* Housman]

(So, because he was no match in strength, he handed over Italy, and, as a fugitive, crossed through the fields of Apulia; Great Pompey withdrew to the safety of the citadel of Brundisium.

The city was settled once by colonists from Crete, who had been carried from their homes across the sea as fugitives in Athenian ships, powered by the sails which spread the lie that Theseus was dead. Here the side of Italy compresses itself into a narrow bow, thrusting forth into the waves its slender tongue, enclosing with its taut and arching horn-tip the Adriatic Sea. But the water that pours through these clenched jaws could not make a port, were it not for an island which cuts off the northerly gales, hurling the tired waves back upon themselves.

On both sides, nature has built mountains of rugged crags to be a barrier against the open sea, and to divert the winds; so ships are held safe at anchor by slack and quivering hawsers, motionless. From here extends the whole expanse of sea, whether ships sail to your harbor, Corcyra, or whether Epidamnos, sloping down to the Ionian shore on the Illyrian coast, is the destination of a more northerly course. But this is also where the sailors come as fugitives when the Adriatic stirs its mightiest waves, when Acroceraunia withdraws into the clouds, and Sason, midway in the sea, is washed with foaming breakers.)

The passage begins by describing Pompey's flight through Apulia to the coast. He comes to Brundisium as a fugitive (*profugus*). Then Lucan, very briefly, tells the foundation myth of the city: it was established by Cretan colonists who were themselves fugitives (*profugi*). Brundisium was a haven to them in their distress, just as it is to Pompey. The reference to Theseus and Crete follows nicely on a theme established just a few lines earlier (600–606), where Pompey is compared to a defeated bull retiring from the pastures to recoup his strength.

But now Lucan raises us to what can only be described as an aerial perspective of the city. He focuses our attention first upon the peninsula of extreme southeast Italy, which narrows itself into a bow shape and projects a thin tongue of land out into the sea. We see the hills behind the city, the harbor, and finally our eyes come to rest for a moment upon a tiny detail of the panorama: the ships at anchor. Lucan's technique here resembles that of

Vergil in *Aeneid* 1 and 2, when he describes Carthage from Aeneas'
vantage point on the hilltop, or the death of Priam from the top
of the royal palace.[29] Vergil, however, gives us the overview
through Aeneas' eyes; Lucan resists the temptation to show us the
scene through Pompey's eyes. Instead, he takes the reader in aerial
flight over the coast. The effect is closer to that Vergil achieves
when, for a moment, we pull back from the description of Priam
lying dead in his palace to the image of the huge, headless body
on the seashore.[30]

Our sweeping panorama is halted momentarily for the single
line of detail about the ships at anchor: "ut tremulos starent
contentae fune carinae." Here is what Haskins has to say about
the line: "*tremulo* and *starent* are the two emphatic words: the
water in the harbour was so still that the ropes by which the ship
was fastened remained slack, and quivered at the slightest motion
of the vessel, caused, for instance, by the crew moving about on
deck, while at the same time the ship remained steady in its
place." [31] To this we might add that *contentae* is a superbly apt
word in this context: not only does it suggest that the ships are
held firm by a slack rope, a curious and clever paradox, but it
also hints at the more common usage of *contentus* as "happy."
Yet surely what is most startling is that Lucan conveys all this in
one line.

The movement which has rested for an instant resumes even
more dramatically in 622: "hinc late patet omne fretum" (the
whole sea opens up in wide expanse). The narrowing of perspectives achieved as we approached Brundisium, to dally for a second
on the motionless ships in the harbor, is suddenly reversed. We
now find ourselves looking far and wide across the Adriatic Sea,
watching the ships sail to Corcyra or Epidamnos. And when our
eyes reach Epidamnos, we see the shores sloping down as if to
greet the incoming sailors. But just as abruptly as we left Brundisium, we are now returned there. The reversal of movement
which we encountered at Epidamnos hurls us back. We reapproach
it now not as a point of departure from Italy to Greece, but as a

29. 1.418–436; 2.453–553. For Aeneas on the rooftop of Priam's palace, see
2.458.

30. 2.554–558.   31. C. E. Haskins, *ad loc.*

place of refuge for storm-tossed sailors when the Greek shores are hostile and inaccessible and the island of Sason, midway between Corcyra and Brundisium, is flooded by the surging waves. But the *fuga nautarum* not only brings us back to port from our own flight across the sea. It brings us back to Pompey. For he, like the sailors, or the Cretans on board Theseus' ships, has sought refuge from troubles in Brundisium.

As we course across the waves in Lucan's description, we are viewing in advance the route Pompey will follow when he leaves Italy for the last time, sailing from the harbor of Brundisium. Almost every detail of the description, then, adds not only to the picture of the place, but to the central themes of the action both before and after the description itself. For all its expansiveness, it is brilliant in its absolute economy and in its continuity of motif.

Throughout the passage the landscape is as much alive and in motion as is the eye of the poet surveying it. Every verb in the narrative except for a descriptive *erat* and the powerful *starent* in 621 suggests some kind of vigorous action or movement. Thus the image of the ships at anchor is doubly effective because the *starent* of 621 contrasts not only with the juxtaposed *tremulo* but with the surge of motion throughout. It quite literally stops us in our tracks.

Is this the sort of description one would expect from a geographer or from a poet? Surely it is the achievement of a poet eager to use his knowledge of geography to impart a new perspective to action and to a landscape. And what is true in this particular passage is true of the epic in its entirety. Lucan brings to bear his knowledge of natural science and history to project poetry into an altogether different dimension. He has not resorted to an elaborate simile to convey the idea of movement and energy as Vergil does in his description of Carthage in *Aeneid* 1.418–440. He has allowed everything to emerge from a carefully phrased narrative, from which we cannot withdraw our eyes even for an instant.

Much the same may be said of the epic as a whole. It is in constant motion, as impressionistically constructed as the description of Brundisium; each part is separate and discrete, yet each is welded into a continuous whole, linked by various motifs to everything around it. It is a kaleidoscope of moods, incidents, and themes, interlocked with great finesse. Lucan's new perspectives, his skill in capturing the moods, faces, and lands of the Roman civil wars, are refreshing and attractive. As even a hostile critic, Robert Graves, admits, he exerts "a strange fascination on even the reluctant reader." [32] Perhaps the readers who bought the *Pharsalia* at the bookseller in such large numbers knew or sensed something that literary critics of the day failed to recognize: that Lucan had written an epic which could have revolutionized Roman poetry.

But there was no literary revolution in the wake of the *Pharsalia*. In fact, the epic form retrenched itself in mythology after Lucan's death. Although Lucan's influence is marked in Silius, Valerius, and Statius, each retreated several crucial steps from the changes Lucan made. To argue that they were disenchanted with Lucan's radical remaking of epic is too simplistic. The ideas on the surface of the *Pharsalia* are powerful undercurrents in the *Punica, Argonautica,* and *Thebaid*. Nor can we truthfully say that Lucan's successors belonged to an altogether different generation. Silius was some fourteen years Lucan's *senior;* Valerius, at a guess (and we can do no more than guess) was around five years younger than Lucan; Statius was rather less than ten years his junior, possibly only five.[33] More important than the differences in age are the differences in the epochs during which they wrote. Silius, Valerius, and Statius are separated from Lucan by the civil wars following Nero's death and by the change of ruling dynasties that followed. The civil strife Lucan prayed for came and went. But it did not bring about the restoration of a less totalitarian regime. On the contrary, the new bloodshed confirmed and strengthened the imperial autocracy.

In the wake of these changes came not only disillusionment, but an increasingly oppressive literary climate. If Vergil proved to be a poet the Flavian writers could not rival, Lucan was one they dared not rival. No matter how attractive Lucan's new approach

32. Graves, 24.

33. For the evidence on Valerius Flaccus, see W. C. Summers, *A Study of the Argonautica of Valerius Flaccus,* Cambridge, 1894, 1–2. For Statius, see O. A. W. Dilke, *Statius: Achilleid,* Cambridge, 1954, 3–8 and D. Vessey, 15–54.

to epic, the *Pharsalia* was too direct and dangerous to follow. Even its author's fate served as a warning. Silius was not the sort of man to take unnecessary political risks; Statius and probably Valerius were not aristocrats, and Statius relied heavily on patronage—imperial patronage at that.[34] At best these writers could admire Lucan from a distance and read of the anguish they knew all too well, but dared not describe. It is little wonder that the *Pharsalia* sold so well in Flavian Rome, where myth had become the only prudent vehicle of truth for a contemporary poet.

History thus conspired against the possibility that Lucan might set a new trend in Roman epic. For Lucan rebelled not only against the literary traditions of the past but also against the tendency to avoid controversial subjects in poetry. Yet the fact that Lucan's revolution did not and could not succeed may well have marked the death of the pagan muse. For all the brilliance of Statius and Valerius, they moved backwards, not forwards. Their new ideas were muffled by the conventions to which they were returned by political rather than purely literary circumstances.

34. See Statius' letter to Marcellus prefacing *Silvae* 4; cf. Juvenal 7.82–87, and the sources cited in Chapter 1, note 1.

CHAPTER 3

Sangre y Arena

A Roman surveying the events of the two hundred years preceding the *Pax Augusta* can be excused for concluding that history was exploiting his city as an object lesson in irony. In 216 B.C. Rome stood on the very brink of catastrophe, her armies crushed by Hannibal. Less than a century later she controlled most of the Mediterranean world. Carthage was leveled; the rest of civilization seemed within her grasp. Yet, no sooner was Carthage destroyed than Rome fell prey, not to a foreign enemy, but to herself. Internal dissent grew steadily and violently as Rome showed herself more capable of military conquest than of controlling her conquering armies.

Dissent finally burgeoned into full-fledged civil war, and in 46 B.C. the climax came. Roman armies clashed at Thapsus, not far from Zama where Scipio Africanus had defeated Hannibal, and the conflict occurred exactly a century after the final destruction of Carthage. As if to drive home the irony, each of the opposing Roman armies was commanded, at least technically, by a Scipio. One was the descendant not only of the Scipios, his adoptive family, but also of the Metellus who had defeated another African foe of Rome, Jugurtha. Allied with him were Cato, a scion of the famous Cato who had urged the destruction of Carthage, and Juba, who traced his line back to both Hannibal and Jugurtha.

Horace, reacting to Pollio's history of the civil wars in *Odes* 2.1, offers one way in which this bizarre cycle of history can be viewed:

> Iuno et deorum quisquis amicior
> Afris inulta cesserat impotens
> tellure, victorum nepotes
> rettulit inferias Iugurthae. [*Odes* 2.1, 25–28]

(Juno—and all the other gods who favored Africa, but had helplessly yielded, leaving it unavenged—brought back the grandsons of the conquerors to be a human sacrifice to Jugurtha.)

Horace adds that conquering Rome has stained the world with her own blood (*ibid.* 29–36), a theme reiterated from *Epodes* 7 and 16. There his bitter conclusion was that Rome had perished by her own hand: "sua / urbs haec periret dextera" (*Epodes* 7.9–10); Rome's own source of strength had been the means of her downfall: "suis et ipsa Roma viribus ruit" (*ibid.* 16.2).

Eduard Fraenkel, in his discussion of Horace's attitude toward the civil wars, comments: "The catastrophe of Thapsus was the means by which the goddess visited upon a late generation of Romans the grim actions of their forefathers—this idea savours of heroic epic and its mythological apparatus rather than of historiography dealing with the recent past." [1] In a way, Fraenkel is right. Horace's idea not only "savours of heroic epic"; it actually is a major motif in an epic—Lucan's *Pharsalia*. As early as *Pharsalia* 1.39 the note is sounded: "Poeni saturentur sanguine manes" (let the ghosts of Carthage be steeped in Roman blood). It is re-echoed in 4.789–790: "ferat ista cruentus / Hannibal et Poeni tam dira piacula manes" (let bloody Hannibal and the Carthaginians have this as a terrible placatory offering); and in 6.309–311:

nec Iuba Marmaricas nudus pressisset harenas
Poenorumque umbras placasset sanguine fuso
Scipio, nec sancto caruisset vita Catone.

(Nor would Juba have lain heavy and naked upon the sands of Africa, nor would Scipio have placated the ghosts of Carthage with the shedding of his blood, nor would holy Cato have been lost to life [sc., if Pompey had won the battle of Dyrrhachium].)

In each of these passages Lucan is referring to the civil wars in Africa between 49 and 46 B.C. The first reference is general enough to encompass both the ill-fated expedition of Curio in 49 and the Thapsus campaign of 46; the second is a specific reaction to the

1. Eduard Fraenkel, *Horace*, Oxford 1957, 239. See also *Epodes* 7 and 16 and S. Commager's useful remarks in *The Odes of Horace*, New Haven, 1962, 160–234. For further discussion of *Odes* 2.1, see also Chapter 2.

defeat of Curio by Juba in 49; the last pinpoints some of the most important incidents of the Thapsus campaign: the deaths of Juba, Metellus Scipio, and Cato.

Although Fraenkel is correct in his observations about the epic nature of Horace's material in *Odes* 2.1, at no point in his discussion does he mention Lucan in connection with these lines. He even suggests that Horace's theme as described here would be ideal for heroic epic and its *mythological apparatus*. Yet Pollio's history of the civil wars could hardly have made less use of traditional mythology than Lucan's *Pharsalia*.

Despite Fraenkel's failure to establish the connection between Horace and Lucan, his observation draws attention to an important and neglected aspect of both *Odes* 2.1 and the *Pharsalia:* the idea that the blood shed in Africa during the civil wars constitutes a placatory offering to the ghosts of Africa and, in particular, to Hannibal and Jugurtha. Horace's use of the word *inferiae* recalls the ritual slaughter of humans as a funeral offering to the dead.[2]

I. The *Munus Gladiatorium*

In Seneca's *Trojan Women,* we see human sacrifice to the dead in a context very suggestive of that in the *Pharsalia*. Early in the play the ghost of Achilles rises from his tomb and demands that Priam's daughter, Polyxena, become his bride in death (*Trojan Women*, 167–202). The force of Achilles' anger is greater than the weight of the earth that oppresses his ashes; in fact, as his ghost arises from the tomb, the earth and sea, along with all the other elements, respond violently to his presence (*ibid.*, 169–184). Achilles' ferocity and thirst for blood are not satiated even in death. The Greek High Command yields to Achilles' demands, and the sacrifice is carried out. Toward the end of the play, a messenger arrives to report to the Trojan women that Polyxena is dead and describes what happened as she was slaughtered:

> non stetit fusus cruor,
> humove summa fluxit, obduxit statim,

2. Cf. *Aeneid* 10.517–520, where Vergil describes Aeneas' capture of men to offer as sacrifices at Pallas' funeral. They are "inferias quos immolet umbris" (419); also *Aeneid* 11.81–82, where the youths captured are actually killed: "quos mitteret umbris / inferias."

saevusque totum sanguinem tumulus bibit.

[*Trojan Women,* 1162–1164]

(But the blood that was shed did not form a pool or flow in streams upon the surface of the ground. That savage grave drew it down immediately and drank it to the last drop.)

The traditional epithet of Achilles, *saevus* (savage), is applied not to the warrior's ghost but to his very tomb. The grave has assumed the identity of the man. It is as if the anger of Achilles' remains has tranferred its power into the very earth in which he lies buried. When the earth drinks Polyxena's blood, Achilles drinks it.

There is a terrifying primitivism here, reminiscent of the barbaric cults associated with much more rudimentary levels of human society, such as those recorded by Sir Edward Burnett Tylor.[3] The whole theory behind human sacrifice seems vindicated. The dead are actually placated by the offering of blood. It is no idle ritual, no anachronistic hangover from bygone days.

We should not pass this off as an example of rhetorical hyperbole for two sound reasons. In the first place, Stoic physics, unlike the physics of Aristotle, do not postulate formal boundaries which clearly define and distinguish one thing from another. The Stoic universe is a dynamic continuum that is infinitely divisible.[4] It is a whole capable of infinite subdivision, *not* an agglomeration of finite entities. And this continuous whole is alive, permeated throughout by the substratum the Stoics called *pneuma,* an animating breath-soul.[5] Since even the soul itself is material in Stoic physics, it is hard to draw a line between organic and inorganic matter. The parts are integrated with the whole and bound together by a material *pneuma.* Thus energy released from one part is capable of being transmitted into anything contiguous to it.

The second reason is far less technically philosophical, but no less complex than the first. The Stoics were by no means the only ancients to believe in the notion of a dynamic continuum. On the

---

3. *Religion in Primitive Culture*[2], London, 1873, 1–447 (especially 41–51); also Schotes, 50–56.

4. S. Sambursky, 1–48 and *passim.*

5. See J. von Arnim, *Stoicorum Veterum Fragmenta,* Leipzig, 1903, 2, nos. 439–481, 522–533, 633–645; *Pharsalia* 7.643–644 and the comments of the scholia on these lines.

contrary, this idea is common to all animistic beliefs in both primitive and more sophisticated society.[6] And this cruder hylozoism was kept very much before the eyes of the Romans by a practice as familiar to them as the bullfight is to the Spaniard: the gladiatorial shows. Tertullian informs us in the *De Spectaculis* that gladiatorial shows were offered as an appeasement to the dead "in the belief that the souls of the dead are propitiated with human blood." This, he adds, is why the gladiatorial show was called a *munus* (an offering or a service).[7] Tertullian's observations are borne out by the fact that the first *munus gladiatorium* was given in 264 B.C. on the occasion of the funeral of Decimus Iunius Brutus Pera. Not until the time of the Gracchi were gladiatorial shows regularly separated from their association with offices for the dead.[8]

Seneca was hardly ignorant of the ritual origins of the gladiatorial *munus*. Certainly Lucan could not have been, since he himself gave a gladiatorial *munus* during his quaestorship.[9] The intelligent Roman reader of Seneca's day knew very well that what the messenger says in the *Trojan Women* comes closer to home than the human sacrifices in *Iliad* 23 or *Aeneid* 11. For Seneca goes to some pains to set the scene for Polyxena's sacrifice in a manner suggestive of a public show: the nature of the site makes it like a theater: "theatri more" (1125). And into this theaterlike hollow pours a great crowd: "concursus frequens implevit omne litus" (1125–1126). In short, the consciousness of the primitive ritual of appeasement of the dead by human sacrifice comes to Seneca no less from the spectacles in the arena than from his Stoic training.

The influence of the gladiatorial shows on Lucan's *Pharsalia* is even more noticeable. His frequent use of the word *par* in the sense of "matched" rather than merely "equal" is only one of the less significant examples. Throughout the epic he seems highly

6. See Tylor, 41–51.   7. *De Spect.* 11–12.
8. Valerius Maximus 2.4.7; Livy *Per.* 16; Servius on *Aeneid* 3.67, and *RE*, SB 3.760–784. (For the Etruscan origins of the *munus* see 760–761); also Athenaeus 4.153 f. = *FHG* 3.416. The early *munera* were fought in the Forum Boarium, the legendary site of the fight between Hercules and Cacus. Hence the Hercules-Cacus fight may well have been very closely associated with the idea of a gladiatorial *munus*.
9. Vacca, *Life:* "gessit autem quaesturam in qua cum collegis more tunc usitato munus gladiatorium edidit."

conscious of the similarity between genuine battle and the arranged fights in the arena. The legions of Pompey and Caesar are matched against each other; their weapons are identical and Roman: "pares aquilas et pila minantia pilis" (1.7). The leaders of the opposing factions do not come to combat equally matched: "nec coiere pares" (1.129). Even on a more ideological level, liberty and Caesar are matched against one another: "par quod semper habemus, / libertas et Caesar, erit" (7.695–696).[10]

But Lucan does not content himself with such oblique allusions:

> coit area belli:
> hic alitur sanguis terras fluxurus in omnis,
> hic et Thessalicae clades Libycaeque tenentur;
> aestuat angusta rabies civilis harena.   [6.60–63]

(The open space (arena, field) of battle closes in. Here the blood which is destined to flow over the whole earth is kept alive; within this space are contained the disasters at Pharsalia and in Libya; the madness of civil war rages on a narrow strip of sand.)

Area is a carefully chosen word. It is commonly used of any open space available for a threshing ground, an arena, or even a graveyard; in addition there is, of course, the basic meaning of field or open space. *Coit* is no less deliberate. It is a verb most often used by Lucan to describe soldiers engaging in battle, as it is in 1.129, quoted above. But in this particular context it suggests that the *battlefield* is being narrowed by the troops. Lucan is describing the action of Caesar in marking off the area for combat at Dyrrhachium by building a rampart for protection against the Pompeian forces. Dyrrhachium is impressionistically reduced to the dimensions of an arena, an enormous amphitheater filled with blood that will spill over the world but is temporarily contained by Caesar's fieldworks. For this is the battle that could have prevented subsequent disasters, had it been a total victory for Pompey.[11]

But even this passage is metaphorical. In *Pharsalia* 4 Lucan re-

10. For further discussion of the ideological aspects of the civil war, see Chapters 6, 7, 8, and 9.
11. 7.312–313.

sorts to direct similes comparing the civil war to a gladiatorial contest. In 4.285–291, the Pompeian forces in Spain are frustrated in their attempts to engage Caesar's army and lose their nerve. Lucan compares them to a wounded gladiator, whose opponent allows him to be weakened by loss of blood and by stiffness before striking the final blow. Later in the same book, the troops of Caesar's lieutenant, Curio, and those of his Pompeian opponent, Varus, are likened to gladiators as they fight against one another (708–710).

The effect of this last simile is especially powerful. It drives home something even the most jaded enthusiast of the games would recognize instantly. Under normal circumstances, pairs of gladiators (*gladiatorum paria*) were equipped with different weapons; they were often of different nationalities.[12] Yet the civil war pits Roman against Roman, legion against legion, javelin against javelin. The unnaturalness of such a pairing is cleverly enhanced by gladiatorial simile. It is appropriate that Curio should use such a simile, for the last part of book 4 brings us back to the point from which we started, culminating in the vision of an offering of blood to Hannibal and the ghosts of Carthage in the land of Africa itself. And Curio's army is to be that sacrifice.

II. Curio

Pharsalia 4.581–824, tells of the arrival of Caesar's legate, Curio, in Africa, the tale of Hercules' combat with Antaeus which he hears there, his victory over the Pompeian general Varus, and his defeat by the African king Juba. We must begin by setting the background to this episode, and, in particular, by giving some account of the central figure in the narrative, Curio.

In 1.171 ff., Lucan outlines the plight into which Rome has fallen in a passage that could almost be a versification of Sallust, *Catiline* 1.10. Might has become the gauge of right: "mensuraque iuris vis erat"; the political system has been broken down by the tribunes; high office is bought, "rapti fasces pretio," and sold by the people every year at the elections: "annua venali referens certamina Campo." Curio occupies a very special place in the midst of all this corruption. He is a tribune, but he is scarcely a *vox*

12. For a full discussion, see *RE* SB3.760–784; also W. Ramsay, *Manual of Roman Antiquities*[15], London, 1895, 406–409.

populi as a tribune ought to be. Lucan sarcastically calls him a *vox quondam populi,* an erstwhile voice of the people. He had been bought by Julius Caesar's gold. His was "a tongue for sale" (*venalis lingua*), and Caesar had purchased its services. Curio's persuasive words proved to be a decisive factor in Caesar's decision to cross the Rubicon. Here, in Lucan's opinion, was a tribune who pursued a course of action in the worst possible interests of Rome.

But Curio is not merely an example of corruption and general worthlessness. Lucan also sees in him a certain ironical greatness:

> ius licet in iugulos nostros sibi fecerit ensis
> Sulla potens Mariusque ferox et Cinna cruentus
> Caesareaeque domus series, cui tanta potestas
> concessa est? emere omnes, hic vendidit urbem.   [4.821–824]

> (Powerful Sulla, fierce Marius, bloody Cinna, and the line of Caesars may have achieved the right to hold their swords at our throats; but who was given such power as Curio? The others all bought the city—he sold it.)

Let us leave aside, for the moment, the acid comment about Sulla, Marius, and Cinna—not to mention the Caesars. We will return to it shortly. What Lucan suggests here is that Curio's greatness transcends even theirs. They merely bought the right to enslave Rome; Curio sold the city to its masters.[13] The greatness and honor involved in this are, of course, ironical. But they are not without purpose. In suggesting that Curio was the great auctioneer of Rome, Lucan is recalling, perhaps, the famous comment made by Jugurtha as he left Rome after bribing the senate:

> urbem venalem et mature perituram, si emptorem invenerit.
> [Sallust, *Jugurtha* 35.10]

> (A city for sale, and doomed to perish soon if she finds a buyer.)[14]

13. Servius (on *Aeneid* 6.261) tells us: "vendidit Curio Caesari XXVII S Romam." See also Velleius 2.48.4; Suetonius *Jul.* 29; Tacitus *Ann.* 11.7; Most significant is Pliny *NH* 36.116–120 (discussed in greater detail in Section VII of this chapter).

14. Cf. Sallust's own editorial comment, *ibid.,* 8.1: "Romae omnia venalia." There are numerous correspondences in the *Pharsalia* with the Sallustian view of Roman history, as we shall note from time to time. Medieval writers have been rather more sensitive to the relationship between Sallust and Lucan

The echo of Sallust's *Jugurtha* is, I suspect, rather more than coincidental. For Curio's special importance in the *Pharsalia* lies in 4.581–824, in which he travels to Africa as Caesar's legate, to put down the Pompeian forces there. Not only does he come to the land of Jugurtha; he is defeated by one of Jugurtha's descendants, Juba; and his blood becomes the first Roman offering upon the graves of defeated Africa. In making Curio the great seller of Rome, then, Lucan presents an individual who not merely completes the final details of Jugurtha's prophecy; he goes beyond them. Lucan knew perfectly well that after Jugurtha's death there was no shortage of would-be purchasers of the city. What was lacking was someone who could actually transact the sale and act as broker for the auction of the corrupt republic.

In general, Lucan's Curio, though unsympathetically treated, is recognizable as the historical personage.[15] But the poet makes certain dramatic changes to use Curio to the best possible effect— changes so slight that they can easily go unnoticed. For example: Lucan informs us that Curio was sent to Africa as Caesar's legate to put down the republican forces under Varus and get rid of the local king, Juba, and that he defeated Varus, but was himself defeated by Juba. This broadly confirms the general outline offered by Appian.[16] But there is a crucial difference. Appian tells that Curio *deliberately* chose to land at a place between Carthage and Clipea, because this was the site of Scipio's arrival in Africa during the Punic Wars. His motive, Appian tells us, was δοξοκοπία—a desire to rival the exploits of his famous predecessor. The Africans, in fact, were so sure that Curio would land in this vicinity that they poisoned all the wells in the area. Although this last suggestion is highly suspect historically, in the view of at least one ancient historian there was nothing *accidental* about Curio's choice of a beachhead.[17]

---

than have modern scholars. The *Rómveriasaga,* for example, is composed of elements drawn from Lucan and Sallust combined, and begins with Jugurtha. See R. Meissner's edition (Berlin, 1910) 5. Cf. Chapter 4, note 2.

15. For a fuller biography of Curio, see F. Münzer, *RE* (Zweite Reihe) 2.867–876 and W. K. Lacey's article, "The Tribunate of Curio," *Historia* 10 (1961), 318–329.

16. Appian *BCiv.* 2.44.

17. See T. Rice Holmes, *The Roman Republic,* 3.427–428.

In the *Pharsalia*, by way of contrast, Curio is surprisingly ignorant of the historical or mythological significance of the area of his
arrival. As he proceeds inland, he comes to a region known as the
Antaei Regna, the "Realm of Antaeus." Curio is baffled by the
name; he is ignorant of the story of Hercules' fight with the Libyan
giant Antaeus. So he asks one of the local peasants why it is so
called; [18] in reply the peasant gives a detailed account of Hercules'
victory.[19] Almost as an afterthought, the peasant adds that the site
is now more famous as the location of Scipio's first African victory
and his base camp.[20] If Curio's joyful reaction is any guide, this is
the first time he realizes precisely where he is.

Why does Lucan make Curio so naive? It is hard enough to believe that an educated Roman would not have known the story of
Hercules and Antaeus.[21] But it is even harder to accept the idea
that the commander of an expedition to Africa would attempt to
land in hostile territory with such scant knowledge of the region.
Curio may have been corrupt, but he was hardly a fool. There are,
perhaps, two reasons, and they are interdependent. The first is that
Lucan is seeking a pretext for narrating the struggle between Hercules and Antaeus, and the second is that he wants the episode to
become a kind of bizarre parallel to Aeneas' arrival at the site of
Rome in *Aeneid* 8.81–369.

III. Aeneas and Curio

When Aeneas arrives at the site of Rome during the celebration
of Hercules' triumph over Cacus, he becomes associated with the
maximus ultor, the great civilizer of the ancient world.[22] Hercules,
by his defeat of the subhuman Cacus, had enabled the primitive
settlement of Evander to grow and live securely; Aeneas, in his
wars against Turnus, will prepare the way for a much greater civi-

18. *Pharsalia* 4.591–592.
19. *Ibid.*, 593–655. See P. Grimal, "L'Episode d'Antée"; and Thompson
and Bruère, "Lucan's Use of Vergilian Reminiscence," *CP* 63 (1968), 1–21.
20. *Pharsalia* 4.656–660.
21. And Lucan makes quite a point of this in 591–592, by using the verb
docēre, suggesting that the *rudis incola* is *teaching* Curio.
22. See G. K. Galinsky, "The Hercules-Cacus episode in *Aeneid* VIII," *AJP*
87 (1966), 18–51 and V. Pöschl, *Die Dichtkunst Virgils*, Innsbruck, 1950, 276.
For a somewhat different discussion, see H. Bellen, "Adventus Dei," *RhM*
106 (1963), 23–30.

lization which will supplant the huts of Evander and go on to
civilize the world. The Romans will continue the mission of Hercules until the last motif on Aeneas' shield is complete, when the
Egyptians and their bestial gods will yield to the might of Rome.
When this occurs, there will be a new age of peace and prosperity
in the triumph of Augustus. Aeneas thus becomes the vital link
between past and future, the visitor to the site of Rome who
shoulders symbolically the destiny of the Roman people and of
the *gens Iulia*. He links, in his person, the fortunes of the Julian
Venus Genetrix with those of *Hercules Invictus*.[23]

The alliance between Hercules and Venus is important, because
these two gods had recently been on opposing sides in the civil war
between Caesar and Pompey.[24] Pompeians made *Hercules Invictus*
their cry at the battle of Pharsalia; Caesarians called upon *Venus
Victrix*. In 46 B.C., Caesar attempted to heal the divisions between
parties and between gods. For sound, if propagandistic reasons, he
linked the name of Hercules with his *ludi Veneris Genetricis,* in
the hopes that some of the wounds within the state could be
patched. Of course, it was important for him to show not just
that Venus and Hercules were natural allies separated only by war,
but that the Roman state and the Julian clan belonged together.
Augustus did much the same on the *Ara Pacis*.[25] Vergil gave literary form to this myth in *Aeneid* 8. In the Hercules-Cacus story
related to Aeneas by Evander at the site of Rome and, later on, in
the scene of Actium upon the shield given to Aeneas by Venus, a

23. See A. Booth, "Venus on the *Ara Pacis,*" *Latomus* 25 (1966), 873–879;
also G. K. Galinsky, *Aeneas, Sicily and Rome,* Princeton, 1969, 3–61 and
191–241.

24. Appian *BCiv.* 2.76: "καὶ ἐς εὐτολμίαν παρακαλοῦντες καὶ τὰ συνθήματα
ἀναδιδόντες, ὁ μὲν Καῖσαρ 'Αφροδίτην νικηφόρον, ὁ δὲ Πομπήιος 'Ηρακλέα ἀνίκητον."
For the cult of *Hercules Invictus,* see K. Latte, *Römische Religionsgeschichte,*
Munich, 1960, 213–331; also *RE* 8.560 ff. The cult of *Hercules Invictus* is associated with the site of Hercules' triumph over Cacus (cf. *Aeneid* 8.102 ff. and
268 ff.). For the association of Hercules with the Forum Boarium, see W. S.
Anderson, "Hercules Exclusus: Propertius 4.9," *AJP* 85 (1964), 1–12. See also
note 8 above. For further discussion of this divine aspect of the civil war, see
Chapter 8.

25. See *RE* 8.560 ff. for a comprehensive list of references, especially 574,
which refers to a relief depicting Venus Genetrix, Victoria, Apollo, and Hercules together. See also the works mentioned above in note 23.

common bond is suggested among Hercules, Venus, Aeneas, the Caesars, and Rome. They are blended together as part of the Roman mythic and historical identity.

Thompson and Bruère rightly argue that the latter part of *Pharsalia* 4 reworks many of the motifs of *Aeneid* 8.[26] They concentrate their attention on the most obvious, and certainly the most startling, resemblance: the fight between Hercules and Cacus in the *Aeneid* and that between Hercules and Antaeus in the *Pharsalia*. The basic scenario is much the same. A man arrives in unknown territory, inquires where he is, and is regaled with the tale of one of Hercules' triumphs. But the land on which each man stands has a much deeper significance for the history of Rome. In the *Aeneid* it is the area that will one day be the city of Rome itself; in the *Pharsalia* it is the site of a camp built many years before by one of Rome's geatest generals; it is the crucible of Rome's greatest victory.

In the *Pharsalia*, however, the man who follows in the footsteps of Hercules and the Scipios is not another Aeneas. He is, rather, a small man in history and a minor figure in Lucan's epic. True, he is one of Caesar's legates, but he is also a man whose decadence and venality Lucan has gone to some pains to stress. He is a pathetic individual, marked for defeat not victory. He is not important enough to fashion the Roman dream or to destroy it. His greatest claim to honor is that he sold Rome to Aeneas' descendant.

Curio is not coming to Africa to seek help as Aeneas sought aid from Evander. His mission is part of the Roman civil war: to win Libya for Caesar.[27] Nor will Africa be the site of any more great Roman victories. Instead it will be the scene of a bitterly contested battle between Caesar and the republicans. If we get the sensation of forward progress when Aeneas arrives at Evander's settlements in the *Aeneid,* we get the feeling that history is undergoing a dramatic turnabout when Curio sets foot in Africa in the *Pharsalia*. For Curio is in almost every respect the complete opposite of

26. Thompson and Bruère, 1–21; also P. Grimal, "L'Episode d'Antée."
27. For Lucan's general attitude to Curio, see 4.689–692 and 1.262–295 and Lacey's article.

Aeneas, a shriveled and degraded caricature of the Roman spirit. But unlike Aeneas, a creation of myth and fantasy, Curio is real. And this petty but historical emissary of the supposed descendant of Venus carries the banner of the Caesarian *Venus Victrix* against the republican Hercules. He is a figure of factionalism, not a champion of unity.

If Curio is an odd counterpart to Aeneas, the peasant, the *rudis incola*, who tells him the tale of Hercules and Antaeus and guides him round the remains of Scipio's camp, gives him suitable company. Curio is a *reductio ad absurdum* of Aeneas; the *rudis incola* is a dwarfed Evander. It is as if Lucan had taken Vergil's Arcadian king, stripped him of his regal and mythical trappings—and, indeed, of his very identity—to reduce him to the level of a nameless, if learned, peasant.

Such procedure verges on parody. But Lucan carefully avoids going too far. He does not allow us to dwell very long on Curio and the peasant. He quickly transfers our attention to Hercules and Antaeus. And if Curio and the *rudis incola* are far inferior to Aeneas and Evander, Hercules in Lucan is far more impressive than he is in Vergil; similarly, Lucan's Antaeus is much more terrible than Vergil's Cacus. Although Vergil assures us that the contest between Hercules and Cacus is that of civilized man against a savage, subhuman creature, Hercules' behavior in Evander's narrative is hardly less bestial than that of his opponent. Once Hercules has trapped Cacus in his cave, he roams around "furens animis" (out of his mind with anger) (*Aeneid* 8.228), and "dentibus infrendens" (gnashing his teeth) (*ibid.*, 230). In fact, the most impressive aspect of Hercules' personality and behavior in Vergil's account is his sheer animal strength and fury.

Cacus makes no attempt to offer battle with Hercules. His first instinct, when his theft of Hercules' oxen is discovered, is to flee, and flee he does. It is only his mighty stone door, suspended by chains which his ancestral skill ("arte paterna," *ibid.*, 226) enabled him to devise, that can protect him from the wrathful Hercules. Ironically, then, Cacus relies on cunning to achieve both the theft of Hercules' oxen and his final self-defense. His dragonlike fire is employed only in the last resort, and it is totally useless to him. Hercules, by way of contrast, would never have discovered what had happened to his cattle had not one of them betrayed Cacus' hiding place with its bellowing.

In the *Pharsalia*, the delineation between Hercules and his opponent is much more distinctly drawn. Hercules is far more credible as the champion of civilization, and Antaeus as the paradigm of raw and unsophisticated violence.

Antaeus' birth and his might make him comparable to Tityos, Briareus, and Typho, the great enemies of heaven whom Hercules had helped defeat in the gigantomachy.[28] His history and background are varied and complex, since he is associated with a number of sites in Egypt and Libya. Perhaps the most astonishing testimony to his barbarity, as we discover from Plato, Pindar, and others—though not, curiously enough, from Lucan—is his building of a temple to his father Poseidon from the skulls of his human victims.[29] In short then, Antaeus is the African monster *par excellence,* and the slaying of Antaeus is one of Hercules' major feats.

Hercules defeats Antaeus not so much by sheer physical strength, though his superior prowess is never questioned, but by his intelligence. He cannot slay his opponent until he discovers the secret of his strength, which is derived from the land of Africa itself: "vires . . . resumit / in nuda tellure iacens" (4.604–605). Hercules' victory over Cacus, on the other hand, is achieved largely by brute force. Cacus, who physically is no match for Hercules, outwits him and is betrayed only by the fact that one of the oxen he has stolen attracts Hercules' attention.

Both Hercules and Antaeus wear lion skins. But this similarity is superficial. Hercules acquired his lion skin as the result of ridding Nemea of the beast that preyed upon its people. Antaeus is himself a predator who slaughters the local residents; and lions, Lucan informs us, were part of his diet. Moreover, Antaeus' lion skin comes from a Libyan lion—a creature of proverbial ferocity in Latin literature. Hercules prepares for the fight by annointing

28. For Antaeus in general and his role in legend and tradition, see K. Wernicke's somewhat patchy treatment, "Antaios," *RE* 1.2339–2343. Astonishingly enough there is no mention of Lucan's account of his fight with Hercules nor of Silius Italicus' reference to an Antaeus in *Pun.* 3.40 in Wernicke's article.

29. Plato *Tht.* 169B; Pindar *Isthm.* 4.56 ff.; Apollodorus 2.5; Diodorus 4.17.4 and 27.3; Hyginus, *Fab.* 31.

himself with the oil used by competitors at the Olympian games; Antaeus pours the sands of Africa upon himself.[30] Lucan may well have had Pindar's *Isthmian* 4 in mind when he saw the contest between Hercules and Antaeus as what K. Wernicke calls "ein Triumph der geistig überlegenen, schulmässigen griechischen Athletik" over the "rohe Naturkraft des Barbaren" (the victory of spiritually superior, educated Greek athletics over the crude natural strength of the barbarian).[31]

This then is the story narrated by the African peasant to the most recent representative of Greco-Roman civilization to arrive at the site of Hercules' victory. As he concludes, however, the peasant adds:

> sed maiora dedit cognomina collibus istis
> Poenum qui Latiis revocavit ab arcibus hostem
> Scipio. [656–658]

> (But greater *cognomina* were given to these hills by the man who forced the Carthaginian enemy [i.e., Hannibal] to be recalled from the citadels of Latium—Scipio.)

Although the region is called *Antaei Regna*, the peasant points out, the site is better known for the camp Scipio established during the Punic Wars, the first step in the campaign leading to the defeat of Hannibal at the battle of Zama.[32] There is an unmistakable suggestion that Scipio's victory over Hannibal surpasses in importance that of Hercules over Antaeus; one great victory for the powers of civilization is overshadowed by another. These lines also contain a neat inversion of epithets. Scipio, who earned his own *cognomen, Africanus,* by defeating Hannibal, is here described as giving what had once been known as the Realm of An-

30. 4.609–616.   31. Wernicke, 2340.
32. For the camp, see Dio 41.41.3; Appian, *BCiv.* 2.102; for the name *Castra Cornelia:* Caesar *BCiv.* 2.24; 25.4 ff. Lucan's identification of the *Antaei Regna* and the *Castra Cornelia* seems to have little purely historical justification, except that this part of North Africa is the general location of both. But surely the basic purpose here is dramatic. The slight modification of geographical detail produces considerable epic effect. On Hercules and Scipio, see E. Basset, "Hercules and the Hero of the *Punica*," in *The Classical Tradition,* ed. L. Wallach, Ithaca, 1966, 258–273 (particularly 259–267); cf. A. R. Anderson, "Hercules and His Successors," *HSCP* 39 (1928), 31–37.

taeus the *cognomen* of his own family. It is worth noting that Hercules' victory over Antaeus occasions no such change of names. Despite his victory, the place remains known as the land of Antaeus. It is only when Scipio is victorious that the *Antaei Regna* assume another (though still secondary) name: *Castra Cornelia.*

But the reminder of Scipio's victory is spoken in a context that relegates it to the distant past:

> en, veteris cernis vestigia valli.
> Romana hos primum tenuit victoria campos. [4.659–660]

("Look," the peasant says, "you can make out the traces of the ancient rampart. This was the first foothold of the conquering Romans.")

Of Scipio's camp only traces remain. There will be no waking of dormant potential here, as there was when Aeneas arrived at the future site of Rome. In the *Pharsalia* Rome's greatness, like Scipio's camp, belongs to the past, and there could be no more poignant reminder of this than the venal Curio himself. He pitches his camp over the remains of Scipio's earlier fortifications, thinking that his chance arrival at so famous a place is an omen of future glory.[33]

Curio's first military engagement is a success. He defeats the Pompeian commander Varus (710–714). The battle is undertaken somewhat precipitously, since Curio doubts the loyalty of his troops who had been, until recently, on Pompey's side. They are, in fact, the cohorts which had come over to Caesar at Corfinium (695–699), and their loyalty to either side is uncertain. Curio reasons that, like gladiators, they will fight in the place they are put:

> veluti fatalis harenae
> muneribus non ira vetus concurrere cogit
> productos, odere pares. [4.708–710]

(As in the offerings [i.e., gladiatorial contests] upon the fatal sand, it is no long-standing anger which leads them forth and pits them against one another; they hate each other because they are matched in combat.)

33. 4.661–665; cf. Thompson and Bruère.

As we shall see in Section VII below, the use of gladiatorial imagery by Curio is singularly appropriate, since he himself had given one of the most dramatic and extravagant *munera* Rome had ever seen. But it also underscores both his own indifference to the issues involved in the conflict and his callous grasp of the fact that there is no genuine reason for the troops to hate one another. They are mere pawns, to be manipulated before they have time to think about what they are doing.

The gladiatorial simile not only reduces the battle between Curio and Varus to the dimensions of a contest in the arena, but it recalls the struggle, fifty lines earlier, between Hercules and Antaeus. For that combat too is suggestive of the arena. On the other hand, distinct issues are involved in the fight between Hercules and Antaeus: civilized man is pitted against the barbarian and is victorious. The dispassionate struggle between Curio and Varus serves only to damage civilization and works to the advantage of neither victor nor vanquished. For no sooner is Varus defeated than the African king Juba moves in to attack the victorious Curio (715). Fifty lines *after* Curio's gladiatorial simile, he lies dead and his troops are slaughtered around him. The unnatural conflict between Roman and Roman has prepared the way for the defeat of Roman by African. In short, Scipio's triumph is replaced by Curio's defeat.

But there is more to it. Curio's blood will be a ritual appeasement to the ghosts of Hannibal and of Carthage:

> excitet invisas dirae Carthaginis umbras
> inferiis Fortuna novis, ferat ista cruentus
> Hannibal et Poeni tam dira piacula manes.
> Romanam, superi, Libyca tellure ruinam
> Pompeio prodesse nefas votisque senatus.
> Africa nos potius vincat sibi.   [4.788–793]

> Let Fortune stir up the hated ghosts of dreaded Carthage with new funeral gifts; let the shades of Hannibal and the Carthaginians have this hideous offering to placate their spirits. But, powers above, this Roman catastrophe on the soil of Libya benefits Pompey and fulfills the prayers of the senate. I wish, rather, that Africa had conquered us while fighting for herself.

Curio, who is so conscious of the imagery of the arena, becomes, along with his army, part of a *munus* himself. And he will not be the last Roman to shed his blood in appeasement of the ghosts of Carthage. If Aeneas at the site of Rome is the harbinger of great things to come, Curio is the harbinger of disaster. At Thapsus and Utica, the Carthaginians will have their fill of Roman blood: "Poeni saturentur sanguine manes" (let the shades of Carthage be drenched in gore) (1.39). This theme is echoed in 6.309–311, where Lucan tells us that if Pompey had followed up his advantage at Dyrrhachium:

Juba would not have fallen naked on the shores of Africa, nor would Scipio have placated the ghosts of Carthage with his blood (*Poenorum-que umbras placasset sanguine fuso Scipio*), nor would holy Cato have been lost to life (*nec sancto caruisset vita Catone*).

Ironically, not even Juba, who exacts this offering to the ghosts of his African ancestors, will gain any long-term benefit from Curio's defeat.

With Curio's arrival and defeat in Africa, the great victories of the past seem strangely hollow. Aeneas may be too huge to enter the small dwellings of Evander, but Curio is no less obviously too small to follow in the footsteps of Hercules and Scipio. All he can do is ready us for the doom of Cato, Metellus Scipio, and the republic, preparing the way for an even greater ritual *munus* at Thapsus and Utica. Perhaps the *Pharsalia*, had Lucan lived to complete it, would not have been without a bizarre version of the traditional funeral games of epic.

IV. Africa, Juba, and Antaeus

The struggles between Hercules and Antaeus, Curio and Varus, and Curio and Juba are dominated by the language of blood, sand, and sweat. The *sangre y arena* of the gladiatorial *munus* could find no better natural landscape than the desert of Libya. In this we can see something of the reason behind the Roman awe for the land of Africa. The sterile sands drain the intruding foreigner of all his energy, but they nurture the native creature such as Antaeus.[34] In fact, Antaeus' greatest ally is the desert. From it

34. See Sallust *Jug.* 89 and R. Syme, *Sallust,* Berkeley, 1964, 150.

he derives the strength to oppose Hercules, who can never be victorious until he learns how to deprive Antaeus of contact with the
land. Antaeus is, in a sense, a born gladiator. The sand thirstily
drinks up his sweat only to replenish his veins with warm blood:

> rapit arida tellus
> sudorem; calido complentur sanguine venae . . .   [4.629–630]

The whole image is paradoxical, for the sand usually *absorbs*
blood no less than it absorbs sweat. But the African enjoys an
enigmatic relationship with his land. It resembles that mysterious
sympathy between the elements we noted in Seneca's *Trojan
Women*—the sympathy between Achilles' ashes and the soil in
which he is buried.

The peasant who tells Curio the tale of Hercules and Antaeus is
quite as puzzled by the phenomenon as is the modern reader. But
he does offer an explanation, and considering that he is supposed
to be a *rudis incola*, it is an amazingly learned one:

> quisquis inest terris in fessos spiritus artus
> egeritur . . .   [*ibid.* 643–644]

(Whatever energy is in the land wells up into his tired limbs.)

The key word here is *spiritus*. It is the Latin equivalent of the
Greek *pneuma*, the Stoic term for the substratum of all matter.[35]
It is the transfer of energy, in this case, from inorganic to organic
matter which can only occur within a material continuum. Here,
in *Pharsalia* 4, primitive animism and Stoic physics merge. No
line can be drawn between man and his universe. Both are alive.

Here we see the similarity between Seneca's idea in the *Trojan
Women* and that of Lucan in the *Pharsalia*. Not only do the successors of Antaeus seek vengeance for their past defeats, so does
the land of Africa itself. In both the *Pharsalia* and the *Trojan
Women*, the graves of the dead are thirsty for a blood offering.
The first *piaculum* to be poured upon the tombs of Africa is that
of Curio. But those tombs, and Africa itself, will not have their
thirst slaked until the battle of Thapsus, a gladiatorial *munus*
fought by the conquerors of Africa as an appeasement to the *manes*
of Hannibal and Jugurtha.

35. See above, notes 3–6.

The horrors of war in Africa and the motif of African vengeance lead Lucan to a rather unsympathetic treatment of Curio's adversary, Juba. This is interesting for a number of reasons, but chiefly because Juba was actually fighting for the Pompeian side in the civil war. Given Lucan's republican sympathies, then, we might wonder why he has no good word to say about Juba in the epic. The explanation is that the historical Caesar had gone to some pains to associate Juba with his African ancestry and to maintain that Metellus Scipio and Cato were fighting for Juba during the campaign of 46, rather than vice versa. In other words, Caesar's propaganda made it necessary for a republican apologist to treat Juba rather gingerly. And Lucan seems intent on making it quite clear that Juba is an independent agent, not an integral part of the republican war effort.

Lucan turns political necessity to artistic advantage. Juba's principal significance is shaped around his African identity rather than around his loyalties to the Pompeian side in the civil war. While Lucan does not deny that Juba's defeat of Curio worked out to Pompey's advantage, he very carefully avoids suggesting that Juba was actually fighting for Pompey. He merely notes that Juba's victory benefited the Pompeian cause: "Pompeio prodesse nefas" (4.792). And the word *nefas* indicates that, in Lucan's opinion, Curio's defeat was something ghastly and *wrong*. Despite the fact that Curio was coming to Africa to free Libya from a tyrant while making Rome a kingdom: "Libyam auferre tyranno / dum regnum te, Roma, facit" (691–692), and despite the fact that, during his tribunate, Curio had supposedly contaminated the gods and human affairs (689), Lucan does not enjoy the spectacle of his defeat in Africa. He shares, fundamentally, the attitude of his Lentulus in 8.429–430. Lentulus, for all his loathing of Caesar, would rejoice if Caesar were to achieve a victory over the Parthians. But Lucan does not go quite so far. Instead of saying that he would be happy to see Juba vanquished by Curio, he exclaims: "Africa nos potius vincat sibi" (4.793) (I would rather that Africa had conquered us while fighting for herself). He thus expresses his distress without going overboard in his condemnation of Juba or in his lament for the fallen Curio.

This still leaves Lucan with the problem of finding a motivation for Juba's role in the war, if his purpose is not that of aiding the republican cause. He argues that Juba engaged in the fight against Curio for personal reasons: "privatae sed bella dabat Iuba concitus irae" (ibid. 688), no less than from interest in the issues of the civil war. Having thus disposed of the problems created by Juba's association with the republican cause without actually falsifying the record, he proceeds to ignore everything about him apart from the fact that he was an African descended from Hannibal and Jugurtha. In 8.284–287, Pompey rejects the possibility of seeking aid from Juba after the battle of Pharsalia on the grounds that Juba is the impious offspring of Carthage who has not forgotten his origins; he is a threat to Italy, since he is related directly to the Numidians, and indirectly to Hannibal himself:

> namque memor generis Carthaginis inpia proles
> inminet Hesperiae, multusque in pectore vano est
> Hannibal, obliquo maculat qui sanguine regnum
> et Numidas contingit avos.

Similarly in 4, Lucan associates Juba with the traditional foes of Rome. At 724–729 he compares him to an ichneumon, a sly and cunning animal with the instincts necessary to match and overpower a snake.[36] This figurative description goes well with the tactics Juba uses against Curio (ibid. 730–748). His deceitful maneuvering evokes memories of Carthaginian warfare. We find Curio fearing "Libycas fraudes" (Libyan treachery) and "infectaque semper / Punica bella dolis" (Carthaginian warfare which is always waged in an underhanded manner) (736–737).

This is why it is wrong to suggest a series of analogies that would align Curio with Antaeus and Hannibal, and Juba with Hercules and Scipio, as Bruère and Thompson have done. That Juba wins, and thus shares something in common with Hercules, is less important than his being an African and an enemy of Greco-Roman civilization. In the case of Hercules and Scipio, the "right" side wins. But in Juba's case, victory has gone to the "wrong" side. Far from connecting Juba with Hercules, Lucan aligns him with Hannibal, Jugurtha, and the forces of the African land inimical

36. For the ichneumon, see Pliny NH 8.88. For the importance of the snakes and their association with Africa, see Chapter 2, Section II.

to Rome. Juba must, as Pompey declares in 8, be feared rather than admired because of his defeat of Curio. He has grown proud and looks down on the affairs of Rome from the vantage point of success: "intumuit viditque loco Romana secundo" (8.288). In fact, as the blood of Curio's army dampens the swirling sand so that Curio can see the full extent of his defeat, a *piaculum* has been made to Carthage, and that *piaculum* has been exacted by Hannibal's descendant, Juba. If Hannibal follows in the tradition of Antaeus, so does Juba.

Juba defeats Curio by relying on the basic source of African strength: the very nature of the land itself, just as Antaeus and Hannibal had done. The secret of depriving the African of the energy transmitted from the land was fundamental to the victories achieved by Hercules, Scipio, and even Metellus and Marius in their wars against Jugurtha.[37] But Curio failed to learn the lesson of his predecessors, and was worn down to defeat.

V. The Roman Africans

Africans were not the only people able to draw into themselves the life force imparted by the Libyan sands and go on to inflict terrible sufferings upon mankind. Marius, who had defeated Jugurtha, learned the secret too.

The anonymous narrator who tells the story of the civil wars between Marius and Sulla in *Pharsalia* 2 reminds us that Marius, in later life, became the avenger of the very nations he had once defeated. When exiled from Rome, Marius traveled to Africa. On his way there, his life was threatened by a Cimbrian, who had good reason to hate him for the carnage he had wrought upon the Cimbrian nation. But just as the Cimbrian raised his sword to kill Marius, there came to him a sudden vision of the destruction Marius would wreak upon Rome:

> si libet ulcisci deletae funera gentis,
> hunc, Cimbri, servate senem. [2.84–85]

> (If you wish to avenge the deaths of your massacred people, Cimbrians, keep this old man alive!)

37. See note 34 above and *Pharsalia* 4.615–617 and 645–651.

The destroyer of the Cimbri is the very man in whom lies their hope of vengeance.[38] Marius, on his return from exile, will drench Rome in blood.

When Marius arrives in Africa, he lies down on the ground in Jugurtha's kingdom and rests upon the ashes of Carthage. He draws the wrathful fury of the African land into himself:

> idem pelago delatus iniquo
> hostilem in terram vacuisque mapalibus actus
> nuda triumphati iacuit per regna Iugurthae
> et Poenos pressit cineres. solacia fati
> Carthago Mariusque tulit, pariterque iacentes
> ignovere deis. *Libycas ibi colligit iras.* [2.88–93]

(This same man, carried across the unjust [*or* stormy] sea, driven into a hostile land [i.e., Africa] full of empty huts, lay down in the deserted kingdoms of Jugurtha whom he had destroyed, and his body pressed down upon the ashes of Carthage. Both Carthage and Marius received solace from fate; for as they lay down in defeat, side by side, they pardoned the gods. *For it was there that Marius absorbed the anger of Africa.*)

Marius, as Haskins rightly points out, renews his *furor* from the Libyan desert just as Antaeus does in 4.604–605: "vires . . . resumit / in nuda tellure iacens." [39] The land that imparted its peculiar strength to its own children, Antaeus, Hannibal, and Jugurtha, now gives renewed vigor to the Roman who will avenge them.

The indiscriminate slaughter of one's fellow-men ranks the perpetrator with the enemies of civilization and of Hercules. It was precisely this African savagery Hercules had set out to destroy in his fight with Antaeus, and which the Romans, according to Livy, had experienced in their life and death struggle with Carthage. Sulla's reprisals following his victory at the battle of the Colline

---

38. Cf. Plutarch *Mar.* 30, where the story of the Cimbrian is also found.

39. Haskins, note on 2.93: "Marius is compared to Antaeus . . . he gathers from the soil of Africa fury against Rome such as Hannibal and Jugurtha had shown, 'true African fury.'" Haskins, following Oudendorp, adduces Manilius 4.44–48 to parallel this passage. For Antaeus' source of strength, see 4.604–605. Cf. Pompey's words in 8.269–270 and Cicero *Pis.* 43; also Juvenal 10.276–278.

Gate are seen by Lucan as surpassing the horrors committed by Lycurgus or Antaeus. Though both Thrace and Libya were noted for their savagery, Sulla succeeds in going beyond them:

> scelerum non Thracia tantum
> vidit Bistonii stabulis pendere tyranni,
> postibus Antaei Libye. [2.162–164]

(Thrace did not see such horrors hanging in the stables of Lycurgus, nor Libya on the doorposts of Antaeus.)

More important than the other *exempla* of Libyan savagery to be found in Latin literature, for our purposes here, is the simile in *Aeneid* 12.4–9, where Turnus is compared to a wounded Carthaginian lion, whose very injury gives him renewed strength to face the enemy:

> Poenorum qualis in arvis
> saucius ille gravi venantum vulnere pectus
> tum demum movet arma leo, gaudetque comantis
> excutiens cervice toros fixumque latronis
> impavidus frangit telum et fremit ore cruento . . .

(Just as a lion in the fields of Carthage, whom hunters have struck with a serious wound in the chest, rallies at last to fight, and takes joy in flexing his muscles, mane erect on his neck; fearlessly he breaks the javelin which the bandit has thrust into him, and roars with blood pouring from his mouth . . .)

G. K. Galinsky, in reference to this simile, points out how crucial it is that Turnus is compared to "not simply any wild lion, but a Punic one. . . . Turnus is identified with Rome's arch-enemy, Carthage." [40] He has, perhaps inadvertently, established a point significant for Lucan also. For in *Pharsalia* 1.205–212, Lucan describes Julius Caesar in almost exactly the same manner:

> sic ut squalentibus arvis
> aestiferae Libyes viso leo comminus hoste
> subsedit dubius, totam dum colligit iram;
> mox, ubi se saevae stimulavit verbere caudae

40. G. K. Galinsky, "*Aeneid* V and the *Aeneid*," *AJP* 89 (1968), 157–185, especially 174–175. Cf. M. C. J. Putnam, *The Poetry of the Aeneid*, Cambridge, Mass., 1965, 153.

erexitque iubam et vasto grave murmur hiatu
infremuit, tum torta levis si lancea Mauri
haereat aut latum subeant venabula pectus,
per ferrum tanti securus volneris exit.　[1.205–212]

(Just as a lion in the parched fields of Libya sees his foe close
at hand, and crouches down in uncertainty until he has
gathered all his anger—(*totam dum colligit iram*); but soon he
rouses himself by lashing his body with his savage tail, makes
his mane stand high, and opens his jaws wide in a ferocious
roar. Then, even if the light lance of a Moor pierces his side, or
hunting-spears penetrate his mighty breast, he passes through
the steel, careless of the great wound that he has suffered.)

The similarity between this passage and *Aeneid* 12.4–9 is obvious. But its implications are very serious indeed. If Lucan is
consciously imitating the Vergilian simile, as seems more than
likely, are we to assume that *Caesar* is being identified with Rome's
archenemy, Carthage?

The answer, as we shall see, is yes. If we go a step further and
compare the expression *colligit iram* in Lucan's simile with the
description of Marius recouping his strength in Africa, cited earlier, our answer receives some confirmation. Just as the lion gathers its anger, so does Marius in 2.93: "Libycas ibi colligit iras." [41]
Like Antaeus and Marius, the lion to which Caesar is compared
renews its energy by sinking down upon the ground. But by far
the most important consideration is this: if Marius and Curio are
responsible for the avenging of Carthage and Hannibal, surely
Caesar is also. For if the petty Curio's defeat by Juba is to bring
about a placatory offering to the ghosts of Africa, the battle of
Thapsus which Caesar will win in 46 B.C. can be nothing less than
the final blood atonement for past African defeats. As Horace
observes in *Odes* 2.1, 27–28, Juno has brought back the grandsons
of the conquerors to be an offering to Jugurtha: "Tellure, vic-

---

41. Haskins, and P. Wuilleumier and Le Bonniec (*M. Annaeus Lucanus:
Bellum Civile, Liber Primus,* Paris, 1962, 20) in their notes on 1.207 all recognize the identity of the expression to that of 2.93. Further, the idea that the
wounded lion can pass through the hunter's weapon recalls the earlier comparison of Caesar to a thunderbolt in 1.157; no *materia* can prevent the thunderbolt's return to the skies.

torum nepotes / Rettulit inferias Iugurthae." The word *inferiae,* even more obviously than Lucan's *piaculum,* makes us aware that what is to occur there is nothing less than a ritual offering to the African dead.

Marius, bloody though his vengeance was, carried out his slaughter in Italy, not in Africa. Curio was at least defeated by an African. But Caesar, at the battle of Thapsus, pitted Roman against Roman in combat over the graves of Libya, as if in some terrible *munus gladiatorium.*

VI. Caesar and Hannibal

The man for whose cause Curio fights in *Pharsalia* 4 stands in direct succession to Antaeus, Hannibal, Jugurtha, and Marius. He will complete the task his predecessors were never able to accomplish. From the very beginning of the *Pharsalia,* Lucan establishes a clear connection between Caesar and the great enemies of Rome.[42] The poet proceeds carefully, step by step. When he first introduces Caesar, he compares him to a thunderbolt whose energy is purely destructive (1.143–157). Our initial impression of Caesar is one of *furor,* and this *furor* is qualified some fifty lines later (1.205–212) as *Libycus furor* by means of the lion simile.

Less than fifty lines after the lion simile, the people of Ariminum complain that they are suffering once again what they have suffered so often in the past: they are on the direct route to Rome which all the great enemies of Italy have followed (1.248 ff.). First came the Sennonian Gauls, then Hannibal, the Cimbri, and the Teutones. This time it is Caesar. Lucan has now advanced his idea a step further: Caesar's actions make him comparable to the worst foreign enemies Rome ever had.

The final link comes in 1.303–305. There Caesar himself observes that the people of Rome are reacting to his presence as if he were some Hannibal:

> non secus ingenti bellorum Roma tumultu
> concutitur, quam si Poenus transcenderit Alpes
> Hannibal . . .

---

42. Just as he seems to envisage a like parallel between Caesar and Achilles in 9.950 ff. See Chapter 6, Section III.

(Rome is stunned by the huge upheaval of war, as if Carthaginian Hannibal had just crossed the Alps.)

Caesar is not, I think, seriously suggesting a close comparison between himself and Hannibal. On the contrary, he is expressing surprise that the Romans are behaving as if he were Hannibal. But surely *Lucan* is serious.

The lion simile, the comments of the people of Ariminum, and Caesar's direct comparison would be effective even if separated from each other in different contexts or in different books. But all three occur not only within the same book, but within a hundred lines. Lucan clearly did not intend us to keep them discrete in our minds. At the same time he proceeds with great caution, advancing the comparison stage by stage. The final touch, the actual identification of Caesar with Hannibal, comes as the powerful climax, though Lucan carefully protects himself from adverse reaction in imperial circles by allowing that crucial identification to be made by Caesar himself, almost in jest. This obliqueness is scarcely surprising, for in suggesting that Caesar and Hannibal were kindred spirits, Lucan is treading on very dangerous ground.

As the *Pharsalia* progresses, Lucan divests himself of this circumspect obliqueness. In 7.408–409 he tells us that the battle of Pharsalia was a more terrible disaster for Rome than either Cannae or Allia.[43] This in itself suggests that Caesar, as victor of Pharsalia, did more damage to Rome than Hannibal did. Finally, in 7.799–803, Lucan openly avows that Caesar's behavior after Pharsalia was worse than Hannibal's behavior after Cannae. At least Hannibal buried the Roman dead; Caesar did not. And Caesar's actions suffer even more by comparison because the Romans were, after all, the foreign foe of Hannibal; but they were Caesar's fellow-citizens.

How much farther and deeper the comparison between Caesar

43. As early as 2.45 ff., the armies begin to wish that they had lived in the days of the great disasters of Cannae and Trebia rather than endure the horrors of a civil war. It is typical of Lucan's hostility to Caesar that he should associate him with Hannibal rather than with Alexander. For allusions to Caesar and Alexander see pp. 222–225. Since the Romans themselves are to be the avengers of Hannibal, it is scarcely surprising that the battles in which that vengeance will be achieved should be considered worse than Hannibal's victories. After all, Cannae, though terrible, was not fatal.

and Hannibal would have gone if Lucan had been able to extend his epic to the battle of Thapsus we can only speculate. But, as we have noted, Caesar's victory on African territory, close to the site of Zama, could hardly escape comparison with the major events of the Punic Wars. His opponents, Metellus Scipio and Cato, far too readily recalled the names of their ancestors who had championed the Roman cause against the African enemies. And last, but not least, Lucan could hardly have resisted noting that Caesar undertook the rebuilding of Carthage once the war was over—the crowning act of historical irony.[44]

The historical Caesar cannot have been unaware of the dangers of appearing to be a Hannibal rather than a Hercules or an Alexander.[45] At the very beginning of the civil war, Cicero, in an unguarded moment, wrote to Atticus: "utrum de imperatore populi Romani an de Hannibale loquimur?" (are we talking about an officer of the Roman people, or about Hannibal?).[46] The African campaign of 46 B.C. posed a real problem for Caesar. His opponents were swift to take advantage of the curious historical accident that had brought the civil war to Africa exactly a hundred years after the destruction of Carthage, and of the fact that the Republican forces were commanded by another Scipio. Metellus Scipio boasted that *only* a Scipio could win in Africa, and in this

44. Dio 43.50.3. Not only did Caesar restore Carthage, he also restored Corinth. Cf. Augustus' restoration of the damage done to Carthage (Dio 52.43), and the rumor that both Caesar and Augustus considered the possibility of transferring the capital to Troy (Suetonius *Jul.* 79). Most scholars reject the idea that either Caesar or Augustus actually contemplated such an action and they are certainly right (R. Syme, "Caesar, the Senate and Italy," *PBSR* 14 [1938], 2, note 6, and the others cited by Fraenkel, 267 ff. in connecwith *Odes* 3.3.17–68). But, given Caesar's preoccupation with connecting his ancestry with Aeneas and Troy, such a rumor probably seemed all too credible at the time. And Lucan cannot resist making insinuations to this effect in 9.950 ff. (See above, note 42.)

45. The mere act of crossing the Alps seems to have conveyed a Hannibal-like image. Perhaps this is why Pompey, when crossing the Alps in 76, followed a route he believed to be different from that of Hannibal (Sallust *Ep. Pompeii* 4). His purpose and direction were also different, of course. He was going to Spain to fight Sertorius (cf. Appian *BCiv.* 1.109). But the fact that Caesar followed what was thought to be Hannibal's path did not help his image.

46. *Att.* 7.11.1. For the parallels between Lucan's Caesar and Silius' Hannibal, see M. von Albrecht, *Silius Italicus*, Amsterdam, 1964, 47 ff. and 185 ff.

boast recalls the peculiar magic of the name Scipio and its strong associations with the Carthaginian wars.

For reasons not quite clear, Caesar decided to take a "tame" Scipio to Africa with him for the Thapsus campaign.[47] Suetonius declares that Caesar's only reason for doing this was that he wished to ridicule certain prophecies that only a Scipio could win there (*Julius* 59). Plutarch is not so sure: "It is difficult to tell whether he put Scipio in charge as some kind of a joke, or whether he was accommodating himself in earnest to the omen" (*Caesar* 52). Caesar's attitude to omens and prophecies, however, is not really the important issue here. What matters is that Caesar took a Scipio —Scipio Salvito—to Africa and actually put him in command of the battle line at Thapsus.[48] Politically, this was an astute move. It was thus much harder for Metellus Scipio to make propaganda for his own advantage on the basis of his family name. Further, it increased the difficulty Caesar's opponents would have in branding *him* as the latter-day Hannibal.

Caesar's keen eye had detected the essential flaw in the republican propaganda, and by neutralizing *their* Scipio, he could exploit it to the full. The flaw was that the republicans were strongly supported by Juba—a powerful, but politically damaging ally. Since Juba claimed descent from Hannibal and Jugurtha, it was easy enough for Caesar to claim that Metellus Scipio had discredited himself by his alliance with Juba. After all, Metellus' ancestors were responsible for the defeat of both Hannibal and Jugurtha; and now this degenerate scion of two great families was fighting for the African cause against the elected officials of the Roman state. Caesar could readily argue that his "tame" Scipio was the real successor of Aemilianus and Africanus and that Metellus was the traitor.

Caesar's success in evading the tag of being a Hannibal would hardly have been very notable if he had been defeated at Thapsus. But he was not defeated. In fact, his propaganda won him an added benefit that military success alone could not have granted him. He celebrated a triumph over Africa on his return to Rome.

47. Plutarch, *Caes.* 52–54; Suetonius, *Jul.* 59; Dio 42.58.
48. Plutarch, *Caes.* 52 τοῦτον ἐν ταῖς μάχαις προέταττεν ὥσπερ ἡγεμόνα τῆς στρατιᾶς.

By maintaining that Metellus Scipio and Cato were fighting for
Juba, rather than vice versa, he was able to pass them off as *hostes*
of the Roman state. By this sleight of hand he circumvented the
tradition that there could be no triumphs in a civil war, arguing
that the African war was not a *civil* conflict.[49]

Although Lucan cannot avoid conceding military victory to
Caesar, he can restore a republican perspective on the propaganda
issue. His approach is very subtle. He could, for instance, have
emphasized that the champion god of the republicans was
Hercules Invictus, and pointedly and geometrically structured his
narrative to show that Caesar, like Antaeus, is an enemy of Hercules the Civilizer. But he does not. Lucan has enough historical
sense to know that the manipulation of divine champions does not
make one side right and the other wrong. As we have seen, however, he runs into more difficulties with Juba. His success in dealing with this awkward ally of Pompey is achieved by assassinating
Juba's character. The Caesarians maintained that Juba was an
enemy of Rome. Lucan conceded this. He does not wish to weaken
his position by making Juba an integral part of the republican forces and attempting to defend him. He thus dissociates
Juba from the republican cause so as to concentrate our attention
on the war's ideological aspects and to leave the way clear for a
much more direct comparison between Caesar and Hannibal in
the epic's later books. By the time Lucan reached the narrative of
Thapsus, the reader would be fully aware that Juba was fighting
for the republicans, not they for him and that his aid was neither
keenly sought nor warmly received. With this problem out of the
way, Lucan could all the more readily maintain that Caesar was
the truly African spirit of destruction, the man who brought the
piaculum to the ghosts of Africa and let the blood with his own
hand.

Thapsus and Utica between them would provide the greatest of
all potential gladiatorial motifs in the *Pharsalia.* The actual battle, where matched Roman armies, each led at least nominally
by a Scipio, would fight in a *munus* of appeasement to the ghosts
of Hannibal and Jugurtha, is powerful enough by itself. But when

49. *Pharsalia* 1.12: "bella . . . nullos habitura triumphos." Cf. 6.260–261;
Cicero *Phil.* 14.23; Valerius Maximus 2.7.7.

we add the quite literal hand-to-hand combat between Petreius and Juba, Roman against African, each seeking death at the hands of the other, perhaps another dimension could be added. Finally, there is the death of Cato.

Of this last potential motif Seneca gives the germ in the *De Providentia* 2.8–9: the usual games and contests in the amphitheater are "puerilia et humanae oblectamenta levitatis" (the childish delights of human vanity). But if one wishes to see a spectacle which god would turn to watch, even though he is busy about his tasks: "ecce par deo dignum: vir fortis cum fortuna mala compositus, utique si et provocavit." This gladiatorial "pair" pits the brave man against evil fortune, with the brave man as challenger. And Seneca's example is Cato, standing amidst the ruins of the state, ready to take his own life: "Catonem, iam partibus non semel fractis, stantem nihilo minus inter ruinas publicas rectum." The battle of Thapsus may be the greatest physical example of the *munus* to the dead. But Cato's suicide is an even greater example of the moral struggle between man and history. With Thapsus the ghosts of Carthage have been avenged. But Cato's suicide marks a new phase in the struggle. It is now his blood and the blood of the Roman state that will cry out for vengeance. Brutus' dagger will be the instrument that achieves the first *piaculum* to the dead republic and keeps in motion the new strife that pits Caesar against liberty. Africa has avenged her defeats by Rome; now the republic must avenge its annihilation by Caesar.

VII. Curio and Rome: A Final Note

Curio's arrival in Africa, then, is an important stage in the development of what Lucan sees as the total reversal of history that awaited Rome as the inevitable consequence of civil war: the vengeance of Africa and the collapse of civilized law and order. It prepares the way for the legalization of crime and a return to the barbaric tyranny of an Antaeus. Thematically, Curio stands between the Rome of Scipio and the Rome of Caesar. His are the qualities that soured Roman greatness and made Caesar's *regnum* possible. But, in an even more literally physical sense, Curio camps on the precise spot where Scipio had once prepared for the battle of Zama and near which Caesar would win his victory at Thapsus. Like Aeneas, Curio is a link between past and future. He also reminds us most powerfully of a comment made by Silius Italicus in *Punica* 3.261: "et Zama et uberior Rutulo nunc sanguine Thapsus" (Zama and Thapsus, richer now with Rutulian blood). Thapsus and Zama are mentioned in the same breath; the two cities are part of the same contingent in Hannibal's army. By juxtaposing the two names, Silius looks forward not only to Rome's victory over Carthage, but to the blood shed later in the civil war. Perhaps it is significant that the blood that enriches Thapsus is *Rutulian*—a reminder that the conflict between Aeneas and Turnus did not bring an end to the conflict between native Italians and the descendants of Venus. The struggle reaches out of myth into history; it does not end as Aeneas' sword falls. Somehow we are not even surprised when Silius tells us that the contingent from Zama and Thapsus was commanded by one Antaeus, whose name recalls Hercules' foe. Rome's greatest victory and her most ominous, self-inflicted defeat are both presided over by that terrible name so deeply associated with the brutality and deadliness of Africa.[50]

Yet perhaps there is one last aspect of Curio that may further explain why Lucan makes him such an important figure in the *Pharsalia*. It is both appropriate and ironic that a man named Curio should bring the first *piaculum* to Hannibal and Carthage in Africa. No Roman reader would have been unaware that Curio's name recalls the *sacerdos curio sacris faciundis*, the priestly *curio* in charge of sacrifices.[51] And Lucan probably knew also that Curio was himself a *pontifex*.[52] Like his priestly namesake, then, Curio presides over a ritual offering. But unlike the usual *sacerdos*, who merely presides, he is also part of it.

A passage from book 36 of Pliny's *Natural Histories* sheds fur-

---

50. The mythical Antaeus is mentioned only once by Silius (*Pun.* 3.40), but he leaves us in no doubt that the Antaeus who commands a unit in Hannibal's army is to be closely identified with Hercules' opponent: "ducit tot populos, ingens et corpore et armis, / Herculeam factis servans ac nomine famam, / Antaeus celsumque caput super agmina tollit" (3.262–264).

51. *CIL* 8.1174; also *CIL* 2.1262; 6.2169; Dion.Hal. 2.7 and 21; Varro *Lingua Latina* 5.83; 6.46. For a full discussion see *RE* 4.1836–1838.

52. Dio 40.62. Cf. *RE* 4.1836–1838.

ther light on both Curio and the ideas discussed to this point.[53] Here are some excerpts referring to Curio's building of a special double theater in Rome on the occasion of his father's funeral, an ingenious and extravagant structure which Pliny calls "insaniam e ligno" (madness in wood).

He constructed side by side two very large theaters made of wood and balanced on a revolving base. . . . Suddenly these theaters revolved so that their ends met and formed an amphitheater. He gave gladiatorial contests there, but the Roman people were in greater danger than the gladiators as Curio whirled them round. . . . Behold the conquerors of the world, the rulers of every nation; they control tribes and kingdoms, they give laws to foreign lands, they are a kind of viceroy of the gods among men. And here they are suspended on a revolving pivot, cheering their own danger! What kind of contempt for life is this? What business have we to complain about Cannae (*quae querela de Cannis!*)?

. . . Behold the entire population of Rome, as if it were loaded into two ships, is suspended upon two axis-points; it watches itself fight to the death (*et se ipsum depugnantem spectat*) doomed to die in a catastrophe at any moment if the contraption collapses.

And this is the means Curio used to win favor for his speeches as tribune, so that he could stir the swaying people to his will (*ut pensiles tribus quatiat*). If he could persuade them to do this, there was nothing that he would not be able to do at a political rally. For if we admit the truth, the whole Roman people was fighting it out in a funereal sacrifice at his father's graveside (*vere namque confitentibus populus Romanus funebri munere ad tumulum patris eius depugnavit universus*).

When the pivots were tired and worn out he modified his magnificence. On the final day, he kept his edifice in the form of an amphitheater and gave an athletic display upon the two stages which were now back to back in the center of the arena. Suddenly the platforms

---

53. 116–120. Pliny corroborates several statements made by Lucan in the *Pharsalia* and deserves closer attention from the Lucan scholar. After all he was an older contemporary of Lucan, and Lucan probably knew him. Perhaps the most notable example is the parallel between *NH* 7.178 and *Pharsalia* 6.333–836 (the necromancy of Sextus Pompey). P. Grenade, "Le Mythe de Pompée et les Pompéiens sous les Césars," *REA* 52 (1950), 28–63, especially 37 ff. notes the similarity between the story of Gabienus' prophecy to Sextus Pompey in Sicily (unknown from other sources) and the necromancy of Lucan. For a fuller discussion of this see Chapter 4, Section IV.

were rushed off, and he produced, that same day, the gladiators who had been victorious in the earlier contests. And this Curio was not a king, a great ruler over nations—in fact, he was not even noted for his wealth. The only thing he had to his credit was the discord between the leaders of the state.

The whole passage is written with fulsome extravagance. Why the comparison with Cannae, for example, why the pointedly allegorical nature of the whole passage? There was no literal catastrophe as the result of the funeral games Curio gave in honor of his father. The theater did not collapse; no one was killed. Surely Pliny is making, in a different way, precisely the same point that Lucan makes in the *Pharsalia*. While Lucan on occasions shrinks the dimensions of the civil war to those of the contests in the arena, Pliny consciously expands the motifs of Curio's funeral games into the larger context of the civil war. The war itself, no less than the funeral games for Curio's father, is the magnificent achievement of a man whose only financial asset is the feud between Caesar and Pompey. For all the superior wealth of the two opposing champions, and for all their greater political stature, they and the whole of Rome are directed into the opposing segments of the great theater, and fight to the death in the arena which Curio built.

Lucan draws us to the same sort of paradox in *Pharsalia* 4.821–824, when he tells us that Curio rivals and surpasses powerful Sulla, fierce Marius, and bloody Cinna—even the long line of Caesars. They merely bought Rome while Curio sold it. With an almost viciously casual stroke of the pen, the more telling because it is unexpected, Lucan suggests that the Caesars are even worse than the villains of the decadent republic. The epithets of Sulla, Marius, and Cinna are set in ascending order of barbarity, *potens, ferox, cruentus*. Then comes the *Caesareae domus series* to top the list. The degeneration of the state in which Curio plays such a key and transitional role will have long-lasting consequences. The small man, Curio, sold Rome not only to Julius Caesar, but to all the Caesars for centuries to come. The pathetic Roman who falls to Juba near the site of Zama has a niche in history that none other could rival. Lucan need not emblazon his shield with scenes from the future to tell of the disasters that lie ahead.

CHAPTER 4

Some Minor Characters
of the *Pharsalia*

The *Pharsalia* is an epic rich in the multiplicity and variety of its minor characters. Indeed, the first six books (especially 3 through 6) are divided fairly evenly between the minor characters and the three protagonists, Pompey, Caesar, and Cato. Lucan has a genius for capturing the moods and faces of the civil wars in brief, colorful sketches of some of its less famous participants. Some are not even names, but merely voices: an old woman lamenting for her sons, an old man recalling the terrible days of Marius and Sulla. They do not require individual personification, for their grief is that of the countless anonymous victims of the struggle for military and ideological control of the Roman world. Others are identified and briefly introduced to add some extra personal, religious, or historical dimension to the narrative. Then there are the women of the epic: Cornelia, Marcia, and Cleopatra whose personalities complement those of the protagonists Pompey, Cato, and Caesar respectively. Only Cornelia is given a truly independent characterization; the others are used chiefly to supply an additional *color* to Cato and Caesar.

The remaining minor characters are drawn chiefly from the military ranks of both sides in the war. Some, such as Cnaeus Pompey, Mark Antony, Metellus Scipio, and Titus Labienus are hardly more than names. Others, such as Afranius, Petreius, and Brutus, are given greater prominence, but do not dominate the scenes in which they are present. They, like most of the minor characters, are best treated in terms of the contexts where they are introduced. A few, however, merit separate treatment because they are the central figures around whom important episodes of the *Pharsalia* are shaped. We have seen two already: Domitius Ahenobarbus (Chapter 1) and Curio (Chapter 3). Four more must be considered now: Cassius Scaeva, Vulteius, Appius Claudius, and Sextus Pompey.

Scaeva and Vulteius differ from Appius and Sextus in several important ways. First, and most obviously, they are on Caesar's side. Second, they are not aristocrats and high-ranking officers but combat soldiers. Third, they are totally dedicated to their leader, Caesar, and highly courageous. Appius and Sextus are degenerate, aristocratic cowards more concerned with their own welfare than with the republican cause. Yet despite these differences, each of the four men demonstrates in his own way something that is wrong with the Roman spirit and with the world in general. They exemplify what Lucan means by the underlying seeds of war that have always brought powerful nations to ruin (1.158–182) and they are thus fit company for Curio. Appropriately, their stories and that of Curio are closely linked both structurally and thematically in the *Pharsalia*. Curio's debacle (4.581–824) is immediately preceded by the suicides of Vulteius and his Gallic troops (4.452–581) and followed by Appius' consultation of the Delphic oracle (5.65–236). The *aristeia* of Scaeva (6.118–262) is followed shortly by Sextus Pompey's consultation of the witch Erichtho (6.332–830). The five incidents comprise about half of the content of *Pharsalia* 4, 5, and 6. Their close juxtaposition allows Lucan to contrast sharply the great, if perverse, bravery of Caesar's men with the cowardice of some major figures of the republican cause.

I. Scaeva and Vulteius

The heroic actions of Scaeva and Vulteius show the attitudes of Caesar's soldiers toward the possibility of defeat. In *Pharsalia* 6, the republicans make a determined effort to break Caesar's blockade of Dyrrhachium and are stopped by the efforts of Scaeva, a common soldier who earned promotion to the rank of centurion because of his heroism in Gaul (6.118–262). In *Pharsalia* 4, Mark Antony tries to escape a republican siege in Illyria by evacuating his men on three rafts. One raft is prevented from getting away; and Vulteius, its commander, persuades his men to kill themselves rather than surrender (4.402–581). On the subject of Scaeva, I have little to add to Berthe Marti's excellent discussion, but more must be said about Vulteius, since his actions are somewhat ambiguously treated by Lucan and have, I think, been misconstrued by W. Rutz.[1] This is why the episodes are discussed here in reverse order.

No sooner is Scaeva introduced than Lucan describes him as follows:

> pronus ad omne nefas et qui nesciret in armis
> quam magnum virtus crimen civilibus esset.   [6.147–148]

(Prepared for any outrage, he did not understand that valor in a civil war is a great and criminal reproach [sc., rather than an action deserving praise].)

I can do no better than append Marti's comments here:

Virtus is here given a precise definition. It is the paradoxical opposite of that highest quality of the Stoics, the *uirtus* which, elsewhere in the poem, is embodied in Cato. Because he is deluded by his ignorance of what is right, Scaeva's valor, ironically, is an evil, the antithesis of what is morally desirable. . . . He had, earlier, reproached his own soldiers for their lack of pietas; but the false nature of his own *pietas* is demonstrated by the aim toward which he strives. For he himself proclaims that those who wish to make peace must first worship Caesar (243, *adorato summittat Caesare signa*), a demand soon followed by his own men's worship of himself as the living image of *Virtus*. (*loc. cit.*, 254)

1. B. Marti, "Cassius Scaeva and Lucan's *Inventio*," in *The Classical Tradition*, ed. by L. Wallach, Ithaca, 1966, 239–257. W. Rutz, "Amor mortis bei Lucan," *Hermes* 88 (1960), 462–475, especially 466–468; cf. Rutz's remarks in "Lucan 1943–1963," 281–282. It is odd that Marti does not see the connection between the Scaeva episode and the story of Vulteius and that she makes no reference to Rutz, who does. For Rutz's discussion of Scaeva, see "*Amor mortis*," 462–466; cf. his "Studien," 87–93. On Scaeva and Vulteius, see also H. Nehrkorn, "Die Darstellung und Funktion der Nebencharaktere in Lucans Bellum Civile," Diss. Baltimore, 1960, 121–132; F. König, "Mensch und Welt bei Lucan im Spiegel Bildhafter Darstellung," Diss. Kiel, 1957, 57–71; E. Longi, "Tre Episodi del Poema di Lucano," *Studi in Onore di Gino Funaioli*, Rome, 1955, 181–188; J. Bayet, "Le Suicide mutuel dans la mentalité des Romains," *L'Année Sociologique* (ser. 3) 1951, Paris, 1953, 70–88; W. Menz, "Caesar und Pompeius im Epos Lucans," Diss. Berlin, 1952, 157–167; H. Flume, "Die Einheit der Künsterlichen Persönlichkeit Lucans," Diss. Bonn, 1950, 69–70. Perhaps the best discussion of the Vulteius episode is that of W. Heyke, "Zur Rolle der Pietas bei Lucan," Diss. Heidelberg, 1970, 147–154, who establishes the connection between Vulteius and Scaeva very well.

Scaeva's virtue is akin to that of another centurion in Caesar's army, Laelius, who declares that he would butcher any of his relatives and sack any temple or city, including Rome, if such were Caesar's orders (1.359–386). Allied with this blind dedication to Caesar is something which Scaeva describes as *mortis amor* (love of death):

> Pompei vobis minor est causaeque senatus
> quam mihi mortis amor.   [6.245–246]

> (The causes of Pompey and senate mean less to you than love of death means to me.)

Scaeva's valor would have made him a good example to others had it been directed against a foreign foe. He would have been *felix*. But, as it is, Scaeva's example is negative and counterproductive (*infelix*) because his virtue established a tyrant (6.257–262). His actions and his rationale for them indeed resemble a perversion of Stoic virtue and the Stoic quest for liberty in death.

In like manner, the Gaul Vulteius seems to be a paradigm of misdirected virtue. His *pietas,* his sense of duty, patriotism and proper conduct is, by his own admission, *militiae pietas* (4.499), dedication to *military* duty. This is the loyalty to individual generals (rather than to any ideal or to the state) that lay at the root of so many troubles in the late republic. What adds further to Vulteius' unconscious irony is that he is fighting and dying for Caesar, the man who will not only deprive Rome of the vestiges of liberty, but who has already enslaved Vulteius' own native land. Vulteius, like Scaeva, seems to think that love of death is the very essence of virtue, even though he never questions the moral worth of what he is dying for. Again, his declarations of resolve are undermined by an unconscious irony:

> totusque futurae
> mortis agor stimulis: furor est.   [4.516–517]

> (I am possessed and driven by the goads of the death I must die: it is frenzy.)

Furor and *virtus* are hard to reconcile. Vulteius, though his principles are more lofty and philosophical than those of Scaeva, is still dying for the wrong reasons. He observes:

magna virtute merendum est,
Caesar ut amissis inter tot milia paucis
hoc damnum clademque vocat. [4.512–514]

(We must display great courage to earn the reward of having
Caesar call this loss of a few men among his thousands a
crippling blow and a catastrophe.)

Like Scaeva he wishes to die with the active approval of his lord.
Compare Scaeva's remark at 6.158–159: "peterem felicior umbras /
Caesaris in voltu" (I would be more blessed as I go to my death if
Caesar could see me). But Caesar, as we shall see in Chapters 7
and 8, is an utterly amoral being. Thus, although no Stoic would
deny that death is, as Vulteius contends, a means of escaping slavery, the kind of dedication he and Scaeva show for Caesar is the
means whereby Caesar is able to destroy freedom. Lucan, however,
does not directly assail the propriety of Vulteius' actions, as he does
Scaeva's. The closest he comes to undercutting the nobility of Vulteius' actions is by innuendo. Vulteius and his men become a miniature of civil nefas (448–449), comparable to the spartai, the men
who sprang from the dragon's teeth planted by Cadmus and who
were a grim omen for Eteocles and Polynices (449–451). Finally,
Lucan points out that suicide, in and of itself, is not lofty virtue:
"non ardua virtus" (576), but something within the grasp of anyone who wishes to avoid slavery. Thus Vulteius, who is not fighting for the cause of liberty, can become an example to those who
think they are fighting for the cause of liberty but who do not
understand, as Vulteius does, that death is a means of gaining
freedom.

Although Scaeva and Vulteius display virtus in the face of danger, it is, at best, military courage, laced in Vulteius's case with a
somewhat perverse Stoic concept of the relationship between death
and freedom. We must not confuse this with the more absolute
virtus which, as Sallust and Lucan both recognize, demands much
more.[2] Yet there is no denying that Scaeva and Vulteius are brave,

2. See D. Earl, The Political Thought of Sallust, Cambridge, 1961, 31, and
Marti, "Cassius Scaeva," 255, where she notes the similarity between Sallust
and Lucan on this point. There are, as we have noted, many striking similarities between Sallust's view of Rome and Lucan's, plus certain stylistic similarities. Scholars have generally ignored the possibility that Sallust may have

as indeed Curio is. Appius Claudius and Sextus Pompey do not even have bravery and mistaken idealism to elevate them above cowardice and corruption. Lucan's attitude to the degenerate nobility recalls that of Sallust who, as Syme notes, "is intent to demonstrate that the heirs of a great tradition had betrayed their trust." [3]

II. Appius Claudius Pulcher at Delphi

The opening of *Pharsalia* 5 finds the republican forces assembled in Greece, awaiting Caesar's arrival. The first 64 lines are devoted to a senate meeting at which Pompey is ordered to assume command against Caesar in the forthcoming campaign—a forceful reminder that Pompey is fighting for the senate, not vice-versa (5.15–49). After such a preamble, we might well expect to see something of Pompey's preparations for war, since he has been conspicuously absent from the epic for almost two books—since 3.45, in fact. Further, Caesar's campaigns at Massilia and in Spain have occupied so much of books 3 and 4 that a return to Pompey might seem appropriate. But Lucan does not oblige. Attention is shifted abruptly from Pompey to Appius Claudius Pulcher, and the change is carefully contrived to take the reader by surprise:

> quae cum populique ducesque
> casibus incertis et caeca sorte pararent,
> solus in ancipites metuit descendere Martis
> Appius eventus, finemque expromere rerum
> sollicitat superos multosque obducta per annos
> Delphica fatidici reserat penetralia Phoebi. [5.65–70]

(While the people and their leaders were making these preparations, not knowing what the result would be, and unaware of what fate had in store, only Appius was afraid to venture into the uncertain outcome of war. He troubles the gods to explore the way things will turn out, and opens up the shrine of prophetic Apollo, which had been shut for many years.)

The surprise is this: after the preamble we might expect Pompey, if anyone, to be setting out to consult the Delphic oracle.

served as a model for Lucan, e.g., Pichon. Stoics generally regarded any emotional or irrational reaction as evil. See Chapter 7, note 11.

3. Syme, *Sallust*, 126.

Odysseus and Aeneas both have encounters with prophets, so why
not Pompey? In terms of conventional epic it would seem almost
mandatory that some consultation of the divine not merely take
place, but involve a protagonist. By introducing Pompey and sub-
stituting Appius at the last moment, Lucan seems to be flouting
tradition to throw his reader off balance. But the reader can complain only of the poet's trickery, not of his historicity. There is no
reason to doubt that Appius actually did consult the Delphic
oracle. Both Valerius Maximus and Orosius tell the story.[4] The
silence of our major historical sources should not be taken too seriously; after all, the consultation is not a crucial incident in the
civil wars from a historian's point of view. But to a poet, Appius'
tale has an obvious attraction, since consultations of the supernatural are a regular part of epic tradition.

A more serious historical objection to Lucan's account lies in
his statement that the Delphic oracle was closed at the time of Appius' visit. H. W. Parke and D. E. Wormell contend that Lucan is
wrong, that the oracle was not closed either in republican times
or in Lucan's own day.[5] But Lucan is emphatic on the subject.
Not only was Delphic closed, it was closed for political reasons:

> non ullo saecula dono
> nostra carent maiore deum, quam Delphica sedes
> quod siluit, postquam reges timuere futura
> et superos vetuere loqui. [5.111–114]

(Our own times feel the loss of no gift of the gods more than
this: the fact that Delphi has fallen silent, after kings came to
fear the future and forbade the gods to speak.)

Juvenal (Satires 6.553–556) appears to substantiate Lucan's
claim: "People will believe whatever an astrologer says has come
from the mouth of Ammon, since the oracle at Delphi has ceased
(quoniam Delphis oracula cessant) and darkness as to the future
encompasses the human race." The scholiasts in the Commenta
Bernensia and the Adnotationes super Lucanum suggest that Lucan's reference to the action of kings in closing the shrine is

---

4. Valerius Maximus 1.8.10; Orosius 6.15.11.
5. H. W. Parke and D. E. Wormell, The Delphic Oracle², Oxford, 1956,
1.283–284 and 2.243 and 597.

prompted by Nero's alleged closure of Delphi after the priestess refused to prophesy to him on the grounds that he was a parricide.[6] But this information, even if true, would not help answer whether or not the oracle was open for consultation in Appius' time. Plutarch, who was an official of the Delphic shrine, admits in the *De Defectu Oraculorum* that declining interest in Delphi had caused the number of priestesses to be reduced from three to one.[7] But he does not say that the shrine was actually closed during the late republic or the first century A.D. Lucan's Delphi still has a priestess, however, even though the shrine is described as closed. Lucan is emphasizing the de facto closing of the oracle, something Plutarch plays down as much as possible, since he and his fellow-priests at the shrine wanted to revive it. Yet Lucan, ironically, cannot exploit one of the most curious testimonia to the decline of Delphi: the fact that the priestess now prophesied in *prose*.[8] This is the only respect in which Lucan presents the oracle as more alive than it was, since even he did not dare interrupt the flow of hexameters with a prose prophecy.

The oracle, whether closed officially or unofficially, was to all intents and purposes defunct in Lucan's time, and probably in Appius' time too. Yet it is clear that Lucan wishes to express some regret about its obsolescence, as lines 111–114 (quoted above) show. In fact, Lucan devotes 50 lines (71–121) to a history of Delphi, laced with comments on its usefulness to mankind, very suggestive of those adduced in Plutarch's *De Defectu Oraculorum*. Despite this, we should not suppose that Lucan is praising Appius for his visit to Delphi. For one of the most disconcerting aspects of Appius' visit is that fear was the main motive for his pilgrimage.

6. *Adnotationes* on 5.113; also the same scholiast on 5.139 and 178, and the *Commenta* on 5.113.

7. *De def. or.* 411E ff. For a discussion of Plutarch's testimony as against that of Lucan and Juvenal, see Parke and Wormell. For more on Plutarch and Delphi, see R. H. Barrow, *Plutarch and His Times*, Bloomington, 1969, 30–35 and 85–86. For a general examination of Lucan's treatment of prophecy, see B. Dick, "The Technique of Prophecy in Lucan," *TAPA* 94 (1964), 37–49, and M. Morford, *The Poet Lucan*, Oxford, 1967, 59–74; also B. Dick, "The Role of the Oracle in Lucan's *De Bello Civili*," *Hermes* 93 (1965), 460–466.

8. In fact, there is a whole treatise by Plutarch on the matter: *De Pythiae Oraculis*; see, however, Eusebius, *Praep. Evang.* 5.16 who refers to a later prophecy in verse.

Further, Cato, whom Lucan clearly admires, has no use for prophetic shrines, even that of Ammon, which both Lucan and Juvenal describe as thriving.[9] The virtuous man does not need reve-
lations about the future.

A further dimension of the Appius episode is revealed in a brief
biographical sketch of Appius Claudius Pulcher. He was a member of a very distinguished senatorial family and had earned the
highest distinctions in public life. He was consul in 54 and censor
in 50. During his censorship he even had the somewhat dubious
honor of expelling Sallust from the senate. Upon the outbreak of
the civil war, he was given Greece as his province. Thus, at the
time of the consultation, he was, in fact, governor of Greece.[10]

Yet the mention of his honors in the *cursus honorum* serves to
sketch in only one facet of his life and, perhaps, not even the major
one for Lucan's purposes here. Appius was also the most noted expert of his day on religious theory and practice. Cicero regarded
him as an important authority on divination, and his book on
augural practice appears to have become a standard work. Appius
himself held the augurate from around 63 B.C. and in that priest-
hood found, no doubt, an ideal opportunity to expand upon his
expertise.[11] In addition to his interests in Roman religion, Appius
was knowledgeable in both psychomancy and necromancy as well
as in the cult of Amphiaraus at Oropus and the Eleusinian mys-
teries.[12] His appointment as governor of Greece must have given
him special pleasure.

Given Appius' distinguished career, it may seem strange that
Lucan offers us so little information about him in *Pharsalia* 5. But

9. *Pharsalia* 9.564–586; cf. Chapter 7, Section VI, and Juvenal 6.553–556.
10. For Appius' consulship see *Schol. Bob. pro Plancio, Tesserae CIL* 1.732
and Caesar *BGall.* 5.1. Appius' colleague in the consulship was Domitius
Ahenobarbus. For his censorship, see Cicero *Fam.* 3.10.3 ff., Dio 40.63, and
Orosius 6.15. For Cicero's reaction to his censorship, see *Fam.* 8.14.4 and *Att.*
6.9.5. For his expulsion of Sallust from the senate see *Inv. in Sallustium* 16
and Dio 40.63.4. See Valerius Maximus 1.8.10 and Orosius 6.15.11 for his gov-
ernorship of Greece.
11. For Appius' augurate, see Varro, *Rust.* 3.2.2; 3.7.1; Cicero *Brut.* 267; *Div.*
1.105; 2.75; *Leg.* 2.32. Cicero also tells us in *Fam.* 3.4.1 of Appius' book on
augury, and in *Tusc.* 1.37 and *Div.* 1.132 of his interest in the occult. Further
sources for details of Appius' biography can be found in *RE* 3.2849–2853.
12. For a discussion of his interests in Eleusis and Oropus, see *RE* 3.2853–
2854.

Lucan's silence should not be mistaken for ignorance. In 5.122 and 145, he demonstrates his acquaintance with Appius' scholarly interest in religion and the occult. In the first of these lines he calls Appius a *scrutator* of the ultimate fate of Italy; not just an enquirer but an examiner—a term suggestive of precise and scholarly investigation. In the second, he calls him a priest, *sacerdos*, thus making it clear that he knew of Appius' augurate. Further, since Lucan was himself an augur, he probably was familiar with the great authority on the subject of augural practice.[13] Lucan's silence on specific details, then, is likely the result of a deliberate withholding of information. If he were to belabor the matter of Appius' biography, the edge of the dramatic irony would be blunted through overemphasis. Even from the preliminary outline offered here, that irony reveals itself to the modern reader. The virtually dead oracle of Delphi is about to be revived by the only person who cares to do so—the famous scholar of religion and the occult. Lucan's contemporary reader, however, would not have needed a thumbnail biography of Appius; he would probably have been quite familiar with his name and his career, and possibly have known of the precise incident. Had Lucan spelled out the details he would have lost the opportunity for suggestive subtlety.

Appius arrives at Delphi only to discover that the priestess is nowhere near the shrine. He finds her wandering around by the Castalian springs without a care in the world: "errore vagam curisque vacantem" (126). His first act is to seize her and force her to break through the doors into the temple: "corripuit cogitque fores inrumpere templi" (127), and after such an abrupt and violent beginning, it is hardly surprising that the priestess is less than eager to cooperate. Although Appius succeeds in getting her to the temple, he finds it harder to entice her to go into the inner shrine and prophesy. Remembering, perhaps, what Lucan has pointed out in 117–120, that the strain of being a priestess tends to shorten life, she is terrified of entering, and attempts to put Appius off with words of deceit: " 'quid spes', ait, '*improba* veri te, Romane, trahit?' " [130–131] (What *unprincipled* desire for truth drags you here, Roman?) The outstanding point here is not so much her unwillingness to cooperate (after all, Appius' treatment of her is

13. Vacca, *Life:* "sacerdotium etiam accepit auguratus."

It is fear of Appius' threats rather than any sense of shame that finally compels the priestess to go to the tripods. She now enters a trance more complex and detailed than that of the Sibyl in *Aeneid* 6. The possessed Sibyl, from the start of her frenzy to the end, merits only a total of 20 lines actual description by Vergil (6.45–53, 77–82, 98–103). In Lucan the Pythia's trance runs from 161–193, a total of 33 lines. If we include her initial quarrelsome words (130–140) and her feigned trance, the difference between the scenes in Vergil and Lucan becomes even more pronounced. Further, while Appius has to resort to violence and threats to persuade the priestess to prophesy, the Sibyl in *Aeneid* 6.37–54 takes Aeneas to task for spending too much time sightseeing in the temple. The frenzy of the god is upon her before Aeneas is ready. As if to remind the reader to keep the *Aeneid* in mind throughout this scene, Lucan twice makes mention of the Sibyl in the course of Appius' consultation, at 5.138 and 183–186. At the second mention he restorts to an elaborate simile, directly comparing the Pythia to the Sibyl of Cumae.

The results of the Pythia's trance, however, are anticlimactic after the long introduction. The whole knowledge of the world from the day of creation to the day of doom fills her frenzied mind, the vastness of the sea and the number of grains of sand upon the beaches: "non prima dies, non ultima mundi, / non modus Oceani, numerus non derat harenae" (181–182). The priestess sifts through this information as the Sibyl does. But whereas the Sibyl selects only information about Rome as the subject matter for her prophecy, the Pythia is not seeking information about Rome, but about Appius, whom she has difficulty locating in the midst of all the important destinies: "te . . . vix invenit, Appi, / inter fata diu quaerens tam magna latentem" (187–189). Out of all the knowledge flooding her mind she grasps only those tiny details affecting Appius—on the eve of a conflict that is to shake the world. When she finally does locate him, she offers the following prophecy:

effugis ingentes, tanti discriminis expers,
bellorum, Romane, minas, solusque quietem
Euboici vasta lateris convalle tenebis.   [194–196]

(You are escaping the threats of war, Roman, you will have no
part in the great crisis. You alone will gain peace in the vast
hollow of the Euboean rock.)

The reader is now completely baffled. And Lucan's own expression of astonishment as to why the gods could reveal nothing more
important than this on the eve of Pharsalia and the imminent collapse of the republic (198–222) does not help. For this is nothing
less than an admission that the whole episode leads nowhere. But
it is not an irrelevant digression; it develops a number of basic
themes in the *Pharsalia*.

If we are outraged by the oracle's refusal to deliver any pertinent information about the future of Rome, we are no less put out
by Appius' reaction to the revelation. The governor of Greece
does not register any anger or disappointment at the outcome; on
the contrary, he goes on his way content with the opportunity, as
he thinks, to save his own life. In other words, the incident tells
us a great deal about the patriotic impulses of this scion of an ancient family. Despite the fact that he came to Delphi for the purpose of finding out what the future had in store for Rome, and is
prepared to use violence to gain this knowledge, he is not really
much concerned about the city. His whole attitude indicates that
the Pythian priestess was quite right to view the world—and Appius—so skeptically.

Appius' response to the oracle is to head for Euboea. The aristocratic governor of Greece simply abandons the cause when he sees
the opportunity to save his own skin. Thus this man who had held
the high office of censor and who numbered among his ancestors
the famous Appius Claudius, the blind censor, commits an act that
makes mockery of his rigorous purging of the senate. Not only is
he shown to be morally degenerate, but also a traitor to his country in its hour of need.

Thus Apollo's oracle *does* reveal something of consequence to
history, for all its reticence. It shows the complete debasement of
the Roman character even among the most notable patricians, such
as makes Curio moderately heroic by comparison. And here is an
important lesson for Rome. The key to the city's future is not to
be found in divination but in the moral character and strength of
its people. The frightened Appius would be *less* dramatically effec-

tive, as would the whole episode, if the oracle had answered in full about the fate of Rome. The impact of Appius' cowardice and degenerate nature and its effect on Roman history is driven home by the next scenes. For as Appius flees to Euboea, Caesar arrives in Greece and braves a mighty tempest in a tiny boat. The key to the future lies in the juxtaposition of Caesar's fearlessness to Appius' cowardice.

There is, of course, a final irony to the sorry affair of Appius. He arrives in Euboea only to die there, earning for himself a grave by the quarries of Carystos. Throughout the consultation he has outwitted the priestess, but the prophecy finally outwits him. The great expert on religion and the occult is brought to grief by a typically Delphic *ambages*. Lucan cannot resist a touch of Delphic irony himself as he comments upon the Pythia's prophecy and its fulfillment. He says of Appius: "secreta tenebis / litoris Euboici" (230–231), which yields two possible interpretations. By poetic convention, the adjective *Euboicus* refers to Cumae as well as to Chalcis, so these words make a nicely ambiguous epitaph for the religious scholar: either "You will grasp the secrets of the shore of Euboean Cumae" *or* "you will gain a hidden place on the Euboean shore." Appius' greatest scholarly desire would probably have been to unravel the secrets of the Sibyl. But instead of knowledge he will find a grave. Appius is as intellectually blind as his famous ancestor was physically blind.

But Lucan does not let the matter rest; Carystos, where Appius was buried, faces toward the town of Rhamnus on the coast of Attica, a place sacred to the goddess Nemesis, and toward Aulis, whence Agamemnon's fleet set sail for Troy. *Aulin,* in fact, is the very last word of Lucan's tale of Appius and the oracle. It is, perhaps, an unhappy reminder of Calchas, Iphigeneia, and the whole legend that begins the chain of events which led the exiled Aeneas to Italy. And in that continuum, Appius has his own little niche, just as he does in the history of prophecy. After all, he is probably one of the last men to have been deceived by the Delphic oracle.

Yet this last word, *Aulin,* directs our attention to the sea. For it is at this moment that Caesar returns from Spain en route to Italy and Greece, an expedition that will be as disastrous for the republic as Agamemnon's expedition was for Troy.

The story of Appius, then, is anything but a digression; it is carefully dovetailed into the thematic structure of the epic. We now know two things that will be of great importance for the books ahead: that men like Appius are more concerned with their own well-being than with that of the republic, and that the gods are not prepared to render aid to Rome in the time of crisis. For the oracle comes out no better from this episode than does the patrician governor of Greece. The Pythia was right on almost every score: Delphi has gone out of business.

III. Sextus Pompey and Erichtho

Since Apollo and the Olympians will tell the world nothing, perhaps the powers of witchcraft will be more successful. And it is to them that Lucan turns his narrative in *Pharsalia* 6.332–830. Here we learn of Sextus Pompey's visit to the witch Erichtho in Thessaly on the eve of the battle of Pharsalia, her reanimation of the corpse of a soldier, and the prophecy delivered to Sextus.

Even the most cursory reading leaves one convinced that Lucan is trying to establish a parallel between Appius' visit to Delphi and Sextus Pompey's consultation of Erichtho. The two episodes are developed almost identically. In 5.71–85, we are told of the history of Delphi; in 6.332–412, the history of Thessaly and its tradition of magic. The brief mention of Appius' decision to consult the oracle, 5.64–70, is paralleled by Sextus' decision to consult Erichtho. In both cases, the men are minor characters in the overall structure of the *Pharsalia,* and in both cases their motivation is fear. In 5.86–101 Lucan debates the source of Delphic *spiritus;* in 6.492–506 the source of the witch's power. The service and usefulness of the Delphic oracle and its present powerlessness in 5.102–120 is counterbalanced by the description of Erichtho and her all-too-evident powers in 6.507–569. Appius' tracking down of the Pythia in 5.121–127 is matched by Sextus' successful attempt to find Erichtho in 6.570–603; the terrified Pythia and her unwillingness to cooperate (5.128–140), by the delighted Erichtho who is quite ready to help (6.604–623). The Pythia's attempted deceit, noticed and stopped by Appius who drags her into the shrine (5.141–146), stands in contrast to Erichtho's deliberate and uncoerced preparations for necromancy, as she dispels Sextus' fears and drags a corpse to the site of her magical activities (6.624–694). Even the Pythia's false trance (5.147–157) is counterbalanced by the refusal of the corpse's soul to reenter the body (6.695–728). Similarly, Appius' threats on the priestess are paralleled by Erichtho's threats on the gods below (5.157–161 and 6.729–749). So are the results of the threats: the Pythia goes into her trance (5.161–189) and the corpse's soul re-enters its body (6.750–776). Finally the prophecy that the priestess delivers (5.188–197) is balanced by the corpse's vision of the underworld (6.777–836).

Yet even from such a synopsis, it is clear that the two episodes, though they follow an almost parallel development, lead to rather different results. While Lucan regrets the passing of the Delphic oracle and goes to some pains to stress its benefits to mankind, he goes to even greater lengths to demonstrate the hideousness of witchcraft in Thessaly. The description of Erichtho that caps his introduction at 507–569 stands as the most horrific portrait in Latin literature.[14] On the other hand, despite Lucan's declared distaste for Thessaly and Erichtho, she is infinitely more informative to Sextus than the oracle is to Appius. To start with, she is willing to cooperate and takes a macabre delight in her work. The

14. This passage has been much imitated by other poets, largely *because of* its gothic qualities. The most notable imitations are in Goethe's *Faust*, where Erichtho acts as the prologue for the *Klassische Walpurgisnacht* (Part 2, 7005 ff.) and in Dante's *Inferno* (9.20–30). Dante's reworking of the Erichtho theme is startling: Vergil claims that he was forced back into his body by her spells. Perhaps because the Erichtho episode is "a careful account of the practice of necromancy, the fullest in Latin literature" (Morford, p. 67), it earned a special place with the many great writers who have been fascinated by necromancy. For a reasonably full account of other Greek and Roman necromancies, see Morford, 66–73. The most notable omissions from his list are: Pliny *NH* 7.178–179; Apuleius *Met.* 2.20; 9.29; Heliodorus *Aethiopica* 6.14–15. Of these various additional passages, the Pliny is by far the most important parallel to Lucan and is discussed in Section V below. For interpretation of the necromancy, the most important article is that of Grenade; see also B. Dick, "Technique of Prophecy" and "Role of the Oracle"; E. Griset, "Lucanea VI: L'Invettiva," *RSC* 4 (1956) 28–33; B. Dick, "The Role of Manticism in Lucan's Epic Technique," Diss. New York (Fordham), 1962. On the notion that Lucan is opposing the optimistic view of Vergil's book 6 with his own pessimism, see L. Paoletti, "Lucano magico e Vergilio," *AeR* 8 (1963) 11–26; Longi; F. Arredondo, "Un episodio de magia negra en Lucano," *Helmantica* 3 (1952), 347–362. Also S. Eitrem, "La magie comme motif litteraire chez les grecs et les romains," *SO* 21 (1941) 39–83. On Goethe and Lucan see O. Schönberger, "Goethe und Lucan," *Gymnasium* 65 (1958) 450–452.

only limitation on her powers that she concedes is her inability to
alter major details of fate; but if all Sextus wants is foreknowledge,
this she can easily provide:

> sed, si praenoscere casus
> contentus, facilesque aditus multique patebunt
> ad verum.   [615–617]

(But if you are content to know what will happen in advance,
many easy doors will open to the truth.)

Erichtho will do what the oracle of Apollo cannot or will not—
reveal the future. Nor does she belittle the quest for truth as the
Pythia does. Instead of greeting Sextus with hostility, she treats
him with great courtesy and feels flattered that he should have
sought her out: "impia laetatur vulgato nomine famae / Thes-
salis" (the impious Thessalian woman is delighted to hear that her
fame is so widespread) (6.604–605). Similarly, Sextus addresses her
as "decus Haemonidum" (the glory of Thessaly) (590).

But there is a careful and deliberate contrast in the Erichtho
episode between the respect with which Erichtho and Sextus treat
one another and the editorial comments Lucan offers about both
of them. Thus, while Sextus introduces himself to the witch as
"Magni clarissima proles" (the most distinguished of Pompey's
sons), Lucan describes him as "Pompei ignava propago" (the cowardly offspring of Pompey) (594 and 589). He is one of the "degenerate souls," driven on by fear to learn what the future has in
store (417–430), a man destined to be "Siculus pirata" (a Sicilian
pirate) (422). Not without a touch of irony, perhaps, Lucan criticizes Sextus for not turning to a respectable source of divination
such as the oracles of Delos, Delphi, or Dodona (425–430). It is
hard to imagine that Lucan does not have tongue in cheek at this
point, knowing full well that Appius' visit to Delphi is quite fresh
in the reader's mind from the previous book.

That Sextus should be *attracted* by hearing of the presence of
Erichtho in the neighborhood of the Pompeian camp says little in
his favor. His motives and character are in question from the episode's beginning and are emphasized from time to time as the
story proceeds. When he sets out in search of the witch, he is ac-

companied by some trusty and practised assistants in crime: "fidi scelerum suetique ministri" (573), and he traces her by following a path of plundered graves. Unlike the diffident Pythia who was wandering carefree when Appius arrived, Erichtho is slavering at the mouth in anticipation of the banquet of slain soldiers upon which she will dine after the battle; her only fear is that Caesar and Pompey will fight elsewhere (579–588). It is hard to imagine a more gruesome duo than Sextus and Erichtho.

Sextus' reason for trying to ascertain the future is more personal than that of Appius. Ostensibly, at least, Appius sought information about the future of Rome, but Sextus is more interested in his own fate and in the destiny of his friends than in the larger issues of the war. He bids Erichtho:

> Elysias resera sedes ipsamque vocatam,
> quos petat e nobis, Mortem mihi coge fateri.   [600–601]

(Open up the gates of Elysium, and compel Death himself to admit to me which of us he is after.)

There is something rather droll about this evil pair having any possible influence over Elysium. Yet Erichtho is quick to oblige. Not only does she fulfill his requests; she supplies him with even more information than he asks for. Sextus learns the doom of the house of Pompey and the whole outcome of the war.

The means Erichtho chooses for making the future known involves the resurrection of a soldier who lies dead in the vicinity. She selects a corpse and attempts to resuscitate it by means of magical potions. When this fails to force the recalcitrant soul back into the body, she rallies all her powers in a threat to reveal the true identity of the gods of the underworld. She even vows to call upon the dread god who lives below Tartarus and who has no fear of breaking an oath sworn by the Styx. Erichtho is prepared to plunge the whole world into chaos if the gods will not cooperate (727–749). Her threats produce immediate results. The corpse comes back to life.

IV. The Corpse and Gabienus

This incident of necromancy, unlike Appius' consultation in 5, is not a matter of historical fact, though it may have a traditional

basis. Lucan knew (8.204–205) that Sextus Pompey was not even
in mainland Greece during the campaign at Pharsalia. He was in
Lesbos. So it is pertinent to ask why Lucan should have decided
to include the episode at all.

The necromancy is hardly flattering to Sextus Pompey and does
little to increase sympathy for the republican cause. It is as if
Lucan were intent on demonstrating the utter worthlessness of
Pompey's son, who was to carry on the war against both Julius
Caesar and Octavian for a dozen years after Pharsalia. Lucan, apparently, does not think very highly of the final years of the struggle against the Caesars. Perhaps his viciousness toward Sextus can
be accounted for on the grounds that he felt that Sextus had done
much to discredit the cause.

But if the necromancy in 6 is unhistorical, it is at least very much
in keeping with what we know about Sextus' character from other
sources. More important still, it bears an astonishing resemblance
to another story about him recorded by Pliny in the *Natural Histories* (7.178–179). During the Sicilian wars of the 30's B.C., one
Gabienus, a soldier in Octavian's army, was put to death in Sicily
on the orders of Sextus Pompey. Gabienus' throat was slit, but he
refused to die until he had spoken a prophecy to Sextus. Here is
Pliny's account of what happened:

In the Sicilian war, Gabienus, the bravest man in Octavian's navies,
was captured by Sextus Pompey, at whose orders his throat was cut. He
lay upon the sea-shore all day, although his head was almost severed
from his body. When evening came and a crowd had gathered around
him, drawn by his groans and entreaties, he begged Sextus to come to
him, or send one of his personal staff instead. *He claimed that he had
been sent back from the dead, and that he had news to announce (se
enim ab inferis remissum habere quae nuntiaret).*

Sextus sent several of his friends, and Gabienus told them that the
Pompeian cause and the party that was in the right was pleasing to the
gods below: the outcome would be what he wanted (*dixit inferis dis
placere Pompei causas et partes pias: proinde eventum futurum quem
optaret*). This is what he had been ordered to announce, Gabienus
said; and as proof of the truth of what he said, he would expire as
soon as he had accomplished his mission: and this is exactly what
happened (*argumentum fore veritatis quod peractis mandatis protinus
exspiraturus esset; idque ita evenit*).

Although Pliny declares in advance that he does not believe the story, there is at least one reason to suspect that, even if apocryphal, it dates back to the Sicilian wars: the fact that Gabienus' prophecy is clearly *wrong*. Sextus presumably wanted to win the war against Octavian, not lose it. Defeat could hardly have been the desired outcome: "eventum . . . quod optaret." If the story of Gabienus' defeat had been concocted after Sextus' defeat, the prophecy would probably have been tailored to fit the outcome of the war. Further, the name Gabienus occurs nowhere else in Latin literature. A piece of pure invention would most likely have settled on a more common name.

Since Pliny was Lucan's contemporary, it is possible that Lucan also knew the story of Gabienus, either directly from Pliny himself or through common source material.[15] This may be at least a partial explanation for the inclusion of the necromancy in *Pharsalia* 6 and its association with Sextus Pompey. What Lucan is probably doing is transposing an incident from the Sicilian wars to the Pharsalian campaign. There are several good reasons for this. Dramatically, Thessaly is a far more satisfactory location for a necromancy than Sicily, given its constant association with witchcraft and the black arts. In Heliodorus' *Aethiopica* there is a very similar account of the revival of a corpse, and it is worth noting that Heliodorus' hero is a Thessalian. But to Lucan Thessaly has an even greater significance: it is the site of the battle of Pharsalia. Necromancy seems, perhaps, appropriate to the forecasting of a battle that was to mark the annihilation of the republic and the triumph of the evil genius of Caesar. In sum, the macabre nature of the tale of Sextus and Gabienus probably seemed too good not to use, even if it involved the reworking of some ingredients.

To be sure, there are differences between Pliny's tale and that of Lucan, quite apart from the matter of the location. Pliny's Sextus is not deliberately engaging in necromancy, as is Lucan's; nor is there any suggestion that he personally came near Gabienus; on the contrary, Sextus sends some friends to hear the prophecy. Further, Pliny explicitly identifies Gabienus as a Caesarian; in Lucan

15. See Grenade's excellent discussion, especially 37 ff. I am much indebted to my colleague Paul Moore for his help in the analysis of the Gabienus story.

the political affiliation of the corpse is not clear. Our only clue comes in 6.716–717:

> ducis omina nato
> Pompeiana canat nostri modo militis umbra.
>
> [716: (om)ina nato *in ras.* U omnia n.o]

There are two immediate problems here. The first is the disputed reading in 716, either *omnia* or *omina*. The second is whether the adjective *Pompeiana* goes with *umbra* or *omina* (*omnia*). To compound the difficulties, there has been some disagreement over the meaning of "nostri modo militis." Haskins (*ad loc.*) takes this to be the equivalent of "Pompeiani modo militis." But this creates a problem. The speaker of these lines is Erichtho. Why should Erichtho think of the dead soldier as "one of ours" in that particular sense? She could as well mean that the soldier is one of her creatures, a man who fought for Caesar or Pompey during his life but is now part of her domain.

We cannot very well argue that because the soldier is to sing the fortunes of the house of Pompey with, as we shall see, a distinctly Pompeian bias, that he is a Pompeian. The passage from Pliny shows that such an argument is untenable. Gabienus was a Caesarian. He was even killed on Sextus' orders. But he still regards, in his prophetic vision, the Pompeian cause as the just cause. Lines 716–717, then, admit of a number of translations:

Let the Pompeian ghost of a soldier who is now mine sing the whole story to the son of the [*or* his] leader. [reading *omnia*]

Let the ghost of a soldier who was once one of ours [i.e., a Pompeian] sing the future of the house of Pompey to the son of the [*or* his] leader. [reading *omina*]

Let the ghost of a soldier who is now mine sing the future of the house of Pompey to the son of the leader. [reading *omina*]

The choice boils down to a matter of personal preference. To me the third alternative seems preferable, if only because *omnia* is more likely to be a corruption of *omina* than vice versa, and given this, it would be hard for the reader not to associate *Pompeiana* with *omina*. This still leaves us in a quandary. We cannot demonstrate one way or the other which faction the corpse belonged to in life. But neither can we rule out the possibility that he was, like Gabienus, a Caesarian.

For all the differences between the story in Pliny and that in Lucan, the similarities are surely more startling. One detail is particularly interesting: that both soldiers die of slit throats.[16] What this means we can only speculate. Possibly the slit throat provided an access for the spirits into the vocal mechanism of the corpse, a kind of "proof" that the individual is speaking not with his own voice but with that of other powers. At the very least, this detail is one of the several echoes of Pliny in Lucan's account. To it we might add that Sextus does not go to meet Erichtho alone. He is accompanied, as we have seen, by trusty assistants in crime. In Pliny, Gabienus' killing is done by Sextus' henchmen, and they are the ones who go to hear the soldier's dying words of prophecy. Finally, in both versions, Sextus emerges as a grim and savage individual. Given his treatment of Gabienus, there is much irony that he should be considered a leader of the *partes piae,* the just cause.

V. The Vision of Tartarus and Elysium

The necromancy of *Pharsalia* 6 is not pure invention on Lucan's part, then, but the modification of a traditional element in the story of the civil wars. Lucan's poetic instincts have triumphed over his drive to maintain historical accuracy in the stricter sense. But with the revival of the corpse, we are ready for a vision of the future and surely this is what Lucan has been preparing us for. The necromancy of 6 serves a purpose not unlike that of the *Nekuia* in *Odyssey* 11 or of Aeneas' visit to the underworld in *Aeneid* 6. Yet, as in the tales of Curio and Appius, we are not watching an episode that features the flower of heroic manhood. On the contrary, the horrible thought lurks in the back of our minds that Sextus Pompey himself claimed leadership of the republican cause once Pompey, Cato, and Brutus were dead.

In preparation for our glimpse into the underworld, Erichtho boasts proudly to Sextus as she delivers her instructions to the reanimated corpse:

16. *NH* 7.178; *Pharsalia* 6.637. Cf. the death of Socrates in Apuleius *Met.* 1.

tripodas vatesque deorum
sors obscura decet: certus discedat, ab umbris
quisquis vera petit duraeque oracula mortis
fortis adit. ne parce, precor: da nomina rebus,
da loca; da vocem qua mecum fata loquantur.   [6.770–774]

(Riddling prophecies are appropriate for the tripods and prophets of the gods. But whoever seeks the truth from the ghosts and
bravely approaches the oracles of harsh death, let him depart in
full knowledge. Spare nothing. Name the events, say where they
will happen, be the voice through which the fates may converse
with me.)

She is openly comparing her prowess with that of the conventional
oracular sources. We have already come to believe in her powers,
and we know at this point that Lucan is not going to beguile us
with a repetition of Appius' futile consultation.

At the same time, the reader is surprised by the brevity of the
revelation after such a long preamble. Even the corpse feels compelled to make an apology to Erichtho. His vision of the underworld, he says, is not complete, because she recalled his spirit
before he could reach the depths. Further, despite what Erichtho
has claimed at 6.777–778, the revelation is enigmatic. Yet we do
learn something—and a good deal more than we learned from the
Delphic oracle.

The corpse offers a vision of Elysium where the Decii, Camillus,
the Curii, Sulla, Scipio, Cato, and Brutus are housed—*optimates*
to a man.[17] Then he gives a brief glimpse of Tartarus where Catiline, Marius, Cethegus, the Drusi, and the Gracchi reside.[18] Thus,
heaven and hell are populated along strictly party lines. Those in
Elysium are solid supporters of the republican, senatorial cause.
The inhabitants of Tartarus, by way of contrast, are all *populares,*
turbulent characters from the last century of republican rule. To
complete the partisan symmetry, all the *optimates,* except for
Brutus, are in tears; the *populares* are overjoyed. Both sides are
aware of the outcome of the civil war. The only reason for the

17. Even though the Elder Cato was, like Cicero, a *novus homo,* his political views, like those of Cicero, took a decidedly conservative bias.
18. 6.785–796.

elder Brutus' happiness must be that his descendant will avenge
the republican defeat.

In this passage, one has the uncomfortable feeling that Lucan is
speaking with tongue in cheek. The *populares* are so ebullient
about events on earth that they are crying out for revolution in
the underworld:

> aeternis chalybis nodis et carcere Ditis
> constrictae plausere manus, camposque piorum
> poscit turba nocens.   [6.797–799]

> (Hands bound in fetters of eternal iron, and locked in Pluto's
> prison clap applause; the crowd of criminals demands to be
> moved to the dwellings of the good.)

It is hard not to see a vein of humor in this extension of the cause
of *res novae* to the world of the dead, reminiscent of Lucian's account in *True History* 2.23–24.

Even stranger is the inclusion of Sulla in Elysium. In 2, 4, and 9
Lucan leaves no doubt that Sulla was at least as bad, if not actually worse, than his enemy and rival Marius. And throughout the
Pharsalia the adjective *Sullanus* is used to evoke ideas of blood-
thirstiness and ferocity.[19] Would Lucan have us believe that all
Sulla's vices are pardonable, in the final analysis, because he was
an *optimate*, a supporter of the senatorial regime? The answer,
I suspect, is yes. Given, however, Lucan's general attitude to visions and prophecy, his hostility to Sulla elsewhere in the epic, and
the humorous touch added to the pictures of Tartarus and Elysium
by the suggestion that Catiline and the others are calling for revolution even after death, we should not eliminate the possibility of
satire here. And the most obvious archetype for this satire is the
catalogue of republican heroes in Anchises' Elysian parade in
Aeneid 6.

---

19. 2.115–232; 4.821–824; 9.204–205. Cf. 1.326; 2.582; 6.303. For *Sullanus*
and its adverse connotations, see 1.330; 2.210; 8.25; also Chapter 7, note 28.
Sallust blames Sulla for the start of the military take-overs at Rome, *Cat.* 5.6.
Cf. Seneca *Ad Marc.* 12.6: "deorum quorum illud crimen erat Sulla tam
felix." Surely Pliny makes the point succinctly (*NH* 7.137–138): "cum Sullam
nemo non oderit."

VI. Anchises and the Corpse

In *Aeneid* 6, Aeneas, motivated by *pietas,* approaches the Sibyl of Cumae, who first prophesies to him and then conducts him through the world of the dead. In the course of his travels through the underworld he finally arrives in the Elysian fields, where he is greeted by his father, Anchises, who, after a brief philosophical excursus on the origins of the world, introduces to Aeneas a carefully selected group of Roman heroes as yet unborn, ranging from Silvius Aeneas to Augustus.[20] Among this group there is only one name that could be associated with the enemies of Caesarism, Cato.[21] But Vergil, by calling him *magne Cato,* leaves us in some doubt as to which Cato he means: Cato *Maior,* or Cato *Minor.* The interpretation the reader gives will depend largely on which Cato he thinks is the *great* Cato. As far as other foes of Caesar and Augustus are concerned, there is the allusion to Pompey in 826–835, but he is not actually *named.*

Marius, Sulla, and other major figures of controversy in Roman history are not to be found anywhere in the *Aeneid,* much less here. The only questionable names are those of the Drusi and the Gracchi (824 and 842). E. Norden's attempt to argue that Vergil is not referring to the Gracchi themselves, but to their sound, republican father is surely nonsensical.[22] If Vergil had intended *Gracchi genus* to mean "the father of the Gracchi" (a usage without any

20. *Aeneid* 6.724–751; 756–853. Dick ("Role of the Oracle," 465) notes the similarity between the Erichtho and Appius episodes and *Aeneid* 6; F. L. Bastet and Le Bonniec reject this identification (*FH* 15.197).
21. *Aeneid* 6.841.
22. E. Norden (*Publius Vergilius Maro, Aeneis, Buch VI²,* Leipzig, 1916, 329–333) argues that Vergil is following Ennian usage. The only parallel he can adduce is *Aeneid* 6.839: "Aeaciden genus armipotentis Achilli" after Ennius *Ann.³* 179 (Vahlen³); and his reasoning on this passage leaves much to be desired. There is, as far as I can see, no good reason to assume that *genus* in this passage does not mean "descendant," which is surely a more likely rendering than "father." There is, so far as I can determine, no undisputed text in Latin where *genus* is used to mean "father." On the other hand, Vergil frequently uses *genus* to mean son or sons: "Augustus Caesar, divi genus" (6.792), where Vergil is neatly playing on both meanings, "son" and "descendant." Augustus is the son of Caesar and the descendant of Venus. Cf. 6.580 (the Titans as *genus terrae*). *Genus* = "descendant" is extremely common: 1.565; 5.45, 117; 6.648, 766, etc.). Finally if *genus* could mean "father," we would expect Vergil to write: *Gracch(or)um genus.*

adequate parallel in the Latin language), he would not, even then, have been paying the elder Gracchus a compliment. To be written down in poetry or history as the father of two revolutionaries would be something less than flattering in *optimate* circles.[23] Obviously Vergil is referring to Tiberius and Gaius Gracchus, "the children of Gracchus."

Although we may argue endlessly as to whether the Gracchi were good or bad, the fact is that Vergil is locating them in Elysium. He even juxtaposes them in his narrative to the Scipios:

> quis Gracchi genus aut geminos, duo fulmina belli,
> Scipiadas, cladem Libyae. [*Aeneid* 6.842–843]

([Or] who does not know the Gracchi [or] that pair, two thunderbolts of war, the Scipios, Africa's doom.)

I have bracketed the word "or" in the translation and inserted it twice to convey something that can only be described as an instant of ambiguity in 842–843: the *aut* in 842 could be taken, at first glance, as a connective between the Gracchi and what has gone before, a confusion heightened by the fact that Vergil introduces the word *geminos* immediately after it. The reader is well aware that there are *two* famous Gracchi. Further, *aut* is inserted in the line at precisely the point where the major caesura usually falls. The reader uncomfortably lurches on after *geminos* and finds that there seems to be a logical break, what appears to be a minor caesura. To increase his discomfort, "duo fulmina belli" (two thunderbolts of war) follows. It is not until the introduction of the Scipios at the beginning of the next line that the confusion is resolved. Then the reader appreciates that the break in 842 comes after *genus,* and that there is no major caesura in the line. Yet when he recalls that the Gracchi were themselves Scipios on their mother's side, the uneasiness returns.

This slight ambiguity rivets our attention to the oddity of Vergil's pairing of the Scipios and the Gracchi. For while the Scipios were associated with the greatest moment of Roman glory, the destruction of Carthage, the Gracchi were no less definitely linked with the beginning of the self-destructive civil wars of the first cen-

23. Besides, the Gracchi were by no means "unacceptable" to the Caesars.

tury B.C. Why does Vergil do this? There is a similar uncomfortable transition earlier in the Elysian parade between the Tarquins and Lucius Brutus, which baffles the reader in much the same way:

> vis et Tarquinios reges animamque superbam
> ultoris Bruti?   [*Ibid.*, 817–818]

(Would you like [to see] the Tarquins and the proud soul of avenging Brutus?)

Since *superbus,* proud, is the traditional epithet of the last of the Tarquins, the very one whom Brutus expelled, it is certainly odd to find it applied, in this context, to *Brutus.* Our uneasiness is increased in that this is the point in Anchises' narrative where Vergil breaks off his catalogue of kings and moves on to give us a panorama of republican heroes. Considering the emotional importance of this particular event in Roman history, such a strange introduction to the transition between monarchy and republic is bewildering. As with the Scipios and the Gracchi, dramatic change in history is not sharply marked but ruthlessly merged in the identities of two famous names which are associated with opposite viewpoints. And in both instances, an attribute of one of the two seems transferred to the other. For a fleeting moment we see Brutus as *superbus,* and the Gracchi as the two thunderbolts of war.

This close association of opposites, where the qualities or characteristics of one group seem to be transferred to the other, cannot be an accident of composition. Vergil must have intended to create a puzzle in his reader's mind or he would have approached the scene differently. He seems intent on blurring distinctions at these watersheds of history, much as he does in his mention of Caesar and Pompey, who, in Anchises' narrative, are identical spirits before incarnation.[24] Perhaps Vergil wanted to avoid marking fundamental changes in Rome too categorically, to avoid a careful distinction between republic and monarchy, Roman triumph and Roman civil war, for a special purpose. Though what this purpose might be is not particularly clear, unless he wishes to glide over as

24. 6.826–831; Vergil seems to be playing on the double-entendre of *pares* in 826, which, of course, can mean either "similar" or "identical" *or* "matched" in the gladiatorial sense (See Chapter 3).

delicately as possible the fact that he has located Augustus in the very center of his narrative of the age of kings.[25]

In short, Anchises' parade has a number of riddles for the reader, each one at least as puzzling as the riddle of Lucan's inclusion of Sulla in his Elysian catalogue. So perhaps some comparisons between the two visions of Elysium may be of help. While Aeneas is motivated by *pietas* to venture into his encounter with the dead, Sextus Pompey is motivated by fear. Further, Sextus does not actually go into the underworld as Aeneas does. The underworld comes to him by means of necromancy. Aeneas and the Sibyl are living beings among the dead, the strangers in an alien world. In the *Pharsalia* it is the prophetic corpse who is away from his proper environment. In place of the courage of Aeneas, lauded by the Sibyl for daring to face death twice, our attention is centered on the pathetic soldier, robbed of the mercy of having to live only once. In Lucan we see the dead among the living, not the living among the dead. Aeneas is given a vision of the great men of Rome to come; Sextus hears of the ghosts of the Roman past and of the doom that awaits him and the whole house of Pompey.

In all this we see a feature of the *Pharsalia* that we already noted in our discussion of the Curio episode in 4. Once again Lucan is taking a Vergilian situation and altering the characters and the outcome in order to convey his cynical view of Rome. In both *Aeneid* 6 and *Pharsalia* 6, for example, it is the dead themselves, rather than the priestess or witch, who provide the insight into the future. But Vergil deliberately by-passes the more horrific aspects of a necromancy by having Aeneas travel to Elysium to meet Anchises instead of resurrecting Anchises himself. Lucan, on the other hand, brings the dead back to life in the longest and most detailed necromancy in ancient literature. For all this, the contrast between the riddling utterances of the Sibyl at the beginning of *Aeneid* 6 and the explicit clarity of Anchises' account in the latter part of the same book is as obvious as the pointed contrast Erichtho makes in *Pharsalia* 6: the dead, as opposed to Apollo's prophets, give very precise forecasts about the future.

Thus the deliberate contrast between Sextus' necromancy and

25. The parade of kings runs from 6.777–815; Augustus is described in 791–805.

Aeneas' visit to the underworld is precisely that—*deliberate*. *Pharsalia* 6 stands in much the same relationship to *Aeneid* 6 as *Pharsalia* 4 does to *Aeneid* 8. Sextus Pompey is to Aeneas as Curio was to Aeneas in 4. Similarly we may compare the role of the reanimated corpse to that of Anchises, and that of Erichtho to the Sibyl, much as we compared the *rudis incola* of 4 to Vergil's Evander.

The contrast between *Aeneid* 6 and *Pharsalia* 6 extends to many details. Not least of these is the vision of Elysium. The Drusi and the Gracchi whom Vergil includes in Elysium are pointedly consigned to Tartarus by Lucan, on the grounds that they are *populares*.[26] The sweeping condemnation of the Drusi is particularly surprising, since by no means all of them were *populares*. One of the most famous members of the family was actually the instrument of Gaius Gracchus' discredit and death. But the Drusi, along with the Gracchi, are labeled as agitators of the same category as Marius and Catiline and expunged from the Elysian scene. It is hard to imagine that Lucan is not trying to offset the Vergilian political bias here—if indeed it is bias. After all, Anchises does not necessarily represent Vergil's personal viewpoint any more than the corpse represents Lucan's. But if Anchises can throw in amongst the select the Gracchi and the Drusi, why can Lucan's reanimated corpse not put Sulla in Elysium? Possibly Lucan is trying to confront us with an *ambages* just as Vergil was, or rather, the parody of a Vergilian *ambages*.

On the other hand, we should bear in mind Lucan's comment earlier in 6 about the failure of Pompey to follow up his victory at Dyrrhachium:

> felix ac libera regum,
> Roma, fores iurisque tui, vicisset in illo
> si tibi Sulla loco. [301–303]

(How blessed Rome would be, free from kings and self-governing, if Sulla had won the victory for you in that place.)

26. For Vergil and the Drusi, see Norden, 329–330. But Norden here, as in the case of the Gracchi, is too eager to dismiss the possibility that Vergil is referring to the more controversial members of the family. Surely the whole point of many of the references in the Elysian parade in *Aeneid* 6 is to leave the reader with an *ambages* to solve. If there is a double entendre in a poet, especially one as careful as Vergil, it is surely sound to assume that it is intentional.

This remark, if meant seriously, suggests that Lucan's attitude to Sulla has undergone a change since book 2. Lucan seems to be wishing that Pompey really had a touch of Sullan *saevitia* in him. Pompey's *pietas*, he implies, cost liberty the war (303–305). The fact that such a thought can even cross Lucan's mind should warn us that he may indeed be quite serious about placing the bloody Sulla among the blessed. At the same time, as we have noted, Lucan seems less than earnest in his description of Tartarus and Elysium. Further, as Housman notes in his apparatus on the opening lines of *Pharsalia* 9, the Stoics, like the Epicureans, rejected traditional notions of Tartarus and Elysium. The spirit of Pompey, as he dies, rises into the brightness of heaven in 9, 1 ff.; it does not descend into the underworld. Most important of all, however, victory in civil war qualifies the conqueror for damnation rather than for glory.

VII. The Corpse's Prophecy

It is fundamental to Lucan's scheme in the *Pharsalia* that it is worse to win a civil war than to lose one. As suggested in Chapter 2, Section II, this notion is forced upon him since he wishes to justify the losing side. In 7.706 Lucan observes: "vincere peius erat" (it was worse to win). This same idea is found in both Seneca and Tacitus. In *Epistles* 14.13 Seneca declares that, though the better man can win, there is no way that the man who has won cannot be worse: "potest melior vincere, non potest non peior esse, qui vicerit." Tacitus, in *Histories* 1.50, adds that the only thing you can know in a war between two opposing parties is that the winner is worse: "deteriorem fore qui vicisset." In keeping with this paradox, Lucan's corpse proceeds, after his description of the inhabitants of Tartarus and Elysium, to tell us that Pluto is preparing to punish the victor of the civil war. He then adds that a place is being prepared in Elysium for Sextus' father. This must make it plain to Sextus that Pompey is not going to win either the battle or the war. As consolation, however, the corpse adds that it will not be long before both victor and vanquished are united in death. "Hasten to die," he continues, "for though your funerals will be undistinguished, you will have a chance to trample under your heels the ghosts of Roman gods" (et Romanorum manes calcate deorum) (6.809). The "Roman gods" are, of course, Caesar and his descendants. With this remark the corpse cleverly points not only to a triumph of the republican cause after death, but to the ridiculous pretense that the Caesars could actually become gods after death.

The only issue at stake in the impending battle, the corpse declares, is which of the leaders will die by the Nile and which by the Tiber. From this, Sextus can deduce that Caesar will not outlive Pompey by long. But, as for Pharsalia itself:

> Europam, miseri, Libyamque Asiamque timete:
> distribuit tumulos vestris Fortuna triumphis.
> o miseranda domus, toto nil orbe videbis
> tutius Emathia.   [6.817–820]

(Unhappy men, fear Europe, Libya and Asia: Fortune has distributed your tombs in the lands that your house has triumphed over. Unhappy house of Pompey, in all the earth you'll see no safer place than Thessaly.)

Sextus' fate is merged with the general doom of the house of Pompey. The corpse fails to give precise details as to the time and place of his death. Instead, Sextus is told that his father will give him more information about the future in Sicily:

> tibi certior omnia vates
> ipse canet Siculis genitor Pompeius in arvis,
> ille quoque incertus quo te vocet, unde repellat,
> quas iubeat vitare plagas, quae sidera mundi.   [*ibid.* 813–816]

(Your father will personally prophesy everything for the future more definitely to you in the fields of Sicily. Yet he too will be uncertain as to where he should tell you to go and where not to go, what shores he would advise you to shun, what lands beneath the stars.)

Sextus now knows that the wars will spell the doom of his whole family, but that he will live until he arrives in Sicily.

This is not quite the precise information Erichtho had promised, but it is more satisfactory than what the Pythia had given Appius. Lines 813–816, however, are somewhat paradoxical. Sextus' father, the corpse says, will provide more certain information to him in Sicily, even though he will be uncertain as to where Sextus should go. In this we get a glimpse of the impasse into which Sextus falls after his defeat by Agrippa in Sicily. The whole world will be closed off to him. He will have no alternative but to seek refuge where he can.

It has been inferred from the corpse's prophecy that Lucan planned to extend his epic to include an appearance of Pompey to his son Sextus during the Sicilian wars more than a decade later.[27] This is highly unlikely. If Pliny's Gabienus is the archetype for Lucan's reanimated corpse, Lucan is shifting a major motif from its original location in Sicily (just as he moves Sextus from Lesbos) in order to make the most of the dramatic possibilities of Thessaly. Further, the poet has left us in no doubt as to what Sextus will do in Sicily or as to the nature of the Sicilian wars themselves: the Sicilian pirate will engage in a slave war. Distinctions of time and space have been blurred to show us, through the voice of Gabienus from the Sicilian wars, that Sextus is the final hope of Pompey's house—a prospect not much less appalling than the defeat which awaits the republican army on the morrow.

Lucan records no reaction on Sextus' part to anything the necromancy has revealed. Instead, he directs our attention to the pathetic second death of the soldier whose grim task is at last complete. Upon his demise, Erichtho and Sextus proceed to Pompey's camp much as the Sibyl and Aeneas are ushered on their way by the ghost of Anchises at the end of *Aeneid* 6.[28] But the dawn of the new day holds vastly different prospects for the houses of Pompey and Aeneas. Although both Lucan and Vergil have used their

27. See L. Thompson, "Lucan's Apotheosis of Nero," *CP* 59 (1964), 147–153. The basis of her argument is that Lucan's expression *Siculis . . . in arvis* (6.813) is a reminiscence of *Aeneid* 5.702, "recalling the verses preceding the appearance of Anchises to Aeneas in Sicily." Since this prophecy is fulfilled in *Aeneid* 6, Lucan presumably would have fulfilled his prophecy in a later book of the *Pharsalia*. There is no particular reason, however, why such a commonplace expression should be treated as a Vergilian reminiscence. Lucan regularly uses expressions with the ablative *arvis* to denote locations: *Arctois . . . in arvis* (1.301); *in arvis Emathiis* (4.255–256; 7.191, 846; 8.266–267); *Libycis . . . in arvis* (4.582); *Phlegraeis . . . in arvis* (4.597); *in Thessalicis . . . arvis* (9.1073) to mention only the most precise parallels. Since Sicilia does not fit into a hexameter Lucan had to use an alternative expression. It would be misleading to make too much of it.

28. *Pharsalia* 6.826–830; *Aeneid* 6.897–899.

sixth books for encounters with the dead and foreshadowings of
the future, the Pompeians cannot look forward to victory and a
glorious line of descendants. The morn brings the catastrophe of
Pharsalia, and the future of their house is the degenerate Sextus,
soon to be no more than an unsuccessful pirate. It is indeed an
evil omen that Erichtho accompanies Sextus back to the tents. For
the camp and those who are in it will be hers before the day is out.

VIII. The Backdrop of Desolation

Given the disaster that is about to overtake the Roman world,
the grisly horror of *Pharsalia* 6 is not only appropriate but indispensable. The spectacle of fratricidal warfare requires the agency
of the hideous rather than the beautiful. A more conventional poet
would have used a Fury to herald the shedding of kindred blood.[29]
But Lucan avoids the traditional Fury just as he avoids traditional
gods. Instead he exploits the fact that Thessaly is, *par excellence,*
the land of witches—and even the most skeptical minds of first-
century Rome were disinclined to treat witchcraft lightly. The
idealized Sibyl or the fictional Tisiphone yield to a creature on the
borderlines of plausibility: the tattered, vulture-like Erichtho.

The necromancy of Sextus Pompey brings to a final climax
Lucan's vignettes of the disintegration of the Roman world. The
remains of Scipio's camp, the defunct Delphic oracle, and the
plundered graves and corpse-littered habitat of Erichtho are all
part of the backdrop of desolation for the last agonies of the republic. Against this backdrop move figures stripped of every vestige of their Vergilian glory, yet still reminiscent of their Vergilian
archetypes. The nameless peasant replaces Evander; instead of the
Sibyl we have the diffident Pythia and the repulsive Erichtho.
Looming larger are men like Appius Claudius and Sextus Pompey,
bearers of great names conjuring up memories of Rome's past
glories, but whose behavior makes them deformed shadows of an
order and a life that is gone for ever. They scurry toward their

---

29. E.g. Statius *Theb.* 1.46 ff. (Oedipus' appeal to the Furies for vengeance
on his sons); Seneca *Thyestes* 1 ff. and *Agamemnon* 1 ff. (blood feuding heralded by the use of Furies in the prologues of both plays); *Aeneid* 7.435–470
(Allecto's maddening of the previously rational Turnus); *ibid.,* 323–405 (her
maddening of Amata). See Hübner, *passim* (34–42 for Vergil's Allecto).

petty dooms in a world that is already, spiritually and physically, a wasteland.

The warring elements within the Roman identity which Vergil assembles to create his hero are irreconcilable in Lucan's view. For *pietas*, the virtue which keeps the individual and the city under control, breaks down in civil war. Indeed, the tale of civil war is, as Lucan notes in *Pharsalia* 2.63, the tale of *pietas peritura*. Thus the role of Vergil's composite hero, and the *pietas* which gives him his completeness, are fragmented. The pathetic Curio visits a site of Roman greatness and hears of Hercules' triumph; Appius and Sextus consult an oracle and the dead because they are afraid. Aeneas' *pietas* is perverted into the *militiae pietas* of Vulteius and Scaeva. Worse still, it becomes the war-cry of the worthless Sextus at the battle of Munda, as Lucan's contemporary reader surely knew.[30] Sextus' claim to *pietas*, in fact, was probably in the forefront of the poet's mind when he chose him as the emissary to Erichtho.

As Lucan's minor characters show, the republic is virtually dead before Caesar administers the final blow. Though it is still standing, it is hollow and rotten, doomed to fall and disintegrate at the slightest push. In this order of things, Sextus' father, Cnaeus Pompeius Magnus, is not just the champion of what remains, he is its very symbol. And it is to him that we now turn.

30. See Appian *BCiv.* 2.104.

CHAPTER 5

Pompey

So far we have made only passing reference to the three major
characters of the *Pharsalia:* Caesar, Cato, and Pompey; this delay
is surely justified since Lucan's primary focus in the first six books
is not on them at all. As we have seen in Chapters 3 and 4, our attention is occupied by a number of diverse characters and situations. *Pharsalia* 1 through 6 is a texture of which Caesar, Cato,
and Pompey are a part, but which they do not dominate. Only
with the beginning of 7 do the minor characters fall into the
background: Pompey dominates 7 and 8, Cato and Caesar 9, and
Caesar 10.

This relatively even distribution of the epic between the major
and minor characters, and indeed among the major characters
themselves, indicates that the search for a hero, in the conventional epic sense, is futile.[1] The diffuse nature and content of 1
through 6 are powerful reminders that *Pharsalia* is not the tale of
the trials and tribulations of any one man. We see, rather, the
agony of Rome in the final days of the republic through a kaleidoscope of different persons and motifs. This diffusion of focus is a
new departure in epic technique, though its novelty is easily obscured by the fact that Silius and Statius proceed in a similar way.
In the *Punica,* for instance, a substantial part of the narrative

1. For a survey of various theories, see Berthe Marti, "Meaning of the
Pharsalia," especially 352–354. Recent scholarship has added little, since the
number of possible hero candidates is obviously limited. Essentially the dispute has centered around Caesar, Cato, and Pompey. The tendency since
Marti's article has been toward Cato. Part of the problem arises from the
incomplete state of the epic (see Chapter 9), part from differing interpretations of Lucan's political or philosophical views and the notion of what is
meant by the term "hero" itself.

dwells on Hannibal. Silius cannot elevate any Roman, even Scipio, to comparable stature without seriously distorting history.[2] As a result, the *Punica* becomes a war between Hannibal and Rome. In historical terms, this is a fair approximation to the truth. But does this also mean that Hannibal is the hero of the *Punica?* The answer depends on what one means by hero.

If hero means the person who occupies our attention for the largest part of a work, then Hannibal is the hero of the *Punica,* and Caesar is the hero of the *Pharsalia.* On the other hand, if hero means the individual protagonist who most clearly engages the writer's sympathies and approval, then the answers will be quite different: Scipio and Cato. The problem, in Silius and Lucan, is that each poet expresses marked hostility to the dominant character of his epic. Both poets, unlike Homer in the *Iliad,* have clearly stated partisan likes and dislikes. In Statius' *Thebaid,* the difficulties are even more complex, since the character for whom Statius expresses most enthusiasm does not even appear until the final book. Theseus is something of a *deus ex machina.*[3] Of the major characters in the first 11 books of the *Thebaid,* Polynices rather than Eteocles seems to engage the poet's sympathies; even then, he does not remain in the forefront throughout the epic. Further, we have the uncomfortable feeling that the difference between Polynices and Eteocles is one of situation rather than character. Eteocles will not share his kingdom with Polynices, and on a smaller but no less illustrative level Polynices will not share the meager shelter of Adrastus' porch with Tydeus.[4]

Post-Homeric epic, however, offers yet another variety of heroism. Although Apollonius, Vergil, and Valerius Flaccus provide a single, central figure in their epics, their heroes do not assume the dominant and impressive characteristics associated with the grand Homeric manner. Apollonius' Jason is godlike in neither strength nor intellect; on the contrary, he is often notable for his difficulties in coping with events and other men. Much the same is true of

2. See E. Bassett, "Hercules" 258–273. For a somewhat different view, see M. von Albrecht, *Silius Italicus.*

3. Although Theseus may represent an ideal of heroic conduct toward which Statius moves in the *Thebaid,* the case for viewing him as the hero is much weaker.

4. *Theb.* 1.401–465.

Aeneas and Valerius' Jason. They all display a mixture of strength and weakness; they are shaped by their environment and heavily reliant on external help.

At least part of the change in treatment of the epic hero after Homer is due to the influence of tragedy and the tragic hero. Obviously tragedy is less diffuse than epic, if only because it is much shorter in length and, with the exception of Aeschylean drama, more weighted toward dialogue than narrative description. Tragedy is also more restricted in its subject matter, since it must above all be stageworthy. The material must conform to the physical limitations of the theater. While Homer may regale us with tales of combat, of man pitted against beasts and nature no less than against his fellow men, such breadth of action is, by and large, beyond the scope of the ancient stage. Not until the time of Shakespeare, in fact, could tragedy become a kind of dramatic epic in miniature. Greek drama focused on themes drawn from the smaller world of the individual: not the tale of the Argo, but Jason and Medea at Corinth. Since tragedy could not easily show the hero in battle or in other violent encounters with the external world, it moved toward a more personal and psychological treatment of human relationships and depicted the struggles among men in terms of verbal battles involving more complex intellectual or moral issues. Most important of all, tragedy directed much of its attention toward the struggle of the individual with himself. The agony of crucial moments of decision and the hero's self-scrutiny became fundamental ingredients of the drama.

The self-scrutiny of an Achilles or Odysseus in Homer is moving and adds depth and plausibility to their characters. At the same time it is only a part of the Homeric hero, a mood of introspection that can change as abruptly as that of Glaucus in *Iliad* 6.[5] But it is the most obsessive feature of Sophocles' Oedipus or Euripides' Orestes. We explore the uncertainties and doubts of the hero; we more often see him in decline or adversity than in ascendency or triumph. But when we take the brooding tragic hero out of tragedy and place him in the context of an epic, we create an altogether different entity. His doubts and tribulations stay in the foreground; they become immensely magnified by the larger world

5. 145–151.

in which he moves. The momentary paralysis in which we discovered him in tragedy becomes almost manic neurosis in epic.

The post-Homeric epic hero is heavily colored by his tragic dimensions. He develops the kind of personality we see in Dostoyevsky's *Notes from the Underground*. He becomes, in short, something of an anti-hero.[6] His doubts and indecision undermine his position within the epic. And with this weakening of the hero comes, of necessity, a counterbalancing tendency to strengthen the forces and ideas of the world in which he moves. Theme and motif become more important than the individual around whom the action is centered. For the dilemma of this new kind of epic hero often renders him incapable of difficult or crucial decisions. Unlike Odysseus, he does not have an answer to every problem; he is not *polumēchanos*. On the contrary, he is, like Apollonius' Jason, *amēchanos*.[7]

Jason is an ordinary human being in a world of demigods. Thus, like the tragic hero, he begins at a disadvantage. He is no match for Heracles, Castor, or the others, much less for the witch Medea. His virtue is caution; his authority as leader must constantly bear the challenges of his more vigorous (and more divine) companions. On several occasions he becomes so entangled in misunderstandings and impasses, that only direct help from the gods can save him.

This *amēchania*, to borrow Apollonius' term, is no less evident in Vergil's Aeneas and Statius' Polynices. Although Aeneas is the man selected by the gods and by destiny to found the Roman race, he is often unable to come to terms with his obligations to

6. Cf. Gilbert Lawall's useful article on Apollonius' *Argonautica*, "Jason As Anti-Hero," *YClS* 19 (1966), 119–169.

7. For *amēchania* as a characteristic of Apollonius' Jason, see Lawall. I am also indebted to a fine unpublished study of this matter by Martha Davis of the University of Texas at Austin. All my observations on *amēchania* in Apollonius are based on her observations and those of Lawall. The word *amēchania* occurs 31 times in the *Argonautica*, and, according to Mrs. Davis, "almost invariably in a series of descriptions of human reaction to conflict. The term is applied eight times to Jason, six times to Medea, five to the group of Argonauts, three to the expedition and twice to abstract qualities. For no other figure in the poem is the scheme of *amēchania* so fully developed as for Jason." Some illustrative examples of Jason's *amēchania* are 1.460–518; 1280–1344; 2.410–418.

destiny. On a number of occasions his decisions result in, or come near to, disaster, for others if not for himself. In *Aeneid* 2, when the Greeks are sacking Troy, he follows the suggestion of the rash Coroebus and dresses his men in Greek armor taken from the slain Androgeos and his band.[8] As a result he and his men are mistaken for Greeks by their own soldiers and are almost exterminated. In 7, Aeneas leaves his camp under the command of his son Iulus when he goes to seek help—an act for which Juno, later on, has some justified scorn and which nearly leads to catastrophe.[9] Most clearly of all, we see in 4 Aeneas' inability to reconcile his own instincts with the demands of destiny. In the *Odyssey* Zeus warns Calypso to release Odysseus so that he may reach his fated destination; in the *Aeneid* Jupiter has to remind *Aeneas* of his obligations in order to entice him to leave Dido.[10]

This paralysis that seizes Aeneas on occasion is caused by the peculiar nature of his role. He is suspended between past and future, Troy and Rome. Dido suffers because she belongs neither in the scheme of his Trojan identity nor in his Roman future.[11] Unlike Odysseus, Aeneas is not going home, except in the purely mythical sense that he is returning to the land of his ancestors. He does not have the advantages of Odysseus, to whom past and future are one and the same.

In the *Thebaid*, Polynices shares much of Aeneas' dilemma. When he leaves Thebes and marries Argia, the daughter of the Argive king Adrastus, he loses part of his Theban identity. Is he now an Argive, or is he still a Theban?[12] Polynices does not perceive the full extent of his dilemma until it is too late. In the battle before Thebes he avoids taking part in the fighting, because he wishes to keep his hands as clean as possible of the bloodshed of his own citizens. On the other hand, he does allow Argives to die for him. His friend Tydeus accuses him of being too forgetful of his *real* friends—a charge that finally strikes home to Polynices when Tydeus dies.[13] The Thebans, including his own mother, address him as if he were an Argive. When all his forces are shat-

8. 370–468.   9. *Aeneid* 10.68–73.
10. *Odyssey* 5.1–115; *Aeneid* 4.198–278.
11. See especially *Aeneid* 4.340–361.
12. *Theb.* 4.74–92.   13. *Ibid.*, 7.546–547; 9.52–56.

tered and he converses with Antigone as she stands upon the walls of Thebes, begging him not to fight his brother, he is a beaten man. He has lost the chance to rule his own city and has lost all his friends at Argos. What can he do? [14]

The closest approximation to this kind of hero in the *Pharsalia* is Pompey. He is neither good nor evil; nor is he strong or invincible. But he has his own curious kind of greatness. This leaves us, then, with three distinct heroic types in the *Pharsalia*, all of them Romans. In Caesar we see the closest approximation to a Homeric Achilles: a man confident in his strength, more sure of his purpose than Achilles himself, invincible in warfare, a man who will bring about a major change in Roman history. Then there is Cato, an altogether new creature in epic, who has no real counterpart in any Greek archetype, though he shares something in common with many heroes of Roman legend and history.[15] He too is confident, but in his goodness rather than in his physical or political expertise. Lastly there is Pompey, fashioned, it would seem, along the lines of Apollonius' Jason and Vergil's Aeneas, though weaker. He is totally lacking in any kind of self-confidence.

Even a hurried glance shows us that Pompey is the odd man out in the *Pharsalia*—at least among the three protagonists. He shares more in common with Curio and Appius Claudius than he does with either Caesar or Cato; but then again, so does the cause for which he is fighting. He is the champion of the republic in its last days—the decadent society of which Appius, Curio, and his own son Sextus are exemplars. But whereas they are shadows of what their forebears were, Pompey is a shadow of what he himself once was in the heyday of his glory. In this sense he resembles Rome as it was in the second half of the first century B.C. Cato, by way of contrast, recalls the idealized, older order of the state before corruption had eaten away at it. Caesar points to the future—the monolithic despotism of the emperors. At one extreme there is Caesar, whose dedication to the fulfillment of self is paramount. At the other is Cato, whose dedication to the state and to virtue is absolute and unwavering. His life is of less importance than the

14. *Ibid.*, 11.354-387.
15. For a fuller discussion of Cato see Chapters 6, 7, and 8.

welfare of the community as a whole.[16] Cato is the perfect Roman, as good for the state as Caesar is bad. Between them stands Pompey.

The *Pharsalia*, then, does not have a single, unifying hero as do the surviving epics that precede it. Rather, it has three paradigms of heroism, of which the most complex and least understood is Pompey.

I. *Pompeius Infelix*

Each of the protagonists of the *Pharsalia* shares something of Aeneas, whose *pietas*, at its best, resembles Cato's *virtus*, whose military prowess recalls that of Caesar, and whose constant inner turmoil and uncertainty resembles that of Pompey. But the most striking correspondence lies between Aeneas and Pompey, if only because both share the characteristic *amēchania* of the post-Homeric hero.

As the *Pharsalia* begins, Pompey is past his prime. Like Aeneas, he is so attached to the past that he finds it difficult to cope with the present, much less grasp the possibilities of the future. Unlike Caesar or Cato, he is not self-sufficient and self-reliant. He needs the response and affection of others to be complete. He can stimulate movement, or be moved, but he cannot move himself. In short, he is *amēchanos*.

Pompey's *amēchania* is best captured by the simile at the beginning of the epic, where he is compared to an old oak tree, leafless and rootless, sustained by his own weight, doomed to topple at the first blast of the east wind.[17] Despite this, he is the sole object of veneration in the grove where he stands, though many thriving young trees surround him.[18] He is verging on old age; he

16. In fact Cato desires to become a kind of *pharmakon* for the sins of Rome. See especially 2.306–319.

17. 1.129–143. Cf. Cicero *Brut.* 239; *Att.* 6.6.4.

18. The motif of the oak tree is common in ancient epic as Wuilleumier and Le Bonniec observe in their edition of *Pharsalia* 1.37. Cf. J. Aymard, *Quelques Séries de comparaisons chez Lucain*, Montpellier, 1951, 77–79. The most important new ingredient Lucan adds to tradition, as Wuilleumier and Le Bonniec observe, is his description of the votive offerings hanging from the branches of the trees "which evoke the primitive cult of sacred trees." Haskins had also noted this in his edition of the *Pharsalia* (note on line 137). But none of the scholars mentioned above adduces Lucan's account of the

has become soft with peacetime living. Above all, he is a seeker of glory and public recognition, enjoying the applause of the people in the theater he himself has built. He bases his hopes for the future on his past achievements, assuming that people will love and follow him because of his previous success. Memories of his great victories haunt him and shape his ideas just as recollection of traumatic defeat stalks Aeneas.

Even before Caesar is introduced, we know that Pompey is going to lose the civil war. For the very tone and form of this opening simile show us that Pompey is only the ghost of what he was: "Magni nominis umbra." [19] He is marked for defeat, not by any divine decree but by his own nature. When Lucan then describes Caesar as a thunderbolt, a savage energy incarnate that destroys all before it, we know that Pompey's opponent is far stronger than he need be in order to win.[20] The war between them will result in the annihilation of Pompey, and everything he stands for will be banished from the face of the earth. A contest between a decayed oak and a thunderbolt can allow only one conclusion.

That Pompey should be described as old and Caesar as young is curious. Pompey, no more than six years Caesar's elder, was in his middle fifties when the civil war broke out.[21] But Lucan seems intent on contrasting Caesar's vigor with Pompey's general lassitude. After all, Caesar's star was still in the ascendant, whereas Pompey's greatest days were already behind him. More important still, the conflict between them is also the conflict between an old order of government and the new Caesarism. For the republic too is old before its time, senile and ready to collapse less than a hundred

---

cutting down of the Druidic grove in 3.388–452, which shows the extent to which Lucan was familiar with the religious significance of sacred trees. Cf. *Aeneid* 10.423; 11.5–7; Lucretius 3.325; 5.554; Ovid *Met.* 9.41; Statius *Theb.* 6.67. Even more important is the fact that the oak to which Pompey is compared, sacred though it be, is also *dead*—as opposed to the oak to which Aeneas is compared in *Aeneid* 4.441–449. Another parallel to Lucan's description of Pompey as the decayed oak is in Seneca *Oedipus* 534–537: "curvosque tendit quercus et putres situ / annosa ramos: huius abrupit latus / edax vetustas; illa, iam fessa cadens / radice, fulta pendet aliena trabe." This passage is also rather similar to Lucan's description of the site of Troy in 9.966–969. See also H. Le Bonniec, "Lucain et la religion," *FH* 15.164–165.
19. 1.135.   20. 1.151–157; see Wuilleumier and Le Bonniec, *ad loc.*
21. 1.129–130. Even Pompey thinks of himself as old (7.382).

years after the destruction of Carthage. If Pompey is, as Lucan describes him in 1.135: "magni nominis umbra" (the ghost of a great name), so also is the republic. Liberty, as Cato points out, is but a fiction in Pompey's day, and liberty, at least in Cato's opinion, means not only the republic but Rome itself. In 2.301–303 he declares that Rome's name is freedom and that he will follow her empty ghost to the grave: "inanem persequar umbram." Rome, like Pompey, is but a shadow of what she once was, and, in this respect at least, Pompey comes close to symbolizing the plight of the decadent republic.

Lucan's Pompey is a paradoxical figure, whose contradictory nature is well analyzed by Cato in 9.190–214. He was, Cato notes, "multum maioribus inpar / nosse modum iuris," far inferior to his predecessors when it came to knowing the limits of power he should observe; yet he was useful in an age when there was no longer any respect for what was right. He was powerful without destroying freedom: "salva libertate potens"; the only man who remained a private citizen even though the people were ready to be his slaves: "solus plebe parata / privatus servire sibi." Though he was the guiding hand in the senate, the senate was still in control: "rector senatus, sed regnantis, erat." He claimed nothing by right of conquest and always wanted the people to have the right to refuse to give him whatever he wanted them to give him: "quaeque dari voluit voluit sibi posse negari." He was too wealthy, but he gave the treasury more than he kept for himself. He took up the sword, but he also knew how to put it down. He preferred war to peace, but loved peace when he was at war. He enjoyed taking power, but he also enjoyed setting it aside. As far as the details of his personal life were concerned, there was nothing to fault. Finally, and perhaps decisively, Pompey represented the last stage when Rome still had any semblance of freedom. True faith in liberty, Cato declares, had disappeared with Marius and Sulla. With Pompey's death, even the fiction of liberty was gone: "Pompeio rebus adempto / nunc et ficta perit."

The highest compliment paid to Pompey by Cato is in the first two words of his encomium: "civis obit" (a citizen has died). Above all else, Pompey had kept himself within the bounds of citizenship, even if at times he had stretched those bounds to the utmost. Over the previous fifty years, liberty had been progressively eroded by a succession of military coups. Pompey stood at the end of the line: he had reached the ultimate power possible within the constitutional framework of the republic. The next step was bound to be the definitive one, marking the transition between republic and despotism. Caesar's victory at Pharsalia accomplished that transition—hence the crucial identification of Pompey with the republic as it was in its final days. No wonder the soldiers at the battle of Pharsalia are afraid not only for the city, but for Pompey: "urbi Magnoque timetur" (7.138)—for it is not easy to differentiate the two. The tottering oak that is Pompey is also the republic.

Unlike the minor characters of the *Pharsalia*—most notably Curio, Appius, and Sextus Pompey—Pompey himself does not reflect an utterly corrupt decadence, even though, as P. Wuilleumier and H. Le Bonniec rightly emphasize, Lucan views him "as a vain demagogue and a general as presumptuous as he is short-sighted." [22] He has a certain pathetic magnificence, a subtlety that makes him one of the finest character studies in Roman literature. He is more carefully drawn than Aeneas or Polynices, more plausible than Dido. Lucan neither spares his weaknesses nor ignores his paradoxical beauty. In this too he is like the republic, decadent and doomed but still capable of eliciting affection. Cicero also saw Pompey in much this same light:

Just as we are put off in love affairs by women who are dirty, silly or brash, so the ugliness of Pompey's flight from Italy and his carelessness made me forget my love for him. He did nothing worthwhile such as might tempt me to become his companion in exile. But now my love is surfacing again (*nunc emergit amor*); I can do nothing to allay my longing for him. My books, my writing, my philosophy are of no avail. Day and night I watch the sea like the proverbial bird—and I want to fly [*Ad Atticum* 9.10]

The historical Pompey, no less than Lucan's, had an ability to draw people to him even against their better judgment and will. Cicero talks of him as if he were a lover rather than a friend and statesman.

22. Wuilleumier and Le Bonniec, 37.

In this sense Pompey provides a bridge in the *Pharsalia* between
Caesar and Cato, who are both, in their own ways, superhuman
To Caesar and Cato, issues are simple and clear-cut, for they are
viewed in terms of an ideal: the quest for personal power, the
struggle for virtue. Neither can tolerate purposelessness or anything less than total commitment. They demand this of their
troops, and they get it. Pompey, on the other hand, is fighting
for something more complex and less accurately definable because
it actually exists in a tangible, material sense. He is the leader of
the republican forces because he has been selected as their leader,
ordered to take command by the consul Lentulus.[23] And here is
the heart of his dilemma, which Lucan presents most dramatically
at the beginning of book 7.[24]

On the very morn of the battle of Pharsalia, Pompey is confronted by an angry Cicero who criticizes his delay in engaging
Caesar's army. The tone of his remarks is accusing and threat-
ening:

> propera ne te tua classica linquant.
> scire senatus avet, miles te, Magne, sequatur
> an comes.   [83–85]

(You had better hurry up or your troops will go on without you.
The senators would love to know, Great Pompey, whether they
follow you as your soldiery, or as your companions-at-arms.)

Cicero plays on the double entendre of *comes*, which can signify
either someone equal in social standing or the member of a pro-
vincial governor's retinue. This adds further bite to the implied
contrast between *miles* and *comes* by means of the sarcastic undertone: "Are we your troops or equals? Are you a general or a peacetime governor?" [25] Pompey is abruptly and brutally reminded of
his position vis-à-vis his army. He was, as Lucan tells us in 5.45–47,
ordered to take command; now the command is, in a sense, being
taken away from him by this overt attack on his strategy of delaying and by the threat that the army will act without him.[26] Cicero

23. 5.45–47.   24. 45–150.
25. Dilke, *Lucan,* note on 7.85, sees only the second meaning.
26. F. Adcock, among modern scholars, finds himself in disagreement with
the consensus of ancient authorities who maintain that Pompey was forced

s going too far in his zeal to demonstrate what Lucan points out
n 5.14: the senators are not on Pompey's side; Pompey is on their
ide: "non Magni partes, sed Magnum in partibus esse."

Caesar, when confronted by rebellious troops, can resort to
prowbeating and even decimating them; Cato can belabor his
men with the rhetoric of liberty.[27] But Pompey can do nothing of
he kind. He is the general of the republican forces by decree of
he senate, and he is suspect because of his past associations with
Sulla.[28] Pompey cannot override Cicero without appearing to be
unwilling to fight, and his unwillingness to fight can be interpreted as a desire to retain power for himself by denying a quick
and speedy end to the war.

Pompey knows that Cicero's words are not a demand for equal-
ty, but a complete reversal of their relative positions:

> ingemuit rector sensitque deorum
> esse dolos et fata suae contraria menti.

---

nto battle prematurely (*CAH* 9.664). See Dilke, *Lucan*, 19–20 for an outline
of the ancient view. Caesar *BCiv.* 3.86 states: "Pompeius quoque, ut postea
cognitum est, suorum omnium hortatu statuerat proelio decertare." Cf. Appian *BCiv.* 2.66–67; Plutarch *Pomp.* 68.1 (and 66.1, 67.2); Plutarch *Caes.* 42.1.
Given the rank and quarrelsome nature of some of the senators on Pompey's
side, notably Lentulus Spinther, Domitius Ahenobarbus, and Metellus Scipio,
and Caesar's observations (*BCiv.* 3.82) that the Pompeians were eager to return to Italy now that the uniting of Pompey's army with that of Metellus
Scipio appeared to promise a quick and satisfactory resolution of the war,
there must have been considerable pressure on Pompey to commit the troops
to battle.

27. See Chapters 6 and 7.

28. Cicero in his letters shows constant fear of Pompey's connections with
Sulla, and of what he takes to be Pompey's Sulla-like disposition: "mirandum
enim in modum Cnaeus noster Sullani regni similitudinem concupivit. εἰδώς
τοι λέγω. nihil ille umquam minus obscure tulit" (*Att.* 9.7). Similarly: "hoc
turpe Cnaeus noster biennio ante cogitavit. ita sullaturit animus eius et
proscripturit iam diu" (*ibid.*, 10). In Lucan, Caesar constantly plays on Pompey's connections with Sulla (especially in 1.325–326 and 7.306–307), but there
is nothing in Lucan's description of Pompey's behavior in the *Pharsalia* suggesting any Sullan *saevitia* left in him. Cf. P. Grimal in *FH* 15.78–81. Lucan,
in fact, expresses regret that Pompey was so unlike Sulla in 6.301–303 (when
he fails to follow up his victory at Dyrrhachium). E. Malcovati," Lucano e
Cicerone," *Athenaeum* 31 (N.S.) (1953) 288–297, argues that Lucan made use
of Cicero's correspondence for his portrayal of Pompey—a convincing argument, made even more plausible by V. Holliday, *Pompey in Cicero's Correspondence and Lucan's Civil War*, The Hague/Paris, 1969, 84–92.

"si placet hoc" inquit "cunctis, si milite Magno,
non duce tempus eget, nil ultra fata morabor."   [85–88]

(The *rector* groaned and perceived that this was the trickery o
the gods, and that the fates were opposed to his intent. "If th
is what you all want," he said, "if the occasion calls for m
services as a soldier, not as a general, I shall delay the fates n
longer.")

The word *rector* is important in this context. For Pompey is th
very man whom Cicero had envisaged as the controller and figure
head of his ideal state and of the fortunes of the Roman republic
the *rector rei publicae.* Cicero, then, who makes here his one an
only appearance in the *Pharsalia,* becomes symbolic of the senate
the whole theory of the republic, and its helplessness in the mc
ment of crisis.

Cicero, however, as scholars have pointed out, was not presen
at the historical Pharsalia.[29] Indeed he was not, physically at leas
But in everything other than physical presence he was. The ful
force of the senate's attitude to Pompey could come more dra
matically from no one else. The man whom Domitius Ahenc
barbus sarcastically called "king of kings," about whom Cicer
and others had so many fears and doubts, yet whom all the re
publicans were prepared to use for their purposes against Caesar
now reaps a harvest as bitter for him as it will be for the state. Th
historical truth of Pompey's dilemma at the historical Pharsalia i
driven home by a historical lie. Surely this is the genius of the poe
which transcends the mere narration of events. For Lucan pro
vides us with the essence of historical truth in defiance of historica

29. Livy *Per.* 111: "Cicero in castris remansit" (though this could simpl
mean that he took no part in the battle); see also Plutarch *Cic.* 39; *Cat. Min*
55; Cicero *Div.* 1.68; and Holliday's general discussion of Pompey at Pha
salia (65–75). Dilke points out (*Lucan,* note on 7.63) that Cicero had actuall
argued in favor of Pompey's prolongation of the war in *Fam.* 7.3. Grimal (*Fl
15.109) comments cryptically: "on ne pouvait pas ne pas le mettre en scène
—not a very convincing argument. Nehrkorn, 249–250, suggests that Lucan a
trying to show us the "real" Cicero; Malcovati, "Lucano e Cicerone," sees i
Lucan's account an attempt at caricature. My own view most closely corr
sponds to that of M. Rambaud, "L'Apologie de Pompée par Lucain au Liv
VII de la Pharsale," *REL* 33 (1955) 258–296, as it does in some other aspec
of the portrayal of Pompey in the *Pharsalia.*

fact (which even as fact has no bearing on the actual outcome of the battle).

The strength of senatorial *libertas* in peacetime becomes its critical weakness in time of war. The confrontation with the senate, represented by Cicero, not the fight with Caesar, is the moment of Pompey's defeat. Pompey rounds in anger upon his critics: "You could have won the war without a single wound. You could have conquered and captured Caesar without slaughter and handed him over for punishment to the peace he had violated. O blind men, what is this mad passion for crime? (*quis furor, o caeci, scelerum?*)—Are men who are intent on civil war afraid that they may win without shedding blood?" (92–96). All the senate has to do, Pompey claims, is wait. Then the victory will be theirs because of the desperate straits to which Caesar's army has been reduced. With great acidity, he adds: "They would rather fight Caesar than conquer him [pugnare ducem quam vincere malunt]" (109). At this point Pompey resigns his responsibility. The steward of Rome's welfare returns his charge to Fortune:

> res mihi Romanas dederas, Fortuna, regendas:
> accipe maiores et caeco in Marte tuere.   [110–111]

(Fortune, you once gave me in trust the welfare of Rome to control. I have increased it for you. Take it back now, and guard it in the blind chances of war.)

Pompey sees no glory in either victory or defeat: all the suffering will fall upon the vanquished, all the guilt and crime upon the victor: "omne malum victi . . . omne nefas victoris erit" (122–123). With these words he falls silent, and, like a helmsman in a storm, leaves control of the ship to the winds:

> sic fatur et arma
> permittit populis frenosque furentibus ira
> laxat.   [123–125]

(So he spoke and his anger allows the people to take up their weapons and looses the reins upon their madness.)

Unlike Neptune in *Aeneid* 1.142–156, he does not attempt to calm the storm and gain control of the dissident elements. Like

Latinus in *Aeneid* 7.594–600, he simply is not strong enough to
do so, and in this is both his greatness and his weakness.

Pompey's sensitivity to the wishes of the senate, or to those of
his army, keeps him within the republican tradition, but it makes
his leadership indecisive. We see a classic example of its results in
2.526–595. There Pompey, at the outset of the war, addresses his
troops with great confidence and even greater boastfulness, minimizing the significance of Caesar's incursion into Italy. The response from his soldiers is silent and unenthusiastic. Perceiving
this, Pompey decides not to fight and withdraws from Italy. He
slinks away from a situation he has swaggered into. By parading
his greatness he has only convinced people of his weakness.

In book 7, as in book 2, Pompey makes no attempt to assert himself against the wishes of those he is leading. But in 7 the situation
he faces is the reverse of that in 2: this time he does not want to
fight, and his army does. As he comes to address his troops in 7, he
is gloomy about the prospects of victory. Forced into battle against
his better judgment, he knows that the outcome has been decided
in the interchange with Cicero. It is hardly surprising, then, that
his speech at 7.342–382 stands in pointed and deliberate contrast
to his boastful and unsuccessful harangue in 2. And it also contrasts sharply with Caesar's address to his forces before Pharsalia.

Lucan sets up the speeches of the leaders at Pharsalia in careful
modal opposition. Not only are they juxtaposed (Caesar: 250–329;
Pompey: 342–382), but Caesar's speech is nearly twice as long as
Pompey's and radiates confidence. Both leaders mention the possibility of defeat. But Caesar promises to kill himself if his army is
put to flight (309–310) and studiously avoids raising the specter of
catastrophe in his closing words. He begins and ends in total sureness of victory. Pompey, on the other hand, begins calmly but
virtually bursts into tears toward the end of his address. He is
terrified of death, and gives no pledge that he will kill himself if
defeated:

> cum prole et coniuge supplex,
> imperii salva si maiestate liceret,
> volverer ante pedes. Magnus, nisi vincitis, exul,
> ludibrium soceri, vester pudor, ultima fata

deprecor ac turpes extremi cardinis annos,
ne discam servire senex. [377–382]

(If I could do so without losing my dignity as your general, I
would throw myself at your feet, along with my wife and children and become your suppliant. Unless you win, Great Pompey
will be an exile, a laughing-stock to Caesar, and a disgrace to
you. I beseech you to save me from this most terrible fate, so
that I will not have to eke out my last years in shame nor learn
to be a slave in my old age.)

But Pompey has already sacrificed his dignity. His fearful words do
not require the physical self-abasement of groveling upon the
ground. He does not contemplate the distinct alternatives Caesar
offers his men: victory or death. To him the alternatives are
victory or slavery. While Caesar foresees rivers of blood flowing
upon the plain, kings trampled underfoot, the body of the senate
ripped asunder, and nations swimming in an immense sea of
slaughter, Pompey dwells on the picture of women on the battle-
ments of a beleagured city, the senate, Rome, and future generations begging the soldiers to fight.[30] Pompey concludes with a plea
that he not end his life in slavery, Caesar with the order that his
army tear down its camp. That night, he declares, they will sleep
in the tents of the defeated foe.[31]

Pompey's speech would have won him no plaudits in a school of
rhetoric. He seems to be saying all the wrong things. But the reaction of the republican army is tremendously enthusiastic, despite
the fact that Pompey offers them a grim picture of what awaits
them and a debased picture of himself.[32] His fear and uncertainty
galvanize the troops into action, as his braggart display in 2 could
not.[33] Why?

Caesar chooses to identify his men with himself and with his
cause. In doing so he is acting intelligently because he quite
literally *is* the cause for which his army is fighting. Without him
there is no cause. But the republicans, even if Pompey himself
does not quite grasp this, are not engaged in a life-and-death

30. 7.292–294; 346–348; 369–372.   31. 7.326–329.   32. 7.382–384.
33. 2.596–597.

struggle to preserve their champion. The Roman people will have
to *live* with the consequences of Pharsalia, now and in the future.
The issue, as Lucan points out in 7.132, is not whether Rome will
live or die, but *what* Rome will be: "Roma quid esset." Thus the
alternatives with which Pompey's cowardice leaves him (freedom
or slavery) are precisely those Rome herself faces. The fearful tone
that dominates the latter part of Pompey's speech coincides with
the fears the republic feels about its future: "metus hos regni, spes
excitat illos" (7.386) (fear of tyranny motivates one side [i.e., the
republicans], hope of tyranny the other). The republicans do not
stand to gain something they do not have if they defeat Caesar;
but if they lose, their cause, freedom, will be struck a devastating
blow. Caesar's men, by way of contrast, stand to gain everything
by victory; if they are defeated, the consequences will be limited
to themselves, their leader, and their generation. As Lucan indicates in 7.639–641, the consequences of a republican defeat at
Pharsalia were far-reaching:

> plus est quam vita salusque
> quod perit: in totum mundi prosternimur aevum.
> vincitur his gladiis omnis quae serviet aetas.

> (We lost more than life and security: we have been cast down
> until the end of time. Every succeeding generation of slaves
> lost its freedom when the swords clashed at Pharsalia.)

The imagery of the beleaguered city which Pompey evokes and
the fears of slavery he plays on obviously strike a responsive chord
in the republican army. Yet Lucan does not wish us to see Pompey
as sustaining, throughout his speech, a calculatedly allegorical approach. True, Pompey asks his troops to imagine mothers exhort-
ing them to fight, aged senators pleading upon their knees, even
Rome herself, fearful of tyranny, coming before them, and future
generations bringing their various prayers (369–376). But his concluding words are a plea for himself. The speech culminates in the
pathetic exhortation of a man whose fears are all too real and all
too personal. The army's warm reaction arises from a curious coincidence of interests: what is at stake for Pompey as an individual
is also at stake for every Roman citizen.

In this we see the delicacy of Lucan's artistry. Since Pompey conjures up the vision of Rome herself, of the senate, and of future generations, we might expect that he would attribute the plea for salvation from slavery to *Rome*. But he does not. Instead, the final appeal is not to the army's love of Rome but to their love of Pompey. In the wake of Cicero's rebuke, Pompey sees his fate as distinct from that of Rome, and can maintain the conventional rhetoric of the city pleading with her troops only for a limited time before succumbing to his own fears. Unwittingly he has allowed himself to become one of the symbolic beings of his own speech: first the anguished mothers, then the senate and Rome, then the unborn generations, and finally Pompey himself.

Unfortunately, the wild applause that greets his words is now bound to mislead him. For it convinces him, since he has ceased to view himself as the *rector rei publicae,* that the army really is fighting for *him,* to save *him* from slavery. When the battle lines clash, and it becomes clear that the republicans are going to lose, Pompey, who is watching the engagement from a high vantage point, resolves to depart:

> "Parcite," ait "superi, cunctas prosternere gentes.
> Stante potest mundo Romaque superstite Magnus
> esse miser." [7.659–661]

> ("Hold back, powers above," he said, "do not destroy all the nations. The world can stand, Rome can survive, even though Pompey must suffer.")

He cannot bear the thought that people should continue to die and add to the slaughter for *his sake.* He fears that, if he dies on the field of battle, the army will insist on dying there with him (671–672). From 647–672, Lucan carefully maintains the illusion that Pompey's motives are of the highest order. He does not even comment on the naiveté of Pompey's assumption that if he leaves the battle, the fighting will stop.

But at 673, Lucan strikes a distinctly less noble chord. He suggests, almost as an afterthought, that perhaps Pompey left the battle so that Caesar would not have the joy of gloating over his corpse: "Caesaris aut oculis voluit subducere mortem." But 674–697 proves to be rather more than an afterthought, for in these lines Lucan unravels the effect produced in 647–672. The heavy

spondees opening line 674 confirm the reversal begun in 673:
"nequiquam. infelix" (in vain. Unfortunate man). Lucan first
reminds his reader of the vanity of Pompey's hope that Caesar will
not be able to see him dead (674–675). Then he suggests that
Pompey departed from Pharsalia because he wanted to see his
wife, Cornelia, again (675–676). From 677–689 he describes Pompey's actual departure from the field, bravely, without groans or
tears. For a moment, the illusion of nobility returns, but it is
rudely shattered in 689–697:

> Fuge proelia dira
> ac testare deos nullum, qui perstet in armis,
> iam tibi Magne, mori. ceu flebilis Africa damnis
> et ceu Munda nocens Pharioque a gurgite clades,
> sic et Thessalicae post te pars maxima pugnae
> non iam Pompei nomen populare per orbem
> nec studium belli, sed par quod semper habemus,
> libertas et Caesar, erit; teque inde fugato
> ostendit moriens sibi se pugnasse senatus.

(Flee from the hideous battle, and bear witness before the gods
that no one who keeps on fighting now is dying for you, Pompey. As in Africa where we will weep our losses, as at guilty
Munda, as in the slaughter by the Nile, so was it at Pharsalia:
the greatest part of the conflict occurred after you had left.
No longer is it a matter of your universal popularity, nor is it
just love of war; it is the conflict which is always with us, between liberty and Caesar[ism]. When you had been routed, the
senate proved by dying that it had been fighting for itself.)

Lucan ruthlessly crushes Pompey's illusion that the battle was
fought for his sake, to clear away once and for all the Caesarian
propaganda that identified republicans by the generic *Pompeiani*
—an identification which Pompey's own conduct had done much
to encourage. The senate is fighting for traditional government at
Rome, not for its latest champion.

Once Pompey is clear of the battlefield, and of the context of
book 7, his behavior changes. Two brief passages illustrate this
transition. In 7.677–689 Pompey is fearless as he gallops away from
Pharsalia, but at 8.5–12 he is frightened by the rustling of leaves in

the woods and by the noises his companions make. We should not conclude that this signifies Lucan's loss of interest in him, since the whole of book 8 is devoted to Pompey—the first time any character in the epic is allocated an entire book.[34] It is wiser to recall that Pompey was very much afraid *before* the battle, when he saw the enemy drawn up on the field:

> vidit ut hostiles in rectum exire catervas
> Pompeius nullasque moras permittere bello
> sed superis placuisse diem, stat corde gelato
> attonitus; tantoque duci sic arma timere
> omen erat. [7.337–341]

(When he saw the enemy forces move out opposite him, and that they would allow no delay in the conflict, Pompey, realizing that this was the day ordained by the powers above, was thunderstruck; his heart froze. It was an evil premonition to so great a general that he should be so afraid of battle.)

Yet Pompey suppressed his fear: "premit inde metus" (341), and rode up and down the lines on his great war-horse. He is capable of putting on a good show when necessary, though, as we have already seen, he is unable to sustain it for long. His address to his troops reveals the very genuine fears in his heart. Similarly, as he leaves the battle, he maintains good face. But at the beginning of 8 the need to repress his fears is gone. Now he needs think only of himself. No longer are his well-known face and the memory of his past exploits a matter of joy; they are a burden to him. He has lived too long:

> sic longius aevum
> destruit ingentis animos et vita superstes
> imperio. [8.27–29]

(Thus his life has lasted too long, it has outlived his power and has destroyed his great courage.)

Now that his luck is past, Pompey is beginning to disintegrate. Although his confidence is restored somewhat after his reunion with

34. Probably Caesar would have dominated 10 in a similar way if Lucan had lived to complete it.

Cornelia on Lesbos, it leads only to his most astonishing act of madness in the *Pharsalia*. This is why we should beware of following Berthe Marti's notion that Pompey approximates to a Stoic *prokopton*.[35] For throughout the *Pharsalia*, Pompey is regressing, not progressing. In the disillusionment of defeat, he is constantly uncertain how he should act. He must have success, he must regain his lost glory. His drive to reestablish himself leads to a total loss of perspective and sense of proportion.

At 8.211 Pompey instructs Deiotarus, one of his eastern vassals, to enlist the aid of Parthia for his cause. Pompey's reasoning is as follows:

> "quando" ait "Emathiis amissus cladibus orbis,
> qua Romanus erat, superest, fidissime regum,
> Eoam temptare fidem populosque bibentis
> Euphraten et adhuc securum a Caesare Tigrim." [211–214]

("Since," he said, "the world—the Roman world, that is—has been lost by the disaster in Thessaly, it remains, most loyal of my kings, to try out the faith of the East and of the peoples who drink from the Euphrates and the Tigris, which Caesar has not yet touched.")

It now becomes much clearer that Pompey sees his own cause as distinct from the cause of Rome. He invites the Parthians to join him, pointing out his generosity to them in the past: he has refrained from conquering them (229–230). Besides, they are his only equals (231–232). It is, of course, untrue that Pompey ever had a real opportunity to conquer Parthia; and his belief that he is an equal of the Parthian king is pathetic. These delusions about past glory and present power, however, are completely over-shadowed by his concluding words to Deiotarus, which take the form of an exhortation to the Parthians: "Pompeio vincite, Parthi, / vinci Roma volet" (8.237–238) ("Conquer for Pompey, Parthians, and Rome will desire to be conquered"). The utter naiveté of these

---

35. B. Marti, "Meaning of the *Pharsalia*," 367: "Pompey . . . represents those men whom the Stoics called *proficientes*." For a critique of this view see Rambaud, "L'Apologie de Pompée," Syndikus, 101–104 and 107–108, and Schönberger, *Untersuchungen*, 113–122. Also Pfligersdorffer, 346, and Holliday, 65–92; also, E. Burck, "Vom Menschenbild in Lucans *Pharsalia*," in *Lucan*, ed. Rutz, 149–159.

words demonstrates that Pompey really believes the battle of Pharsalia was fought for him alone, that what Rome wants, above all, is her Pompey, regardless of the cost. Lucan refrains, however, from a withering denunciation of Pompey. The poet, it appears, would rather let the condemnation come from another of his dramatis personae, just as Vergil allows the censure of Aeneas to come from Fama, Iarbas, Jupiter, Mercury, and Dido, in *Aeneid* 4.

When the remnants of the republican forces gather at Syhedra, Pompey makes no reference to his despatch of Deiotarus to the Parthians. Instead, he suggests that the senate consider seeking aid from one of three sources: Libya, Parthia, or Egypt (8.276–278). This suggests some deviousness on Pompey's part, and drives home the fact that his consultation with and sending of Deiotarus is the only instance of genuinely independent and positive action on his part in the entire epic. Parthia, Pompey argues, should be favored because of its invincibility, its resistance to Alexander, and its defeat of Crassus (8.299–302). Even more tellingly, he reminds his colleagues that, once upon a time, Marius had been able to restore himself to power by relying on a foreign nation:

> an Libycae Marium potuere ruinae
> erigere in fasces et plenis reddere fastis,
> me pulsum leviore manu fortuna tenebit?   [8.269–271]

(The ruins of Africa could elevate Marius to the consulship and give him a place once more on the honor lists filled with his name. Shall Fortune hold me down when she has thrown me with a gentler hand?)

To suggest an alliance with Parthia and adduce the massacre of Crassus' army in support of his contention is bad enough in Roman eyes. And, given Lucan's own reactions to the inability of Rome to avenge Crassus, the poet himself can hardly have approved.[36] But to propose a return to Rome in the style of Marius is even more dreadful.[37] Not only would this rank Pompey with the great criminals of Roman history, it would put him on the opposite side of the political fence, in the number of the *populares* in whose steps Caesar is following. To restore himself to power, Pompey is ready to do everything Caesar does and more. It is

36. 1.10–12.   37. See Chapter 3, Section V.

surely no accident that his words "Roma, fave coeptis" at 8.322 are a verbatim echo of what Caesar says to Patria as he crosses the Rubicon in 1.200. But Pompey's contemplated action is worse than what Caesar does; at least Caesar would not subjugate Rome with the troops of Rome's great enemy. The paradoxical benefits of the Parthian alliance which Pompey touts before the senate scarcely justify his proposal: if the Parthians are brought in, they too will suffer from the civil wars, and the outcome will avenge either himself or the Crassi: "aut me Fortuna necesse est / vindicet aut Crassos (326–327)." But in the midst of this, Rome and liberty have been forgotten—as has the fact that his wife Cornelia was married to one of the Crassi who died at Carrhae.

"Non omnis in arvis / Emathiis cecidi" (266–267) (I did not fall in total destruction at Pharsalia), Pompey cries. We now perceive that if Pompey were to gain his request at this juncture, liberty would fall beyond all hope of redemption, and Caesar's cause would become, both morally and politically, the better. Pompey's love of glory has degenerated into madness, and he must be stopped.

It is Lentulus who speaks up against Pompey's suggestion, in a lengthy speech running from 331–453.[38] He instantly strikes at the very crux of the matter: "quid causa obtenditur armis / libertatis amor?" (339–340) (Why was love of liberty employed as the excuse for war?). Pompey's words and actions have made it patent that he is concerned only for himself; now Lentulus dismembers his arguments point by point. He demonstrates the vanity of Pompey's belief that the Parthians will still respect him; then he demolishes Pompey's contention that the Parthians are invincible in war; with a particularly clever but vicious stab at Pompey's love for Cornelia, he points out that it will be her fate to endure the lust of the Arsacid king, who will find her particularly attractive since she has been the wife of both Pompey and the younger Crassus. Lentulus adds that he would be happy to see even Caesar triumph over the Parthians, which is a rather broad hint that if Pompey were, somehow, to pursue his plan against the wishes of the senate, the senate would take up arms on Caesar's side.[39]

38. For some other implications of this speech, see Chapter 1, Section II.
39. 8.429–430.

Lentulus offers the counterproposal of going to Egypt, an alternative Pompey rejected at 281–282. Ironically, this is the one instance in the confrontation between Lentulus and Pompey where Pompey's judgment is sounder than Lentulus'. Pompey distrusts the Egyptian king Ptolemy because of his extreme youth, suggesting that a problematic alliance requires the assent of a maturer ruler (281–282); Lentulus argues the opposite (450–453). When Lentulus' proposal is approved by the senate, however, it guarantees, though Lentulus does not realize it, Pompey's death. At the same time, the success of Lentulus' suggestion reemphasizes Pompey's subordination to the senate. Pompey does not even raise the slender protest he registers against Cicero in 7. Still, for an uncomfortable moment, we have a glimpse of that dimension of Pompey to which Caesar alludes: the man who licked the sword of Sulla.[40] But the illusion is fleeting. Pompey is incapable of joining the ranks of the great domestic foes of Rome. Caesar may fashion events, but events fashion Pompey. Suitably, if brutally, Lentulus has pointed out the vanity of Pompey's dreams of vengeance. He knows that, though the idea of seeking aid from Parthia is horrendous, the man who makes the proposal is now too insignificant to take seriously. "Quis nominis umbram horreat?" (Who would tremble at the ghost of a name?), Lentulus cries at 8.449–450. The initial image of Pompey as the ghost of a great name, "Magni nominis umbra" (1.135), is recalled. But to Lentulus, no less than to the Parthian king, the name is no longer even great.

II. Pompey the Lover

In the midst of this tangle of frailty, vanity, and temporary *furor,* there is a warmth in Pompey which is utterly lacking in either Cato or Caesar, and which makes him unquestionably the finest character study in the *Pharsalia.* Whereas Lucan carefully uses mythic *color* to enhance Cato's glory and accord him divine stature, and no less carefully uses myth to demonstrate Caesar's demented megalomania, he presents Pompey in purely human terms without mythic coloration. Pompey's goals are admiration and respect—which are to him the same as love. Cato, in contrast,

40. 1.324–331; 7.307.

is impervious to mere human love; Caesar more concerned with inspiring fear than affection.[41]

Much of the pathos aroused by Pompey stems from the fact that, for all his desire to love and be loved, the joy and pleasure of love usually evade him. Sometimes he simply fails to recognize the affection others have for him, because he equates love with applause, approval, and success. If not applauded, if not successful, he cannot believe he is loved. When he is applauded, and when the promise of success remains, he assumes that he is loved. His fulfilment, then, is dependent upon the response of others, as Caesar's or Cato's is not. As a result, Pompey's behavior almost always takes us by surprise, as does the response of others to his actions or words. His inner confusion, his often illogical actions, and his ultimate failure mark him off from his fellow protagonists.

In 7, for example, after the battle of Pharsalia, Pompey arrives at the city of Larisa.[42] The townspeople offer to help him so that the struggle with Caesar can continue. Pompey's reaction to their offer is brief and perfunctory: "quid opus victo populis aut urbibus?" (7.720) (What use are cities and peoples to a conquered man?). Yet, as he gallops away, the inhabitants of Larisa weep and inveigh against the savagery of the gods. They are not angered by Pompey's curtness, but sorrowful at his defeat. "Here was your chance," Lucan says, "to have a real belief in the popularity you sought, Pompey, the chance to know its bounty":

> nunc tibi vera fides quaesiti, Magne, favoris
> contigit ac fructus: felix se nescit amari.   [7.726–727]

What is the meaning of this last phrase, "felix se nescit amari"? Is it just some kind of proverb: "A happy man does not know that he is loved"? I must admit that I am unable to detect the existence of any such proverb. Given the common meaning of *felix* as fruitful and productive, it is hard to imagine that anyone would have coined such an odd apophthegm, much less that it would have become proverbial. Surely this is a paradox, authored by Lucan himself: "Happy man, he does not know that he is loved." To know that the people love him would be more than Pompey could

41. See Chapter 6, Section II, and Chapter 7, Section III.
42. 7.712–727.

endure at this point. He is a helpless refugee, rejected by Cicero and the senate, defeated by Caesar. He is happy in his ignorance of the affection of Larisa; for there is nothing he could do to respond to it. Had he known that he was loved at this juncture, he would have been truly *infelix*, as Cornelia is at the end of 5, when she cannot embrace the husband whom she loves so dearly (5.799).

The desire to be loved is at the very core of Pompey's being and explains most of his actions in the epic. Unless his suggestions meet with immediate approval, he backs off, as in 2 when his troops show no enthusiasm for a confrontation with Caesar, or when Cicero attacks his strategy of delaying in 7. As defeat looms ever larger and finally become reality, he is rendered incapable of doing anything that provokes displeasure amongst his supporters. Each disapproving word or gesture becomes a sign that he is no longer loved.

When he arrives in Lesbos in a tiny skiff in the course of his flight from Pharsalia, his wife collapses on the beach where she has been awaiting his arrival. She is as distraught on seeing him again as she was when he left her at the end of 5.[43] In fact Lucan goes to considerable pains to resume the portrait of Pompey and Cornelia in the same sort of setting as that in which he broke off in book 5. At the end of 5, Cornelia had wept on the beach as her attendants escorted her to the ship that was to carry her to Lesbos. Now, at the beginning of 8, she weeps as Pompey's small vessel and handful of supporters arrive. In neither scene does she receive much sympathy from Pompey, who fails to understand her grief.

Pompey's first reaction as he comes ashore at Lesbos in 8 is to berate Cornelia rather than console her. He insinuates that she loved him not for himself but for his fame:

> vivit post proelia Magnus
> sed fortuna perit. quod defles, illud amasti. [8.84–85]

(Great Pompey is alive after the battle, but his Fortune has perished. What you are weeping for is what you loved.)

Pompey's words astonish us with their defensive obtuseness. For a man who so desires love, he is extraordinarily unable to under-

43. 8.40–108; 5.722–815.

stand what it is or to detect it in others. He can see love only in
terms of the joy and the applause, never in terms of the tears.
Cornelia, he declares, should love him all the more *because* he has
lost the senate, his power, and his entourage of kings. "Love me
for myself," he declares, "*because* I have been conquered [ipsum
quod sum victus ama]" (77–78). Though this is what he asks of her,
his own rationale of why she should still love him is marred by
that same touch of vanity we see everywhere in his behavior. He
argues, in effect, that Cornelia should be delighted now that she
has the great man all to herself and no longer has to share his love
with all his other suitors—the senate, the people, and even Rome
herself. In his happier days, he declares, Cornelia could rejoice in
the glory of his extensive power and influence; now she can glory
in him even more, because she is his only follower.[44]

Cornelia reacts to this extraordinary outburst not by pointing to
its hypocrisy, but by taking all the blame for Pompey's defeat
upon herself.[45] This ploy breaks down Pompey's defensive hostility, perhaps because it recalls the words of Julia's ghost who
appeared to him at the beginning of book 3, as he left Italy. Julia,
Pompey's first wife, angrily and scornfully referred to Cornelia as
Pompey's *paelex*—his whore, not his real wife.[46] Cornelia is the
woman who will sour his luck. In 8, Cornelia almost concedes that
she is everything Julia called her; not only does she blame herself
for Pompey's defeat, she even refers to herself as a *paelex*.[47]

In short, Pompey has a pretext, irrational though it may be, to
find in Cornelia's words some cause for exonerating himself from
full responsibility. After she has finished speaking, he takes her in
his arms and weeps:

> duri flectuntur pectora Magni,
> siccaque Thessalia confudit lumina Lesbos. [8.107–108]

(The heart of harsh Pompey is moved; the eyes which had been
dry at Pharsalia weep at Lesbos.)

44. 8.72–85.   45. 8.88–105.
46. 3.21–23. We need not necessarily infer that Pompey had told Cornelia
of his dream. Lucan often has one of his characters echo words said by another (or even by Lucan himself in his capacity as narrator). The most notable is that of Lentulus in 8.449–450, which picks up the theme of 1.135.
47. 8.104.

This is one of the rare moments of close and warm human contact in Latin epic. It is all the more remarkable in the *Pharsalia,* since Lucan hardly ever shows his major protagonists, Caesar, Cato, or Pompey, in physical encounters of any kind, even on the battlefield. More important still, it underlines a disturbing and all-too-human facet of Pompey himself. Not only does the shift of guilt from himself to Cornelia permit him tears rather than anger; it shows him readier to respond to individual, human grief than to national catastrophe.

A nagging question lurks in the back of our minds: what is it that Pompey is weeping for? His own words earlier, "What you are weeping for is what you loved," make us wonder whether the tears spring to his eyes because he realizes that Cornelia really loves him, or because he recalls everything that he has lost in the war. Lucan does not give us an answer immediately; it emerges as the scene proceeds.

When Pompey thanks the people of Lesbos for taking such good care of Cornelia, he offers fulsome praise of the island and its kindness to him: "hic sacra domus carique penates, / hic mihi Roma fuit" (8.132–133) (This is where my sacred home and beloved household gods have been. This has been Rome to me). Perhaps this is merely a courteous hyperbole for the occasion, to please the people of Lesbos, who have offered him refuge and all the gold in their temples. But perhaps it is something more. Rome, Pompey suggests, is not the physical city; it is wherever Cornelia is. In his mind there is an equation between Rome and Cornelia. The city and the woman are both objects whose love Pompey seeks to earn by doing great deeds and winning applause. In adversity he thinks he can no longer be loved by either.

But Cornelia and, we might add, the people of Lesbos have shown that he is still loved in defeat. They bestow the affection Rome no longer gives, or is no longer able to give. And it is they, henceforth, who define the limits of Pompey's love. Whatever loves him, this is his Rome. He has no abstract dedication to Rome, "whose name is liberty," as Cato does (2.302–303). Pompey's tears on Lesbos, then, are both for Cornelia and for himself. Once Rome had been the great lady who showered her fullest affection on him. But now the great lady, Rome, is no more than a woman and a small island. Just as Cornelia should love him the more because she has him all to herself, so he can love her because she is all he has left. She is all of Rome that is left to him; so to him she is now Rome itself. In this lies both his sadness and his joy—sadness at what he has lost, joy at what he still has. So he weeps.

To gain a perspective on the love between Pompey and Rome in the happier days, we must turn back to book 7, and the "Dream of Pompey" (7–44).[48] Here we see the expansion of a motif, first stated in 1.132–133, where Lucan informs us that the height of Pompey's ecstasy is to sit in his own theater at Rome and bask in the plaudits of the citizens: "totus popularibus auris / inpelli plausuque sui gaudere theatri." Lucan now takes this idea and develops it into perhaps the supreme moment of beauty in the *Pharsalia*:

> At nox felicis Magno pars ultima vitae
> sollicitos vana decepit imagine somnos.
> nam Pompeiani visus sibi sede theatri
> innumeram effigiem Romanae cernere plebis
> attollique suum laetis ad sidera nomen
> vocibus et plausu cuneos certare sonantes;
> qualis erat populi facies clamorque faventis
> olim.   [7.7–14]

(The night before, that final chapter of his happiness in life, Great Pompey dreamed deceitful dreams, empty visions for a troubled soul. He saw himself in his own theater at Rome; and all around, the countless voices and faces of the Roman people, thunderously chanting his name, making the skies echo

48. For the dream, see H. J. Rose, "The Dream of Pompey," *Acta Classica* 1 (1958) 80–84. Rose is, I think, too influenced by Artemidorus in his interpretation of the passage. I can find no rational grounds for his inference that 7.24 suggests a prophecy that Pompey will return to Rome; though we cannot rule out the possibility that Lucan perhaps contemplated transporting his remains to Rome from Egypt after the completion of the Pisonian conspiracy, if we are to take 8.843–845 at face value. See also W. Rutz, "Die Träume des Pompeius in Lucans *Pharsalia*," *Hermes* 91 (1963) 334–345, and H. Cancik, "Ein Traum des Pompeius," in *Lucan*, ed. Rutz, 546–552; also A. Guillemin, 217 ff., and A. Grillone, *Il Sogno Nell' Epica Latina*, Palermo, 1967, 96–98.

their shouts of joy, section competing with section in applause. It was like this so many years ago.)

The heady ecstasy of Pompey's dream returns him to the happy days of old when he was the darling of the Roman people, the conquering hero whom senate and knights rose to cheer. But now, on the eve of Pharsalia, that hour has passed:

> seu fine bonorum
> anxia mens curis ad tempora laeta refugit,
> sive per ambages solitas contraria visis
> vaticinata quies magni tulit omina planctus,
> seu vetito patrias ultra tibi cernere sedes
> sic Romam Fortuna dedit.   [*ibid*. 19–24]

(Now that the good days were past, perhaps his mind, fretful with anxiety, found escape in recollection of past happiness. Dreams love to tell us riddles; perhaps, prophetically, they told the opposite of what they seemed to say, foreshadowing great sorrow and grief for the great man. Perhaps, though, Pompey, this was Fortune's way of bringing Rome to you once more, the homeland you would never see again.)

At this point Lucan intrudes upon his own reflections. He has already moved away from Pompey's actual dream and is developing his motif in a slightly different direction:

> ne rumpite somnos,
> castrorum vigiles, nullas tuba verberet aures.
> crastina dira quies et imagine maesta diurna
> undique funestas acies feret, undique bellum.   [*ibid*. 24–27]

(Do not disturb his sleep, men of the watch, don't let the trumpet's blast shatter anyone's dreams tonight. Tomorrow's dreadful sleep, haunted by recollections of the day, will torment dreaming minds trapped in bloody combat, trapped in war.)

Editors and translators have unnecessarily, yet regularly, fallen foul of these lines, largely because they feel that Lucan is limiting their application to Pompey. Postgate and Dilke searched for parallel usages of *nullas* (25) in the sense of "not at all" in order to justify this.[49] They failed to note that Lucan is in the habit of startling us with a sudden expansion of his motif. More serious still, this oversight leads them to conclude, erroneously, that with these lines the "Dream of Pompey" ends. Postgate finishes his translation of the dream at line 27, and Armstrong, in a review of Graves' translation, makes the same same error.[50]

But Lucan is about to present us with the conclusion of his montage, an unfulfilled vision of his own: the grief of Rome over her beloved Pompey's death:

> Unde pares somnos populis noctemque beatam?
> O felix, si te vel sic tua Roma videret!
> donassent utinam superi patriaeque tibique
> unum, Magne, diem, quo fati certus uterque
> *extremum tanti fructum raperetis amoris.*
> tu velut Ausonia vadis moriturus in urbe,
> illa rati semper de te sibi conscia voti
> hoc scelus haud umquam fatis haerere putavit,
> sic se dilecti tumulum quoque perdere Magni.   [*ibid.* 28–36]

(But whence could the people derive a sleep such as his, and so happy a night? How blessed would Rome be to see you even in a dream! If only the powers above had granted to your country and to you one day, in mutual, full awareness of impending doom, so you could part with a last, fleeting token of a love so great. But, as it is, you go your different ways, you thinking you will die at Rome, she knowing that her every prayer for you has always been answered, never believing that fate could be so hideous, that she would lose the right to be the tomb of her beloved Pompey.)

We are now confronted with a portrayal of Pompey and Rome as lovers, capturing the touching sadness of the doom that robbed them of the opportunity to take their farewells, the final fruit of their great love. I have italicized line 32, because here Lucan re-echoes the earlier parting of Pompey and Cornelia in 5. Cornelia's

---

49. Dilke, *Lucan,* note on 8.25; cf. J. P. Postgate's 1917 edition (*M. Annaei Lucani Liber VII*) which has basically the same comment *ad loc.* Similarly Haskins, *ad loc.* Neither Rutz nor Cancik ("Ein Traum") have any observations on this crux.

50. R. D. Armstrong, "Roman Epic," *Arion* 7.3 (1968), 448–453.

abrupt departure for Lesbos had deprived them of their chance to
enjoy a lovers' farewell: "extremusque perit tam longi fructus
amoris" (5.794). In 7 we find the same picture in almost identical
words. The parting of Pompey and Cornelia is recalled in the
imagined parting of Pompey and Rome. It is not surprising, then,
that Rome and Cornelia are inextricably bound together in Pompey's mind. For Pompey is, in Lucan's terms, the lover of Rome
as surely as Cato is the city's father or husband (2.387).

There is, as we shall see in greater detail in Chapter 7, a pointed
contrast between Pompey's relationship with Cornelia and Rome,
and that of Cato with Marcia and Rome. Pompey needs the
warmth and closeness of love; Cato seeks to be the protector of the
ideal in a cold dedication to principle. The ascetic sexlessness of
the relationship between Cato and Marcia is offset by the emphat-
ically physical nature of the bonds between Pompey and Cornelia.[51]
When Pompey asks Cornelia to leave him, instructing her to find
refuge in Lesbos, they are lying together in each other's arms
(5.734–798). Cornelia's desolation on the following night is reflected in her consciousness of the empty place beside her in the
bed, as she sleeps alone, burning with love for her absent husband:
"flamma tacitas urente medullas" (5.811).

Lucan now concludes the "Dream" with the imagined grief of
the city at Pompey's death, offsetting the remembrance of the
happy days at the beginning of the passage:

> te mixto flesset luctu iuvenisque senexque
> iniussusque puer; lacerasset crine soluto
> pectora femineum ceu Bruti funere volgus.
> nunc quoque, tela licet paveant victoris iniqui,
> nuntiet ipse licet Caesar tua funera, flebunt,
> sed dum tura ferunt, dum laurea serta Tonanti.
> O miseri, quorum gemitus edere dolorem,
> qui te non pleno pariter planxere theatro.   [7.37–44]

(Young and old in universal grief, they would have wept for
you; no need to tell a child that he should cry. Women, hair
blowing in the wind, would rip their breasts with fingernails,
as they did once for Brutus. Perhaps they fear the weapons of

51. Compare 2.326–379 (the remarriage of Cato and Marcia) with 5.722–
815; see also Chapter 7, Section III.

their brutal conqueror, perhaps they'll even hear about your
death from Caesar's own lips; yet even as they bring their offerings of laurel-wreaths and incense to the altars of the thun-
dering kings of gods, compelled to celebrate their victor's victory, they'll weep. Poor Romans, groan by groan they gnawed
the bitter food of grief; they cannot purge their sorrows in one
communal cry, as once they roared their joy, massed in your
theater.)

We have been moved from the fanciful but misleading recollection of the very real joys of the past, from the crowded theater
ringing with applause, to the empty stillness of terrified silence;
from the unbridled triumph of victory to the cramped and silent
heartache of defeat. Yet it is in these two false visions that dream
merges with reality. When Pompey lived, Rome could openly
express its joy. When Pompey dies, it cannot even give vent to its
grief.

The human warmth and personal appeal which radiate from the
love that Pompey inspires give him a beauty lacking in either
Caesar or Cato and supply an aura of pathos which makes his
passing from life a deep and genuine loss to Rome. Even at the
moment of death's approach, Pompey cannot abandon the hope
that he will be loved if only he can show bravery in dying. He
must suppress his cries of pain as the murderers strike him down
in the small boat off the Egyptian coast, for Cornelia and his son
Sextus are watching: "gnatus coniunxque peremptum, / si miran-
tur, amant" (8.634–635) (If my son and wife watch me as I die,
they love me).

"Love," *amant*, is the very last word on his lips. Pompey has an
audience again, and this gives him the courage and comfort he
needs in his last moments of life. For the first time he feels confident that he really is loved: not *amabunt*, they will love, but
amant, they love. This pathetic yet touching vanity of a great man
fallen low is heightened by the shocking brutality of his murderers, who hack off his head even before he expires and cannot
make a clean job of decapitation. The tottering oak has fallen, and
Pompey, now that he is dead, can become a symbol of the fallen
republic. If he had lived and won the war, he would have been its
destroyer. Throughout the epic Lucan has called him by his

cognomen, Magnus, "The Great," a title which all too often carries with it a touch of irony and pathos. But he, like Shakespeare's Caesar, becomes, perhaps, more mighty after death.

III. Pompey, Dido, and Aeneas

If we were to view Pompey as an allegorical figure, as Dante views Lucan's Cato, we could see him as the epitome of human frailty, vanity, and beauty, crushed in a conflict of absolutes. His actions bear the mark neither of the *virtus* or *pietas* of the dedicated nor the demonic *furor* of the destructive and the depraved. In short, he is neither a Cato nor a Caesar. What we see in Pompey is *amor,* a love that at its most sublime approaches *pietas,* and at its lowest comes close to *furor.* He is neither totally good nor totally evil; his conduct hovers between altruism and self-seeking.[52]

In this sense, Pompey is very much like Aeneas. But there are several crucial differences. Pompey, like the republic, is trapped by his flaws and imperfections; Aeneas is not. Vergil's hero is favored by fate and bolstered by external powers when his weakness threatens to undermine him. Even when the gods do not actually intervene to save Aeneas, his luck seems to hold. From *Aeneid* 8.9 to 11.225–295, we are kept in suspense wondering whether the Greek Diomedes will enter the war on the Rutulian side. But the Greek who could outmatch Aeneas does not enter the lists. Aeneas triumphs, at least partially, through Diomedes' default.

There is no Olympus to save either Pompey or the republic, and there is nothing except the dagger of Brutus to stay the mighty hand of Caesar. Here, I think, is the heart of the matter. For though there are similarities between Pompey and Aeneas, the two men move in opposite directions, as do their respective epics. In the *Aeneid,* Rome and its founding genius are at the beginning of their fortune and divine favor; in the *Pharsalia,* Pompey and Rome are nearing the end.[53] Aeneas proceeds from

52. On this point I am in agreement with Marti, "Meaning of the *Pharsalia.*"

53. The *Aeneid* ends with the slaying of Turnus (12.950–951); the *Pharsalia* begins with the motif of the conquering sword thrust into the vitals of the nation that wields it (1.1–7). The notion of the suicide of the state is thus established by Lucan at the very outset and comes very close to what Anchises prays will be averted in *Aeneid* 6.826–835. For more on this see Chapter 9, Section III.

defeat to triumph, Pompey from triumph to defeat; Aeneas is haunted by memories of the annihilation of Troy, Pompey by recollections of his former greatness.

Two motifs from *Aeneid* 4 and two from *Pharsalia* 8 accentuate both the similarities and the differences between Pompey and Aeneas, and show, in germ, how the two epics proceed by kindred means to utterly different ends.

In *Aeneid* 4 and *Pharsalia* 8, the protagonists are either contemplating, or actually engaged in, activities which would, in Roman eyes, merit great censure. Aeneas is discovered building Carthage, attired in oriental robes woven by Dido (4.259–264); Pompey is proposing to enlist the aid of the Parthians against Caesar (8.211–327). Both are prevented from continuing on their respective courses by external intervention: in Aeneas' case, Jupiter sends Mercury to stop the building of Carthage and remind the hero of his obligations; in Pompey's case, the senate and Lentulus intervene and vote down his proposal. Neither Aeneas nor Pompey changes his conduct as the result of an inner reevaluation of what he is doing or proposes to do. Each is forced back into line by humiliating denunciation.

Yet the aftermath of these humiliations is markedly different in the two epics. When Lentulus crushes Pompey by referring to him as the ghost of a name: "nominis umbra" (8.449), he not only recalls the very words with which Pompey was introduced into the epic (1.135), but the simile that goes with them: that of Pompey as the tottering oak, sapless and doomed to fall. And with this recollection comes a striking contrast between Aeneas and Pompey. After Mercury's rebuke in *Aeneid* 4, Vergil's hero not merely regains his composure but earns comparison with a massive oak, whose roots are established in the very bowels of the earth, unshakable and immovable.[54] The humiliation has strengthened Aeneas' resolve rather than weakened it. In the *Pharsalia* the reverse is true. Pompey, who begins the epic as the shadow of a great name, "Magni nominis umbra," is deprived of the epithet *Magnus* by Lentulus in 8.449. He is now simply "nominis umbra." But

54. *Aeneid* 4.441–449; see note 18 above (particularly the resemblance between Pompey the dead oak and the site of Troy in *Pharsalia* 9) and Chapter 6, Section III.

worse is to come. The oak to which Pompey is compared casts a shadow not with its leaves, but with its trunk: "trunco non frondibus efficit umbram" (1.140). By the end of 8, Pompey's own headless trunk will lie upon the shores of Egypt, as the frenzied woman in 1.685–686 foresaw: "hunc ego fluminea deformis truncus harena / qui iacet agnosco" (The man who lies, a shapeless trunk on the sandy shores of the Nile, him I recognize). After Pompey's death the devout Cordus finds his body tossing among the breakers. He has difficulty discerning it because of the grudging light of the moon and the heavy clouds:

> lucis maesta parum per densas Cynthia nubes
> praebebat, cano sed discolor aequore truncus
> conspicitur.   [8.721–723]

> (Through the dense clouds, sorrowing Cynthia provided little light; but the trunk can be seen, for it differs in color from the gray sea.)

The rotting oak is now no more than a piece of battered driftwood; in the dim light it almost merges with the water in which it floats, unable even to cast a shadow. Book 8 ends where it begins, with Pompey upon the beach of an alien land.

Aeneas' indecision and neglect of duty results not in his own death, but in that of Dido. Pompey's indecision is visited upon himself and upon Rome. This draws attention to yet another parallel between the *Pharsalia* and the *Aeneid,* the similarity of Pompey's plight to that of Dido. Both are the victims of divine indifference. Jupiter, for all his wrath at Aeneas' dallying in Carthage does not have a word to say about Dido.[55] Even Juno is interested in the city's future rather than its queen. Only Venus shows much concern about Dido herself, and her interest extends no further than a desire to prevent her causing any damage to Aeneas. In the *Pharsalia,* Fortune deserts Pompey on the morn of the fateful battle. Both have completed their historical destinies; they simply do not matter any more. Yet neither really dies alone. Each represents something that transcends individuality. Pompey's death marks the end of the republic, and Dido's, symbolically, the end of Carthage.

55. *Ibid.,* 223–237.

Vergil goes to some pains in *Aeneid* 1 and 4 to remind us that the city of Dido is Rome's future enemy. Aeneas' crime in dallying with her lies primarily in the fact that she is the founder of the nation that will produce the direst challenge to Rome's destiny of greatness—though, we should note, Aeneas is *never* told this. Unlike the royal houses of Greek legend, that of Dido is accursed not for what has been done, but for what will be done.

Here we see an example of the peculiar time-perspectives of the *Aeneid,* which are brought to our attention from the beginning of the first book. The opening seven lines tell of the hero who came from Troy to Italy as fate demanded, who had suffered much because of the unrelenting anger of Juno. In lines 8–11, Vergil asks his Muse to tell the reasons for this anger. Then, lines 12–14:

> Urbs antiqua fuit (Tyrii tenuere coloni)
> Karthago, Italiam contra Tiberinaque longe
> ostia, dives opum studiisque asperrima belli.

> (Once there was an ancient city [Tyrian settlers inhabited it]; it was Carthage, faced against Italy and the Tiber estuary from afar, rich in resources, ferocious in the art of war.)

Familiarity with the passage tends to dull our awareness of its peculiarly startling qualities. To begin with, we expect Vergil to adduce Troy, not Carthage as his ancient city. The reader knows that Juno had good reason to dislike Troy after the judgment of Paris. Secondly, *fuit,* "was", is an emphatic perfect, informing us that this city did indeed exist once, but is no more. Finally there comes the mention of Tyrians, not Trojans, Carthage, not Troy; the careful juxtaposition of *Karthago* and *Italiam* and the ambiguous use of *contra* which suggests, in this context, not just "opposite to" but "opposed to." But, most surprisingly of all, the newly founded city of Dido is called *antiqua,* "ancient."

In Vergil's narrative perspective—no less than in the Augustan historical perspective—both Troy and Carthage are dead cities of the past. Two levels of the past, over a millennium apart, are merged in the opening lines of the epic, and with this merging of time comes a merging of identities which gives both Dido and Aeneas a dimension they themselves do not fully grasp. Aeneas has

an inkling of his Roman destiny, but no notion as to why there
should be anything ominous about his relationship with Dido. It
is, rather, Dido herself who sees the relationship as Vergil and the
reader can see it, as a Herodotean *archē kakōn*, the beginning of
ills between Rome and Carthage. At 4.624–629, she cries a vow of
eternal enmity between their nations. With prophetic insight she
promises that someone will bring fire and the sword in pursuit of
the Trojan settlers in Italy, an avenger sprung from her ashes who
will exact a *munus*, a ritual appeasement for her death.

At the same time, however, we can see in Dido's death a foreshadowing of the destruction of Carthage. Although Aeneas himself does not wield the sword that kills Dido, she dies by the sword
he leaves behind in the bedchamber of their love. And in the
flames that cremate the founding genius of Carthage lie the seeds
of a much greater flame that will destroy the entire city. We are
reminded as the Trojans leave Carthage of the way in which that
city was first introduced: "urbs antiqua fuit" (there was once an
ancient city).

The variable, complex time perspectives of the *Aeneid* sometimes leave us with a most uneasy feeling that Vergilian allusions
run much more deeply than we care to state explicitly. For example,
consider Dido's curse upon Aeneas himself in 4.620: "cadat ante
diem mediaque inhumatus harena" (Let him fall before his time
and lie unburied in the middle of the sand). A corpse lies unburied on the seashore. We recall, as perhaps Dido herself recalls,
Aeneas' description of Priam's headless body lying on the shores
of Asia (2.557–558). Is Aeneas to die as Priam did? Perhaps. But
even then, the death of Priam, as described in *Aeneid* 2, left us
with the feeling that Vergil had more than just Priam on his mind.
For Priam was killed in the palace, not on the seashore, where
Aeneas somewhat oddly locates his truncated corpse. In short,
Dido's enigmatic curse recalls another enigma.

Granted that Dido is symbolic of the city of Carthage and her
curses and death foreshadow the revenge and disaster which the
future holds, may we not also argue that Aeneas himself becomes
a prefiguration of Rome's future in this context? In other words,
if Dido's suicide and self-cremation suggest the destruction of Carthage, perhaps her prophecy of Aeneas' death is suggestive not so

much of the fate that awaits him as an individual, but of the fate that awaits his city. Few Romans could have forgotten, in Vergil's day, the hideous moment in the autumn of 48 B.C. when Pompey was decapitated and his headless body lay on the seashore of Egypt, unburied. Perhaps Dido is wishing upon Aeneas the fate of Priam; but given the perspectives of the *Aeneid*, she could be wishing upon Rome the fate of Pompey. It is not so much Aeneas himself who will fulfill Dido's curse, as Pompey, whose death will mark the end of the Roman republic and of a whole chapter in Roman history as surely as Priam's death marked the end of Troy and as Dido's death foreshadows the doom of Carthage.

With Pompey, the curse of Dido comes to fruition; no longer will alien nations suffer for Roman error. As Dido suffered because history had passed her by, so will Pompey and the republic. If Aeneas' last farewell to the ghost of Creusa in *Aeneid* 2 carries with it a reminder that there lies before him the more prosperous marriage with Lavinia, the apparition of Julia to Pompey before his final departure from Italy is no less powerful a reminder that before him lies nothing but defeat and death.[56] What happened to Carthage will now happen to Rome. Rome too must pay the penalty for her greatness. Perhaps this is what Lucan has in mind when he suggests, by his echoes of *Aeneid* 4, that there is a striking resemblance not only between Pompey and Aeneas, but between Pompey and Dido.

Yet, with the death of Pompey, as with the death of Priam or of Dido, the end is not total and complete. In fact, as Pompey dies, it is almost as if the soul of Rome were released from its weak and ravaged body, much as Pompey's soul is released at the beginning of *Pharsalia* 9.[57] The decadent republic and the ghost of a man who championed its cause are no longer adulterated by an imperfect existence. Thus Pompey's death is, as Cato points out, a *benefit* to the cause of liberty and to the defense of the ideal.[58] In

56. *Pharsalia* 3.8–35; *Aeneid* 2.771–795. It is odd that Rutz, "Die Träume," does not establish the parallel between Pompey's vision of Julia and Aeneas' encounter with the ghost of Creusa, especially given the similar manner in which both apparitions flee through the arms of the embracing husband (*Pharsalia* 3.34–35; *Aeneid* 2.790–794). Rutz does see the similarity between Pompey and Dido.

57. 9.1–18.   58. 9.263–266.

much the same way the destruction of the Old Troy and the death
of Priam open the way for the establishment of something greater.
But one vitally important difference undercuts our analogy. True,
there were indeed a Cato and a Brutus to avenge the republic.
But Lucan, like many others, must have asked himself this question about Pompey and *libertas:* can the ideal, however much
more magnificent than Pompey it may be, ever become a reality
again, or will it wander the seas and through time as an Aeneas
whose vessel will never more touch land?

In this unanswered question we see why Pompey, for all his
shortcomings, enjoyed a place close to the heart of every devotee
of the republican cause. Indeed, Lucan prays that he himself may
bring Pompey's remains back to a tomb in Italy (8.840–845)—an
act which doubtless symbolizes his personal ambition to participate in the restoration of the republic. This will herald, he declares, the coming of a more blessed age when the notion that
Pompey is dead will seem as absurd as the Cretan belief in Jupiter's death: "veniet felicior aetas" (819). For the republic, and
with it Pompey, will be restored to Italy once more. In the meantime, the poet consoles himself with the thought that Pompey's
lack of proper burial has an advantage: there is no marble vault
to last through the ages as a reminder that Pompey really is dead.[59]

59. For a detailed discussion of the death of Pompey, see H. Schnepf,
"Untersuchungen zur Darstellungskunst Lucans im 8. Buch der *Pharsalia*,"
Diss. Heidelberg, 1953, particularly 125–151, reprinted in *Lucan*, ed. Rutz,
380–396. Lucan's comment on the absence of a tomb for Pompey is reminiscent of Caesar's reaction to the possibility of death at sea (*Pharsalia* 5.668–
671). The crucial difference, of course, is that uncertainty as to Pompey's
death provides hope, not fear.

CHAPTER 6

Caesar

Lucan faces a much larger problem with Caesar than with Pompey. In the first place, Caesar had left his own version of the history of the civil wars. Compared with other major works of Roman history, it is plain and unextravagant, calculated to give the impression of impartial objectivity and almost autistic self-detachment. Caesar knew the art of conceding just enough credit to his foes to suggest that his account was composed without anger or partisanship. It is propaganda at its most plausible. This low-key approach suited his behavior during the war. The might of his Gallic veterans and his personal tactical skill annihilated the opposition on the battlefield; but then he "pardoned" his defeated foe. Even though his clemency may have been as calculated and sinister in its purpose as a wholesale purge, it was *humanely* sinister. This left the rhetoric of his opponents' propaganda floundering. Tyrants are supposed to eliminate their enemies, not spare them. More important still, those who received a pardon from Caesar and accepted it appeared to have conceded that they were wrong to oppose him.

Lucan's task would have been easier if he had been well-disposed to Caesar and to the consequences of his victory. Since he was not, he had to face numerous rhetorical and historical difficulties. His portrait of Caesar had to be plausible historically. Certain things about Caesar had to be conceded. He had won the war militarily; he had shown phenomenal tactical skill. The sheer power of his personality and his charismatic appeal could not be denied. In short, Lucan had to portray Caesar as a great man. On the other hand, the poet had considerable freedom to question Caesar's motives and to shed an unfavorable light upon the consequences of his victory. It could be argued that Caesar's genius was founded upon a distorted and self-seeking megalomania and that his military prowess and forcefulness of character were vices not virtues, since they worked against the best interests of the state.

Lucan is more concerned with undermining Caesar's claim to moral justification for his actions than he is with disputing the actions themselves. The Caesar of the *Pharsalia* is endowed with superhuman vigor and energy, but it is an energy used to attain ends dictated by narrow self-interest, culminating in a destructive rather than creative victory. At the same time, Lucan is not so naive as to portray Caesar as an evil genius running amuck in a world of pristine goodness. His sketches of the decadence of the Roman republic and even of such characters as Sextus Pompey and Appius Claudius show that he is not prepared to make Caesar appear black by whitewashing those who opposed him. Even Pompey himself is treated in far less than grand heroic style. Lucan has too keen a sense of rhetoric to make such an error. Caesar destroys an order already debilitated and infirm, yet his annihilation of it demonstrates that he is as corrupt spiritually as the world he destroys.

Caesar does not use his talents to cure the ills of the sick republic. He ends the sickness by killing the patient. Lucan thus contrasts Caesar's behavior with that of Cato, who does offer the possibility of curing the disease. Rhetorically and historically, Lucan's choice of Cato as Caesar's ideological opponent was perfect. Cato's reputation had survived all the onslaughts of Caesarian propaganda, and politically and morally his credentials were, from a republican point of view, beyond reproach.

Yet the subversion of Caesar's claims to moral justification requires more than a pointed contrast of his actions with those of Cato. It demands that those moments where Caesar's behavior was questionable, such as his failure to bury the Pompeian dead after Pharsalia, be underscored, and that those where his behavior seemed noble be shorn, as far as possible, of their nobility. Of these, the first presented relatively few problems. The latter, however, proved much harder. As noted, Caesar could make a strong claim to moral virtue on the grounds of his clemency alone. Not only was his clemency beyond dispute but difficult to attack as amoral or immoral.

Before undertaking a general assessment of Lucan's Caesar, we must take into account the poet's efforts to minimize Caesar's clemency. It was, I think, his most awkward task and, perhaps inevitably, his least successful.

I. The Problem of Caesar's *Clementia*

Lucan's treatment of Caesar's activities in Spain during 49 B.C. (*Pharsalia* 4. 1–401) seems, at first glance, thoroughly inconsistent with his attitude toward him in the rest of the epic. Although he characterizes Caesar as *saevus* in 4.2, Lucan makes no effort to maintain the picture of ferocity and fiery impatience seen in the remainder of the *Pharsalia*. It would, I think, be overhasty to assume a temporary change of heart on Lucan's part. The difference is, rather, the by-product of dealing with an irrefutable case of Caesarian *clementia*.

Lucan's principal difficulty centers on an incident in which Caesar's troops and those of the Pompeian commanders Afranius and Petreius find themselves encamped so close together that they can see one another from the walls of their respective forts. Hostility yields to fraternization (4.168–182) until Petreius orders the friendliness to stop and massacres the Caesarian troops whom he finds in the republican camp (4.205–253). Caesar renews his efforts to force the Pompeians to surrender, and when they do, he pardons them (4.254–401). To get a better perspective on Lucan's account, let us first comment briefly on the same incident as recorded in the Caesarian *Bellum Civile*, 1.74–75.[1]

Caesar's version indicates that, while Afranius and Petreius are temporarily away from camp, their troops go over to Caesar to thank him for his clemency and to negotiate a surrender. Their embassy is successful. Caesar promises to spare them and even assures them that Afranius and Petreius will not be harmed. When

---

1. For a different treatment of this incident, see Heyke, 60–76. The principal weakness in her interpretation is her failure to compare Lucan's account adequately with Caesar's. For a view closer to my own, see Syndikus, 17 and 63–65; cf. W. Metger, "Kampf und Tod in Lucans *Pharsalia*," Diss. Kiel, 1957, 138 ff. For the flood preceding the truce, see H.-W. Linn, "Studien zur Aemulatio des Lucan," Diss. Hamburg, 1971, 15–29.

the commanders return to camp and discover what has transpired, Afranius does not care much one way or the other. But Petreius retains his presence of mind: "non deserit sese" (*BCiv.* 1.75). He assembles his personal slaves, throws the Caesarian troops out of his camp, and executes those he finds hiding. Hostilities resume. Later, after Caesar has successfully kept the Pompeians hemmed in, depriving them of water and supplies, Afranius negotiates a surrender (*ibid.* 84). Caesar, though he has good cause to be angry and indulge in reprisals, remains true to his earlier offer. Afranius and Petreius are spared, and the troops are exonerated not merely from punishment but from any obligation to continue the war on Caesar's side.

If the Caesarian account is an approximation of the truth, Lucan is confronted with an episode that not only shows the Pompeian troops in a very bad light, unwilling to fight and prepared to sell out to Caesar, but is evidence of Caesar's clemency. Lucan's task is to reduce the impact of Caesar's clemency and of the overall damage the incident causes to the republican image.

The Caesarian account tells us that the fraternization occurs because the Pompeians want to negotiate their capitulation to Caesar; it is made possible by Caesar's grant of clemency, negotiated behind the backs of the republican commanders. Lucan, however, suggests that the fraternization arises spontaneously (4.169–188). The proximity of the two camps enables friend to recognize friend across the ramparts. As they swarm out to greet one another, Lucan exhorts them not to heed the bugle's summons to war (186–187). If they maintain this concord, he asserts:

> iam iam civilis Erinys
> concidet et Caesar generum privatus amabit.
> nunc ades, aeterno complectens omnia nexu,
> o rerum mixtique salus Concordia mundi
> et sacer orbis amor. [4.187–191]

(In an instant the fury of civil war will abate, and Caesar will become an ordinary citizen again and love his son-in-law. Now, Concord, salvation of all things and of the universe which you blend in harmony, be present, and embrace everything in your eternal web of closeness. Be present too, holy and universal love.)

By using "universal love" as the motivating force, Lucan not only removes all trace of the republican army's treachery by sublimating it into a yearning for peace and brotherhood, he also blots out Caesar's clemency. He wickedly suggests that universal love cannot but affect Caesar too. Thus Caesar, who was the real catalyst of the fraternization, is left out in the cold. More seriously still, Lucan's suppression of the real causes for the momentary concord between Caesarians and Pompeians diverts our attention from a simple but crucial fact: permanent peace could be achieved in this situation only by the surrender of the Pompeians to Caesar. And Lucan *is* holding back on the real causes for the fraternization as we discover a few lines later:

> nam postquam foedera pacis
> cognita Petreio, *seque et sua tradita venum*
> *castra* videt . . .   [4.205–207]

(Once the truce became known to Petreius and he perceived that *he and his camp had been sold . . .*)

The reader unfamiliar with the Caesarian account must surely find these lines inexplicable. Lucan has given no inkling of any treachery behind the fraternization. Petreius' stern rebuke to his troops upon his return to camp does not mesh with Lucan's earlier claim that the truce arose spontaneously. The reader familiar with the Caesarian account will know that Petreius has every right to be outraged. Caesar's own comment (*BCiv.* 1.75) that Petreius did not lose his presence of mind (as Afranius did) seems to suggest that even he approved, on military grounds at least, Petreius' refusal to be defeated by promises of clemency.

Possibly Lucan is relying on his readers to supply the relevant details from their own knowledge of history, as he does in the Appius episode in 5. The following excerpt from Petreius' speech seems to suggest this:

> ibitis ad dominum damnataque signa feretis,
> utque habeat famulos nullo discrimine Caesar
> exorandus erit? ducibus quoque vita petita est?   [4.217–219]

Will you go over to a master and carry the banners that you [until now] condemned? Must you beg Caesar to have you as his slaves on the same terms as his other slaves? Have you also bargained for the lives of your generals?)

Consider the comments about the negotiations of the Pompeian troops in *BCiv*. 1.74. They ask whether they may rightly entrust themselves to Caesar: "rectene se illi sint commissuri"; they plead for the lives of Afranius and Petreius: "de Petrei atque Afranii vita petunt." When their requests are granted they will come over to Caesar's side immediately: "se statim signa translaturos confirmant"; some of the centurions and tribunes offer their services to Caesar: "compluresque tribuni militum et centuriones ad Caesarem veniunt seque ei commendant." In short, they have been doing everything of which Lucan's Petreius accuses them.

What does Lucan gain by this curious treatment of the incident? First he sidesteps the uncomfortable truth that the Pompeian soldiers did not want to fight Caesar at all. He would rather damn them and Petreius for a breach of *pietas* so he can portray them as heroically resisting Caesar until thirst and hunger compel them to capitulate. At the same time, he saves Petreius from total censure by alluding to the real version of what happened, relying on his reader's knowledge of history. Most important of all, he subverts Caesar's claim to extraordinary clemency in the situation by omitting the fact that Caesar had offered the most generous terms to the Pompeians during the fraternization. He would rather concede that a crime against *amor* and *pietas*, brought about by Petreius' words, made Caesar's cause the better one: "dux causae melioris eris" (259) than acknowledge that Caesar's clemency in sparing the republicans even after their murder of his men and resumption of war made his cause better.

The surrender later negotiated by Afranius also shows Lucan attempting to salvage what he can from the debacle. Afranius is described as maintaining his dignity unbroken by misfortune: "maiestas non fracta malis" (341). He has the bearing of a conquered man, but one who is still a general: "gerit omnia victi,/ sed ducis" (342–343). The only reason he surrenders, he claims, is his belief that Caesar is worthy to grant him his life. We were fighting, he declares, not out of partisan zeal: "non partis studiis agimur" (348), but in support of the cause we chanced to be supporting at the outbreak of war: "dum potuit, servata fides" (351). Lucan's Afranius concludes with the plea that the Pompeians not be required to fight for Caesar: "hoc petimus, victos ne tecum vincere cogas" (362). In Julius Caesar's account, however, Afranius' final plea is for the lives of himself and his men:

Itaque se victos confiteri; orare atque obsecrare, si qui locus misericordiae relinquatur, ne ad ultimum supplicium progredi necesse habeat. Haec quam potest demississime et subiectissime exponit.
[*BCiv.* 1.84]

(So they confessed themselves beaten. They begged and implored, that if any place for pity were left, he should not consider it necessary to exact the supreme penalty. This he asked in the most groveling and humble manner possible.)

There is no trace of residual nobility in Caesar's Afranius. It is, perhaps, in the contrast of the verbs *petimus* (in Lucan) and *orare atque obsecrare* (in Caesar) that the difference of manner comes across most clearly.

Lucan cannot deny Caesar's clemency in dealing with the surrendering army, but he can and does minimize it. He has Afranius make the suggestion that the Pompeians not be required to fight for Caesar. In Caesar's account, it is not Afranius' request, but Caesar's clemency that suggests this idea (*BCiv.* 1.85). By putting all of this into Afranius' mouth, Lucan is able to wriggle out from the obligation to make more than passing reference to Caesar's clemency. This is the only response we get to Afranius' request:

> dixerat; at Caesar facilis voltuque serenus
> flectitur atque usus belli poenamque remittit.   [4.363–364]

(Afranius finished speaking. Caesar, easy and serene of countenance, is moved; he excuses them from military service and from punishment.)

In Julius Caesar's version, a whole section (*BCiv.* 1.85) is devoted to Caesar's grant of clemency.

Throughout this passage, then, Lucan is trying to make the best of a bad situation. One has only to compare Domitius' unwilling surrender to Caesar in 2.507–525 to perceive how galling this episode must have been. Here is Lucan's reaction to the pardoning of Domitius:

> heu, quanto melius vel caede peracta
> parcere Romano potuit fortuna pudori!
> poenarum extremum civi, quod castra secutus
> sit patriae Magnumque ducem totumque senatum,
> ignosci. [2.517–521]

(Alas, how much better and more merciful Fortune would have been to Roman honor if Domitius had been cut to pieces! It is the ultimate penalty for a citizen that he be *pardoned* because he has followed the cause of his country, Pompey, and the whole senate.)

If Lucan cannot entirely rob Caesar of his claim to humanity and clemency, he certainly does his best to diminish it. Yet he does so at a price, as we can see in 4.382–401. There, in order to extoll the blessings of the republican army and blur the shame of their defeat, he ventures into an apostrophe, praising the joys of disinvolvement in the civil war, which concludes with the following words: "sic proelia soli / felices nullo spectant civilia voto" (400–401) (Thus they alone are prosperous, watching the battles of the civil war without a prayer for either side). As we shall see in Chapter 7, Section II, this is a flat contradiction of Lucan's own avowed position in *Pharsalia* 7, and of his justification for Cato's entry into the civil war. Lucan has sacrificed the overall consistency of his theme in a vain attempt to salvage a patently unsalvageable episode. For, despite all Lucan's efforts, Caesar's *clementia* still comes through in the Spanish campaigns of *Pharsalia* 4.

The important thing is not the degree of historical and rhetorical manipulation Lucan uses to minimize Caesar's clemency, but the simple fact that he *is* trying to play down Caesar's moral qualities. His portrayal of Caesar in Spain seems favorable not because he intended it to be so but because, despite his efforts, he could not make it unfavorable.

II. Caesar's Control of Man and Nature

With the exception of the episode of the Spanish Wars in 4, Lucan develops his portrait of Caesar in a relatively logical and coherent manner, advancing steadily in rhetorical intensity during books 1 through 9. Caesar's basic nature is apparent the moment Lucan first introduces him in 1.143–157. In contrast to Pompey, who is the hollow, tottering oak, Caesar is the thunderbolt, bursting through the clouds, forced out by the winds to the roar of the stricken aether and to the crackling of the universe.[2] He flashes and shatters the light of day, striking fear into the hearts of the people, extending his light in the slanting thunderbolt. Nothing can stop him; he wreaks havoc far and wide in his own domain, only to gather his energy back for yet another onslaught.

The power described is superhuman. Caesar is energy incarnate, a Zeus-like being whose attacks wither and destroy all in their way. Unlike Pompey, who has been softened by peacetime living (1.129–131), Caesar is totally unable to endure peace and respite from war: "numquam patiens pacis longaeque quietis/armorum" (2.650–651). He rushes headlong into everything: "in omnia praeceps" (*ibid.* 656), considering nothing done while anything else remains to be done: "nil actum credens cum quid superesset agendum (*ibid.* 657). This is not just the way Lucan views Caesar; it is the way Lucan's Caesar views himself. During the seige of Massilia in 3, for example, he compares himself to wind and fire:

> ventus ut ammittit vires, nisi robore densae
> occurrunt silvae, spatio diffusus inani,
> utque perit magnus nullis obstantibus ignis,
> sic hostes mihi desse nocet, damnumque putamus
> armorum, nisi qui vinci potuere rebellant . . .
> . . . dabitis poenas pro pace petita,
> et nihil esse meo discetis tutius aevo
> quam duce me bellum.   [3.362–366; 370–372]

(Just as the wind loses its strength unless forests thick with trees get in the way—it dissipates into empty space; just as a great fire dies when there is nothing in its path, so it is damaging to me to be without enemies. I think myself defeated un-

2. For the contrast between Caesar and Pompey in Lucan, see W. Menz, 49–65 and 168–170, reprinted in *Lucan,* ed. Rutz, 360–379; and W.-H. Friedrich, "Cato, Caesar und Fortuna bei Lucan," *Hermes* 73 (1938), 391–421 for Caesar and Cato; also Rutz, *Studien,* 128–157 and 171–182, and Heyke, 99–143.

less those who could be conquered fight against me. . . . You
will pay the penalty for the peace you seek [people of Massilia]
and you will learn that in the age of Caesar nothing is safer than
war—with me as your leader.)

These figurative descriptions of Caesar as a cosmic force are remarkably reinforced in 3.399–452 by Caesar's quite literal felling
of a sacred oak in a Druidic grove during his seige of Massilia.
Finding himself in need of lumber to bolster his blockading
mound, he orders a Druidic grove cut down, even though it is so
sacred that woodland deities, wind, and lightning stay clear of it
(3.399–411).[3] Not even the Druidic priest enters it without fear
(*ibid.* 423–424). Since Caesar's men refuse to obey his command,
Caesar picks up an ax and splits a tall oak tree, crying out: "Iam
nequis vestrum dubitet subvertere silvam, / credite me fecisse nefas"
(436–437) ("Believe that it is I who have committed sacrilege; now
none of you should hesitate to destroy this forest"). If the horrific
grove of the Druids is no obstacle to Caesar, the tottering oak that
is Pompey will certainly not stand in his way. More important
still, Caesar ventures to do what even the powers of nature shun.
When wind and lightning will not strike, Caesar will.

Lucan does not content himself with comparisons between
Caesar and the elements. For although these establish a picture
of massive destructive power, they do not establish that this power
is specifically inimical to Rome. If the notion of Caesar as the
thunderbolt in 1.143–157 is one of Jovian *furor,* the simile comparing Caesar to a Libyan lion some fifty verses later (1.205–212)
is one of African *furor,* suggesting comparisons with Hannibal, as
pointed out in Chapter 3. This identification of Caesar with forces
hostile to Rome is continued in the observations of the people of
Ariminum (1.248–257) and in Caesar's comment that Rome is
reacting to his presence as if he were some Carthaginian Hannibal
(1.303–305). Finally, Lucan's insistence that the battle of Pharsalia
was a worse catastrophe for Rome than Cannae and that Caesar's
behavior after the battle was more savage than Hannibal's after his

3. For further discussion of the Druidic grove, see Chapter 5, note 18; cf.
O. Phillips, "Lucan's Grove," *CP* 63 (1968), 296–300, and S. Dyson's brief but
useful note: "Caepio, Tacitus and Lucan's Grove," *CP* 65 (1970), 36–38; also
Heyke, 131–138.

great victory leaves little doubt that the poet wants us to see
Caesar as the most destructive foe the city ever encountered. At
least Hannibal was a foreign foe devastating an alien land. Caesar,
like the thunderbolt, rages in his own territory. And, unlike
Hannibal, he succeeds in making the city his own.

Caesar's ability does not rest solely on his thunderbolt-like
energy or his Hannibalic disposition. His ferocity, unlike that of a
conventional epic warrior, is not a matter of sheer physical prowess. Although Lucan never questions Caesar's martial valor, he
never shows him in the thick of battle, sword in hand, engaged in
a Homeric *aristeia*. Caesar's strength lies rather in his supreme
self-confidence and indomitable will, which bends first his soldiers
then the world to his command.

What gives Caesar his peculiar power in the *Pharsalia* is that he
is fighting for himself; he is both leader and cause, as Pompey and
Cato are not. He does not have to consider the good of the senate
and has no desire to draw men to love of liberty by his example.
Because his cause is evident and uncomplicated by ideological considerations, his soldiers easily see what they are fighting for:
Caesar. And they respond with deeds of great, if perverse, bravery
and audacity. Yet the simplicity of Caesar's cause makes it particularly sinister. Since he is both man and cause, he is not bound
to evaluate his decisions and actions in terms of any external
criteria of morality. To him, military success decides what is good
and what evil (7.259–263). It is the philosophy of might is right in
its crudest form, irreconcilable with a society based upon the rule
of law. Caesar's victory can mean only the legalization of behavior
which, to civilized man, is criminal: "ius . . . datum sceleri"
(1.2).

The soldiers who follow Caesar place loyalty to him above all
considerations of civilized behavior. The most extreme example
is to be found in Laelius' speech to Caesar in *Pharsalia* 1:

> Per signa decem felicia castris
> perque tuos iuro quocumque ex hoste triumphos,
> pectore si fratris gladium iuguloque parentis
> condere me iubeas plenaeque in viscera partu
> coniugis, invita peragam tamen omnia dextra;

si spoliare deos ignemque inmittere templis,
numina miscebit castrensis flamma monetae;
castra super Tusci si ponere Thybridis undas,
Hesperios audax veniam metator in agros.
tu quoscumque voles in planum effundere muros,
his aries actus disperget saxa lacertis,
illa licet, penitus tolli quam iusseris urbem,
Roma sit.   [1.374–386]

(I swear by your standards which have prospered in ten campaigns and by your triumphs, no matter what enemy you conquer, that if you were to order me to bury my sword in my
brother's heart, my father's throat, or the womb of my pregnant
wife, I would do all this, even if my right hand was unwilling.
If you command me to despoil the gods and burn their temples,
the furnace of our military mint will render down the gods. If
you tell me to build a camp by the waters of the Etruscan Tiber,
I will boldly step forward to mark out the ground of Italy for a
site. Whatever walls you want leveled, these arms of mine will
drive the battering-ram against them, scattering the stones, even
if the city you wish to annihilate is Rome itself.)

To Laelius there are no deities save the victories of Caesar; there
is no loyalty, no *pietas*, to family, religion, or city. What motivates
him is precisely what motivates both Scaeva and Vulteius: *militiae
pietas*. They have given themselves to Caesar, body and soul. The
only vestige of traditional values to be found in Laelius is the suggestion that his right hand may be unwilling to respond to the
order to commit parricide. Yet he does not doubt that he can over-
come the instinctive piety of a mere limb. Laelius, like the rest of
Caesar's army, hesitates at the thought of an invasion of his homeland, as Lucan notes in 1.353–355; but counterbalancing and
finally overswaying such considerations is love of warfare and fear
of their leader: "sed diro ferri revocantur amore / ductorisque
metu" (1.355–356). It is grimly ironic that Laelius should be wear-
ing, as he speaks, the *quercus civilis*, the soldier's highest honor,
awarded for saving the life of a fellow-citizen in battle (1.356–358).
   Yet this transference of loyalty from state to individual is not

incomprehensible. Caesar appeals to his troops for practical as well as personal reasons. When he addresses his army in 1.273–351, he emphasizes the problems facing his Gallic veterans, the perennial problems confronting general and troops in the late republic:

> quae sedes erit emeritis? quae rura dabuntur
> quae noster veteranus aret? quae moenia fessis? [344–345]

> (Where will the soldiers settle when they retire? What lands will be given the veteran to plow? What walls will shelter the exhausted?)

They are men denied a stake in their homeland. But the import of these lines does not begin and end with this simple statement of the soldier's grievances. Lucan's reader has a feeling of déjà vu, for the sentiments expressed bear a striking resemblance to those of Aeneas when he visits the temple of Apollo on Delos in Aeneid 3.85–89. "Da propriam, Thymbraee, domum; da moenia fessis," Aeneas cries at line 85 ("Give us a home of our own, Apollo, give walls to shelter the exhausted"). Then, at 88 he asks: "quem sequimur? quove ire iubes? ubi ponere sedes?" ("Whom shall we follow? Where do you bid us go? Where shall be build our settlements?").

Caesar's apparently ingenuous questions assume another and much larger dimension because of this echo of Vergil. This is not the only, or even the first, time that Lucan uses such an echo to suggest that Caesar regards himself as another Aeneas. Lucan is hinting at the Caesarian propaganda that linked the Julian clan with the founder of the Roman race. Lucan's Caesar would have his men believe he is exercising the same mandate as Aeneas, to find a home for the dispossessed and build the foundations of greatness. But Caesar is not so much championing the rights of the dispossessed as he is utilizing them as a basis for his personal ambitions. And, as we have already seen, the troops under his command are much more ready to destroy walls than to build them.

Until he reaches Rome, however, Caesar can delude his troops with the claim that he is championing their rights. But once Rome is his, the pious facade is shattered. At 5.237–316, he is confronted

by a mutiny in his army.[4] Caesar has achieved the goal he declares
to his troops in 1: he has control of Rome and Italy. Now the men
can have their pensions, or so they think. It soon becomes clear,
however, that Caesar has no intention of laying down arms, and
this angers his soldiers. His critics cannot understand why they
must go on fighting since they are home where they wanted to be
in the first place (5.261–295). They begin to realize that Caesar is
not really fighting for them, but that they are pawns in his game
(5.261–269). Yet the scope of his ambition mystifies them: "quid
satis est, si Roma parum est?" (274) (what is enough if Rome is too
little?). Lucan himself echoes this question at line 315: "saeve,
quid insequeris?" (savage man, what is it that you pursue?).

Caesar faces a challenge to his command as Pompey does in 7.
His soldiers feel that while Caesar was their legal commander in
Gaul, he is their equal in Italy, since they are all present illegally:
"Rheni mihi Caesar in undis / dux erat, hic socius" (5.289–290).
Whereas Pompey faces the possibility that his troops will act with-
out him, Caesar must cope with the opposite dilemma, fighting
without troops: "irato milite, Caesar, / pax erit" (294–295) (since
the soldiers are angry, Caesar, there will be peace).

Caesar does not back off from war, as Pompey would have done;
nor does he wait for tempers to cool down (303–304). He calmly
confronts the troops, standing high upon a mound, his face unmoved, and *earns the right to be feared because he is not afraid:*
"meruitque timeri / non metuens" (317–318). His approach to the
crisis is not one of tactful diplomacy, but of utter contempt. He
begins (319–320) by offering his breast to their swords; he ends by
ordering the execution of the ringleaders of the mutiny (360–364).
Caesar browbeats his men into submission by two ploys: first by
declaring that *he* does not need *them* any more, which undermines
their notion that the war cannot go on without their help; then he
accuses them of being cowardly and unfit for war, thus turning
their desire to retire from conflict into evidence of their spiritless-
ness. They are "imbelles animas" (322) (spirits unfit for war). The
very least they can do, if they are tired of fighting for him, is to
join Pompey, to *weaken* the enemy army (343–351). The rebellion,

4. For another discussion of this scene, see Rutz, *Studien,* 94–116; cf. Menz,
128–138 and Nehrkorn, 161–168.

in fact, turns out to Caesar's advantage. For it enables him to establish, once it is put down, that the troops are fighting for him:

> iam certe mihi bella geram. discedite castris,
> tradite nostra viris ignavi signa Quirites.
> at paucos, quibus haec rabies auctoribus arsit,
> non Caesar sed poena tenet. procumbite terra
> infidumque caput feriendaque tendite colla.
> et tu, quo solo stabunt iam robore castra,
> tiro rudis, specta poenas et disce ferire,
> disce mori.   [5.357–364]

(Now I am clearly fighting for myself. Get out of this camp, you
cowardly civilians, give my banners to *men!* But a few of you,
those at whose instigation this madness began, will stay. It is
not Caesar that detains them, but their punishment. Fall down
upon the ground and stretch out your necks and treacherous
heads. You will be beheaded. And you, new recruit, on whose
strength alone my cause will stand, watch their punishment.
Learn to strike, and learn to die!)

The sheer ferocity of Caesar's speech is, in itself, amazing, considering the circumstances. But it has its full effect. His men are
cowed, and they obey. The ringlanders' heads are duly lopped off,
and Caesar is more firmly in command than he was before the
trouble started. After such successful treatment of this crisis,
Caesar now ventures to enter Rome without an army (5.381–384)
—something he could not have done in book 3:

> ipse petit trepidam tutus sine milite Romam
> iam doctam servire togae, populoque precanti
> scilicet indulgens summo dictator honori
> contigit et laetos fecit se consule fastos.

Caesar enters the terrified city safe without an army. Rome has
already learned to be a slave to an unarmed man. As if to please
the people on their knees before him, the dictator takes the
supreme office of state, and makes the records happy with his
consulship.)

There is no longer any doubt as to Caesar's intentions or Rome's
willingness to acquiesce. By taking the consulship *and* the dictator-

ship, Caesar has acquired the authority to act as he sees fit for the welfare of the state. As supreme official of Rome, invested with extraordinary military and constitutional powers, he prepares to cross the Adriatic in pursuit of Pompey and the senatorial rebels. Caesar has turned the tables on his foes; he is transformed from rebel to magistrate, and they are the outlaws in the new Rome of Caesar. Crime now has the sanction of law. The dictatorship that came into being to protect the fabric of the state in time of crisis has become an instrument for transforming the republic into a monarchy.

Republican adversaries, even mutiny among his own forces, have proved only modest obstacles to Caesar's progress. Emboldened by his success, he even dares to challenge the elements when they seem to oppose him. Later in *Pharsalia* 5 we find him in Greece contemplating a hurried return to Italy. He is fretful because his second contingent, under Mark Antony, has not yet arrived (5.476–503). Suspecting—and rightly, Lucan implies—that Antony is seeking power for himself, Caesar decides to return to Italy alone to find out what is going on. He goes to the seashore and requisitions the boat of a fisherman, Amyclas.[5]

When Caesar mentions the voyage, Amyclas reacts with fear, and warns him, on the basis of meteorological signs, that a storm is to be expected (540–556). The admonition does nothing to deter Caesar, who orders him to put to sea forthwith. As the winds and waves begin to rise, Amyclas becomes terrified that they will be killed. But Caesar responds:

"sperne minas" inquit "pelagi ventoque furenti
trade sinum. *Italiam si caelo auctore recusas*
me pete. sola tibi causa est haec iusta timoris,
vectorem non nosse tuum, quem numina numquam
destituunt, de quo male tunc fortuna meretur
cum post vota venit. medias perrumpe procellas

5. On Amyclas, see Rutz, *Studien*, 154–157, and Nehrkorn, 154–160. The fullest and best descriptions of the storm are those of Linn, 60–132, and Morford, 20–58. For other sources, see Morford, 20, note 3; also König, 35–39, and Menz, 143–150. The story of Caesar's attempted crossing of the Adriatic is found in most ancient sources except Caesar himself: Suetonius *Julius* 52, Plutarch, *Caesar* 38, Appian *BCiv.* 2.57, Dio 41.46.3, Valerius Maximus 9.8.2 and Florus 4.2.37.

tutela secure mea. caeli iste fretique,
non puppis nostrae labor est." [578–585]

("Disregard the threats of the sea, give full sail to the raging
wind. *If the heavens do not prompt you to make for Italy, then
do so at my prompting.* The only just pretext for your fear is
that you do not know who your passenger is—a man whom the
divine never fails, whose ill-will Fortune deserves if she comes
after I have prayed to her. *I will protect you.* It is the sea and
sky that must suffer, not our boat.")

Caesar, unlike Aeneas, is not going to Italy against his will. On the
contrary, he is prepared to go whether the heavens want him to or
not. The gods and their protection are nothing compared to what
he, Caesar, can achieve. His comment at 582–583 that Fortune
deserves his ill-will if she does not come to him before he requests
her aid echoes Lucan's words in book 4 after Caesar had suffered
setbacks from adverse weather conditions during his Spanish campaign. But as the weather improved:

> sed parvo Fortuna viri contenta pavore
> plena redit, solitoque magis favere secundi
> et veniam meruere dei. [4.121–123]

(But Fortune, satisfied with frightening her hero a little, returns
full force; and the gods, by favoring him more than usual,
earned his pardon.)

It is he who pardons the gods, not they him.

As Lucan's words in 4 are surely not without a touch of sarcasm,
so Caesar's words in 5 are no less touched with megalomania. No
sooner does Caesar utter them than the storm swells to its howling
crescendo. His attempt to reach Italy is futile; the elements make
mockery of his boast. The issue at stake now is whether he will
even survive the abortive voyage. It finally occurs to Caesar that
he may die, for the tempest is unearthly and the full forces of the
elements batter his tiny vessel. His response is to believe that the
dangers are now worthy of his destiny: "credit iam digna pericula
Caesar / fatis esse suis" (653–654). His arrogance increased rather
than diminished, he addresses nature and the storm:

me superis labor est, parva quem puppe sedentem
tam magno petiere mari! si gloria leti
est pelago donata mei bellisque negamur,
intrepidus quamcumque datis mihi, numina, mortem
accipiam. licet ingentis abruperit actus
festinata dies fatis, sat magna peregi.
Arctoas domui gentes, inimica subegi
arma metu, vidit Magnum mihi Roma secundum,
iussa plebe tuli fasces per bella negatos;
nulla meis aberit titulis Romana potestas,
nec sciet hoc quisquam nisi tu, quae sola meorum
conscia votorum es, me, quamvis plenus honorum
et dictator eam Stygias et consul ad umbras,
privatum, Fortuna, mori. mihi funere nullo
est opus, o superi: lacerum retinete cadaver
fluctibus in mediis, desint mihi busta rogusque,
dum metuar semper terraque expecter ab omni.   [655–671]

(Is it so difficult for the powers above to destroy me that they
hurl the mighty force of the sea against me as I sit in a tiny
boat? If the honor of my grave is to be given to the sea, and I
am denied a death in battle, I will accept, divinities, whatever
doom you give me. Although my days end prematurely, breaking off my great achievements, I have had enough success. I
have tamed the people of the north, I have conquered my
enemies by fear alone. Rome saw that Pompey was second to
me. I gained the consulship denied to me in war by command-
ing the people to give it to me. No Roman power will be missing from my titles. No one, except you, Fortune, will know
that, although I go to the land of the dead loaded with honors
as dictator and consul, I am still dying on the lowest rung of
my ambition. This you alone, confidante of my prayers, know.
Gods, I do not need a funeral. Keep my shredded body in the
midst of the sea. Deprive me of pyre and cremation, so long as I
am always feared, and people expect me to appear from every
corner of the world.)

Caesar does not make it to Italy; but neither is he drowned. The
tenth wave, which in Latin, as in Celtic poetry, is the greatest and
most powerful, rises to strike Caesar and his boat.[6] But instead of

6. Compare the description of the great storm in *Odyssey* 5.313–340, which
is in some ways similar to Lucan's narrative here; see Morford, 38–48. For the

sweeping him to his death, it carries him safely back to the shore of Greece.

Although Lucan uses a variety of sources, including Vergil and Ovid, in his description of the storm (as Morford has shown in his excellent discussion of Lucan's storms), the end product is utterly different from that of any epic predecessor.[7] There is not the slightest suggestion that Lucan's tempest arises from the intervention of any deity. On the contrary, its occurrence is predicted on the basis of meteorological signs by Amyclas before Caesar puts to sea. Thus Lucan precludes the possibility that the storm is generated for the express purpose of harassing or destroying Caesar. In this sense it is quite unlike the opening tempest of the *Aeneid*, despite the verbal reminiscences.[8] It is Lucan's Caesar, not the poet himself, who suggests that the storm was stirred up by divine powers in order to annihilate him. This omission of divine agency has the effect of enhancing Caesar's megalomania: the storm did not just happen to arise; it arose because he was upon the sea.

No less interesting is Caesar's reaction to the possibility of death at sea, a prospect that reduces Odysseus and Aeneas to cries of lamentation. At first blush this might suggest that Caesar is greater than his epic predecessors. But we should recall that Odysseus and Aeneas are not afraid of death but of an *unheroic* death far from the battlefield. They wish to be remembered as having passed from life gloriously. Although Caesar concedes that drowning would be a slightly disappointing conclusion to his career, he takes consolation from the thought that the uncertainty surrounding his demise would leave him as an object of fear for mankind. He would gain a perverse kind of immortality in death.

What this incident shows more than anything else is that there is nothing Caesar cannot somehow construe to his own advantage. Adversity simply increases his megalomania. He thinks of himself as a cosmic power; he dares to act when the forces of nature

significance of the tenth wave, see Ovid *Met.* 11.530 and *Tristia* 1.2. 49–50. In Welsh poetry the ninth wave is the largest; but since the Welsh do not practise inclusive reckoning, as did the Romans, they clearly mean the same wave: "o dwfr ton nawvet" (the ninth wave's foam) (*Book of Taliesin*, 25) and, of greater interest here: "Aduvyn gaer yssyd ar ton nawvet" (there is a fine fortress above the ninth wave) (*ibid.*, 43).

7. Morford, 38–48.   8. *Aeneid* 1.124–147.

shrink back (as in the felling of the Druidic grove in *Pharsalia* 3);
it therefore follows that he would view his braving of the storm as
a contest between himself and the elements. From Caesar's point
of view, the outcome is at worst a stand-off. The tempest prevents
him from reaching Italy, but it returns him safe to land—and to
all his kingdoms, cities, and good Fortune (5.676–677).

III. The New Troy and the Old

We have already noted that Caesar's words in 1.344–345 seem to
be a reminiscence of Aeneas' appeal to Apollo in *Aeneid* 3.85–89.
This anachronistic echo of the *Aeneid* by Caesar invites both a
parallel and a contrast with Vergil's hero, especially when viewed
in conjunction with Caesar's address to Patria in *Pharsalia* 1 and
his prayers to the gods of Troy in 9.

If Pompey seems weaker than Aeneas, Caesar seems immeasur-
ably stronger. Aeneas, when addressing his plea to Apollo to find a
home for the exhausted and dispossessed Trojans, really does not
know where he is supposed to be going. He has either forgotten or
repressed the memory of Creusa's instructions to sail for Italy.[9] No
less evident is Aeneas' unsureness as to who should lead the exiled
Trojans. During the sack of Troy he shows both unwillingness
and inability to assume command of the Trojan resistance; it is
all he can do to grasp the fact that Troy is, in fact, doomed. At the
beginning of *Aeneid* 3 it is Anchises, not Aeneas, who assumes
command. Caesar, by way of contrast, shows neither reluctance nor
inability to take control, and he knows precisely what his goal is.
He does not move from oracle to oracle seeking reassurance and
hoping to find a resting place from his toils. Whenever he addresses the gods, it is to demand their aid in completing something
he has undertaken on his own initiative. And rest is alien to his
impatient nature.

9. In *Aeneid* 2.780–784. Aeneas never again mentions Creusa (though As-
canius refers to her in 9.297). Aeneas' ability to repress or sublimate the
traumatic is evidenced on several occasions in the epic; e.g., 2.268–297, where
he tells Dido of his reaction to the vision of Hector on the night of the fall
of Troy. Obviously Aeneas, when conscious, knows that Hector is dead; but
in his dream he is baffled by Hector's long and unexplained "absence" (282–
285) and cannot account for the wounds and general disfigurement of the
vision before him (285–286).

It is, of course, arguable that Aeneas has some of the qualities of a savage Achilles, particularly in *Aeneid* 10 through 12. But in the earlier books, the trail of destruction he leaves behind is not of his own making. Dido, admittedly, dies by his sword; but the blow was inflicted by her hand, not his. Nor is there any reason to suppose that he desired to destroy her or *consciously* grasped the fact that she would die if he abandoned her. Only in the later books does Aeneas' destructiveness seem consciously undertaken, and much of this is in reaction to the death of Pallas. In *Aeneid* 10.510–605 his slaughter of Magus and Lucagus who are begging for their lives, his capture of the sons of Sulmo and Ufens for human sacrifice, and his denial of burial to Tarquitus show an anger and savagery that is a match for Achilles. Aeneas' worst passions always seem aroused by the desire to avenge Troy and the death of friends. And this is where, even in his bloodiest moments, he differs from Caesar. His actions are not undertaken for the purpose of self-aggrandisement. His mission, the foundation of the Roman race, is one imposed upon him against his own personal inclinations, not as a result of them. Finally, Aeneas' goal will yield, ultimately, constructive results: the foundation of a New Troy in Italy.

Lucan's Caesar clearly views himself as Aeneas' successor. As early as *Pharsalia* 1.195–203 this becomes apparent. When he is about to cross the Rubicon, the figure of Patria confronts him, demanding to know where he is bound and what his purpose is, warning that if he and his men are to be considered citizens, they may advance no farther (1.190–192).[10] Caesar hesitates for a moment, horror-stricken, but then he answers:

> o magnae qui moenia prospicis urbis
> Tarpeia de rupe Tonans Phrygiique penates
> gentis Iuleae et rapti secreta Quirini
> et residens celsa Latiaris Iuppiter Alba
> Vestalesque foci summique o numinis instar
> Roma, fave coeptis. non te furialibus armis

10. On Caesar's crossing of the Rubicon, see also Chapter 8 and H. Dubourdieu, "Le Passage du Rubicon d'après Suétone, César et Lucain," *IL* 3 (1951), 122–126; 162–165; E. Hohl, "Caesar am Rubico," *MH* 80 (1952), 246–249, Heyke, 11–34 and 165–166, and L. Herrman, "Le Prodige du Rubicon," *REA* 37 (1935), 435–437.

persequor: en, adsum victor terraque marique
Caesar, ubique tuus (liceat modo, nunc quoque) miles.
ille erit ille nocens, qui me tibi fecerit hostem.   [195–203]

(O Jupiter, you who watch over the walls of the great city from
the Tarpeian rock, and you, Trojan household gods of the
Julian clan, mystery of Romulus assumed to heaven; Latin
Jupiter residing in the high citadel of Alba, fires of Vesta, and
Rome, equal to the greatest of the gods, favor my undertaking.
I am not persecuting you with a madman's war. Behold, I am
the victor over land and sea, I am Caesar, who, if you permit,
will be your common soldier throughout the world! The man
who made me your enemy, he will be the guilty one—he, not I.)

With this, Caesar crosses the Rubicon and begins the civil war.
The appeal of his homeland is simply brushed aside.

This prayer to the gods of Troy and Rome is almost unique in
the *Pharsalia*. Aside from the pitiful echo of Caesar's "Roma, fave
coeptis," made by Pompey in 8.322, there is only one major parallel, as we shall see shortly.[11] Obviously it is ironic that Caesar
should appeal to the gods to favor his cause which is, in effect,
the subjugation of Rome to himself, and that he should offer such
a response to a vision of his homeland. He even concedes that he
is what Patria has accused him of being—the enemy of Rome. But
then, in a foretaste of his perverse logic, he argues that the man
who *will be* guilty is the man who made him Rome's enemy: not
est (1.203), but *erit*. As we noted in the last section, victory will
establish who is innocent, as far as Caesar is concerned; and he is
confident of victory. What makes Caesar's actions even worse is
that his reference to the Trojan household gods of the Julian clan
(196–197) indicates he is fully aware of himself as descendant and
heir of Aeneas. True, he does not actually name Aeneas here. Indeed, Aeneas is named only once in the entire *Pharsalia* (9.991)—
and, we should add, by Caesar. But the very fact that Caesar is the
only character in the epic ever represented as praying to the gods
or thinking of Troy as anything but a ruined city makes even this
slight reference noteworthy. Further, Patria, to whose rebuke this
prayer is a response, is the only symbolic or divine being introduced into the action of the *Pharsalia*.

11. For a discussion of Pompey's echo of Caesar see Chapter 5, Section II.

The unusual qualities of this passage are not necessarily evident upon first perusal of the *Pharsalia*, since it comes so early in the epic, before the absence of conventional deities and myth has fully dawned on us. But when viewed in conjunction with Caesar's visit to Troy and arrival in Egypt in 9.987–1108, its importance becomes clearer. By then the reader knows more about Caesar and far more about Lucan's attitude to the civil war and its outcome.

In 9.950, we find Caesar where Lucan left him at the end of 7, gloating over his victory at Pharsalia. Our attention, during the intervening period has been focused exclusively on Pompey and Cato, who occupy the whole of 8 and the first 949 lines of 9 respectively. Events have proceeded apace without the benefit of Caesar's presence. Pompey has been murdered, and his spirit has transcended its corporeal limitations. He is now more of a symbol than a man, purified at last of the shortcomings that dogged him throughout the later stages of his life. The spirit of the republicans is now housed in Cato who, for the first time in the epic, takes an active part in the war and enters the major action. The reintroduction of Caesar in 9 is abrupt, as transitions often are in the *Pharsalia*. Yet the abruptness has, I believe, a profoundly dramatic effect upon the whole scene.

It juxtaposes, for the first time, Caesar and Cato, who would presumably be the principal figures in the next books of the *Pharsalia* if Lucan had lived (or intended) to continue his narrative to encompass the battle of Thapsus. More important still, it allows the poet to compress the events between Caesar's departure from Pharsalia and his arrival in Egypt. At 9.950, he leaves Pharsalia; at 1010, not only is he in Egypt, but he has been presented with the head of Pompey. We might conclude that Lucan is just attempting to bring us up to date as quickly as possible, by hurrying through Caesar's actions during this time. But there is, I think, more to it than this. The compression of events and time perspectives in this way has the ultimate effect of establishing a very close thematic continuity between actions that would otherwise be separated in time, space, and narrative. At one moment Caesar is surveying the carnage he has wrought at Pharsalia; at the next he is gazing at the overgrown and formless site of Troy, where he stops en route to Egypt. Finally, before we can catch our breath, he is staring at the head of Pompey. In the space of 60 lines, we are confronted with the ruins of the republic at Pharsalia, the ruins of Troy, and the disembodied head of Pompey, three *exempla* of greatness now past and gone.

Line 950 invites us to turn back to the description of Caesar's reaction to the slaughter at Pharsalia, since we now learn that he has had his fill of the spectacle of destruction: "Emathia satiatus clade." Here, then, is Caesar on the morning after the conflict:

> postquam clara dies Pharsalica damna retexit,
> nulla loci facies revocat feralibus arvis
> haerentis oculos. cernit propulsa cruore
> flumina et excelsos cumulis aequantia colles
> corpora, sidentis in tabem spectat acervos
> et Magni numerat populos, epulisque paratur
> ille locus, voltus ex quo faciesque iacentum
> agnoscat. iuvat Emathiam non cernere terram
> et lustrare oculos campos sub clade latentes.
> fortunam superosque suos in sanguine cernit.
> ac, ne laeta furens scelerum spectacula perdat,
> invidet igne rogi miseris, caeloque nocenti
> ingerit Emathiam.   [7.787–799]

(When the clear light of day disclosed the catastrophe at Pharsalia, no aspect of the place repels him; his eyes remain fixed upon the hideous battlefield. He sees rivers flooding with gore, and heaps of bodies as high as the tall mountains, and watches the mounds of corpses slowly rotting. He makes a count of the Pompeian dead. A lavish breakfast is prepared for him at a vantage point from which he can distinguish the faces and expressions of the dead, deriving pleasure from the fact that he cannot see the soil of Thessaly or make out the plain, since they are hidden by the slaughter. In the blood, he sees reflected his fortune and the gods who are now his. In his criminal obsession he forbids the burning of the wretched dead, for fear that he will lose the pleasure of the spectacle before him. Heaven is guilty; and Caesar parades Thessaly before the gods.)

Caesar's morbid delight in the panorama of death evokes, in the lines following, a comparison with Hannibal, to Caesar's detriment. It also recalls the description of Erichtho in 6.573–588, as she anxiously awaits her feast at Pharsalia. Although Caesar does not consume corpses as Erichtho does, the macabre touch of dining on the battlefield is perhaps as gruesome a counterpart to Erichtho's behavior as could be entertained, even by Lucan. Caesar, like Tolstoy's Napoleon, finds that the spectacle of death on the battlefield whets the appetite.

For Caesar, of course, this is the fulfillment of a dream. To his troops before Pharsalia, he had said:

> videor fluvios spectare cruoris
> calcatosque simul reges sparsumque senatus
> corpus et inmensa populos in caede natantis.   [7.292–294]

(I seem to be watching rivers of blood, kings trampled underfoot, the body of the senate ripped asunder and the people swimming in an immense sea of slaughter.)

In 9.950, then, Lucan reminds us of the dream and its fulfillment at Pharsalia.

This recollection serves as a powerful preamble to Lucan's description of the desolate site of Troy at 9.964–979:

> circumit exustae nomen memorabile Troiae
> magnaque Phoebei quaerit vestigia muri.
> iam silvae steriles et putres robore trunci
> Assaraci pressere domos et templa deorum
> iam lassa radice tenent, ac tota teguntur
> Pergama dumetis: etiam periere ruinae.
> aspicit Hesiones scopulos silvaque latentis
> Anchisae thalamos; quo iudex sederit antro,
> unde puer raptus caelo, quo vertice Nais
> luxerit Oenone: nullum est sine nomine saxum.
> inscius in sicco serpentem pulvere rivum
> transierat, qui Xanthus erat. securus in alto
> gramine ponebat gressus: Phryx incola manes
> Hectoreos calcare vetat. discussa iacebant
> saxa nec ullius faciem servantia sacri:
> "Herceas" monstrator ait "non respicis aras?"   [9.964–979]

(Caesar walked around the famous name of burned-out Troy and searched for the great remains of the wall of Phoebus.

Barren forests and tree-trunks with rotting timber have crushed the dwellings of Assaracus, and, though their roots are weak with age, they are the only binding force which holds the temples of the gods together. The whole of Pergamum is covered with scrub-thickets—even the ruins have collapsed. He sees the rocks of Hesione, the woods that concealed the marriage of Anchises and Venus, the cave where Paris judged the goddesses, the place where Ganymede was snatched from earth to heaven, the hill-top on which the nymph Oenone played. There is no rock that does not have its own identity. He crossed, without realizing what it was, a creek winding its way across the dry dust. This was once the river Xanthus. A Phrygian inhabitant tells Caesar not to trample underfoot the grave of Hector. The stones were lying scattered and broken, preserving no semblance of anything sacred. "Take care!" says the guide, "Do you not see the altar of Hercaean Jupiter?")

The picture is brilliantly surrealistic. Troy is an archaeological site, nothing more, as is Scipio's camp in 4.[12] Though each stone has its tale to tell, one needs the services of a guide to find the stone and tell the tale. Even the forests growing over the city are rotting.

Lines 966–969 recall the description of Pompey as the rotting oak in book 1, and the suggestion that Troy itself is now merely a *memorabile nomen* brings to mind the rendering of Pompey as *Magni nominis umbra*. But, even more powerfully, the passage revives memories of Lucan's description of the consequences that the battle of Pharsalia would have for Italy:

> tunc omne Latinum
> fabula nomen erit; Gabios Veiosque Coramque
> pulvere vix tectae poterunt monstrare ruinae
> Albanosque Lares Laurentinosque penates,
> rus vacuum, quod non habitet nisi nocte coacta
> invitus questusque Numam iussisse senator.
> non aetas haec carpsit edax monimentaque rerum
> putria destituit: crimen civile videmus

12. On the question as to whether this description is founded on Lucan's own observations of the site of Troy see B. Bilinski, "De Lucano Troiae periegeta observationes," *Eos* 42 (1947), 90–121; Heyke, 139–143, and F. Bastet, "Lucain et les Arts," *FH* 15.137–138.

tot vacuas urbes. generis quo turba redacta est
humani! toto populi qui nascimur orbe
nec muros implere viris nec possumus agros:
urbs nos una capit. vincto fossore coluntur
Hesperiae segetes, stat tectis putris avitis
in nullos ruitura domus, nulloque frequentem
cive suo Romam sed mundi faece repletam
cladis eo dedimus, ne tanto in corpore bellum
iam possit civile geri. Pharsalia tanti
causa mali.   [7.391–408]

(Then [i.e., after Pharsalia] the Latin League [or Latin name]
will be a folk tale. The ruins covered with dust will scarcely
show a trace of Gabii, Veii, Cora, the Lares of Alba and the
Penates of Laurentum. It will all be empty countryside which
no-one would live in—except the senator who stays there for the
night the law demands, stays there against his will, complaining
that Numa ordered this to be done. It is not greedy time that
has gnawed all this away, and left the monuments of men's
achievements rotting. We see the crime of civil war, so many
empty cities. Where, then, have all the throngs of people gone?
We nations who were born throughout the world cannot fill the
walls of our towns or the fields of our countries. One city embraces us all. The harvests of Italy are brought in by a reaper in
chains. The house with lifeless, rotting roof still stands; and
when it falls, no one will be crushed. Rome is crowded, but not
with its own citizens. It is filled with the scum of the earth. Such
a catastrophe did we inflict upon the city that, though many
years lie between Pharsalia and our own day, we could no longer
fight a *civil* war. And of all this misfortune, Pharsalia was the
cause.) [13]

The resemblance between the descriptions of Italy and Troy is
too close to be accidental. Lucan is saying that the civil war and,
in particular, the battle of Pharsalia, has utterly ruined Italy. It
would be truer to say that the civil war had completed the process
of destruction already begun. Appian tells us that the greater part
of Italy had been devastated during the Roman conquest (*Civil
Wars* 1.7); Lucretius implies that the fields were losing their fertility, possibly through intensive farming (2.1144–1174). But, at

13. Cf. *Pharsalia* 1.21–32.

worst, what Lucan says is only an exaggeration. Rural Italy was dead. Horace observes in *Epistles* 1.11.7–8: "scis Lebedus quid sit: Gabiis desertior atque / Fidenis vicus" (you know what Lebedus is: a hamlet, emptier than Gabii and Fidenae). Propertius in 4.1.33–34 comments:

> quippe suburbanae parva minus urbe Bovillae
> et, qui nunc nulli, maxima turba Gabi.

(And then there's neighboring Bovillae—though it was less of a neighbor when Rome was smaller; and the crowded streets of Gabii where no-one lives now.)

H. E. Butler and E. A. Barber observe, in fact, that Gabii was "a by-word for desolation"[14] Cicero tells us that no one from the Latin cities can be found to come and claim his share of the food at the Latin Feast, the *Feriae Latinae* (*Pro Plancio* 23). Add to this Propertius' gloomy epitaph on Veii:

> Heu Vei veteres! et vos tum regna fuistis,
> et vestro posita est aurea sella foro:
> nunc intra muros pastoris bucina lenti
> cantat, et in vestris ossibus arva metunt.   [4.10.27–30]

(Alas, ancient Veii! You were, in those days, a kingdom, and a golden throne stood in your forum. Now the slow-moving shepherd plays his pipes within your walls; men reap the harvests growing on your bones.)

Strabo, a more impartial commentator, confirms this picture of annihilation.[15] The Latin cities are dead; they are ghost towns, like Troy.

Lucan in his description of the Latin cities cannot resist a word-play on the term for the Latin League—*Latinum nomen*. The *nomen* of Latium will become a *fabula*, a folk tale, in the aftermath of the war. We recall Propertius' similar wordplay in *Elegies* 1.5.26, where the poet informs his rival, Gallus, that if Cynthia is angered by Gallus his great name will become a rumor: "quam cito de tanto nomine rumor eris." And *fabula* (from *fari*) can

14. H. E. Butler and E. A. Barber, *The Elegies of Propertius*, Oxford, 1933, note on 4.1.33–34.
15. Strabo 5.3.2.

mean "idle talk" just as *rumor* can. Yet even the word *nomen* itself frequently has the connotation of "name without substance" or suggests an appellation that belies the true nature of the thing to which it is applied, particularly in Lucan and Vergil. In *Pharsalia* 1.668, the crime of war will pass under the *nomen* of virtue, and in 4.222, peace will be the *nomen* given to slavery. Similarly in *Aeneid* 4.172, Dido will hide her shame (*culpa*) under the *nomen* of marriage. In *Aeneid* 7.411–413, the desolate town of Ardea is a *magnum nomen*, a great name; but its fortune and its great days have passed: "sed fortuna fuit." Similarly Troy in *Pharsalia* 9.964 is a *memorabile nomen* and Pompey (*ibid.*, 1.135 and 8.449) even less, the ghost of a name, *nominis umbra*. Just as Ardea has only its name as a reminder of former glory, since the substance, the very existence of the town, has disappeared, so Priam in *Aeneid* 2.558 is a *sine nomine corpus*, a body without identity. An even more curious parallel is to be found in *Aeneid* 6.773–776, where Anchises describes to Aeneas the various peoples who will found the cities of the Latin League, only to conclude with the remark: "haec tum nomina erunt, nunc sunt sine nomine terrae" (776) (These then will be names; now they are lands without names). It is hard to imagine that Vergil's contemporaries would not have found something ironical in Anchises' comment here, knowing as they did that the cities of Latium were dead in their own time. Given the prophetic vision Aeneas' father seems to have, it is odd that he supplies no hint of the future emptiness of Latium. Perhaps, though, there is an ambiguity in what Anchises says. For it would certainly be possible to translate *Aeneid* 6.776 as follows, in the light of our discussion of the meaning of *nomen:* "These then will be names (without substance); now they are substance without name."

The conclusion to be drawn from the parallel between the devastation of Italy and that of Troy begins to emerge. What the conquering Greeks had inflicted upon Asia, civil war has inflicted upon Italy. And Caesar, as victor of Pharsalia, is, to Lucan, the agent of that destruction as surely as Achilles and Pyrrhus were the architects of Troy's annihilation. The parallel is further enhanced by Lucan's mention of Troy as one of the cities sending a contingent to Pompey's army in 3.211–213:

Iliacae quoque signa manus perituraque castra
ominibus petiere suis, nec fabula Troiae
continuit Phrygiique ferens se Caesar Iuli.

(Bands of men from Ilium also joined the standards and the
camp of the doomed army, bringing their Trojan luck with
them. The myth of Troy and Caesar's claim of descent from
Phrygian Iulus did not hold them back.)

The Trojans have no more use for Caesarian propaganda than
does Lucan. And, ironically, their bodies, along with those of
Romans, lie upon the field at Pharsalia. Caesar has also destroyed
what was left of Troy.

At 9.963, in the midst of his description of Troy and the memories it evokes, Lucan reminds us of the debt the past owes to literature. Only through poets do the ghosts of the famous men of
Troy live on: "multum debentis vatibus umbras." This isolated
comment is developed more fully a few lines later:

> o sacer et magnus vatum labor! omnia fato
> eripis et populis donas mortalibus aevum.
> invidia sacrae, Caesar, ne tangere famae;
> nam, siquid Latiis fas est promittere Musis,
> quantum Zmyrnaei durabunt vatis honores,
> venturi me teque legent; Pharsalia nostra
> vivet, et a nullo tenebris damnabimur aevo.   [980–986]

(O labor of poets, how holy and great you are! You snatch
everything from fate and give life to mortal peoples. Caesar, do
not be envious of the poet's holy fame. For, if Latin Muses are
allowed to produce anything which will endure as long as the
honors rendered to Homer, people in time to come will read
both you and me. Pharsalia, our tale, will live, and no age shall
condemn us to the shadows.)

We will reserve for a later chapter the controversial interpretation of lines 985–986, and concentrate here on some of the other
things that emerge from this passage. Lucan seems to envisage a
parallel between himself and Homer, Caesar and Achilles. The
passage is indeed highly reminiscent of the story of Alexander's
visit to the tomb of Achilles, where the great conqueror is re-

minded of the debt that heroes owe to the written word, if their greatness is to be remembered.[16] But there is something particularly disturbing about the whole business if we take it any further, as I think we should. Lucan makes no suggestion that Caesar, like Alexander, felt any need of a poet to celebrate his deeds. We must note that Lucan talks of giving life to the peoples, *populis*, not to the victorious warrior. The poet, not Caesar, is moved to comment on the transitory fortunes of mankind, and the focus is on the debt *Troy* owes to the poets, not the debt Caesar owes them. Of course the Old Troy Homer wrote of was defunct when Homer wrote, but the New Troy in Italy was still alive as Lucan composed the *Pharsalia*. Or was it? Perhaps this is precisely Lucan's point. The Italy of 7, like the Troy of 9, is name without substance, a *fabula*, the merest recollection of a name.

The parallel between Italy and Troy is further emphasized as Caesar turns from his contemplation of the ruins to erect an altar (9.987 ff.). He prays to the gods of the ashes in his capacity as the descendant of Aeneas and the representative of the New Troy in Italy, founded by the Phrygians:

> Di cinerum, Phrygias colitis quicumque ruinas,
> Aeneaeque mei, quos nunc Lavinia sedes
> servat et Alba, lares, et quorum lucet in aris
> ignis adhuc Phrygius, nullique aspecta virorum
> Pallas, in abstruso pignus memorabile templo,
> gentis Iuleae vestris clarissimus aris
> dat pia tura nepos et vos in sede priore
> rite vocat. date felices in cetera cursus,
> restituam populos; grata vice moenia reddent
> Ausonidae Phrygibus, Romanaque Pergama surgent.
>
> [9.990–999]
>
> (Gods of the ashes, whoever you are that now dwell in the ruins, and the household gods of my Aeneas, whom the Lavinian land and Alba now preserve, and whose light, still Trojan, burns upon the altars, and you, Pallas, hidden from male eyes, whose memorable gift lies as a pledge in Vesta's innermost sanctuary, the most distinguished descendant of the Julian clan gives pious offerings of incense, and calls upon you with proper ceremony in your former home. Grant me a prosperous course for what

16. Cicero *Arch.* 24.

remains to be done, and I shall restore your people. In return for your favor, the people of Italy will give pleasing walls to Phrygia, and a Roman Troy will rise.)

The household gods of Alba are scarcely preserved among the dust-covered ruins Lucan describes in 7. If they have any existence at all, it is no more than the survival of an antique ritual. *Di cinerum*, gods of the ashes, is a title as suitable to the Alban as to the Phrygian deities. Thus Caesar's proposal is as ironic as it is outrageous, recalling his effrontery in 1, when, in reply to Patria, he calls upon the Roman gods to aid his cause.

Caesar is, as he points out, the descendant of Aeneas, and 9.991 is the only occasion in the *Pharsalia* where the name of Aeneas occurs. The offspring of Aeneas, at the battle of Pharsalia, destroyed the Italian Troy his ancestor had founded. Now the destroyer of the New Troy stands in the midst of the ruins of the Old, appealing to the gods of both to support his cause. He even suggests that his ritual offering is pious. And the new Roman Troy Caesar promises to found in return for the favor of the dead gods will be in Asia, not in Italy. The Trojan myth has run its full cycle.

Yet the picture cannot be quite complete without the head of Pompey, with which Caesar is presented on arrival in Egypt at 9.1010. Again Lucan recalls the battlefield at Pharsalia:

> qui duro membra senatus
> calcarat voltu, qui sicco lumine campos
> viderat Emathios, uni tibi, Magne, negare
> non audet gemitus.   [9.1043–1046]

(The man who, with face unmoved and harsh, had trampled the limbs of the senate, who had looked without a tear upon the plains of Thessaly, did not dare deny to you, and only you, Pompey, a groan.)

Caesar's feigned tears over Pompey's shrunken head go well with his feigned piety to the ashes of Troy.

Given the reader's awareness of the implicit comparison between the destruction of the republic at Pharsalia and the ruins of Troy, the head of Pompey comes to represent the final doom of the republic, much as Priam's head symbolizes the demise of Troy, marking not merely the death of a man, but the end of an era. When Vergil locates Priam's corpse on the seashore in *Aeneid* 2.554–558 instead of in the flames of the royal palace where he actually died at the hands of Pyrrhus, the recollection of Pompey's death must have welled up in the reader's consciousness, bridging the gap between myth and history, past and present.[17] Similarly, in *Pharsalia* 9 the foreshortening of perspectives draws our attention to the parallel between the fate of the New Troy and the fate of the Old.

It is fundamental to the irony of the *Pharsalia* that the man who destroys Rome should claim association with the legendary founder of the Roman race. While Lucan himself wants no part of the Aeneas legend and studiously avoids mentioning it in his capacity as narrator (except to dismiss it as a *fabula* and Caesarian propaganda in 3.211–213), he is more than happy to use it to Caesar's disadvantage.[18] Caesar's use of mythological propaganda during the civil war invited such retaliation, and Lucan turns it back on Caesar very effectively. The poet succeeds here as obviously as he fails to subvert Caesar's clemency in 4.

Yet what Caesar says about rebuilding the Old Troy in *Pharsalia* 9 reminds us that there will be a new, if bizarre beginning. The Roman world will experience the results of the credo Caesar enunciates in—of all places—his address to his mutinous troops: "humanum paucis vivit genus" (the human race lives for the benefit of a few) (5.343).

IV. Caesar at Alexandria

Caesar, like his mythical ancestor, Aeneas, enjoys sightseeing. The reliefs on the temple of Juno in Carthage and the Daedalus motif at Cumae hold the attention of Vergil's hero to such an extent that, in the latter instance, he draws a direct rebuke from the Sibyl: "non hoc ista sibi tempus spectacula poscit" (*Aen.* 6.37) ("This is not the sort of sightseeing the occasion demands").

17. See Chapter 5, Section III.
18. On the use of the mythological against Caesar, see O. Phillips. For the rumor that Caesar proposed to transfer the capital of the Roman empire to Troy, see Chapter 3, note 44.

Caesar, however, prefers the spectacle of human blood, the desolate site of Troy, and the grave of Alexander to the purely artistic. While Aeneas is fascinated and not a little jealous of Dido's Carthage and Andromache's Buthrotum, Caesar shows little interest in what is living and growing.[19] Though Aeneas is relegated to the position of an observer, for the most part, during the sack of Troy, bewildered and stupefied by the slaughter, there is no indication that he enjoys what he sees, as Caesar does at Pharsalia.

When Caesar arrives at Alexandria at the beginning of *Pharsalia* 10, he is not attracted by the cultural wealth of the city, though it has much to attest to the ancient strength of Macedonia (10.14–19). None of the charming sites captivates him: "nulla captus dulcedine rerum" (10.17). Instead, he eagerly descends into a cave hollowed out for tombs: "effossum tumulis cupide descendit in antrum" (10.19). He is not interested in the by-products of Macedonian arms, but only in the grave site of the "insane offspring of Philip of Pella, the successful bandit *(felix praedo)*" (10.20–21). Lucan leaves us to guess Caesar's motivation for the visit and offers no suggestion as to how it affected him. On this occasion, Caesar's sightseeing serves as an opportunity for Lucan to launch into a searing attack on Alexander the Great, and, by implication, on Caesar.

I mention the name Alexander the Great for purposes of identification only. For Lucan accords him neither name nor greatness. He is merely a creature of blood who devastated the world, driven on by the prompting of destiny. "He coursed through Asia leaving piles of dead humanity behind him, running his sword through every nation, polluting rivers he had never seen before: the Euphrates with Persian, the Ganges with Indian blood" (10.30–33). His utter bestiality is underscored by the contemptuous word *proles* (offspring) (10.20), which could as easily be animal as human offspring; he leaves the "latebras . . . suorum" (the lairs of his ancestors) (10.28); he perpetrates a slaughter of humans: "humana cum strage ruit" (10.31), as if he were a creature of some different order.

The mere existence of a sanctified tomb for Alexander is repugnant to Lucan. That his grave has not been plundered and his

19. For Aeneas at Buthrotum, see *Aeneid* 3.493–499; at Carthage, 1.437.

ashes scattered is testimony to the continued rule of kings (10.22–24). The poet would deprive Alexander of a grave as surely as he would love to provide a Roman shrine for Pompey. For Alexander set "a precedent that was not helpful to the world, namely that so many lands could be under the control of one man":

> . . . non utile mundo
> editus exemplum, terras tot posse sub uno
> esse viro.   [10.26–28]

Clearly Caesar is following in his footsteps, and the parallel is driven home in lines 34–36. Alexander is:

> terrarum fatale malum fulmenque quod omnis
> percuteret pariter populos et sidus iniquum
> gentibus.

> (A deadly blight upon the earth, a thunderbolt which cuts down all nations indiscriminately, and a star of doom to all mankind.)

Alexander, like Caesar, is a thunderbolt—though Alexander's destructive energies are directed outside, not within, his homeland. In this sense, Caesar is even worse than his predecessor. Further, Alexander left no successor to his vast empire; it disintegrated when he died (10.43–45). But Caesar obviously did leave a successor. The temporal limits placed upon Alexander were not placed upon Caesar.[20]

Although this may suggest that Caesar is a "greater" man than Alexander, if only in terms of outrages committed at the expense of civilization, Lucan introduces other elements in his denunciation of Alexander to cut Caesarian pretensions down to size. Alexander's spirit was venturesome, ever moving in search of new lands to explore and conquer. Lucan exaggerates the scope of his travels, suggesting that he even drank from the source of the Nile (10.40). Thus Caesar seems cautious and conservative when he observes to Achoreus, the Ptolemaic sage:

> spes sit mihi certa videndi
> Niliacos fontes, bellum civile relinquam.   [10.191–192]

> (Were there a positive hope that I could see the sources of the Nile, I would abandon civil war.)

20. For further discussion of Lucan's use of recollections of Alexander, see Chapter 7, Section VIII.

Caesar, unlike Alexander, will not gamble with the unknown. He and his successors were never able to retrace Alexander's path of victory in the East. In fact, as Lucan points out in conclusion, the peoples of the East were more afraid of Alexander than of Rome; Parthia was a secure province of tiny Pella, but untouchable by mighty Rome.

Lucan contrives to present Caesar's visit to Alexander's tomb in a manner that shows both men in the worst possible light. Yet the connection established in this back-handed way is used to further advantage in the following scene between Caesar and Cleopatra. By using the adjective *Emathius* to describe the royal palace in Alexandria (10.58), Lucan establishes some further common ground between Caesar and the Macedonian. Caesar is fresh from his Emathian slaughter and suitably finds himself in residence at the Emathian palace of the Ptolemies. By allowing the adjective to encompass both Thessalian and Macedonian geography, Caesar and Alexander can share a common identity, one as the victor of the battle on the Emathian plain, the other as the offspring of Emathian Pella.

Yet the Caesar of *Pharsalia* 10 is Caesar at his most vulnerable. The city that holds Alexander's grave and Pompey's ghost very nearly adds Caesar to its list of notable dead. We find him, at the conclusion of the epic, uncertain as to whether he should fear or wish for death: "dubiusque timeret / optaretne mori" (10.542–543). The onslaught of the Egyptians leaves him, "the man for whom there was not enough room in the Roman world, like a boy who cannot fight or a woman in a captured city trying to find the safety of a house":

> hic, cui Romani spatium non sufficit orbis . . .
> ceu puer inbellis vel captis femina muris,
> quaerit tuta domus. [10.456; 458–459]

For the first time in the epic, Caesar is afraid, and Lucan makes the most of it. He describes Caesar as wandering aimlessly around the palace with the young king Ptolemy as hostage, ready to kill him, if necessary, to keep his foes at bay (10.459–464). This suggests to Lucan a comparison with the barbarous Colchian, Medea (464–467). Comparison with a woman would, in Roman eyes, be

bad enough; but since that woman is Medea, the comparison becomes one of the most insulting comments Lucan makes about
Caesar in the *Pharsalia*. The simile, of course, has a certain perverse appropriateness. Medea dismembered her own brother, Ab-
syrtus, to hold up Aeetes' pursuit; Caesar is ready to dismember
Cleopatra's brother. Not only does this reverse the male and fe-
male roles—Caesar plays Medea to Cleopatra's Jason—but Caesar
is killing not his own, but his mistress' brother. Even in a comparison with Medea, Caesar comes off second best.

Caesar's weakness in 10 may be ascribed to a variety of causes.
Lucan was probably well involved in the Pisonian conspiracy by
this time, and perhaps he found that this gave him the confidence
to diminish Caesar's stature in the *Pharsalia*. Although the poet's
political activities may have played some part, the change can be
explained on the basis of the content of book 10. For, under the
influenec of Cleopatra and her decadent court, Caesar becomes softened in his purpose and determination. Like Aeneas, he dallies at
the court of a future enemy of Rome, learning there the taste for
luxury: "discit opes Caesar spoliati perdere mundi" (10.169)
(Caesar learns how to dissipate the wealth of a plundered world).
He neglects his destiny—the destruction of the remains of the republic—while squandering his time in debauchery with an Egyptian love and preferring not to conquer for himself (79–81).
Echoes and reminiscences of *Aeneid* 1 and 4 are frequent in
Lucan's account of Caesar's stay at Cleopatra's court.

While Aeneas' affair with Dido sheds a not altogether favorable
light on Vergil's hero, Caesar's affair with Cleopatra elicits a
Juvenalian *saeva indignatio* from Lucan:

> et in media rabie medioque furore
> et Pompeianis habitata manibus aula
> sanguine Thessalicae cladis perfusus adulter
> admisit Venerem curis, et miscuit armis
> inlicitosque toros et non ex coniuge partus. [10.72–76]

(In mid-madness and mid-rage, in the court haunted by the
ghost of Pompey, soaked in the blood of the massacre in
Thessaly, the adulterous Caesar allowed Venus access in the
midst of his anxieties and intermingled an illicit liaison and
bastard children with warfare.)

Venus, the goddess of his family, is reduced to mere "Lust." Cleopatra, like Caesar, is reduced to a sordid, amoral creature. She is a painted whore sagging beneath the weight of necklaces and jewels (137–140). As her foe Pothinus observes, "She controls Egypt; and Rome is hers for services rendered (Aegypton habet Romamque meretur)" (359). There is no trace of the nobility of Vergil's Dido, and the negative effects of Caesar's liaison are far greater than those of Aeneas'. Although we find Aeneas tricked out in luxurious Carthaginian clothing in *Aen.* 4.261–264, there is no suggestion that Aeneas maintained this kind of attire after leaving Carthage. Lucan, on the other hand, accuses Caesar of having his luxurious tastes whetted by the visit to Alexandria (10.146–171). Not only does he feel ashamed of the low-cost war he fought with Pompey (171), but he establishes the precedent for the subsequent affair between Antony and Cleopatra, the dissipation of the world's wealth, and the importation of extravagant living to Rome. Along with these offenses, he leaves behind in Egypt a *parvulus Caesar,* and a woman eager to control the Roman world. He had, Lucan notes, kindled Cleopatra's ambition to hold an Egyptian triumph in Italy itself, and to lead in that procession a Caesar as prisoner (10.60–67).

Not only does Caesar act against Roman interests; he acts against his own. "Dum hon sibi vincere mavolt" (10.81) (he prefers, at this point, not to conquer on his own behalf). His bastard child by Cleopatra, Caesarion, is a potential rival for his adopted son Octavian. Thus it is not altogether surprising that he loses some of his great, if demented, courage, much of which has been predicated upon the fact that he and his cause are one and the same. Gold is no longer a means to power, power is a means to acquire gold and the luxuries of a decadent life. This, surely, is the reason for Lucan's comparisons of Caesar to an unwarlike child and a terrified woman—or even Medea. He has been softened and effeminized by the court of Alexandria.

Perhaps it is more than coincidence, then, that Caesar, not Cleopatra, seeks to stretch out the night in conversation (10.172 ff.). In the *Aeneid,* by way of contrast, it is Dido who cannot bear to let her guest depart (*Aen.* 1.748–749). While Dido wants to learn about Aeneas and Troy, Caesar wants to learn the

secrets of Egypt from Achoreus the sage (*Aen.* 1.748 ff., *Pharsalia*
10.176–193). Yet we should not infer that Caesar's megalomania
has lapsed under the influence of the Alexandrian court. It is
merely given a different coloring, as Caesar's words to Achoreus
show. "Betray the [secrets of] the gods to me; they want to be be
trayed (noscique volentes / prode deos)" (10.180–181). Then he
continues:

> Si Cecropium sua sacra Platona
> maiores docuere tui, quis dignior umquam
> hoc fuit auditu mundique capacior hospes?
> fama quidem generi Pharias me duxit ad urbes,
> sed tamen et vestri; media inter proelia semper
> stellarum caelique plagis superisque vacavi,
> nec meus Eudoxi vincetur fastibus annus.
> sed, cum tanta meo vivat sub pectore virtus,
> tantus amor veri . . .   [10.181–189]

(But if your ancestors taught Athenian Plato their holy rites
was there ever a visitor more worthy than I to hear them—a
visitor more capable of grasping the universe? It was the rumor
about my son-in-law that brought me to the cities of Egypt, I
admit; but it was also your reputation. I always have enough
time, between battles, for the regions of the stars and the skies
and for the powers above. My year will not be outdone by
Eudoxus' calendar. But since such great virtue flourishes in my
heart and such great love of truth . . .)

Caesar now claims for himself philosophical, not just military vir
tue. He has won his battle with Eudoxus, as well as with Pompey;
his calendar will rule the year as he will rule the cities of the
world. Surely the honor accorded Plato cannot be denied him, for
he has made himself master and regulator of the cosmos. Megalomania could hardly extend further.

In sum, the Caesar of the *Pharsalia* stands in stark contrast to
the quietly understated Caesar of the *Civil Wars.* It is a study of
demonic megalomania handled with sufficient skill to elicit a
sardonic smile as often as a shudder. Lucan's Caesar is simultane-
ously awesome and preposterous. Unlike the superstitious and

earful Eteocles of Statius' *Thebaid* or Seneca's Lycus, he is not a
mall man made large by his despotic position.[21] He does not fence
imself with steel against the consequences of his actions through-
ut most of the epic. On the contrary, he exposes himself freely to
ll the threats that man and nature can hurl against him, firm in
he belief that there is nothing that will not bow to his command.
Only when his sense of purpose is weakened by his affair with
Cleopatra and by his taste for Egyptian luxury does he begin to
ssume the dimensions of the rhetorical tyrant figure. And Cleopatra is as worthy a woman for Caesar as Cornelia is for Pompey
r Marcia for Cato. While Cato and Marcia share an ascetic dedi-
ation to the interests of the state and treat sex solely as a means
f procreation, while Pompey and Cornelia share a deep and
personal love, Caesar and Cleopatra use one another sexually as
hey do politically: to satisfy their amoral lusts.[22] Lucan gives no
int that Cleopatra reciprocates Caesar's passion; she merely suc-
umbs to it for her own political purposes. Thus Caesar very
early passes on to her the world that Rome, according to Curio,
as conquered for him.[23]

Caesar's ultimate victory in the civil wars, then, brings to Rome
he trappings of Eastern luxury, religion, and monarchy—and
very nearly an Egyptian woman to rule it. Pothinus, Achillas, and
Ganymede are but forerunners of the mercenaries and eunuchs
who were to control the Roman empire, people who, until the
ime of Caesar, had no place in the politics of Rome. To Lucan's
contemporary reader, the scenario of Alexandria in *Pharsalia* 10
must have been something all too familiar in the Rome of their
own day. This, presumably, is why Lucan stresses that Caesar was

21. For a different view, see Syndikus, 95: "Lucan seinen Caesar nicht als
ebendige Person, sondern nur als Verkörperung des Tyrannentypus gesehen
und geschildert hat." This is an oversimplification, in my opinion. The conventional tyrant is usually portrayed as struggling with a sense of fear or per-
onal inadequacy; his viciousness is generally a sign of some inner weakness.
Other characteristics of the "typical" tyrant missing in Caesar are vengeful-
ess and treachery.

22. See Chapter 5, Section II, for Pompey and Cornelia; Chapter 7, Sec-
ion III, for Cato and Marcia.

23. For Curio's comment, see 1.284–291; for Lucan's reaction to Cleopatra's
hreat to Rome, see 10.63–66.

CHAPTER 7

Cato

Caesar and Pompey are introduced early in the first book of the *Pharsalia*. Cato, though mentioned in book 1, does not enter the action until book 2. The most obvious reason for this delay is that introduction of a third major figure would destroy the symmetry of Lucan's antithesis between Caesar and Pompey. But not only is Cato introduced later than the other protagonists, he is presented in an altogether different way. While Lucan gives brief thumbnail sketches of Caesar and Pompey, highlighted by metaphor and simile, he painstakingly prepares for Cato's entrance. Further, he uses allegory rather than more simple figures of speech to suggest Cato's relationship to his theme. Cato cannot be summed up in a relatively straightforward comparison with an oak tree or a thunderbolt; Lucan does not want to simplify him in this manner.

Lucan's best-known line warns us even in book 1 that Cato functions on a different plane from either Caesar or Pompey:

victrix causa deis placuit sed victa Catoni. [1.128]

(The conquering cause pleased the gods, but the conquered cause pleased Cato.) [1]

Cato is matched against the gods as one of the great judges whose protection the warring factions seek (1.127). Yet this early glimpse

1. See also Chapter 8, especially Section III. On Cato's political signficance see A. Afzelius, "Die politische Bedeutung des jüngeren Catos," *CM* 4 (1941), 100–203 and Wünsch, *passim*. Other discussions are in Nehrkorn, 229–233; W. M. Alexander, "Cato of Utica in the Works of Seneca Philosophus," *TRSC* 3 ser. 40 (1946), 59–74; Due, "Lucain et la philosophie," 203–232; Burck, "Vom Menschenbild"; Marti, "Meaning of the *Pharsalia*"; Syndikus, *passim*, and especially 98 ff.; Pfligersdorffer, 344 ff.; Friedrich, "Cato, Caesar und Fortuna bei Lucan," 405 ff.; other sources are cited in note 33, Chapter 1.

of Cato catches us so unprepared that we might almost mistake it
for an ironical suggestion that Cato's ideals are futile (as Caesar
implies they are in 1.131). Having thus presented Cato, briefly
but memorably, Lucan moves on. Enough has been said to distinguish him from other characters. Any more would link him
too closely with the origins and causes of war. Lucan, I suspect
wanted all this out of the way before Cato entered. Further, after
Cato is introduced in book 2, he is to all intents and purposes
abandoned by Lucan until book 9. He is carefully separated from
the actual conflict until Pompey is dead.

By way of a preamble to our discussion of Cato it is necessary
to study the context into which Lucan inserts him in *Pharsalia* 2
Only by examining the first 233 lines of this book can we appreciate the subtlety with which Lucan develops the imagery essential
for his presentation of Cato.

I. Preparing the Way

In the concluding sections of *Pharsalia* 1, Lucan subjects the
reader to a barrage of prodigies and prophecies demonstrating that
the outbreak of civil war is heralded and approved by the universe
as a whole. Indeed, as the opening lines of 2 show, the cosmos is
ready for the conflict.[2]

> Iamque irae patuere deum manifestaque belli
> signa dedit mundus legesque et foedera rerum
> praescia monstrifero vertit natura tumultu
> indixitque nefas. [2.1-4]

> (Now the anger of the gods was revealed; the universe gave clear
> indication of war. Nature, knowing in advance what would
> occur, reversed the laws and bonds of matter in a tumult of
> prodigies, and declared [the rule of] crime.)

Lucan establishes an important rhetorical point here, which will
be vital for the portrait of Cato: the whole universe, not just

2. On the phenomena at the end of 1, see C. Floratos, Ἡ προφήτεια τοῦ
P. Nigidius Figulus, Athens, 1958; R. J. Getty, "The Astrology of P. Nigidius
Figulus," *CQ* 35 (1941), 17 ff., and "Neo-Pythagoreanism and Mathematical
Symmetry in Lucan, *De Bello Civili* I," *TAPA* 91 (1960), 310-323; E. Dutoit
"Le Thème de 'la force qui se détruit elle-même' et ses variations chez quel-
ques auteurs latins," *REL* 14 (1936), 365-373; and Morford, 59-74.

Caesar, Pompey, and the Roman people, is morally responsible
for the outbreak of civil war.[3] Jupiter earns special censure for
permitting foreknowledge of disaster:

> cur hanc tibi, rector Olympi,
> sollicitis visum mortalibus addere curam,
> noscant venturas ut dira per omina clades?   [4–6]

(Why, ruler of Olympus, did it seem right to you to add this
anxiety to harrassed humanity—that they should learn of the
catastrophes ahead through hideous omens?)

Yet Lucan does not commit himself to a simplistic explanation, as-
signing all blame for the crime of civil war to Jupiter. This would
be too close to the conventional epic mode. Perhaps, he suggests,
the course of events has been predetermined from the beginning
of time, binding even the creator of the universe, as the Stoics believed (7–11). On the other hand, perhaps the Epicureans are
right: nothing is fixed, and chance rules supreme (12–13). The
philosophical dilemma is left unresolved.[4] Lucan returns to Jupiter
to make a special plea:

> sit subitum quodcumque paras; sit caeca futuri
> mens hominum fati; liceat sperare timenti.   (14–15)

(May whatever you plan come unexpectedly. Let the mind of
man be blind to fate; let him have hope when he is afraid.)

Fear of the future becomes a prominent motif for the next two
hundred lines. In lines 16–19, the city is paralyzed by fear:

> ergo, ubi concipiunt quantis sit cladibus orbi
> constatura fides superum, ferale per urbem
> iustitium; latuit plebeio tectus amictu
> omnis honos, nullos comitata est purpura fasces.
> tum questus tenuere suos magnusque per omnis
> erravit sine voce dolor.

3. For the guilt of the Roman people, the *publica semina belli*, see *Pharsalia* 1.158–182; and U. Piacentini, *Osservazioni sulla tecnica epica di Lucano*,
Berlin, 1963, 22–27; also Chapter 3 above. In attributing guilt to nature and
making it almost evil, Lucan goes beyond usual Stoic convention. A more
typical view is that of Marcus Aurelius *Commentaries* 2.17: "οὐδὲν δὲ κακὸν κατὰ
φύσιν." Lucan's view can be most readily paralleled in Senecan tragedy.
4. One Lucan's view of fate and the gods, see Chapter 8.

(Therefore, when they realize what the reliability of the gods is
going to cost the world in terms of disaster, business is suspended in mourning; high-ranking officials conceal themselves
in plebeian clothing; no more do consuls wear the purple. People suppress their complaints, and their great grief wanders
among them, voiceless.)

The atmosphere that pervaded Ariminum when Caesar arrived
(1.257–258) now grips Rome. Lucan compares it to the first shock
of death upon a household, the moments before the reality of what
has occurred fully registers upon the bereaved (2.21–24). Then
parents begin to crowd around the altars of the gods, and the
mourning begins. A nameless mother utters her prayer, begging
only for the end of the war, indifferent to which side wins (28–42).
Others complain that they were not born in the days of Hannibal;
then, at least, they would have died fighting a foreign foe (45–63).
General complaints spill forth from anonymous voices. They are,
Lucan observes, the result of torn and confused loyalties: "talis
pietas peritura querellas / egerit" (63–64). The last emanates from
an old man, who recalls in detail the hideous sufferings of Rome
during the power struggle between Marius and Sulla (68–232).
His final sentiment is that, no matter which of the two adversaries
wins, neither will stop even where the bloody Sulla stopped:
"neuter civilia bella moveret / contentus quo Sulla fuit." (231–
232).

Several important themes emerge from these passages. First,
that of parental grief and death in the household; second, the sensation that there is little or no choice between the combatants. But
dominating all is the fear and anxiety caused by the divine prodigies which forecast disaster.

At line 234, Lucan introduces Brutus, and contrasts him with
the general atmosphere of anonymous fear suggested by the first
233 lines of book 2: "at non magnanimi percussit pectora Bruti /
terror" (but terror has not stunned the heart of great-souled
Brutus). While others are terrified of the divine portents, reduced
to utter inactivity by self-pity and gloomy prognostications of the
future, Brutus knocks upon the doors of Cato's unpretentious
house: "atria cognati pulsat non ampla Catonis" (238). Lucan's
use of the word *cognatus* subtly underscores the relationship be-

tween Brutus and Cato: they are, in fact, *gener* and *socer* respectively and, as such, a curious doublet of Pompey and Caesar. While Pompey and Caesar put their own interests to the forefront, the prime concern of Brutus and Cato is with the welfare of the state. Brutus finds Cato wide awake and deep in thought although it is night:

> invenit insomni volventem publica cura
> fata virum casusque urbis cunctisque timentem
> securumque sui . . . [239–241]

(He finds him pondering affairs of state in sleepless anxiety: the fates of men, the plight of the city; full of fear for everyone else, but untroubled about himself.)

Brutus has come with a complex moral and political problem for Cato to solve. He confesses he is unsure what to do in the crisis and calls upon Cato for guidance: "tu mente labantem / dirige me" (244–245). Others, he declares, may follow Pompey or Caesar, but Cato is his only leader: "dux Bruto Cato solus erit" (247). If Brutus is distinguished from the crowd by his fearlessness, this appeal distinguishes Cato not only from the crowd but from Brutus, setting him apart from even the most courageous men.

What is Cato to do now that civil war has broken out? Brutus asks. Is he to stand aside as the world is plunged into chaos (247–248), or is he to involve himself in the struggle on one side or the other (249–250)? If he chooses the latter course, he runs the risk of condoning the civil war, and even of justifying it (*ibid.*). Perhaps, though, he finds war pleasing in and of itself: "tibi uni / per se bella placent?" (255–256). If this is true, Brutus contends, does it not make mockery of Cato's attempts to live a pure and unsullied life? After all, he stands to gain nothing personally from the conflict, as Caesar and Pompey do, since his goal is virtue, not power (256–257). War will inevitably make him guilty; for people will rush to die beneath his holy sword (259–266)) in an attempt to die a noble death in an ignoble conflict. Above all, Cato's involvement in the war will seem to justify, and will certainly please, Caesar, even if he joins the other side (273–276).

Brutus' arguments closely resemble those adduced by Seneca in
Epistle 14.13:

Potest aliquis disputare an illo tempore capessenda fuerit sapienti res
publica. "Quid tibi vis, Marce Cato? iam non agitur de libertate; olim
pessumdata est. quaeritur, utrum Caesar an Pompeius possideat rem
publicam; quid tibi cum ista contentione? nullae partes tuae sunt;
dominus eligitur. Quid tua, uter vincat? Potest melior vincere, non
potest non peior esse qui vicerit."

(One can easily dispute as to whether a wise man should have taken
up the cause of the republic at this point. "What do you want for
yourself, Marcus Cato? This is not a battle for liberty, which is long
gone. The issue is whether Caesar or Pompey will gain possession of
the republic. What has this conflict to do with you? Neither cause is
yours. A tyrant is being selected. What does it matter to you who wins?
The better man has the ability to win, but the one who finally wins
cannot fail to be the worse.")

Seneca never adequately resolves the dilemma, though he
promises to return to the subject later. His tentative advice in the
meantime is that one should follow the example of those Stoics
who have chosen to withdraw from politics.[5] Lucan, however,
chooses to tackle the issue as soon as Cato is introduced. Brutus
becomes the spokesman for the school of thought which advocates
noninvolvement in politics.[6] Cato should either stand aside until

5. "Sed postea videbimus, an sapienti opera rei publicae danda sit; interim
ad hos te Stoicos voco, qui a re publica exclusi secesserunt ad colendam vitam
et humano generi iura condenda sine ulla potentioris offensa" (*Ep.* 14.14).
Seneca seems to feel that a Stoic's course of action in this matter is determined by his own personal character. But at no stage does he adequately
answer the question as to whether the wise man should participate in politics.
See note 16 below for the paradox that the one who finally wins must be the
worse.

6. Lucan's personal attitude seems to favor political involvement. But see
Chapter 6, Section I for the problem of his observations in *Pharsalia* 4. Some
further insight may be gained on this problem by comparing the interchange
between Cotta and Metellus in *Pharsalia* 3.112–168. While Cato in 2 opts for
involvement, Cotta recommends acquiescence in Caesar's usurpation of power,
and dissuades Metellus from confronting Caesar. On balance, at least insofar
as Lucan represents them, Cato's decision seems more laudable than that of
Cotta (3.143–149). Cotta suggests that the ghost of liberty can be preserved
if you are willing to do whatever you are ordered to do: "si quidquid iubeare
velis." But Cotta also concedes that the surrender of Rome is shameful and

a victor emerges, then fight him (2.281–284), or remain totally aloof:

> melius tranquilla sine armis
> otia solus ages, sicut caelestia semper
> inconcussa suo volvuntur sidera lapsu.
> fulminibus propior terrae succenditur aer,
> imaque telluris ventos tractusque coruscos
> flammarum accipiunt; nubes excedit Olympus.
> lege deum minimas rerum discordia turbat,
> pacem magna tenent. [266–273]

(You would be better advised to observe a solitary, tranquil peace of mind. Don't take up arms. The stars in heaven rotate for ever unshaken in their course. The air which is closer to the earth is scorched by thunderbolts, and the low places of the earth endure the winds and the flash of lightning. But Olympus rises above the clouds. Discord troubles the smallest elements; great things stay at peace. This is the law of the gods.)

Brutus' language in this passage is reminiscent of Lucretius' description of the gods and their abode in *De Rerum Natura* 5.146–155. In other words, it is suggestive of Epicurean *ataraxia* no less than of Stoic *apatheia*. Lucan cleverly subverts the position of those Stoics who argue against political involvement by stating their view in imagery evocative of Epicurean rather than of Stoic thought. This weakens the case for disinvolvement even before Cato's rebuttal. And, we should add, Brutus' speech is carefully arranged to facilitate that rebuttal.

Yet Lucan's primary concern is not the refutation of Stoics who advocate withdrawal from politics. After all, Seneca, for all his uncertainty on the issue of the sage and the republic, never questions Cato's Stoic sainthood. Lucan's real foes are those who might utilize this division in Stoic thought to undermine the contention that Cato really was the totally moral creature his followers believed him to be. He was doubtless aware that Caesarians could—

---

that its only justification lies in the fact that he and others could do nothing to stop it. Lucan studiously avoids directly censuring Cotta. Presumably he wants his reader to decide the issue for himself and, to tilt the scales against the policy of disinvolvement, relies on the fact that Cotta's argument is a rather lame rationalization.

and probably did—utilize these philosophical differences for political ends. By treating the problem of Cato's participation in the civil war in the philosophical context of a meeting between Brutus and Cato, Lucan avoids the necessity of a propaganda war with the Caesarians. Further, he enhances Cato's moral position by showing that Cato has given the problem of political neutrality very deep thought, and by providing him with the opportunity to state his opposition to it in a detailed response during his first appearance in the epic. Lucan realizes that this major moral dilemma must be solved immediately so that it will not interfere with the impact of his ideas at a later and more crucial stage.

Hardly less subtle is the manner in which Brutus' words at 266–273 are calculated to evoke impressions of Caesar as well as of the Epicurean gods. In emphasizing the vulnerability of earthly things to lightning, Lucan recalls the comparison of Caesar to a thunderbolt in 1.151–157. Cato, by withdrawing into Olympian tranquillity, can separate himself from the destruction wrought by Caesar upon the world. In short, Lucan has added a dimension to Brutus' speech of which Brutus is unaware but of which the reader is well aware.

The philosophical and political implications of Brutus' address can easily distract our attention from his treatment of Cato as a holy and oracular being. While keeping us occupied with a key issue of Stoic thought, Lucan has deified Cato. Further, the imagery he employs to suggest the divinity of Cato is drawn from the same source as the imagery used to suggest that Stoics who advocate withdrawal from politics are Epicurean—Lucretius:

> at illi
> arcano sacras reddit Cato pectore voces. [284–285]

(But Cato gave in reply these holy words from the shrine of his heart.)

Lucan is imitating, and indeed venturing beyond, Lucretius' comment about Empedocles and others in *De Rerum Natura* 1.737–739:

> ex adyto tamquam cordis responsa dedere
> sanctius et multo certa ratione magis quam
> Pythia quae tripodi a Phoebi lauroque profatur.

(They gave responses as if from the oracle of their hearts, with more sanctity—and a good deal more sound reasoning—than the Pythia who speaks from the tripod of Apollo, and with the blessing of Apollo's laurel.)

Lucretius almost apologizes for his boldness with *tamquam* (as if). What is a simile in Lucretius becomes a simple statement in Lucan. Cato is indeed an oracle. Lucan is doing with Cato what he accuses Fortune of doing with Caesar in 1.264–265:

> iustos Fortuna laborat
> esse ducis motus et causas invenit armis.

(Fortune works hard at justifying Caesar's actions, and finds reasons for his taking up of arms.)

In fact, Lucan's suggestions as to the divinity of Cato, combined with the Olympian imagery Brutus employs throughout his speech, give us the strange feeling that we are witnessing the equivalent of what would be, in a more conventional epic, a council of the gods. Since Lucan elsewhere ascribes to Brutus a sanctity similar to, though lesser than, that here ascribed to Cato, such an inference does not seem unreasonable. The usual formula involves a visit to Jupiter by a lesser deity who is perplexed or annoyed about the course of events on earth. Jupiter, when unable to offer moral justification for what is occurring, tends to fall back on the plea that the fates are responsible.[7] This is essentially the same course Cato adopts here in *Pharsalia* 2 when he responds to Brutus. The crucial difference, however, is that Cato clearly finds the evolution of events unjust and reprehensible, whereas Jupiter usually implies that what is happening is justified simply on the grounds that it is fated.

II. Cato's Reply

Cato immediately concedes that civil war is the highest of crimes: "summum . . . nefas" (286), but then argues that the

7. A typical example is Jupiter's reaction to the quarrel between Juno and Venus at the council of the gods in *Aeneid* 10.104–113, where he declares that he is a partisan of neither side: "rex Iuppiter omnibus idem. / fata viam invenient" (112–113). Contrast this with his clearly partisan declaration in *Aen.* 1.257–296.

fault is not his, but the gods'. They have set the course of things, and they are to blame for any guilt he himself incurs: "crimen erit superis et me fecisse nocentem" (288). This argument is not only uncomfortably similar to a typical *apologia* of Jupiter; it is reminiscent of Caesar's response to Patria in 1.203: "ille erit ille nocens, qui me tibi fecerit hostem" (He will be guilty, he who made me your enemy). But Cato, unlike Caesar, is not attempting to shrug off his guilt completely. He does not say that he is innocent, but that the gods have made him guilty. We realize now why Lucan so carefully establishes at the end of 1 and the beginning of 2 that the gods and nature are, in fact, guilty of the *nefas* of civil war in which Cato is about to become embroiled.

We may even detect a note of something resembling heresy (in Stoic terms) in Cato's opening words. In 2.287, Cato declares: "sed quo fata trahunt virtus secura sequetur" (But virtue will follow unconcerned wherever the fates drag her). This expression bears a strong resemblance to a recognized catch phrase of Stoicism. Yet a comparison with the famous line of Cleanthes, translated by Seneca in *Ep.* 107.11, shows something odd: "ducunt volentem fata, nolentem trahunt" (The fates lead the willing man and drag the unwilling). Similarly, in *De Providentia* 5.4, Seneca notes: "boni viri . . . non trahuntur a fortuna, sequuntur illam" (good men are not dragged by fortune, they follow her). Lucan's attribution to Cato of the word *trăhunt* rather than *dūcunt* here may be more then merely *metri causa,* for it suggests unwillingness on Cato's part to follow the path prescribed by destiny, even though he has no fears about doing so. In short, he follows, but he disapproves.

Lucan's dilemma in dealing with Cato's entry in *Pharsalia* 2 is reminiscent of the problem Vergil faces with Aeneas in *Aeneid* 2. Aeneas is, like Cato, endowed with the appropriate instincts to perish along with his city.[8] Vergil has to cope with the Roman notion that the proper thing for Aeneas to have done was to die in the defense of Troy. Only a traitor would act otherwise.[9] Vergil's

8. Particularly *Aeneid* 2.314–317, 348–354, 668–670. The second of these passages shows Aeneas in an almost Cato-like frame of mind, particularly line 354: "una salus victis nullam sperare salutem."

9. For a discussion of the tradition of Aeneas *proditor* and Vergil's reaction to Aeneas' *pietas,* see Galinsky, 3–61.

approach to the dilemma is to imply that Aeneas' suicidal impulses are irrational and then to dwell in detail upon the painful steps whereby Aeneas is finally induced to leave. When Venus appears to Aeneas and reveals that the gods themselves are actively engaged in the destruction of Troy (*Aeneid* 2. 594–620), she points out that the inclemency of the gods, not any human action, is to blame: "divum inclementia, divum" (602). She makes the same point about divine malevolence that Lucan and Lucan's Cato make in *Pharsalia* 2. But, in Venus' case, the argument is made, first, to persuade Aeneas not to kill Helen and, second, to get him to leave Troy, since it is doomed. Divine guilt exculpates Aeneas and the Trojans and makes self-sacrifice futile. Instead, Aeneas is asked to become the instrument of those very powers whose inclemency has destroyed his homeland.

In the *Pharsalia,* Lucan wishes to reestablish the notion that self-sacrifice in a doomed but worthy cause is not futile, that clinging to the ghosts of the past may, in fact, be morally correct. His difficulty lies in how to maintain the facade of Cato's morality in light of the fact that Cato involved himself in a civil war that Lucan regards as immoral. Perhaps this is why the opening passages of *Pharsalia* 2 seem so suggestive of *Aeneid* 2. The visions of doom, the depredations of Marius and Sulla that are recalled by the anonymous old man remind us of Vergil's description of the fall of Troy. But Cato's reaction to all that is going on around him is diametrically opposed to Aeneas' jumbled perceptions. Cato knows that Rome is doomed. Aeneas has to be convinced by a series of portents that Troy is really lost; in fact, his unconscious mind has not even grasped that Hector is dead.[10] Aeneas' desire to die at Troy stems from passion; Cato's desire to die for Rome is the result of calm deliberation and reflection, as we shall see in the next section.[11] Most poignantly of all, however, we must note

10. See also Chapter 6, Section III and note 9.

11. For Aeneas' madness see the passages cited above in note 8. Note line 314: "arma amens capio; nec sat rationis in armis"; lines 317–318: "furor iraque mentem praecipitat"; cf. Venus' remarks at 2.594–598, and Galinsky's discussion of Aeneas' behavior in 2. Such emotional reaction indicates loss of self-control; as such, it is in Stoic terms morally evil. See E. V. Arnold, *Roman Stoicism,* Cambridge, 1911, 352, and E. Zeller, *The Stoics, Epicureans and Sceptics* (trans. O. J. Reichel), London, 1880, 236–237; Cicero *Fin.* 3.10.35; *Tusc.* 4.22; and Seneca *Prov.* 2.1.

the contrast between Aeneas and Creusa on the one hand, and
Cato and Marcia on the other. But first let us turn to Cato's decision to fight and die for what is left of Rome.

Cato rejects out of hand the idea that he should assume an attitude of divine indifference to the impending civil war, as Brutus
recommends.[12] He compares the chaos of civil war to the collapse
of the universe—a notion Lucan first develops in 1.72–80, and
which Lucretius uses for different reasons in *De Rerum Natura*
5.380–383. Obviously a human being cannot survive alone when
the universe is consumed, as he can, presumably, during a civil
war. But Cato argues that, just as no one would *want* to survive
cosmic catastrophe, so no one would *want* to remain untouched
in the midst of national disaster (289–292). Cato's reasoning fits in
with the rhetorical and political view Lucan maintains throughout
the *Pharsalia*, that the fate of Rome in the civil wars will be, to all
intents and purposes, the same as the fate of a city that falls to an
alien conqueror. Just as it is better to die than to live to see your
people overrun by a foreign foe, so it is better to die than to see
your people succumb to a native-born tyrant. Lucan is merging
traditional notions of patriotism with the Stoic idea of the individual's reaction to universal catastrophe. But it is worth noting
that, in this passage at least, the philosophical seems to be used to
strengthen Cato's political dimensions rather than vice versa. Cato,
unlike the Epicurean ideal man, is not in the least apolitical. He
considers it nothing short of madness to stand aside from a war in
which nations from all over the world will be fighting (292–297).
The contrast with Lucretius' vision of the pleasure of disinvolvement is marked:

> Suave, mari magno turbantibus aequora ventis,
> e terra magnum alterius spectare laborem;
> non quia vexari quemquamst iucunda voluptas,
> sed quibus ipse malis careas quia cernere suave est.
> suave etiam belli certamina magna tueri
> per campos instructa tua sine parte pericli.
>
> [*De Rer. Nat.* 2.1–6]

---

12. For another discussion of Cato's entry into the civil war, see A. Kopp,
"Staatsdenken und politisches Handeln bei Seneca und Lucan," Diss. Heidelberg, 1969, 139–164.

(It is pleasant, when the winds are churning up the surface of the sea with mighty waves, to watch the mighty struggle of someone else from dry land; not because it is a joyous sensation to see someone in trouble, but because it is pleasant to behold evils which you yourself are free from. It is also pleasant to gaze upon the great conflicts of war, battlelines drawn up across the plains, when you have no part in the danger.)

Cato, far from desiring to separate himself from the civil war, sees his relationship to Rome as that of a bereaved parent to his dead children:

> ceu morte parentem
> natorum orbatum longum producere funus
> ad tumulos iubet ipse dolor, iuvat ignibus atris
> inseruisse manus constructoque aggere busti
> ipsum atras tenuisse faces, non ante revellar
> exanimem quam te complectar, Roma; tuumque
> nomen, Libertas, et inanem persequar umbram.   [297–303]

(Grief bids me marshal the long funeral procession to the grave, just as it bids a bereaved parent to do so when his children die: you want to put your hands into those black flames, and bring black torches to kindle the fires when the pyre has been built. I shall not be torn away from you, Rome, before I embrace your lifeless body and your name, Liberty; and I shall follow your empty ghost to the grave.)

Cato, like Pompey, sees his relationship to Rome in very personal terms.[13] But, as Lucan points out in 9, and as Cato points out here, it is that of parent to child; he is the protector of the city, not its lover, as Pompey is.[14]

13. See note 6 above and Chapter 6, Section I, for a discussion of whether Lucan shares Cato's view. Lucan's personal comments in 7.134–137 and 9.598–604 suggest he does.

14. The idea of Cato being the father of the city gives him a certain god-like quality. Compare Seneca's observations about the paternal attitude of god: "patrium deus habet adversus bonos viros animum" (Prov. 2.6); ibid., 1.5: "parens ille magnificus" and Ep. 110: "deus et parens noster." Since, in Seneca's judgment, Cato is not just the exemplar of the Stoic wise man, but something more: "vereor ne supra nostrum exemplar sit" (Constant. 7.1), the divine qualities become even more apparent. For the wise man is similar to god in everything but his mortality: "sapiens . . . vicinus proximusque deis

This passage should warn us that we will severely misconstrue Lucan's Cato if we regard him solely as a Stoic hero, more dedicated to pure philosophy than to political ideals.[15] It should also remind us that Cato differs from the anonymous mother who prays only for the safety of her children at the beginning of *Pharsalia* 2. For, though Cato's funereal imagery picks up the earlier atmosphere of gloom (16–21) and vastly expands the funereal simile of 21–28, Cato realizes that the civil war marks the end of the republic, of Rome, and of Liberty. While others grieve for individual children, he is determined to attend the last rites of Rome herself. Though Brutus envisages the possibility that people will attempt to die upon Cato's sword, Cato wishes that he could become a sacrificial scapegoat for Rome, the target of every spear (306–318).

Cato's desire to undergo *Opfertod* for the sake of Rome and its peoples places him in the succession of self-sacrificing heroes that Roman literature extols so often: the Decii, Lucius Brutus, Regulus, Mettus Curtius, and Mucius Scaevola. Needless to say, it also had a very substantial impact on Lucan's Christian readers generations later. When Cato says, at 2.312: "hic redimat sanguis populos" (may this blood redeem the people), he is speaking a language Dante understands well, as we shall see shortly. Cato, unlike the gods, is not prepared to remain indifferent to, or to condone, the horrors which are about to occur. He would give his life to prevent them and thus provide the moral exemplar which the Olympians are unable—or unwilling—to provide. We begin to see what

consistit, excepta mortalitate, similis deo" (*ibid.*, 8.2); cf. *Ep.* 73.13, *Prov.* 1.5, and H. Usener, *Epicurea*, fr. 386. Further, as Seneca notes in *Prov.* 6.6, man is in some respects greater than god: "hoc est quo deum antecedatis; ille extra patientiam malorum est, vos supra patientiam"; cf. *Ep.* 53.11. Thus Cato is something more than the divine parent, in that he can, unlike god, die for his "children."

15. The view, that is, of Marti and Brisset. Yet O. S. Due, "An Essay on Lucan," *CM* 23 (1962), 68–132 goes a little too far in the opposite direction when he observes (86): "we may not regard Lucan as a philosopher"—a view that Syndikus maintains throughout his discussion of Lucan. I see so little difference between Lucan's view of Cato and that of Seneca that I find it hard to accept either extreme in this argument. Seneca's remark in *Ad. Marc.* 20.6 should warn us against too narrow an interpretation of Cato: "virum libertati non suae tantum sed rei publicae natum." He is a man born not just for his own freedom, but for that of the state.

Lucan meant earlier when he observed: "the conquering cause pleased the gods, but the conquered cause pleased Cato" (1.128). For what Cato approves is based on considerations of morality, of right and wrong, not on the inevitable historical outcome of events, as is usually the case with the epic Jupiter.

But Lucan has not solved the more pressing moral problem— how to have Cato enter the war on one side or the other when neither side is really good. The power of Cato's response to Brutus is such that it can easily obscure the abrupt and somewhat surprising decision Cato makes: to enter the war on Pompey's side (2.319–323). Lucan points out in 1.125–126, that it is not just impossible, but criminal, to decide whether Caesar or Pompey was more correct in taking up arms: "quis iustius induit arma / scire nefas." In fact, the only thing that seems to make Pompey's cause better at this stage is that he has Cato's approval (1.128 and 2.319–323). But Brutus suggests that if Cato were to join Pompey, Caesar would be left as the only free man in the world: "toto iam liber in orbe / solus Caesar erit" (280–281); in short, Caesar alone would be fighting for himself. This difficulty is evaded rather than answered by Cato, for Cato's decision to join Pompey is political rather than moral: [16]

> quin publica signa ducemque
> Pompeium sequimur? nec, si fortuna favebit,
> hunc quoque totius sibi ius promittere mundi

16. Seneca does not fare any better than Lucan on this score. Seneca clearly wants to see Cato as distinct from either the Caesarians or Pompeians: "alii ad Caesarem inclinarunt, alii ad Pompeium, solus Cato fecit aliquas et rei publicae partes" (*Ep.* 104.30); *ibid.*, 31: "illinc plebem . . . hinc optimates et equestrem ordinem . . . duos in medio relictos, rem publicam et Catonem"; also *ibid.*, 32, where Cato is determined to condemn himself regardless of who wins the war: "ait se, si Caesar vicerit, moriturum, si Pompeius exulaturum." It is evident from the last excerpt that Cato regards Pompey as the lesser of two evils, though *why* we never learn. In *Ad Marc.* 20.6 Seneca comments on the ill-fortune of Cato who, a few years after his annexation of Cyprus, was forced "Caesarem fugere, Pompeium sequi." The simplest justification for Cato's support of Pompey is, perhaps, the fact that Pompey lost. Lucan, Seneca, and Tacitus all suggest that it is better to lose a civil war: "potest melior vincere, non potest non peior esse qui vicerit" (Seneca *Ep.* 14.13); "vincere peius erat" (*Pharsalia* 7.706); see also 6.799–802, where Pluto prepares to punish the victor of the civil war: "paratque poenam victori" (801–802); "inter duos quorum bello solum id scires, deteriorem qui vicisset" (Tacitus *Hist.* 1.50).

non bene conpertum est: ideo me milite vincat
ne sibi se vicisse putet. [2.319–323]

(Shall we not follow the banner of the state and its [official] leader? I am well aware that, if Fortune favors him, he promises himself control of all the world. So let him conquer with me in the ranks so that he will not think he has conquered for himself.)

Pompey is the commander whose power is legally ratified by the senate; Caesar no longer legally holds office.

To add to the confusion, the impact of Cato's response on Brutus is expressed in somewhat ambiguous terms:

> sic fatur, et acris
> irarum movit stimulos iuvenisque calorem
> excitat in nimios belli civilis amores. [2.323–325]

(So he spoke, and goaded on the sharp anger of Brutus. He aroused the young man's passion to too great a love of civil war.)

Not only do Cato's words move Brutus from neutrality to active partisanship, but, unless I mistake Lucan's meaning, they produce an overreaction on Brutus' part. Haskins explains (ad loc.) that Brutus' passion is excessive because it leads to the murder of Caesar and the battle of Philippi. Yet Lucan appears to approve of the tyrannicide and of the struggle against Caesarism.[17] Perhaps the answer lies in this passage from 7, where Lucan comments on Brutus' attempt to kill Caesar at Pharsalia:

> o decus imperii, spes o suprema senatus,
> extremum tanti generis per saecula nomen,
> ne rue per medios nimium temerarius hostis,
> nec tibi fatales admoveris ante Philippos,
> Thessalia periture tua. [588–592]

(O glory of our power, last hope of the senate, the final name of a family so great throughout the centuries, do not rush too rashly through the enemy's ranks and bring fatal Philippi upon yourself before your time. You will die in your Thessaly.)

Again Lucan points out Brutus' penchant for hastiness and overreaction: compare *nimium temerarius* in 7.590 with *nimios belli*

17. See 7.586–596; 10.341–344.

civilis amores in 2.325. Brutus' reaction to Cato's speech, then, implies little more than Lucan's awareness of Brutus' fiery temperament as contrasted with Cato's calmer and stabler nature. Lucan presumably knew that Brutus, for all his republican greatness, was not a Stoic, much less a Stoic sage, as was Cato.[18]

Lucan's introduction to and apologia for Cato's involvement in the civil war is by no means completely watertight. But it is done with considerable ingenuity. Even the logical flaws he attempts to disguise with rhetoric are evidence of his desire to justify Cato, something he makes no effort to do in the cases of Caesar and Pompey. We are presented with a Cato who is the perfect Roman, the perfect sage—a man worthy of divine honors. But the scene between Cato and Brutus is not an end in itself. It is the crucial preface to the Cato-Marcia episode at 2.326–391, where all the carefully spun motifs of the first 325 lines are finally woven together.

III. Cato and Marcia

Dominant throughout the early sections of *Pharsalia* 2 are the funereal motifs. We move from the stunned grief of the city, which Lucan compares to the first shock of death upon a household, to the anxiety of a mother fearful for the lives of her children. Then the theme is developed in Cato's vision of himself as the bereaved parent of Rome, mourning the death of the city and of liberty as a father would mourn his children. Marcia's arrival takes us a step further. She comes to Cato's door grief-stricken at the death of her second husband, Hortensius (326–328). Lucan's epithet for Marcia, *sancta,* shows that he regards her with the same veneration he feels for Cato. And, as the episode progresses, we begin to appreciate why. Cato was Marcia's first husband; after the birth of their children he sent her to become the wife of Hortensius, so that Hortensius too could have children by Marcia.[19]

18. It has sometimes been assumed that Brutus was a Stoic, e.g., Brisset, 148 and note 1. See, however, Cicero *Att.* 13.12.3; 25.3. According to Cicero, Brutus' philosophy was the typical eclecticism of the Academy, "modo huc, modo illuc"; see Grimal, "Le Poète," 97.

19. 2.330–333. It is hard for the modern reader to comprehend, much less sympathize with, Cato's attitude to Marcia which resembles that of a farmer to a good breeding cow. But clearly Lucan comprehends and expects his reader to do so.

But now that Hortensius is dead, Marcia returns, asking that she
be permitted to become Cato's wife once more:

> dum sanguis inerat, dum vis materna, peregi
> iussa, Cato, et geminos excepi feta maritos:
> visceribus lassis partuque exhausta revertor
> iam nulli tradenda viro. da foedera prisci
> inlibata tori, da tantum nomen inane
> conubii; liceat tumulo scripsisse 'Catonis
> Marcia', nec dubium longo quaeratur in aevo
> mutarim primas expulsa an tradita taedas.
> non me laetorum sociam rebusque secundis
> accipis: in curas venio partemque laborum.
> da mihi castra sequi: cur tuta in pace relinquar
> et sit civili propior Cornelia bello?   [2.338–349]

(While there was blood in me, while I had the vitality for
motherhood, I carried out your orders, Cato. While I was fertile
I had two husbands. But now my womb is tired; I am worn out
from giving birth, and I return. Never again will I be given to
another man. Give me the right to return to the marriage bed
that I never shamed—give me at least the empty name of wife,
so that the inscription upon my tomb may read "Cato's
Marcia." Let it not be debated for years as to whether I married
another because you had driven me out of your house, or because you had given me to someone else. You will not be taking
me back to share in happiness and success; I come to share your
troubles and distress. Give me a cause that I can follow. Why
should I be left safe and far from war? Why should Cornelia be
nearer to the civil war than I?)

Marcia, like her husband, is aware that she is pursuing something
that no longer has any real existence. She wants the "nomen inane
conubii" (the empty name of marriage) (342–343); and his desire
is to embrace Rome, whose name and whose empty ghost, "inanem
umbram" (303), he will follow to the grave. Both are dedicated to
death not to life. The remarriage Marcia asks is little more than
the honor of dying as Cato's wife. She is old and tired, no longer
productive, ready to die. And Cato takes her back.

   In a stark ceremony, in bare and joyless surroundings, Cato and
Marcia are remarried with only Brutus as witness. Both display

the signs of mourning, not of joy. Cato has kept his beard un-
trimmed through grief at the civil war; Marcia wears her funeral
attire. The atmosphere is enhanced by Lucan's stress on the lack
of traditional features of a wedding ceremony. There are no flowers, no ritual crossing of the threshold to a bed decorated with
gold coverlets, no maidenly blushes from the bride.[20] Marcia kisses
Cato as she would kiss a son rather than a husband: "quoque
modo natos hoc est amplexa maritum" (366). Although she had
asked for the right to return to the marriage bed she had never
shamed: "da foedera prisci / inlibata tori" (341–342), Lucan tells
us that Cato will abstain from sexual intercourse with his wife.
And, to add emphasis to his comments, he uses words designed to
echo Marcia's request: "nec foedera prisci / sunt temptata tori"
(378–379).

Their reunion, then, will be ascetic and sexless. As far as Cato
is concerned, the sole (or essential, if we read *maximus* for *unicus*)
purpose of sex is the procreation of children:

> Venerisque huic unicus usus
> progenies: urbi pater est urbique maritus,
> iustitiae cultor, rigidi servator honesti,
> in commune bonus. [387–390]

(To him the sole purpose of sex is procreation; he is a father
to the city, and a husband; a man dedicated to justice, a pre-
server of uncompromising honesty, a man good for the community.)

Lucan now makes explicit what is already implicit. Cato's reunion
with Marcia is indeed an allegory. The republic, worn out and no
longer productive, will be reunited with the man who is the embodiment of the ideals upon which it was founded. The Roman
state, like Marcia, had been entrusted to other less worthy men;
now it returns to the ideal, in a marriage that is really a preparation for death. As Marcia embraces Cato, the shadow of her funeral robe eclipses the shining senatorial purple of Cato's toga:
"obsita funerea celatur purpura lana" (367). And there could be
no more appropriate witness to this moment than Brutus, the de-

20. 2.350–364.

scendant of the founder of Roman freedom who will himself avenge liberty lost.

The scene with Marcia emphasizes the importance of Cato in Lucan's eyes. He is a man who believes himself born not merely for himself, but for the whole world: "nec sibi sed toti genitum se credere mundo" (383). While Pompey is unable to escape the temptation to reduce the world to his own scale, confusing *Roma* with its anagram, *amor*, Cato would expand himself to encompass the universe. As if to reinforce the contrast with Pompey, when Lucan turns from Cato in 391, it is to Pompey's fearful retreat through Italy that he directs our attention: "interea trepido discedens agmine Magnus" (392) (Meanwhile Pompey, departing with his trembling army . . .).

To Dante the Cato-Marcia episode is an allegory in which Cato represents God and Marcia the noble soul returning to its master after a life of obedience to his will.[21] No doubt Lucan would have agreed with Dante that there is no earthly man more worthy to symbolize God than Cato.[22] For what Cato represents, even what Cato is, transcends the purely concrete and perishable. Dante, of course, views the scene in Christian rather than in pagan terms, but his construction of it reminds us how Christlike Lucan's Cato is, here and elsewhere in the *Pharsalia*. Yet Cato, unlike Christ, is dedicated to political as well as moral idealism. While it is true that he follows the guidelines of the Stoic sage, he is no less dedicated to his country: "naturamque sequi patriaeque inpendere vitam" (2.382) (to follow nature and to give his life for his coun-

21. *Convivio* 4.28. This is, by and large, a line-by-line, allegorical interpretation of *Pharsalia* 2.338–345. The only major alteration Dante makes is in his reading of 344–345, which appears as: "L'Altra che dopo me si dica che tu non mi scacciasti, ma di buono animo mi maritasti." Marcia's concern (in Lucan) with clearing up whether Cato had thrown her out of his house or simply given her to Hortensius is obviously not congenial to Dante's purposes. Major references to Cato in Dante seem to be drawn directly from Lucan: *Convivio* 4.5—*Pharsalia* 2.285 (cf. *Aeneid* 6.841); *Convivio* 4.27— *Pharsalia* 2.383; *Purgatorio* 1.31–36; 71–75—*Pharsalia* 2.372–378 and various other passages from 1 and 2. Obviously the Cato-Marcia scene was of particular interest to Dante, possibly because it was suggestive of his own relationship to Beatrice; see *Purgatorio* 1.78–79. *Purgatorio* 2.119–124 is possibly modeled on *Pharsalia* 9.256 ff. Similarly *Vita Nuova* 19.

22. Compare Dante's: "E quale uomo terreno più degno fu significare Iddio, che Catone? Certo nullo," with Lucan's praise of Cato in 9.601–604.

try). He will not concede that one should give unto Caesar, for, in his opinion, Caesar has no right to what he demands.

The funereal remarriage of Cato and Marcia stands in obvious contrast to the parting of Aeneas and Creusa in *Aeneid* 2, and draws our attention once more to the difference between the two epics. When Aeneas reenters the dead city of Troy in quest of his lost wife, he encounters only her ghost. Creusa tells him to go on his way to Italy, to look to the future and to the welfare of their son, Iulus. Aeneas' attempt to embrace her is futile, for she is an *umbra*, a ghost, as insubstantial as Aeneas is real. Husband and wife now exist on two distinct and irreconcilable planes. She has died with the city, Aeneas has not. Vergil seems to suggest not only the futility, but the impossibility of clinging to what is past and gone.[23] Aeneas can no longer have children by Creusa; he must find another wife. Troy is dead; he must find another city. His paternal and marital obligations must be redirected, along with his patriotism, to a new land. The remarriage of Cato and Marcia, on the other hand, reminds us that one may indeed embrace a ghost if one is dedicated to death rather than to life. Lucan presents the paradox that liberty, if not attainable in life, can be attained in death. Whereas Aeneas must continue to live to preserve the remnants of Troy, Cato must die to preserve the notion of liberty. Thus Cato's death is not something essentially negative. For an ideal does not require *physical* transmission from generation to generation, as the Trojan blood of Aeneas does. It demands, rather, an individual capable of bringing the ideal into tangible, living dimensions. This is the role Cato fulfills as father of the city. But, in ideological terms, the father of the city is also the husband of the city, in the sense that his example is the regenerative force that inspires others to follow in his footsteps. Without Aeneas, the remains of Troy would not have come to Italy; without Cato, the ideal of liberty might have perished along with the republic. As Lucan points out in 9.601, Cato is the true father of his country: "ecce parens verus patriae." And surely by this he

---

23. In the first six books of the *Aeneid*, Vergil seems intent on demonstrating the pointlessness of trying to relive or recreate the past. This can, perhaps, be best seen in Aeneas' visit to Buthrotum, especially the encounter with Andromache (3.294–355).

means its spiritual and moral father. Dante did not go far from the mark.

Throughout his appearance in book 2 Cato is remote, divine, and shadowy, as are those things to which he dedicates himself. It is, perhaps, not surprising that he who seeks to embrace the ghost of Rome and of liberty should take the side of Pompey, who is himself the ghost of a name. Caesar suggests in 1.313 that Cato too is an empty name and, to diminish his importance still further, refers to him in the plural: "nomina vana Catones" (the Catos, those empty names). The amoral Caesar does not grasp the importance of the ideal and the abstract as Cato does. But clearly Lucan perceives it. For the disappearance of such abstract moral principle is, in Lucan's view, fundamental to the disintegration of the Roman world.

IV. Pompey's Successor

Though Cato is mentioned from time to time in *Pharsalia* 3 through 8, he is not reintroduced into the action until book 9. This long absence is partially explicable in terms of history. Cato's actual contributions to the Pompeian war effort prior to Pompey's death were hardly of major importance. But Lucan turns this historical fact to rhetorical advantage. It enables him to keep Cato unsullied by the partisan struggles culminating in the battle of Pharsalia and Pompey's death:

> Ille, ubi pendebant casus dubiumque manebat
> quem dominum mundi facerent civilia bella,
> oderat et Magnum, quamvis comes isset in arma
> auspiciis raptus patriae ductuque senatus;
> at post Thessalicas clades iam pectore toto
> Pompeianus erat.   [9.19–24]

(While the outcome was hanging in the balance and it was uncertain as to whom civil war would make master of the world, Cato had hated Pompey too—even though he had joined his camp, judging this to be in the best interests of his country, and prompted by the leadership of the senate. But after the disaster in Thessaly he was wholeheartedly Pompeian.)

By the time Cato enters the scene again the war has devolved into a fight between Caesar and the republic rather than between

Caesar and Pompey: "totae post Magni funera partes / libertatis erant" (29–30) (After the death of Pompey, the cause was that of liberty). Pompey's widow, Cornelia, goes so far as to suggest that Pompey left explicit instructions to his sons that when he died they should follow only one man, Cato—provided that he undertook to embrace the cause of freedom: "uni parere decebit, / si faciet partes pro libertate, Catoni" (9.96–97). Although he disapproved of Pompey, Cato is, in fact, Pompey's successor. But the spirit of Pompey that enters the breasts of Cato and Brutus at the beginning of 9 has been purified and filled with the pure light of the aether beyond the terrestrial sphere (1–18).[24]

Cato gathers the remnants of the Pompeian army and sails to Africa. His forces are broken and defeated, as were those of Aeneas after the fall of Troy; indeed Lucan's mention of the fact that Cato's landing point in Africa is the coast of Palinurus suggests that the poet intends us to see a parallel with the hero of the *Aeneid*.[25] Cato's arrival in Africa marks the beginning of a new and crucial phase of the civil war. The first steps have been taken in the campaign that will culminate in the battle of Thapsus and the death of Cato at Utica.

It is, I believe, significant that Lucan gives immediate prominence to Cato in this preamble to the African war, but has little whatsoever to say about Metellus Scipio who, throughout the *Pharsalia*, merits hardly more than passing mention. This suggests that Lucan may well be more interested in Utica than in Thapsus itself.[26] Further, the shift of scene to Africa brings about something unique in Lucan and extremely rare in his epic predecessors: return to a location already visited. As a result, it is hard to avoid comparing Cato's arrival, and its consequences, with that of Curio in 4.581 ff.[27] Although the scene is much the same, Cato, the embodiment of the ideal of *libertas*, is as different from Curio, the epitome of Roman venality and decadence, as he could possibly be. Finally, Cato's behavior toward his troops during the march

---

24. For the location of Pompey's soul after death, see A. E. Housman's discussion in the apparatus criticus of his *M. Annaei Lucani Belli Civilis*, 255.

25. 9.39–47.

26. Especially if we note that Thapsus is never named in the *Pharsalia*.

27. See Chapter 3.

through Libya seems to be set in careful contrast to Caesar's behavior earlier in the epic.

V. Caesar and Cato

The contrast between Caesar and Cato emerges early in *Pharsalia* 9 and is sustained throughout the entire book. Cato's experiences in the first 949 lines recall Caesar's exploits in many details. But it is well to note that Lucan shuns explicit comparisons between the two men. He relies instead on the reader's recollection of Caesar's actions, particularly those of book 5, to make the necessary associations. His oblique approach has numerous rhetorical advantages. It allows the poet to establish that Cato is as capable of energetic and heroic action as Caesar is; in fact, as we shall see, he is able to surpass Caesar. Yet one cannot surpass without being compared, and direct comparison, flatly stated, would do Cato more harm than good, since Caesar's energy and bravery are associated with his inhuman capacity for destruction. The unstated parallels between Cato and Caesar enable Lucan to show how high moral principles can be combined with the ability to take swift and decisive action. Book 9 answers the question as to how Cato's ideals will work when put to the practical test. In 2 we saw only their theoretical and philosophical side in the relative calm of his house in Rome. Will they work on an extended military campaign in the hostile environment of North Africa?

The moment Cato assumes command of the republican forces in Africa he is confronted with a mutiny reminiscent of the one that faced Caesar in 5.237–273. His ideals, then, are immediately put to the test. Certain elements in the army feel, now that Pompey is dead, that the struggle with Caesar is over, just as Caesar's troops felt that the reason for further fighting had gone once Italy was in their hands. Cato lashes out at their hypocrisy:

> ergo pari voto gessisti bella iuventus,
> tu quoque pro dominis, et Pompeiana fuisti
> non Romana manus? quod non in regna laboras,
> quod tibi, non ducibus, vivis morerisque, quod orbem
> adquiris nulli, quod iam tibi vincere tutum est,
> bella fugis quaerisque iugum cervice vacanti
> et nescis sine rege pati . . .

> . . . meruistis iudice vitam
> Caesare non armis, non obsidione subacti.
> o famuli turpes, domini post fata prioris
> itis ad heredem.   [9.256–262; 272–275]

(So you were fighting the war with the same prayer in your hearts, young men. You too were fighting for tyranny. You were Pompey's soldiers, not Rome's, weren't you? You give up the struggle because you are not living and dying for your generals, because you are not conquering the world for someone, because it is now safe to fight for yourselves. You are looking for a yoke to wear, now that there is none upon your necks; you do not know how to endure without a king . . . You, who have neither been conquered in battle nor reduced by siege, deserve a life with Caesar as your judge. You vile lackeys! As soon as your first master is dead, you run to his heir.) [28]

Cato finds it hard to grasp the unwillingness of men to fight for freedom—to fight, that is, for themselves. This unwillingness is, in his opinion, a perversion of the human spirit. Soldiers such as these are in constant danger of confusing true *virtus* or *pietas* with what Vulteius calls *militiae pietas*. They are, in effect, transposing their dedication from the ideal of *libertas* to an individual leader. For this reason Cato regards Pompey's defeat and death, which is to some republicans the final defeat of their cause, as a benefit to the struggle for liberty rather than a loss. He, like Brutus, appreciates that liberty is doomed even if Pompey wins.[29] When Pompey dies, the triumvirate which had overshadowed the final years of the republic is reduced to one man.[30] The contest now is not between Caesar and Cato, since Cato seeks no power for himself, but between Caesar and the liberty which Cato champions. If the cause of the republic is victorious, liberty can triumph.

28. Cato's contemptuous use of the adjective *Pompeianus* seems to be paralleled in Senecan usage. G. Viansino has noted (*L. Annaei Senecae De Providentia—De Constantia Sapientis*, Rome, 1968, 77) that adjectives derived from a personal name, and ending in *-anus* are often disdainful in Seneca: *Prov.* 2.10, 3.7; *Ep.* 95.70; *De Ira* 3.1.1. Note, however, that Lucan uses the adjective *Pompeianus* of Cato in 9.23–24 without any unflattering connotations.
29. 2.77 ff. See note 30 below.
30. 9.265 ff. Cicero expresses a similar view in *Att.* 9.7.

Cato's method of dealing with recalcitrant troops is based on an appeal to their sense of shame and to their nobler instincts. He asks them, ironically, to take the chance to act for themselves and in their own interests—something they have, it appears, forgotten how to do. Caesar wants his soldiers to fight for his glory; Cato wants his soldiers to fight for their own freedom, for *libertas*. As far as Cato is concerned, Rome and freedom are synonymous. Keeping Rome free and keeping the individual citizen free are one and the same thing. To Caesar, the very word "citizen" is an insult.[31] Thus, while Caesar spurns his rebellious troops as unworthy of him, "cowardly civilians" who do not deserve to be called soldiers, much less *his* soldiers, Cato spurns those who would desert the republican cause as unworthy of Rome and a disgrace to themselves.

But Cato, unlike Caesar, is not prepared to go beyond the limits of reason, rhetoric, and persuasion. He will not attempt to punish those who would ground arms and return home. To do so would undercut the very message he is trying to convey. He cannot compel them to fight for themselves, he cannot make them fear him, as Caesar instills fear into his men. Cato can lead only by example and with the consent of his soldiers; he cannot terrorize them with threats and decimation. Should he attempt to do so, the cause of *libertas* would be ruined, for he would become like Caesar.

The contrast between Cato and Caesar becomes even clearer if we compare a later speech of Cato to his troops with an excerpt from Caesar's address to his army before Pharsalia:

> o quibus una salus placuit mea castra secutis
> indomita cervice mori . . . [9.379–380]

> (You men who have joined my forces, men who know but one salvation you can tolerate: death, free from the bonds of slavery . . .)

While Cato makes it clear that he expects loyalty to principle, not to himself, Caesar identifies his men with his own huge ambitions:

> o domitor mundi, rerum fortuna mearum,
> miles . . .

31. 5.358.

in manibus vestris, quantus sit Caesar, habetis.

$$[7.250-251; 253]$$

(Master of the world, guiding genius of my success: my soldier.
. . . You have in your hands the power to decide how great
Caesar will be.)

Cato draws men up to his own level; he invites them to emulate him; he ennobles them. Caesar reduces them to the level of
minions.

Everything about Cato marks him as an individual who behaves
in a way that distinguishes him from other men; he propounds
and practises a code of action that runs counter to the value system of popular ethics. Things that would please others offend him.
As his troops march through the arid wastes of North Africa, one
of his soldiers finds a small pool of water in the desert, scoops it
up, and offers it to him; Cato is angered by this action and threatens to punish the soldier by making him drink the water:

> "mene" inquit "degener unum
> miles in hac turba vacuum virtute putasti?
> usque adeo mollis primisque caloribus impar
> sum visus? quanto poena tu dignior ista es,
> qui populo sitiente bibas!"   [9.505–509]

("Degenerate soldier," he said, "did you think that I was the
only man in this band who lacked courage? Did I seem to be so
soft and unequal to the first hot weather we have encountered?
How much more worthy you are of this punishment than I am.
You are the one who should drink when everyone else is
thirsty.")

Haskins misses the whole point of the incident when he tries to
explain "poena . . . ista" as "this punishment which I inflict
upon myself, viz. to go without drinking." [32] Surely what Cato
means here is that it is a punishment to be obliged to drink when
others are thirsty. The offering of water constitutes, to his mind,
a slight upon his ability to endure. When Cato suggests that he

---

32. C. E. Haskins, note on 9.508. This episode stands in deliberate contrast
with 9.607–618 where Cato does drink first—though only because he suspects
that the water is poisoned.

might require the soldier to drink the water in front of the army, he is returning this "insult": he would humiliate the soldier as the soldier would have "humiliated" him. Cato's attitude may seem unnecessarily brusque and unreasonable, since there is no hint that the soldier meant anything other than a gesture of kindness and consideration, even of self-sacrifice. But Cato wants his troops to understand that he will not tolerate special privileges. This he has vowed to his men from the beginning of their journey:

> sitiat quicumque bibentem
> viderit, aut umbras nemorum quicumque petentem
> aestuet, aut equitem peditum praecedere turmas
> deficiat: siquo fuerit discrimine notum
> dux an miles eam.   [9.398–402]

(Any man who sees me drinking may feel thirst; any man who sees me heading for the shade of trees may feel hot; any man who sees me riding in front of the infantry may feel faint, or if there is ever anything to distinguish whether I am your general or just a soldier.)

Should Cato drink the water offered him, his whole army would feel thirst. Therefore his final action is to cast the helmet upon the ground so that the water spills out. Then, paradoxically, there was enough for everyone: "suffecitque omnibus aquam" (9.510) although there was none for anybody.

This incident has two interesting parallels in ancient literature, of which Lucan probably knew one. The first is in 2 Samuel 23: 14–17, where David rejects the water brought to him, though for very different reasons. The other is quite possibly the archetype for this scene: Alexander the Great's rejection of the water offered him by a soldier when the whole army is thirsty, recorded in Arrian 6.26. The reminiscence of Alexander would surely have been familiar enough to Lucan's reader and is, no doubt, intended to enhance Cato's stature here.[33] By rejecting the water Cato affirms, as Alexander does, that he is prepared to suffer as his men suffer. But Alexander's action is intended to secure greater devotion from

---

33. For a discussion of the Alexander passage and its relationship to Lucan's Cato, see W. Rutz, "Lucan und die Rhetorik," *FH* 15.242–243.

his troops for the furtherance of his personal ambitions. Cato wants his men to know that he really is just one of their number, not a leader seeking special consideration. He also wishes to convey the notion that it is wrong for any man to be satisfied while others are suffering—the same principle that led Cato to involve himself in the civil war in the first place. Finally, he underscores something of cardinal importance in the *Pharsalia:* the inseparability of political and moral principle if a society is to remain free.

Here, essentially, is the difference between Caesar and Cato. Though Lucan matches the two point for point, the parallels serve to distinguish rather than associate them. True, Caesar's courage is described as "nescia virtus / stare loco" (a courage that does not know how to stay put) (1.144–145) and Cato's merits the comparable "inpatiens virtus haerere" (a courage that cannot bear to stay still) (9.371). But Cato's *virtus* is based on knowledge and moral principle, whereas Caesar's is, paradoxically, *nescia*. In Stoic terms, there is no such thing as *nescia virtus,* and even though Lucan qualifies *nescia* with an infinitive, the paradox remains. Cato's *virtus,* on the other hand, is not *ignorant of* how to stay still, but *unwilling to* endure inactivity—not the same thing at all.

Cato's physical trials in Africa seem designed to outdo Caesar's tribulations in *Pharsalia* 5 on almost every score. Not only is he able to win men to him by inspiring their emulation rather than their fear, but each of his hardships is willingly shared by his accompanying troops. In 5, Caesar ventures alone upon the Adriatic and endures the perils of a great storm. In 9, Lucan gives Cato and his men an *aristeia* against the forces of nature. It begins with the republicans' attempt to cross the Syrtes from Cyrene to join up with Juba (9.300–347). Nature forbade the undertaking, Lucan tells us, but virtue hoped to force nature to yield (301–302). The attempted crossing is, like Caesar's, a failure. The treacherous nature of the sandbanks combined with the fury of a tempest wreck several republican ships and drive the remainder far off course. Fortune, then, is not as favorable as she is to Caesar in 5; at least Caesar arrives back at the point from which he started. But Cato and the republicans are stranded in a remote part of Africa, at the site of the Garden of the Hesperides and close to the river Lethon (348–367).

The reference to the Hesperides is surprising. We know that Lucan dare not portray Cato strolling in an orchard of golden apples unless he is prepared to sacrifice all claim to historical credibility. Lucan acknowledges the problem in a curious way:

> invidus, annoso qui famam derogat aevo,
> qui vates ad vera vocat. [9.359–360]

> (Hateful is he who strips fame from aged tradition and calls upon the poet to speak the truth.)

He is writing somewhat ironically. For the limitations on the use of myth are, in Lucan's case, substantially self-imposed. Here is an instance where he would really like to use myth to enhance Cato. And, in a roundabout way, he does so despite the inference that he will not. The mere mention that Cato lands in Africa at the Garden of the Hesperides adds an exotic quality to the narrative. And the association of Hercules with the Hesperides affords Lucan an opportunity to suggest a comparison between Hercules and Cato—to Hercules' disadvantage.[34]

Even before critics demythologized the Garden of the Hesperides, Hercules had robbed it of its chief glory, its golden apples: "pauper spoliatis frondibus hortus" (358) (The garden is now poor, its boughs despoiled). Thanks to the critics and to Hercules, then, there are no golden apples to bring back. So Cato cannot rival Hercules on this score. On the other hand, Hercules gave the apples to Eurystheus, tyrant of the Argolid: "rettulit Argolico fulgentia poma tyranno" (367). This, we infer, is something Cato would never have done.

Thus what begins as a tempestuous voyage like Caesar's in 5 is given a much broader significance. It is Cato's first step on a journey to death and a kind of immortality like that purchased by Hercules with the golden apples of the Hesperides.

The republican army would have been content to stay in the

34. Lucan's location of the Hesperides and the Triton in the same area is in accord with Strabo 17.3.20. On this passage see J. Aumont, "Cato en Libye," *REA* 70 (1968), 304–320. For Hercules and the Hesperides, see the comprehensive list of sources in R. Littlewood, "The Symbolism of the Apple in Greek and Roman Literature," *HSCP* 72 (1968), 163–165; G. Martin, "Golden Apples and Golden Boughs," in *Studies Presented to David Moore Robinson* (ed. G. Mylonas and D. Raymond) St. Louis, 1953, 2.1191 ff.

area of the Garden, Lucan tells us at 368–371. This simple observation gains from the site's proximity to the river Lethon whose waters induce forgetfulness (355–356). Once again, Lucan adds mythic *color*. The magic of the Garden is not altogether gone. Cato's refusal to succumb to such delights, like Odysseus' determination not to abandon the travails of mortal existence for the bliss of Calypso's isle or the land of the Lotus-eaters, attests to his belief that virtue requires confrontation with, not avoidance of, the struggles of life. So he summons his men to follow him around the Syrtes on foot, to brave the dangers of snake, thirst, and sand: "serpens, sitis, ardor harenae" (402), three perils they will shortly encounter, though in reverse order. The allegorical nature of the march is stressed by Cato at the outset: "durum iter ad leges patriaeque ruentis amorem" (385) (The road to the rule of law and to love of our falling country is a hard one). He undertakes the journey at the harsh command of virtue: "hac ire Catonem / dura iubet virtus" (444–445).

The harshness of the Libyan landscape, described in detail at 411–444, its virgin sterility and barbarous inhabitants, lend force to Lucan's sense of awe at this venture into the unknown. The geographical preamble gradually merges with the narrative of the march itself at 445–465, as the blowing sandstorms which afflict the native inhabitant apply themselves with unusual vigor to Cato's army.[35] In the description that follows (447–497), the ground is swept from beneath the feet of the marching soldiers; they are overwhelmed by huge mounds of blowing sand; they are buried beneath the surface and unable to rise; landmarks disappear, and they must guide their steps by the stars. The similarity of the sandstorm to a tempest upon the sea is obvious, and Lucan does not belabor the point with a single nautical simile or metaphor. We have only his one comment at the very outset:

illic secura iuventus
ventorum nullasque timens tellure procellas
aequoreos est passa metus. [445–447]

(There the young men, though they did not anticipate winds and had no fears of storms on the land, experienced the terrors of the sea.)

35. On the nature of and Lucan's sources for this storm, see Morford, 49–51.

Lucan is again recalling Caesar's attempt to cross the Adriatic. Cato must suffer twice what Caesar suffers once. In contrast to the storm in 5, however, this episode is brief and unextravagant. Cato voices no cries for a death beneath the billowing sand, and this trial is but a prelude to even greater sufferings.

Yet it would be misleading to suppose that Lucan's aim is solely to elevate Cato beyond Caesar. Cato's arrival in Africa and his journey across the Libyan desert evoke memories of Hercules and Alexander as well as of Caesar. Indeed, there are sufficient similarities between *Pharsalia* 9.294 ff. and Apollonius' account of the Argonauts crossing the same desert in *Argonautica* 4.1219–1460 to indicate that Lucan is echoing Apollonius and matching his Cato with Apollonius' Heracles. Argonauts and republicans alike face death in the desert. From this fate they are saved by Heracles and Cato respectively. But Heracles provides salvation from afar and almost accidentally, whereas Cato accompanies his troops every step of the way. Heracles' quest for freedom is a very personal one: delivery from servitude to Eurystheus and from the anger of Hera, and this personal quest keeps him apart from the Argonauts. Cato's goal is freedom not only for himself but for all men.[36] Lucan's intent, then, is to have Cato surpass not only Caesar but the greatest heroes of myth and history, as we shall see more fully in Sections VI through VIII.

VI. Cato and the Oracle

Cato emerges from the sandstorm to find himself at the threshold of one of the great oracles of antiquity, that of Jupiter Ammon at Siwah (9.511–586). This episode begins in much the same way as the incidents involving Appius and Sextus discussed in Chapter 4, with a descriptive preamble telling of the site, its importance, and the powers associated with it. But it develops in such a way that we perceive the major differences not only among the men involved, but in many other details of the scenes. First, Cato merely happens to arrive at the oracle; he does not

36. A full treatment of the parallels between the desert crossings in *Pharsalia* 9 and *Argonautica* 4 is pending in R. A. Shoaf's forthcoming article "Certius Exemplar Sapientis Viri: Rhetorical Subversion and Subversive Rhetoric in *Pharsalia* 9."

make a detour for the specific purpose of visiting it, as Appius does when he visits Delphi, or as Sextus does when he consults Erichtho. Second, a visit to the oracle of Ammon could hardly fail to remind the Roman reader of the story of Alexander the Great's journey to the same oracle and the tradition that Hercules too visited the shrine.[37] Third, the oracle of Ammon is still very much alive—unlike that of Apollo at Delphi. It still functions because it has been protected, Lucan assures us, from the corruption of Roman gold by the staunch, good life of its people (9.511–521). The Libyans enjoy the blessings of fruitful poverty, "fecunda paupertas," which Rome had long since lost.[38] Finally, as we shall see, Cato does not attempt to consult the oracle. Unlike Appius, Sextus, and Alexander, he is not concerned with the kind of information the oracle has to dispense.

Not only does this introduction contrast the virtues of poverty with the corruption engendered by wealth—a theme Roman writers had worn threadbare long before Lucan's time—but it strongly suggests that a consultation of this particular oracle would not be futile, as Appius' consultation of Delphi was. We come to anticipate some momentous revelation as the result of Cato's arrival at the shrine. At the same time, however, the possibility that Cato might be given prophetic insight into the future kindles uneasiness. For the reader knows that, if Cato consults the oracle, he may well learn of the catastrophe awaiting the republican cause at Thapsus, and, perhaps, of his own death at Utica. While such foreknowledge would probably not affect Cato detrimentally, it would certainly jeopardize the morale of his troops.

Cato's lieutenant, Labienus, broaches to him the matter of

37. Arrian 3.1 tells us that Alexander went to visit the oracle because his forebears Perseus and Hercules had done so. For the significance of Alexander's visit, see A. Gitti, "Alessandro Magno e il responso di Ammone," *RSI* 64 (1952), 531–547 and J. Larsen, "Alexander at the Oracle of Ammon," *CP* 27 (1932), 70–75; W. Tarn, *Alexander the Great,* Cambridge, 1948, especially 2, app. 25; and E. Badian, "Alexander the Great and the Unity of Mankind," *Historia* 7 (1958), 425–444.

38. Cf. 1.165–166 and Horace *Odes* 1.12.37–44, and 3.6.37 ff. Juvenal *Satires* 6.553–556 implies, obliquely, that the oracle of Ammon was more alive than that of Delphi in his day. For a further discussion of Cato and the oracle, see Dick, "Role of Manticism" and his articles: "Technique of Prophecy" and "Role of the Oracle." Also W. Wünsch, 86–108 and Morford 73–74.

consulting the oracle, suggesting that this would be an ideal opportunity to discover the outcome of the war. Knowing Cato's philosophical disposition, he tries to make the consultation more attractive by pointing out that this is also a fine moment to enquire what virtue is and ask for an example of right conduct: "quaere quid est virtus et posce exemplar honesti" (9.563). There is humor in Labienus' naiveté. Standing before his eyes is the exemplar he would have Cato ask about—Cato himself. Lucan adds a touch of ambiguity to Labienus' own words in 561–562: "tua pectora sacra / voce reple." Since *sacra* is the very last word in 561, and since, as a result, its final syllable is of indeterminate length, Labienus' request yields one of two meanings: either "Fill your heart with that holy voice [i.e., the voice of the *oracle*]," or "Fill your holy heart with your voice." Labienus clearly intends the first of these. But what follows is the fulfillment of the secondary meaning. For it is Cato, not the oracle, that answers Labienus; Cato, rather than the priest of the shrine, has a god within his heart:

> ille deo plenus tacita quem mente gerebat
> effudit dignas adytis e pectore voces.   [9.564–565]

(He, filled with the god whom he carried with him in the silent reaches of his mind, poured from his heart responses worthy of an oracle.)

The reader now perceives that the suggestions about Cato's oracular nature in *Pharsalia* 2 were hardly more than a foretaste of what was to come. As in Cato's reply to Brutus, so here Lucan recalls Lucretius 1.737–739.[39] But the effect is now much more powerful since Cato is actually standing before the shrine of Ammon himself.

This, surely, is a major reason why Lucan emphasizes that the oracle of Ammon is in good working order. A comparison between Cato and a defunct shrine, such as that of Apollo at Delphi, would be less than flattering to Cato. The value of Cato's words must be weighed against the value of an oracle that might indeed reveal

---

39. See above, Section I. Seneca, like Lucan, refers to the sacred heart of Cato: *Ep.* 67.13; *Prov.* 2.11; *Epigr.* 9.1.

something of consequence about the future, even if it is an African
shrine. But Lucan does not sustain the illusion of Ammon's worth
very long. Cato's response makes it clear that he regards the very
idea of an oracle as absurd. Jupiter, he maintains, is not confined
in this way, he does not bury his truth in the sand:

> estque dei sedes nisi terra et pontus et aer
> et caelum et virtus? [9.578–579]

> (Is there a dwelling-place for god apart from the land, the sea,
> the air, the heavens and virtue?)

Though Cato doubts the possibility that the oracle has any truth
to communicate, his prime attack is directed against the *kind* of
knowledge to be gained from such a consultation. He already
knows all that he needs to know:

> Quid quaeri, Labiene, iubes? an liber in armis
> occubuisse velim potius quam regna videre?
> an sit vita nihil sed longa an differat aetas?
> an noceat vis nulla bono fortunaque perdat
> opposita virtute minas, laudandaque velle
> sit satis et numquam successu crescat honestum?
>
> [9.566–571]

> (What would you have me ask, Labienus? Whether I would
> rather die free than live to see a tyranny? Whether the quality
> of life does not matter, but only its length? Whether any force
> harms the good man, or whether Fortune loses its threats when
> opposed by virtue? Is it not enough to desire goals which merit
> praise? Does right conduct ever improve with success?) [40]

Cato responds to Labienus with questions whose answers, to his
Stoic mind, are self-evident. The only knowledge that matters per-

40. Stoics had ready answers for most of these questions: "neque enim
rerum natura patitur ut umquam bona bonis noceant" (Seneca *Prov.* 1.5);
"nihil accidere bono viro mali potest" (*ibid.*, 2.1); "ne a fortuna quidem,
quae quotiens cum virtute congressa est numquam par recessit" (*Constant.*
8.3); "omne humanum genus, quodque est, quodque erit, morte damnatum
est . . . quid est ergo quare indigner aut doleam, si exiguo momento publica
fata praecedo?" (*Ep.* 71.15. These words are attributed by Seneca to Cato);
"incipe virtutibus illum, non annis aestimare; satis diu vixit" (Seneca's advice to the bereaved Marcia, *Ad Marc.* 24.1).

tains not to historical events but to moral conduct. And *virtus* is more than adequate to cope with any challenges events or Fortune throw before it. If Cato were to consult the oracle, he would undermine his own philosophical position. More important still, such a consultation would link him too closely with the land of Africa, Rome's traditional foe. As we have seen in Chapter 3, the alliance with Juba was embarrassing enough for the republicans in the civil war. Any ties between Cato and Ammon, then, are best avoided. Cato must not appear to be a Marius, renewing his strength from the Libyan desert, but the embodiment of the qualities of Hercules, Regulus and Scipio who were able to triumph over all the terrors of Africa. Therefore Lucan takes Cato to the shrine of Ammon only to have Cato, not the god, prophesy.

Cato, then, is the oracle of civilized man, the wise man *par excellence*. But he is also something more. He is the last repository of Roman greatness, the shrine of *libertas*. Now that the republic has succumbed to Caesar, the very essence of Rome is in Cato.

As Cato departs from the shrine, Lucan confronts us with an enigma:

> servataque fide templi discedit ab aris
> non exploratum populis Hammona relinquens.   [9.585–586]

> (He departed from the altars, keeping the credibility of the oracle intact and leaving Ammon to his people without putting him to the test.)

Possibly Lucan intends a secondary connection between *templi* and *aris*, which would change the meaning of the first line to "Keeping his faith intact, he departed from the altars of the temple." Cato's own credibility has been on trial here, as has the faith of his troops in their goal. Not only would a consultation of Ammon have revealed, perhaps, the doom of the army at Thapsus, it would have sapped the soldiers' confidence in both leader and cause.

Cato's example inspires the troops, and it inspires Lucan as well:

> si veris magna paratur
> fama bonis et si successu nuda remoto

inspicitur virtus, quidquid laudamus in ullo
maiorum, fortuna fuit. quis Marte secundo,
quis tantum meruit populorum sanguine nomen?
hunc ego per Syrtes Libyaeque extrema triumphum
ducere maluerim, quam ter Capitolia curru
scandere Pompei, quam frangere colla Iugurthae.
ecce parens verus patriae, dignissimus aris,
Roma, tuis, per quem numquam iurare pudebit
et quem, si steteris umquam cervice soluta,
nunc, olim, factura deum es.   [9.593–604]

(If great fame is gained by true merits, if we strip virtue bare by
removing the trappings of success, we see that what is praised in
any of our ancestors was really the work of Fortune. For who
won so great a name as Cato, whatever his victories in war,
whatever people he annihilated? I personally would rather
lead this triumphal march through the remote regions of Syrte
and Libya than ride three times up to the Capitol in Pompey's
chariot, or break Jugurtha's neck. Here was a real father of his
country, a man, Rome, who truly deserves an altar in your city.
This is a man by whose name you will never be ashamed to
swear. If ever you stand again with neck unchained, one day you
will make this man a god.)

Lucan's apotheosis of Cato is an attempt not only to accord him
divine status in his own right, but to outdo the tale of Alexander's
visit to the oracle of Ammon. For Alexander supposedly received
a secret response from the oracle and was greeted by the priest as
the "son of god." It has been argued that at this point Alexander
recognized his own status as son of god.[41] Lucan is probably familiar with this tradition. Thus the echo of Alexander is surely
intended, as is the parable of the rejection of the water, to bolster
Cato's claims to greatness and, in this instance, divinity. But Cato's
divinity, unlike that of Alexander, is self-evident, requiring no
prophetic affirmation. It has therefore a far more solid basis than
Caesar's claim to godhood, which lacks both the blessing of
Ammon and the sanctity accorded by virtue.

Here we see one of the most curiously ironic consequences of

41. See L. Edmunds, "The Religiosity of Alexander," *GRBS* 12 (1971),
379–386; cf. the sources cited in note 37 above.

Caesarism. Absolutism of one kind produces, as a backlash, absolutism of another kind. The prerogatives of Olympus have been usurped by Caesar who, after death, is officially declared a god. Now Lucan swears that, if ever Rome regains her freedom, Cato will become a god. The devotee of virtue will supplant the champion of Fortune. But freedom never did return to Rome. The notion of the divinity of the truly virtuous man, who offers himself as a sacrifice for all humanity and promises victory even in the teeth of apparent defeat, however, did remain. It is not altogether surprising that, as the hope of political freedom died, Cato should yield to the similar—but essentially apolitical—Christ, who offered the promise of reward in another life for the tribulations experienced in this.

VII. Cato and the Snakes

No sooner has Lucan finished his encomium of Cato than he launches on one of the most bizarre episodes in the *Pharsalia*. We have already discussed some aspects of Cato's encounter with the Libyan serpents.[42] It remains now to explore some further dimensions of this passage, most notably the contrast with the tale of Curio in 4.581–824. Curio arrives in Africa to destroy the Pompeian opposition and to make Rome Caesar's kingdom. He camps on the ruins of Scipio's camp, defeats Varus, and is himself defeated by Juba. In 9, Cato, the very embodiment of *libertas,* arrives in Africa at the plundered orchard of the Hesperides with a band of men dedicated to the goal of dying free and confronts the perils of the Libyan desert. Although Lucan did not live to tell the full tale, hints elsewhere in the epic, supplemented by information from other historical sources, complete the picture. Metellus Scipio placates the ghosts of Africa with his blood, and Cato takes his own life at Utica.[43]

There are some interesting similarities in the way Lucan narrates the tales of Cato and Curio—enough to suggest that he is inviting comparison. The adventures of both these very different men are embellished with something Lucan rarely uses—a lengthy,

---

42. Above, Chapter 2, Section II.
43. *Pharsalia* 6.305–311; see Chapter 3 above.

mythological excursus.[44] The tale of Hercules and Antaeus in 4 and that of Perseus and Medusa in 9 are two of only three passages in the entire epic where Lucan expounds a mythic event in detail.[45]

There are, of course, some differences in the way the myths of Hercules and Antaeus, Perseus and Medusa are handled. In the first, Lucan does not tell us the story "himself," but puts it in the mouth of an African peasant, and his own reference to the tradition as "non vana vetustas" (4.590) suggests that he believes it. In the second, Lucan narrates the myth "personally," and apologizes that he can offer nothing more plausible. He introduces Perseus and Medusa to explain the origin of the serpents in Africa, telling in considerable detail how they were born from the blood that spilled from Medusa's head as Perseus carried it over the desert. "Non cura laborque / noster scire valet," he declares at 9.621–622 ("my careful research could not come up with an [alternative] answer"). The story of Perseus and Medusa is, he avows, a folk tale, which has deceived people for centuries; it is a substitute for the truth: "volgata per orbem / fabula pro vera decepit saecula causa" (ibid., 622–623).

Yet this breakdown, allegedly due to ignorance, of Lucan's normal, scientific approach to phenomena is somewhat less ingenuous than Lucan would have us believe. For we recall that earlier in 9, when telling the tale of the Hesperides, he expressed annoyance that the poet is obliged to abandon mythic tradition in favor of the truth (9.359–360). Yet the Hesperides myth is deliberately introduced to give Cato a more than Herculean stature at the outset of his journey in Africa. The myth of the origin of the African snakes serves a similar purpose. It introduces the subsequent narrative of Cato's encounter with the serpents against a backdrop of the mythical, and separates Cato still further from the realm of the other protagonists of the *Pharsalia,* associating him with the mythical conquerors of the bestial and subhuman— including Hercules himself. In fact, Lucan's reminder that no one

44. On Lucan's use of excursus, see L. Eckhardt, "Exkurse und Ekphraseis bei Lucan," Diss. Heidelberg, 1936, *passim.*

45. On the tales of Medusa in 9 and Antaeus in 4, see I. Cazzaniga, "L'Episodio dei serpi libici in Lucano e la tradizione dei 'Theriaka' Nicandrei," *Acme* 10 (1957), 27–41; P. Grimal, "L'Episode d'Antée"; Piacentini, 36–39.

really knows the facts about the origin of the Libyan serpents *adds* to this effect. These creatures still belong to the province of myth in Lucan's own day; he does not have to fall back on literary convention to show that Cato is pitting himself against forces as terrifying and inexplicable as they were in primitive times. Cato confronts the monstrous and unknown just as Hercules did, under the same conditions as the legendary hero.

The snake, like the lion, is one of the African creatures *par excellence*. In some ways it is even more terrible than the lion, for it is traditionally regarded as no less cunning than vicious. Livy (*Per.* 18) and Silius Italicus (*Punica* 6.140–260) tell of a monstrous Libyan snake Regulus fought during the Punic Wars—a creature which, like Lucan's Antaeus, fed on lions. Silius even compares it to the snakes that armed the giants' feet when they assaulted Olympus.[46] More important, Regulus' battle with it merits, in Silius' opinion, comparison with the Hydra which Hercules fought or with Juno's snake that guarded the golden apples of the Hesperides (*Punica* 6.181–184).

Regulus regards the snake as a threat to the civilized world, especially to Rome. It becomes the very symbol of the raw forces of Africa against which Italy is struggling and thus presents a challenge that cannot be turned down. When Regulus fights this monster, he responds as the champion of civilization:

> serpentine Itala pubes
> terga damus Libycisque parem non esse fatemur
> anguibus Ausoniam?   [*Punica* 6.242–244]

(Are the young men of Italy to flee at the sight of a snake? Are we to say that Italy is not a match for the serpents of Libya?)

It is quite possible that Lucan intended his reader to see a parallel between Cato's march through snaky Libya and Regulus' struggle with the serpent. He found in the historical tradition of Cato's march the opportunity to give him an *aristeia* against the bestial to rival that of Regulus. But, as we noted earlier, in Chapter 2, Section II, it is typical of Lucan's technique to reduce the

46. *Pun.* 6.181–183; see E. Bassett, "Regulus" and "Hercules"; also A. R. Anderson. Other sources for Regulus and the serpent are Valerius Maximus 1.8; Pliny *NH* 8.37; but the most detailed is that of Silius in *Pun.* 6.62–551, especially 117–293 and 299–551.

archetypal monster to a number of smaller—and thus seemingly more credible—creatures. Obviously Lucan wants to make as much as he can of the incident without trespassing too much on historical credibility.[47]

It is not only the coincidence of the situations in which Cato and Regulus find themselves that attracts our attention. As types of the Roman hero, Cato and Regulus share much in common, above all in their refusal to compromise on matters of principle, regardless of personal cost.[48] When the Carthaginians captured Regulus and sent him back to Rome to negotiate a truce on their behalf, Regulus not only denounced the Carthaginian proposal to his Roman countrymen, but dismissed their attempts to dissuade him from returning to certain death at Carthage. He had given his word to his captors that he would return, and return he did. It is this same dedication to principle that leads Cato to take his own life rather than compromise with Caesar. A greater contrast with Curio is hard to imagine.

VIII. Cato, Hercules, and Alexander

Although Lucan makes no explicit comparisons between Cato and Regulus or Cato and Alexander the Great and only obliquely

47. An interesting example of how far Lucan is prepared to go to justify Cato, even in details, can be seen in his lengthy digression on the Psylli (9.850–937). Plutarch *Cat. Min.* 56, tells us that Cato took the Psylli with him on the march because of their famed prowess in dealing with snake bites. Such caution is not becoming to Lucan's Cato. In the *Pharsalia,* Cato and his men do not encounter the Psylli until *after* their encounter with the snakes. Lucan's account of the Psylli bears a striking resemblance to that of Pliny *NH* 7.13 and probably they drew their material from the same source, whom Pliny says was Agatharchides. The Psylli are also mentioned by Herodotus (4.173), but he does not mention their power over snakes, nor does he intimate that their race survived their defeat by the Nasamonians.

48. Roman writers associated Regulus and Cato very closely. Horace *Odes* 1.12.33–40 does so, and Seneca does so frequently: *Prov.* 3.4–4.3, where Cato is named along with Regulus, Mucius Scaevola, Fabricius, and Socrates; similarly *Ep.* 98.12 (Cato, Mucius, Regulus, Rutilius, Socrates); *Ep.* 71.17 (Cato, Socrates, Regulus). More significant still are the following: *Tran.* 16.4: "ego Herculem fleam, quod vivus uritur, aut Regulum, quod tot clavis configitur, aut Catonem, quod vulnera vulnerat sua"; *Constant.* 2.1: "Catonem autem certius autem exemplar sapientis viri nobis deos immortales dedisse quam Ulixen et Herculem prioribus saeculis." An interesting similarity between Cato and Regulus is also worth noting: both had wives named Marcia. For a comparison between Cato and the Scipios, see *Ep.* 70.22.

touches on the similarity between Cato and Hercules, such comparisons are certainly implicit in *Pharsalia* 9. Cato's exploits in Africa are clearly suggestive of Hercules' quest for the golden apples of the Hesperides—an offering that secured for Hercules, according to some accounts, his accession to Olympus. Just as Hercules will triumph over death, so will Cato.[49] Similarly Lucan's references to Cato's rejection of the water and his visit to the shrine of Jupiter Ammon recall similar actions by Alexander.[50] Finally, the epithet, *invictus*, "the unconquerable one," which Lucan uses of Cato in 9.18, is strongly evocative of both Hercules and Alexander.[51]

But the detection of such implicit comparisons should not give us carte blanche to exploit these parallels too far. Surely Lucan avoids making a direct, explicit parallel between Hercules and Cato because he wants to hint at Cato's Herculean aspects without importing any of the less savory elements of Hercules' nature. Although Hercules is the great civilizer, he is not free from fits of homicidal rage and brutal sexual passion. Lucan understands the disadvantages of direct comparisons with the heroes of the past as well as the advantages, since he wants his Cato to be greater than, not just equal to, Hercules. Direct comparisons would have been of little use. For Hercules' exploits belong to the realm of myth and legend and cannot possibly be rivaled in kind by a hero whose deeds belong to an age of well-documented history and skepticism about tall stories. Seneca states the matter succinctly:

Cato non cum feris manus contulit, quas consectari venatoris agrestisque est, nec . . . in ea tempora incidit quibus credi posset caelum umeris unius inniti. [*De Const. Sap.* 2.2]

(Cato did not fight with wild beasts—that's the sort of thing a hunter or a peasant does. . . He was not born in an age when one could believe that the heavens rest on the shoulders of one man.)

49. See L. Farnell, *Greek Hero Cults and the Ideas of Immortality*, Oxford, 1921, 171, and the sources cited in note 34 above.
50. See above, Sections V and VI and note 33.
51. For the use of the epithet *invictus* of Cato elsewhere see Plutarch *Cat. Min.* 71. Tarn, 2.338–339, argues that the epithet *anikētos*, *invictus*, was not applied to heroes until *after* its use as an epithet of Alexander; Cf. S. Weinstock, "Victor and *Invictus*," *HThR* 50 (1957), 214. Thus *Hercules Invictus*

We have seen in Section V how Lucan copes with this dilemma. Cato cannot rival Hercules by finding golden apples when he arrives at the traditional site of the Hesperides. But since he did arrive at the site, an allusion to the Garden and its golden apples is quite in order. Thus the parallel between Cato and Hercules is established. Then, by pointing out that Hercules gave the golden apples to a tyrant to secure his own freedom, Lucan undermines Hercules' mythological advantage. So the poet uses the associations of Hercules' exploits to build up Cato, then exploits Hercules' weaknesses to elevate Cato beyond Hercules.

Much the same is true of Lucan's more oblique parallels between Cato and Alexander. Because he campaigned in exotic lands where the fantastic was still believable, the aura of myth and mysticism Alexander drew around himself allowed him to vie with the greatest heroes of mythology. Thus Alexander, though historical, shared Hercules' advantage over Cato. Once again direct comparisons had to be avoided. Besides, Alexander, unlike Hercules, was not a very popular figure with the Stoics. He came closer to being the antithesis of the wise man than the exemplar, and it is hard to see how Lucan could possibly have used any direct comparison between Alexander and Cato without harming Cato's image. For this reason, Lucan never actually mentions Alexander's exploits in the context of Cato's journey through North Africa in *Pharsalia* 9, even though there are obvious parallels. Alexander, like Cato, refused to drink water offered to him by a soldier; he also visited the oracle of Ammon. Lucan relies on his reader to adduce the parallels and contrasts. As noted earlier, Alexander rejects the water so that his men will become devoted minions, not to entice them to emulate him in the fight for their own freedom. And Alexander's arrival at the oracle of Ammon is an occasion for him to receive an oracle not to bestow one. The unstated but implicit contrast between Cato and Alexander enhances Cato's image at Alexander's expense.

Later, when Lucan has established the effect that he wants, the process can be reversed. He can attack Alexander by means of unstated parallels with Cato. In 10.14–52, Lucan launches into a

owes much to *Alexander Invictus* rather than vice versa. How aware Lucan was of this is another matter.

withering attack on Alexander. He calls him a *felix praedo,* a
lucky bandit (10.21), recalling, perhaps, his description of Sextus
Pompey 6 as a Sicilian pirate (6.422). Alexander cuts a path of
slaughter across the world, like a thunderbolt which strikes all
nations indiscriminately: "fulmen . . . quod omnis / percuteret
pariter populos" (10.34–35). Here Lucan echoes his own description of Caesar in 1.151–157 and with it all the megalomania and
savagery that characterizes him. But then he cannot resist adding
this:

> non illi flamma net undae
> nec sterilis Libye nec Syrticus obstitit Hammon.   [10.37–38]

(Not fire, not water, not sterile Libya nor African Ammon stand
in his way.)

The same, of course, could be said of Cato; in fact, this is the
major theme conveyed in much of *Pharsalia* 9. But comparison
with Cato now serves to cut Alexander down. For, in this context,
it underscores the difference between the two men, not their
similarity. Cato does what he does not to enslave or murder mankind but to offer them the chance of attaining freedom.

The purpose, then, of these oblique allusions is quite simple.
Lucan wants us to see Cato as a match for Caesar and Alexander,
the great conquerors; a match for the great patriot, Regulus, and
the civilizing Hercules. He has all their strengths and none of
their weaknesses. As Seneca suggests in *De Constantia Sapientis,*
2.1, Cato is a more positive exemplar of the wise man given to us
by the immortal gods than Ulysses and Hercules in earlier centuries. His is the greatness recognized by the people of Utica, who
call him, according to Plutarch, *Cato Minor* 71, μόνος ἀήττητος, or,
in Latin terms, *solus invictus,* the only unconquerable man. He
is, in short, the greatest man of all time.

IX. *Pietas, Furor,* and *Virtus*

The reader of the *Pharsalia* may well find that Lucan treats both
Caesar and Cato as ideas rather than people. Indeed, what they
symbolize seems more important to the poet than what they actually are. In this sense they are more like the forces operating upon

man than man himself. If Lucan had adopted a more conventional approach to epic, it might be possible to equate Cato and Caesar with the notions of *pietas* and *furor* respectively. In Roman terms, *pietas* is the force that binds men and society together in selfless dedication.[52] The man who is *pius* respects the laws of the gods, the state, and the elders of the family, and molds his life in accordance with the most stringent demands that these obligations place upon him. *Furor* is the diametric opposite of *pietas*. It is the uncontrolled assertion of self, as irrational and amoral as *pietas* is both rational and moral. *Furor* is most often compared to a fire that consumes everything in its path and finally, when there is nothing left to destroy, consumes itself. When Aeneas leaves Carthage, *furens* Dido kills herself.[53] Since the object of her passion has been removed, the fire of passion that consumes her mind is translated into the literal fire that devours her body upon the pyre she built herself.

Within the state, as within the individual, there is often, in Roman epic, a struggle between *furor* and *pietas*. When man becomes more concerned with his own well-being than with the welfare of the state, *furor* begins to get the upper hand. If the ultimate act of *pietas* is to offer one's life in defense of the city and of freedom, then the ultimate act of *furor* is to turn one's energies against

52. On the idea of *Pietas* in general, see Koch's article in *RE* 20.1221–1232; also E. Burck, "Drei Grundwerte der römischen Lebensordnung (labor, moderatio, pietas)," *Gymnasium* 58 (1951), 174–183; also T. Ulrich, *Pietas (pius) als Politischer Begriff im Römischen Staate bis zum Tode des Kaisers Commodus*, Breslau, 1930, and J. Liegle, "Pietas," *Zeitschrift für Numismatik*, 42 (1935), 59–100. The classic republican definition of *pietas* is in Cicero *Rep.* 6. 15.15: "pietatem, quae cum magna in parentibus et propinquis, tum in patria maxima est." The dominant notion in almost all definitions of *pietas* is that of dedication to those who have given one life: one's parents, one's country—in the sense that it is the fatherland—and the gods. In short, it demands conformity to national and ancestral traditions and values, and respect for those to whom one is related, by blood, marriage, or citizenship. For *pietas* in Lucan, see W. Heyke. Heyke, strangely enough, says little about Cato and *pietas* although she concludes: "Pietas ist an die conservative republikanische Ideologie gebunden. Sie ist eine Eigenschaft der Pompeianischen Partei, die im Bürgerkrieg besiegt wird; *pietas* ist der Ausdruck *des politisch-moralischen Widerstandes gegen Caesar*, welcher die höchste Ausprägung in Cato erreicht, der für seine pietas erga patriam in den Bürgerkrieg zieht und seinem Leben ein Ende setzt" (158).

53. *Aeneid* 4.634 ff.

the city in an attempt to overthrow it. There is no greater *pietas* than to defend Rome against a foreign foe; there is no worse *furor* than to engage in civil war.

The tale of civil war, in Lucan's terms, is the doom of *pietas:* "pietas peritura" (2.63), since the object of *pietas* is to preserve and honor the lives of one's kin, not to destroy them. The same is true in the *Thebaid*. When Statius' Menoeceus prepares to cast himself from the walls of Thebes in a ritual *Opfertod* to save his city, he expresses the hope that his death may be of some avail:

> at Tyriis templa, arva, domos, conubia, natos
> reddite morte mea . . . [*Theb.* 10.768–769]

> (But, in exchange for my death, give back to the Thebans their shrines, their lands, their homes, their wives and children.)

His cry, *reddite,* is not, as it so often is in the mouths of other characters in the *Thebaid*, a call for the shedding of blood in vengeance.[54] It is the hope that, somehow, his individual death will be an offering for the safety of the whole state. Suitably enough, *Pietas* and *Virtus* bear Menoeceus' body gently down to the ground.[55] Similarly in the *Pharsalia*, Cato expresses the desire to undergo ritual *Opfertod* for all the sins of Rome, past and present (2.306–325). This too, it would appear, is *pietas* at its highest point.

Curiously, however, Lucan does not describe Cato as *pius,* nor does he explicitly describe his attitudes and actions in terms of *pietas*.[56] There are, I suspect, a number of reasons for this. First, Lucan may wish to avoid using the epithet *pius* of Cato for fear of evoking comparisons with Aeneas' *pietas,* which Lucan probably regarded as something of a perversion, since it required blind obedience to the demands of the gods regardless of any principles of justice and goodness. Second, *pietas* had become the slogan of the younger Pompeys after their father's death—and Lucan's attitude toward Sextus, in particular, is one of revulsion.[57] *Pietas* had

---

54. Compare *Theb.* 2.452–453; 6.174–175; 10.207–208.
55. *Theb.* 10.780–782.
56. See, however, Heyke's comments cited in note 52 above.
57. See above, Chapter 6, Section III.

also—worse still—been Octavian's pretext for war against his adoptive father's assassins.

Yet there is another and, I think, more persuasive explanation of Lucan's reluctance to call Cato *pius:* Cato must be comprehensible in Stoic, no less than in purely Roman, terms. To the Stoic, *pietas* would be a manifestation of *virtus* rather than the other way around. The difference between *pietas* and *virtus,* from a Stoic point of view, is the difference between unquestioning dedication to the *mores maiorum* and conscious, intellectual commitment to what is good. Cato's desire to sacrifice himself for the city is not the product of *furor,* as in Aeneas' case, but of calm, rational thought. Cato's *virtus,* unlike Aeneas' *pietas,* is founded upon knowledge. His virtue makes the epithet *pius* not only unnecessary, but misleading; for, in Lucan's terms, he is the parent or husband of the city, rather than its child—the object of *pietas* rather than its exemplar.

Both Caesar and Cato differ from the protagonists of the *Aeneid,* because they behave according to their own wills and purposes. Although Caesar's actions are frequently described as or associated with *furor,* they are responses to stimuli from within, not the by-product of external influences, as in Dido or Turnus. Caesar is not, like Turnus, a fundamentally normal person goaded into madness by a fury any more than Cato is, like Aeneas, a hero driven to his destiny by the commands of the gods. Thus the differences between Cato and Caesar in the *Pharsalia* are at once more subtle and more obvious than those between Aeneas and Turnus in the *Aeneid.* Aeneas is marked for victory, Turnus for defeat; there is no real question of which is morally superior since neither actively seeks the role for which fate and history need him. In the *Pharsalia,* the course of events is shaped by the character of the protagonists; the principal line of distinction to be drawn between Cato and Caesar is that Caesar's energy lacks the directed moral purpose of Cato's and thus is destructive and evil, whereas Cato's is ennobling and good.[58]

Lucan's emphasis on Cato's morality and on Caesar's amorality is at least partially explicable in terms of his own view of history

58. Cf. W. Fischli, *Studien zum Fortleben der Pharsalia des M. Annaeus Lucanus,* Lucerne, 1943, 32–40.

and indeed of the verdict of history itself. As we have noted before, if the losing cause is to be "better," it can be "better" only in moral terms. Lucan cannot deny the verdict of history, but he can attack it by suggesting that what happened was morally wrong: "vincere peius erat" (it was worse to win).[59] To offset Caesar's victory, Lucan must make Cato the paradigm of goodness and must rob Caesar, as far as possible, of all claims to positive, moral qualities. That, presumably, is why Lucan would rather blacken Petreius' actions in 4, and accuse the republicans of impiety than concede any more of Caesar's clemency than he has to.[60] By ennobling Cato, the cause for which he is fighting can be ennobled. Thus the development of Cato as a Stoic *sapiens* is rhetorically and politically necessary to Lucan's theme. Cato's Stoic heroism is as much a means to a political end in the *Pharsalia* as it is an end in itself.

The conventional opposition of *pietas* and *furor* simply would not be adequate for Lucan's purposes. The more important tension he must establish is between what happened and what was right and good, between *Fortuna* and *virtus*. In his terms, Caesar is the darling of history, Fortune's favorite, victorious over those who oppose him on his own, secular ground. Cato, dedicated to *virtus*, cannot be defeated by history or by Fortune. *Furor* may destroy *pietas*, but *Fortuna* cannot destroy *virtus*. By employing the Stoic paradox that nothing can harm the good man, Lucan is able to transform the defeat of Cato and the republic into a moral victory for *libertas*.[61] For freedom, if unattainable in life, is attainable in death.

Though Cato functions on a different plane from everyone else in the epic, the import of what he does is, in its own way, just as political as the action of Caesar.[62] For Lucan has grasped the fact that a state can only be free as long as a substantial number of people are prepared to make freedom their personal, philosophical goal, not just a slogan. A free state is an association of free individuals; if the impulse to individual freedom dies, then freedom

59. *Pharsalia* 7.706 and note 16 above.
60. On Petreius and Caesar's *clementia,* see Chapter 6, Section I.
61. See above, note 40.
62. For a different view, see F. Gundolf, *Caesar, Geschichte seines Ruhms,* Berlin, 1924, 102–103.

itself is dead. When Cato decided to enter the civil wars, he was pointing out, as Lucan notes, that he was born not only for his own freedom, but for that of the republic.[63]

63. *Pharsalia* 2.380–383. Cf. Seneca *Ad Marc.* 20.6 (cited in note 15 above).

CHAPTER 8

Aspects of the Divine

In *Aeneid* 2.604–620, Venus tells Aeneas that he must not blame Helen or Paris for the fall of Troy but rather the inclemency of the gods: "divom inclementia" (*ibid.* 602). The Olympians are using their massive powers to annihilate a city and its people. They have rejected clemency, the most sublime of divine and kingly virtues, in favor of a callous ruthlessness.

It would not be hard to view the fall of the Roman republic in a similar way. Indeed, one would not have to resort to assertions of divine inclemency. Lucan's Rome is not, like Vergil's Troy, a healthy society ruined by the implacable hostility of the gods, but a decadent and corrupt city which deserves divine punishment. Yet Lucan studiously avoids any suggestion that the civil wars are a punishment inflicted upon Rome by the gods or a manifestation of Olympian inclemency. Instead he expresses regret that the gods have *failed* to exact retribution for the crimes Rome has committed.[1] In his account of the floods in Spain, for instance, his narrative almost exactly corresponds to that of Caesar in the *Bellum Civile,* dwelling on the meteorological and geographical causes of the disaster.[2] But then, unlike Caesar, he comments ruefully that the impiety of civil war merited another great flood to inundate the whole of Spain.[3] Human actions deserve a punishment they do not get. He strikes a similar chord in *Pharsalia* 7: the crime of civil war in Thessaly demands the thunderbolt of retribution from the hand of Jupiter.[4] The force of the hyperbole in both in-

1. 7.445–459; cf. Horace, *Odes* 1.2.
2. *Pharsalia* 4.48–120; Caesar *BCiv.* 1.48–52. For similar descriptions of floods in Lucan's predecessors, see Morford, 44–49, and the sources cited there; also Linn, 44–59.
3. 3.110–120.
4. 7.445–448; see P. Jal, "Les Dieux et les guerres civiles," *REL* 40 (1962),

stances underscores Lucan's regret that no divine power will check or punish errant mankind. The inactivity of the gods or nature in a corrective capacity bolsters his bitter thesis of 7.454–455, that human affairs are of concern to no god: "mortalia nulli / sunt curata deo."

In Lucan's scheme of things, the fates of men and cities are not determined by divine powers acting independently or through the intermediacy of human agents, but by human beings themselves. Thus a Helen or a Paris can be blamed for the fall of Troy, or a Caesar for the annihilation of the republic. Surely this is a major reason why Lucan would rather explain the sufferings of the civil war in terms of divine passivity than of divine activity in the Vergilian manner even though it forces him to abandon the popular Stoic notion of a beneficent, divine providence.[5] He does not want to lessen Caesar's guilt (as Venus would lessen that of Paris or Helen) by suggesting that men are merely pawns manipulated by the gods and consequently not really responsible for their actions. In the *Pharsalia* as in most Senecan tragedy, there is no power external to man that is interested in punishing, much less preventing, human error and crime. The Olympians have ceased to function and no longer wield any power in human affairs.[6] They are as grossly indifferent to man as man is to them.

---

170. Jal stresses the paradox of Lucan's condemnation of divine passivity in the civil wars and the simultaneous condemnation of the civil wars as irreligious; also H. Le Bonniec, 168–170.

5. Stoics had considerable problems reconciling the notions of a divine providence and a world created for man's benefit with the obvious and strong presence of evil, as opponents of Stoicism liked to point out. See Aulus Gellius, *Noctes Atticae* 7.1.1. Seneca tried to resolve the dilemma in his *De Providentia* by emphasizing the invulnerability of the good man to external (evil) circumstances. Yet he is not entirely consistent in his views. Contrast the optimism of the *De Providentia* or the *Consolatio ad Helviam* (particularly 8.2–5) with the pessimism of *Trojan Women* 371–408 and 1009–1055. Similarly Lucan, though agreeing that the good man, such as Cato, cannot suffer harm, argues that mortal affairs are of concern to no god. We should, perhaps, infer that, in Lucan's view, we need not postulate a divine providence to account for the good man's ability to resist evil. For a discussion of the possibility that Cato's view of the gods differs from Lucan's see Linn, 55, note 2. On the identity of Zeus and providence in Stoic thought, see J. M. Rist, *Stoic Philosophy*, Cambridge, 1969, p. 163.

6. 7.445–459.

The gods, then, have no dramatic role in the *Pharsalia*. Individual Olympians are rarely mentioned and never assume any distinct personality. Even the words *deus* and *superi*, though common throughout the epic, are employed so vaguely that little change would be wrought in most contexts if the poet had substituted "Nature," "Fortune," or "Fate." [7] Indeed, when Cato describes Jupiter in 9.580 it is in philosophical not poetic terms: "Iuppiter est quodcumque vides, quodcumque moveris" (Jupiter is whatever you see and whatever you contemplate). The scholiast rightly reminds us in his comment on 9.578 that Lucan (or perhaps we should say Cato) is thinking in terms of Poseidonius' observation: "God is a rational *pneuma* [breath-soul, *spiritus*] permeating all matter." [8] In short, he is a far remove from the usual epic king of gods.

It is precisely this mode of thinking that enables Lucan to treat the elements of the cosmos, from the individual human thought to the outermost star, as belonging to the same, unbroken order of being where everything is somehow in motion and sensate, and consequently (in ancient thought) alive. Thus, although the Olympians are inactive in the epic, there is a strangely animate quality about nature itself. We have already seen something of this earlier. The ashes of Carthage thirst for Roman blood; so do the sands of Africa. [9] Similarly the sun rises slowly on the morning of the battle of Pharsalia, reluctant to view the debacle. [10]

When one thinks of nature itself as being alive, there is no reason to be concerned with an obsolescent order of gods. As a result, we find in the *Pharsalia* what we find in most Senecan tragedy: the interaction of man with man and of man with nature without the intermediacy of god. Nature, however, is scarcely more

7. Cf. Plutarch *Quomodo adul.* 24B; also note 36 below.

8. θεός ἐστι πνεῦμα νοερὸν διῆκον δι' ἁπάσης οὐσίας (*deus est spiritus rationalis per omnem diffusus materiam*); SVF 2, nos. 439–481; 522–533; 633–645; and Sambursky, 1–48 and *passim*. For the primitive nature of hylozoism, see Tylor, 1–447; also Chapter 3 above.

9. 1.39; 4.788–790; 6.309–311. The *spiritus* of the African land seeps up into Antaeus (4.604–605; 643–644), into Marius (2.88–93), and, metaphorically, into Caesar in 1.207. For more discussion of this see Chapter 3.

10. 7.1–6; of the sun also replenishes its powers from the sea; cf. the manner in which the *spiritus* of Delphi takes possession of the priestess of Apollo in 5.86–101; 161–192.

successful in correcting human error than the gods are. But even if nature cannot act to redress the balance of justice, at least it responds to wrongdoing, as the gods do not.[11]

In such an order of things it is difficult to distinguish between individual calamity and cosmic disaster.[12] The universe is a single, unified entity. Thus Herington's remarks on Senecan tragedy can equally well apply to Lucan:

> Seneca . . . however eclectic he is . . . is still Stoic enough by habit to draw little or no distinction between spiritual, moral and material realities. Though he protests in theory against some excesses of the earlier Stoics in this matter, in practice he treats *all* phenomena as belonging to the same order of being. His discourse slips, without warning . . . from the vastness of the soul to the vastness of the starry sky. The stormy wanderings of Ulysses are equated with the daily experience of the soul.[13]

Something of the same occurs in Lucan. The role of the gods in traditional epic is superseded by a kind of Stoic hylozoism; the Olympians yield to the workings of natural phenomena. For between man and nature there is still a bond that no longer exists between man and the gods.

Curiously enough, the end product, for all its differences from Homer, has something in common with Homer. All life, in both Homer and Lucan, belongs essentially to the same order of being. In neither the *Iliad* nor the *Odyssey* is there ever much more than a shade of graduated distinction between the lower orders of life and the gods themselves. Though Thetis is immortal and Achilles mortal, they can still communicate as human mother and son. Homer's world allows an infinite mingling of what later came to

---

11. Chrysippus, unlike Lucan, held that the gods punished evil: "τὸν θεὸν κολάζειν φησὶ τὴν κακίαν καὶ πολλὰ ποιεῖν ἐπὶ κολάσει τῶν πονηρῶν" (Plutarch *De Stoicorum Repugnantiis* 35 (1050 E) = *SVF* 2.1176). On the other hand, the Stoics ridiculed the notion that the fear of god was in any sense a deterrent to wrongful action (Plutarch *ibid.*, 15 [1040 A–B]). It is possible, however, that what Chrysippus meant is being obscured by Plutarch in this latter passage; perhaps what Chrysippus actually said was that fear of individual punishment now or in an afterlife was not a deterrent; cf. Cicero *Nat. D.* 2.5; 3.86.

12. *Pharsalia* 2.289–292; 5.620–624; 7.134–138, and 447–455.

13. Herington, 433.

be discrete entities. Pantheism and Stoic animism are not really very far apart.[14]

After Homer, human and divine elements within the universe become more separate and distinct. In the *Aeneid* there is no closeness between Venus and Aeneas to match that of Thetis and Achilles in the *Iliad*. True, they are mother and son; but this is as hard for the reader to grasp as it is for Aeneas himself. Vergil distinctly draws the line between gods and men; the Homeric continuum is gone. Ironically, Lucan restores the continuum by leaving out the gods: man and the influences external to him are once again part of the same order.

Because of his omission of the gods Lucan is able to build Caesar and Cato into the great forces they are in the *Pharsalia*. They are not gods with the weaknesses of men, but men with the might of gods. There is, then, more than a passing similarity between Caesar and Cato and the Homeric gods. And that similarity is of great importance.

Cato is not only the most perfect man in the *Pharsalia;* he is the most perfect presence of any kind. He never suffers from weakness or self-doubt. Even his closest counterpart in Latin literature, Seneca's Hippolytus, cannot approach Cato's perfection. Hippolytus is flawed by his separation from human society and human behavior and by his pathological aversion to women.[15] Cato is bound up with and dedicated to his fellow-men, not withdrawn from them.[16] Likewise Caesar goes far beyond either Seneca's Atreus or Homer's Achilles. Achilles has his moments of breakdown and impotence. He is not always a man of steel. And even Atreus is conscious of the enormities he is perpetrating.[17] But in Lucan's Caesar we rarely sense any slackening in his pursuit of purpose.[18]

Although neither Caesar nor Cato is immortal, both are un-

14. Stoic hylozoism also shows some remarkable similarities to the ideas of the Milesian philosophers. See E. Bevan, *Stoics and Sceptics,* Oxford, 1913, 40–44.

15. See especially *Phaedra* 483–564.   16. *Pharsalia* 2.286–323.

17. Seneca *Thyestes,* especially 491–505.

18. Some initial hesitation is shown before the speeches of Curio and Laelius in 1, particularly at the crossing of the Rubicon in 183–227.

afraid of death and thus triumph over death. They do not have the absolute power of Zeus, but they guide the destiny of Rome and shape the affairs of the world. And there is something still more important that they share with the gods of Homer: both men are too superhuman to stir any sense of pity or sympathy. They are both beyond the agony and suffering of man.

Much of the tension and motivating force of the *Pharsalia* stems from the opposing principles and ideologies of Caesar and Cato. They are the driving energies of the epic in much the same way Venus and Juno are in the *Aeneid*. But, unlike Vergil's opposing deities, who differ only in political affiliation, Cato and Caesar are quite distinctly marked as good and evil respectively, as we have seen in the previous chapter. Thus the *Pharsalia* supplies an ideological tension lacking in the *Aeneid*. Venus is no better and certainly no more just than her rival Juno. Consequently Vergil is less able—or less willing—than Lucan to direct our attention to the rightness or wrongness of what is happening.

By setting up Cato and Caesar as opposing forces in the *Pharsalia*, Lucan is able to examine the morality of human action, not just assess its failure or success. That he favors Cato indicates his belief that virtue, not history, determines what is good; or to put it in the Stoic terms of Seneca, that *virtus*, not *Fortuna*, is the measure of man's achievement.[19] This is the point of Cato's words to Labienus at 9.570–571: "laudandaque velle . . . satis" (it is enough to desire a goal that is praiseworthy); "numquam successu crescat honestum" (righteousness does not increase with success). The ultimate struggle envisaged in the *Pharsalia* is between Cato and Caesar, between the exemplar of *virtus* and the champion of *Fortuna*. But to leave the matter there would be to oversimplify Lucan's work. For virtue cannot pass from a wise man unless he lapses into ignorance, but Fortune can and does change her champions regardless of their wishes. Thus Cato's hold on virtue is firmer than Caesar's hold on Fortune. Fortune has an independent existence of its own, and its presence in the *Pharsalia* is by no means restricted to Caesar.

---

19. See the passages cited in Chapter 7, note 40.

I. Venus and *Fortuna*

An epic poet who followed Vergil's example could easily have turned to considerable advantage the fact that the champions of the republican cause and of Caesar's army were, respectively, the gods Hercules and Venus. Paul Jal, for example, comments that the battle of Pharsalia could be viewed by a Roman as "a conflict which, in certain respects, is a battle between Hercules and Venus."[20] We might even go a step further and suggest that the whole war could be so viewed.[21]

Jal's observation drives home the fact that Lucan is deliberately eschewing such overt divine symbolism. The name Venus occurs in the *Pharsalia,* but only in reference to sexual intercourse, love, or the planet Venus. It is never used to signify the Olympian goddess. We are given no inkling that Caesar's battle cry was *Venus Victrix,* and only passing reference is made to Caesar's worship of her as *Venus Genetrix.* Hercules, of course, is present in the *Pharsalia,* most notably in the Curio episode in 4.[22] At the same time, Lucan does not attempt to make explicit the obvious connection between Hercules and the republican cause.

It is all very well to argue that the complete omission of Venus stems from Lucan's desire to stay as close as possible to history, but even historians could not resist establishing the connections among Pompey, Caesar, and Venus. Appian and Plutarch, for example, tell us that Pompey had a dream of Venus Victrix the night before the battle of Pharsalia.[23] According to Appian, Pompey saw himself dedicating a temple to her; according to Plutarch, he saw

20. "Les Dieux," 194–195: "Pharsale devait être aussi, à certains égards, une bataille entre Hercule et Vénus. . . . Certaines divinités paraissaient avoir été victorieuses, d' autres vaincues." Cf. Jal's "La Propagande religieuse à Rome," *Ant. Class.* 30 (1961), 395–414.

21. The Caesarians probably used the war-cry Venus Victrix throughout the war. At Munda the Pompeian war-cry was *Pietas* rather than Hercules. For the battle of Pharsalia see Appian *BCiv.* 2.76: "καὶ ἐς εὐτολμίαν παρακαλοῦντες καὶ τὰ συνθήματα ἀναδιδόντες, ὁ μὲν Καῖσαρ Ἀφροδίτην νικηφόρον, ὁ δὲ Πομπήιος Ἡρακλέα ἀνίκητον." For Munda, see *ibid.,* 104. Cf. Chapter 3 above, especially notes 24 and 25; also J. Bayet, *Les Origines de l'Hercule Romain,* Paris, 1926, 325–332, for the epithet *invictus;* cf. S. Weinstock, "Victor and Invictus."

22. 4.581–824.

23. Appian *BCiv.* 2.69; Plutarch *Pomp.* 68.2. Caesar also had similar dreams (Appian 2.68).

himself entering his own theater at Rome and adorning her shrine with laurels.

The dream, as Plutarch points out, is ambiguous. For both Pompey and Caesar were closely associated with the cult of *Venus Victrix*, as Sulla before them had been. She was not specially— much less exclusively—Caesar's goddess; she was also the patron goddess of Pompey's theater.[24] Thus the dream could be favorable to either Caesar or Pompey, since both generals had claims on her affections. Her name was Caesar's battle cry, and he had vowed to dedicate a temple to her if he was victorious. Pompey would quite naturally decorate her shrine with garlands if he won, since, in every account of his life, his theater is the symbol of his happiness and enjoyment of public acclaim.

But in Lucan's account of Pompey's dream, there is no mention of Venus. He merely informs us that the dream that night was the last phase of Pompey's productive, happy life: "at nox felicis Magno pars ultima vitae." [25] The only possible reminiscences of the traditional appearance of Venus are in the word *felix*, "fruitful" or "productive," and the notion permeating the whole dream that the relationship between Pompey and Rome is like a love affair.

It is possible that there is some direct connection between Venus and the adjective *felix*. We have noted above that Sulla engaged in the cult of *Venus Victrix*. He also adopted the cognomen *Felix*. The hint of a connection between these two ideas comes in Plutarch's *Sulla*, 34. Plutarch attempts to explain to his Greek readers what Sulla's epithet *Felix* means. The nearest Greek equivalent, he asserts, is Ἐυτυχής, "Lucky." But, much more in-

---

24. Both Sulla and Pompey had been associated with the Cult of *Venus Victrix*, and both thought of themselves as *Felix* (C. Koch, "Venus," *RE* 8A.859–887; Jal, "La Propagande"; Dilke, *Lucan*, 21 is mistaken in assuming that *Venus Victrix* was particularly *Caesar's* goddess. Perhaps he is confusing the cult of *Venus Victrix* with that of *Venus Genetrix*. Venus Victrix was the patron goddess of Pompey's theater (Plutarch *Pomp.* 68; Tertullian, *De Spect.* 10) and appears as such to Pompey in his dream before Pharsalia in both Appian and Plutarch (above, note 23). For Pompey and Hercules, see Vitruvius 3.3.5 (the *aedes Herculis Pompeiani*), Pliny *NH* 7.95, and *RE* 8.555–560 (s.v. *Hercules*). See also R. Schilling, *La religion romaine de Vénus depuis les origines jusqu' au temps d'Auguste*, Paris, 1954.

25. The dream runs from 7.7–44; see Chapter 5, Section II.

teresting, he adds that Sulla, in his correspondence with the Greeks
and in inscriptions in the Greek language, called himself
Ἐπαφρόδιτος, "Blessed by Venus". Surely Sulla thought that "Lucky"
or "Fortunate" did not quite convey what he understood to be the
full meaning of *Felix*. To Sulla, *Felix* suggested something more:
that he enjoyed the special bounty of the goddess Venus.[26]

Sulla's association of Venus with good fortune and productivity
is, of course, quite natural, since Venus was a fertility goddess.
Throughout Latin literature *felix* is used in the sense of "fertile"
or "productive," and its opposite, *infelix*, suggests barrenness,
sterility, unproductiveness. An interesting case is found in the
Einsiedeln Eclogues, where the writer makes an ironical reference
to what he calls the "infelix gloria Sullae" (2.33) (the barren
glory of Sulla). Although Sulla himself may have been *felix*, Rome,
which was also supposed to be *Felix* (and one of whose major
national gods was Venus) went through such a grim experience
under his rule that she lost hope, as she died, in her great but
fatal wealth: "moriens cum Roma supremas desperavit opes"
(*ibid.* 34–35). Sulla may have enjoyed the bounty of fruitfulness
and productivity, but Rome did not.[27]

Similarly in the *Aeneid*, Dido is constantly referred to as *infelix*.[28] Not only does she fail to achieve any further greatness after
Aeneas' arrival in Carthage, but, as she complains, she does not
even produce a child from their liaison. Perhaps it is more than
pure coincidence that her greatest foe, the real architect of her
downfall, is Aeneas' mother Venus, who draws her into this barren
and fatal romance. For at the very moment Venus softens Dido's
heart with love for Aeneas the Carthaginian queen first receives
the epithet *infelix* from Vergil.

If we now return to Pompey and his dream in *Pharsalia* 7, we
may see the importance of this connection between Venus and

26. See H. Ericsson, "Sulla Felix," *Eranos* 41 (1943), 77–89; cf. Cicero *Att.*
10.4.4; *Rosc. Am.* 8.22; Sallust *Jug.* 95.4; Appian *BCiv.* 1.98; Seneca *ad
Marc.* 12.6; *Prov.* 3.7; *Clem.* 1.26.5. For Lucan's comments on Sulla, see 2.221
and 464–465; 6.787. This last line is particularly odd, and some of its implications difficult to decide upon. It is discussed in Chapter 4, Section 5.

27. Compare, however, Lucan's comments on Pompey and Sulla in 6.301–
303; see Chapter 4, Section V.

28. *Aeneid* 1.712, 749; 4.68, 450, 529, 596; 5.3; 6.456.

the adjective *felix*. A less subtle poet would, no doubt, have lessened the dream's pathos by showing us that the goddess *Venus Victrix* was about to bestow all her affection upon Caesar. But Lucan leaves us only with the word *felix*, to remind us that this is the last moment in Pompey's life when he can be considered great and fortunate. It is the faintest echo of the Venus in Plutarch and Appian, but it is not the only echo. Later in the dream (7.29–32), Lucan bemoans the fact that Rome was not given a chance to see Pompey as he saw her:

> o felix, si te vel sic tua Roma videret!
> donassent utinam superi patriaeque tibique
> unum, Magne, diem, quo fati certus uterque
> extremum tanti fructum raperetis amoris.

(How blessed, if your Rome could see you, even in this way! If only the powers above had granted to your country and to you one day, in mutual, full awareness of impending doom, so you could part with one last kiss, a fleeting token of a love so great.)

The use of *felix* is rather ambiguous in this context. It is not clear whether it refers to Pompey or to Rome: "How blessed Rome would be" or "How blessed Pompey would be." As noted in Chapter 5, Lucan portrays Pompey and Rome as lovers in this passage. Line 32 of 7 is almost a verbatim echo of 5.794, and underscores the parallel between the parting of Pompey from Cornelia in 5 and the imagined parting of Pompey and Rome in 7. Pompey and Rome would both be *felices* if they had the opportunity to share this last moment of love. But they cannot. Thus the city—which does not even experience a vision of her beloved —must be *infelix* and suffer the pangs of unrequited love, just as Cornelia is *infelix*, and specifically described as such, in 5.802, when deprived of the company of her beloved Pompey. Rome, like Cornelia, will be widowed and lost now that Pompey is no longer with her, as surely as Pompey himself will cease to be blessed and productive.

Lucan is taking the traditional Venus and transposing her into something far more personal and delicate. Our final vision is not, as in Plutarch, that of Pompey dedicating laurel wreaths in the temple of *Venus Victrix*, but that of the Roman people forced against their will to pay homage to their conqueror, Caesar, by bringing laurel wreaths to the altars of Jupiter the Thunderer, the god of sheer, raw power, the immortal counterpart of the thunder-bolt-like victor. It is Rome, not Pompey, who will really be *infelix*.

What brings this vision of delusive happiness to Pompey? Lucan speculates that it may be the anxiety of a tense mind, seeking escape in recollection of the past. Yet perhaps "this was Fortune's way of giving Rome to you—the homeland you would never see again."

> seu vetito patrias ultra tibi cernere sedes
> sic Romam Fortuna dedit.   [7.23–24] [29]

It is not just an Olympian that lurks in the back of Lucan's mind, but Fortune. Just as the motifs of love and of lost *felicitas* are ghosts of Venus, so, in a way, is Fortune.

Fortune and Venus are closely linked in the Roman mind. Even in gambling terminology, the highest throw of the Roman dice was the *iactus Venereus,* the Venus throw. The lowest was the "dog throw." In the symbols of dicing, the languages of luck and love merge. You win everything at best; at worst you are excluded completely. As Plutarch, quoting Menander, points out, Fortune has a greater share in Aphrodite than night has.[30] It was thus more than coincidence that beside the altar of Venus of the Basket at Rome was a shrine of *Fortuna Virilis*.[31]

Caesar, as an offspring of *Venus Genetrix,* felt that he had some special claim to Venus' favors. But he felt no less grateful to *Fortuna*. Plutarch, Suetonius, and Dio tell of the gardens Caesar

29. The notion of dream contraries is common in ancient literature. One of the most interesting parallels to this passage is Apuleius *Met.* 4.27, where the young captive Charite tells of a dream in which she sees her husband killed; the old robber woman consoles her with the thought that dreams often presage the opposite of what they appear to say, then launches into the tale of Cupid and Psyche. Ironically, the young woman's husband is, in fact, killed later—though not by the bandits as her dream suggested. See also Pliny the Younger, *Ep.* 1.18.2. For further discussion of Pompey's dream and of the vision of Julia in 3, see Chapter 5, Section II, and the articles cited in Chapter 5, note 48.

30. Menander *frag.* 739 (Koch) = Plutarch *De fort. Rom.* 318D.

31. Plutarch *De fort. Rom.* 323A; the temple of *Fortuna Virilis* itself was built shortly after Caesar's death (42–38 B.C.).

bequeathed to Rome upon his death; in them the Romans built
a temple of *Fortuna* "because they believed that he also achieved
greatness because of the favor of Fortune, as he himself testi-
fies." [32] Quite possibly, then, Caesar had in mind both his debt
to Venus and his debt to *Fortuna* when he crossed the Rubicon
with his famous remark: "iacta alea esto" (let the dice be cast)
(Suetonius *Julius* 32).[33] Since his patron goddess was *Venus Genetrix* and his battle cry *Venus Victrix*, he had more than a casual
interest in the highest possible throw of the dice.

But just as Lucan avoids direct reference to Pompey's connection with Venus in 7, he avoids the chance to introduce her in
book 1 as Caesar crosses the Rubicon. Even the imagery of the
dice is removed. Lucan merely has Caesar say: "Te, Fortuna,
sequor" (Fortune, I follow you) (1.226). In other words, the role
that might have been assigned to Venus in the epic begins to
devolve upon *Fortuna*.

An even clearer example of this can be found in 3.8–35, when
Pompey has a vision of Julia, his first wife. The incident occurs on
the eve of Pompey's departure from Brundisium. The vision of
Julia in 3, like the dream of his theater in 7, comes at a critical
juncture in his life. It is the moment when he breaks with the
past, though he does not realize it. For he leaves Brundisium never
to return.

The apparition of Julia serves a purpose at once similar to and
quite opposite to the appearance of Creusa to Aeneas in *Aeneid*
2.[34] It emphasizes the watershed in Pompey's life, just as Creusa's
ghost does in the case of Aeneas. But the change for Pompey is
not to be for the better. He is to leave Italy; Aeneas is to journey
there. Lavinia will bear great children for Aeneas, but Cornelia,
Pompey's second wife, will bring her husband nothing but un-
happiness. His marriage will be quite literally *infelix*. Julia cries:

32. Plutarch *ibid.* 319B; Suetonius *Jul.* 83; Dio 44.35.3. There is, however,
much justice in Appian's complaint that people (particularly Caesar's foes)
ascribed everything, including their own blunders, to Caesar's Fortune (*BCiv.*
2.97).

33. On Caesar's crossing of the Rubicon, see Chapter 6, Section III and the
sources cited in Chapter 6, note 13; also L. Herrman, "Le Prodige du Rubicon," *REA* 37 (1935), 435–437.

34. *Aeneid* 2.771–795; see also Chapter 6, note 9.

coniuge me laetos duxisti, Magne, triumphos:
fortuna est mutata toris. [3.20–21]

(When I was your wife, Pompey, you paraded in joyful triumphs. But when you changed wives, then Fortune changed
too.)

Julia brought Pompey the victory associated with her family. But
Cornelia had been married previously to Crassus, the son of the
triumvir, who had died, along with his father, at the battle of
Carrhae in 53 B.C. By marrying her, Pompey associates himself
with defeat.

It is hard to imagine that another poet would have resisted the
opportunity to point out that Julia was the daughter of Julius
Caesar and thus directly associated with the family goddess, Venus.
When Pompey was married to Julia, he shared the blessings of
Venus Genetrix and, to no lesser degree, those of *Venus Victrix*.
His infidelity to his first love Julia by marrying Cornelia before
Julia's ashes were cold marks the turning point of his life. But
Lucan studiously avoids saying that the goddess Venus changed
sides as a result. On the contrary, what occurs is a change of *Fortuna*
(3.21): "Fortuna est mutata toris." This close association of *Fortuna* with marriage and love allows the reader to be aware of the
connections with Venus, by innuendo at least. But the poet clearly
wishes to avoid making explicit what is no less powerful when
cautiously understated: that Pompey's association with the *victrix
causa* of the Iulii and of Venus comes to an end with the death
of Julia and his marriage to Cornelia.

Lucan is adumbrating a divine presence without actually introducing a god. Instead of Venus, we find her closest counterpart
outside the Olympian pantheon, *Fortuna*. The choice is perfect.
Fortuna is un-Olympian enough to be consistent with the poet's
policy of avoiding conventional deities, yet divine enough to
suggest them. Most important, perhaps, is that Lucan, by resort-
ing to *Fortuna* rather than Venus, keeps our attention strictly
upon human relationships and upon the significance of individual
human action. Whatever decisions men make in the *Pharsalia*,
be they good or bad, are their own. And the crucial transitions in
Pompey's life are prefigured not by a goddess, but by two women

who shared Pompey's physical love. The imagery and language associated with Julia's appearance invite comparisons with traditional epic gods and Furies. But for all that she is still only the ghost of a woman—real enough to gain our attention, yet elusive enough to make Pompey wonder, when he awakens, whether his mind has been playing tricks on him.[35]

II. *Fortuna* and History

Fortune in the *Pharsalia* exercises a control over events not altogether dissimilar from that exercised by the Olympians in earlier epic, even though no attempt is made to define her in terms of a conventional deity. She is a personalized force rather than an actual character or being. Plutarch, in the *Quomodo adulescens poetas audire debeat,* suggests that Homer's gods represent those forces of causation which his contemporaries would describe in terms of Fate and Fortune. Commenting on *Odyssey* 8.81, where Homer tells us that the beginning of troubles came upon the Trojans and Greeks because of the plans of Great Zeus, he explains: "This is to be interpreted as a reference to Fortune (*Tyche*) or Fate (*heimarmenē*); it is a means of representing those aspects of causation which transcend our powers of comprehension, and with which we are completely unable to grapple." [36]

Although this explanation would be of dubious value to Homeric criticism, it has some significance in the criticism of Lucan. For Lucan is systematizing, to some degree, the forces external to man that appear to be operating upon him. Thus it

35. *Pharsalia* 3.36–40.
36. Plutarch *Quomodo adul.* 24B. For some modern discussions of *Fortuna, Fatum,* and the gods see W. Friedrich, "Cato, Caesar und Fortuna," 391–423; H. Le Bonniec, 170–174; B. Dick, "Fatum and Fortuna in Lucan's *Bellum Civile,*" CP 62 (1967), 235–242; O. Schönberger, *Untersuchungen,* 92–113; cf. W.-H. Friedrich, "Caesar und sein Glück," *Thesaurismata* (Festschrift für Ida Kapp), Munich, 1954, 1–24; H. Canter, "Fortuna in Latin Poetry," SP 19 (1922), 64–82. A particularly useful study of *Fortuna* in Sallust, whose usage resembles that of Lucan, is D. J. Stewart, "Sallust and Fortuna," *History and Theory* 7 (1968), 298–317. For a fuller bibliography, see the notes of Friedrich ("Cato, Caesar und Fortuna") and Schönberger, *Untersuchungen,* 172–176, particularly notes 7, 8, and 11. My own discussion follows in Section III. See also Pliny *NH* 2.22, and the excellent exposition of W. Warde Fowler, *The Religious Experience of the Roman People,* London, 1911.

would be wrong to conclude that *Fortuna* is merely one of the Olympians dressed in a more philosophical and prosaic guise. *Fortuna* encompasses in a more general way the role a conventional poet would have assigned to a number of Olympians. Given the subject-matter of the *Pharsalia*, of course, Venus would probably have dominated a "conventional" epic on this subject in much the same way as she dominates the *Aeneid*.

Besides, Fortune is a separate entity all to herself, with countless shrines all over Rome and other Italian cities, notably at Praeneste, which dated far back into the Roman tradition. She is a native Italic deity with a quasi-animistic rather than an anthropomorphized Olympian nature, quite discrete from the Greek *Tyche*.[37] As Plutarch somewhat sarcastically observes: "As of the present moment, however, there is no temple [at Rome] dedicated to Prudence, Magnanimity, Constancy or Self-Control. But Fortune has enjoyed her ancient and magnificent temples virtually from the day the city was founded." [38] Fortune, he declares, is Rome's presiding genius, her *megas daimōn*, much more so, in fact, than *Virtus*.[39] Although Plutarch pays tribute to the *virtus* of the Horatiuses and Scaevolas, he points out that in the final analysis Fortune, not any intrinsic moral superiority, handed the world to Rome. Ironically this is essentially the same argument Lucan makes for Caesar's victory over Cato.

In this sense Fortune is the force of historical destiny. And at times Lucan addresses Fortune personally as if she were akin to what we might call the process of history. When he voices his complaint that Rome has lost the freedom given her by Brutus, he cries, "De Brutis, Fortuna, queror" (Fortune, I complain about the Bruti) (7.440). His lament that freedom should be given to the city, only to be taken away again, is addressed to Fortune, as if she were the goddess supreme of history.

But Fortune is not quite as passionless as the name History implies. When Horace speaks of the Roman civil war as the *ludus Fortunae*, the game of Fortune, what comes to mind is a curiously

37. See Fowler, 235 and note 30 (245); and his *Roman Ideas of Deity*, London, 1914, 61–80.
38. *De fort. Rom.* 324B; cf. Babbitt's note in vol. 4 of the Loeb *Moralia* (London, 1936), 320.
39. *Ibid.*, 318E.

demonic being shaking the *turris* in which the dice are held, ready for Caesar's crossing of the Rubicon.[40] In fact, as the dicing metaphor suggests, she is not unlike Caesar himself. Though Fortune may be the closest approximation to the process of history, she has too much divine color to be *just* that. But for the moment, let us say that to Lucan or to Horace, Fortune is a force external to man, which confers its blessings upon individual countries and men, but which is unpredictable enough to appear whimsical and inscrutable. It is Olympus without the divine trappings, but with more than a trace of its divine nature.

In dispensing with the Olympian veneer, however, Lucan has opened the door to the issue of the morality of human actions. In the *Aeneid*, the presence of the Olympians provides an almost impenetrable barrier to any discussion of justice, goodness, or truth. If Aeneas follows the gods' directives, we are invited to presume that he is acting properly. Our dismay at his behavior from time to time can always be rationalized by arguing that he is fulfilling his duty, that he is "right" to permit himself to become the instrument of destiny; and epic tradition dulls our concern with the rightness or wrongness of the directives the gods give him. The absolute morality of Aeneas' actions is hardly ever before our eyes. It lurks, rather, as an uncomfortable question in the back of our minds.

But when Fortune becomes the principal divine force in an epic, the question of the propriety of individual actions can be raised more easily, as Lucan demonstrates in the *Pharsalia*. There is no Venus, no Olympian god, to carry the unwilling Caesar to his great destiny. Instead, Caesar willingly follows Fortune; his actions become an amoral response to what Shakespeare's Brutus calls the "tide in the affairs of men."

When Caesar ventures upon the Adriatic in his tiny boat, he gives a quite literal illustration of the force of Shakespeare's metaphor.[41] He is entrusting himself wholly to Fortune, on the assump-

40. *Odes* 2.1.3.
41. See above, Chapter 6, Section III, and the sources cited in Chapter 6, note 5. Plutarch selects Caesar's attempt to cross the Adriatic as an example of his *Fortuna*: "ἐτόλμησεν εἰς ἀκάτιον μικρὸν ἐμβὰς καὶ λαθὼν τόν τε ναύκληρον καὶ τὸν κυβερνήτην ὥς τινος θεράπων ἀναχθῆναι. σκληρᾶς δὲ πρὸς τὸ ῥεῦμα τοῦ ποταμοῦ γενομένης ἀντιμεταμβάσεως καὶ κλύδωνος ἰσχυροῦ, μεταβαλλόμενον ὁρῶν τὸν κυβερνήτην

tion that he will be treated appropriately. Similarly, in book 1, when he crosses the Rubicon and takes his first illegal steps into Italy, he makes no effort to disguise the amoral nature of his actions:

> te, Fortuna, sequor. procul hinc iam foedera sunto;
> credidimus fatis, utendum est iudice bello.
>
> [1.226–227] [227: *satis his,* Housman]

(Fortune, I follow you. Let treaties stand aside. We have put our trust in fate. War must be the judge.)

Pompey, in a rather different way, and to a much lesser degree, shares Caesar's attitude. After his confrontation with Cicero in 7, when he senses that the tide of history has turned against him, he resigns all responsibility for the conduct of the war. He will not oppose the turn of events, even though he knows the battle of Pharsalia should not be fought. No Vergilian Allecto robs him of his wits. The responsibility is all his own. Curiously, Lucan does not use Fortune at this particular juncture but supplies instead fate and the gods:

> sensitque deorum
> esse dolos et fata suae contraria menti. [7.85–86]

(He realized that this was the trickery of the gods and that the fates were opposed to his intentions.)

This is an appropriate moment for Lucan to insinuate the idea of divine treachery into his narrative, since the confrontation with Cicero follows immediately after the echoes of the traditional Venus in Pompey's dream. Pompey realizes that he—and Rome—have been duped by the gods. For a moment, Fortune is unmasked, exposing her Olympian *color.* But when Pompey addresses

---

ἀφεῖλεν ἀπὸ τῆς κεφαλῆς τὸ ἱμάτιον, καὶ ἀναδείξας ἑαυτόν, 'ἴθι,' ἔφη, 'γενναῖε, τόλμα καὶ δέδιθι μηδέν, ἀλλ' ἐπιδίδου τῇ Τύχῃ τὰ ἱστία καὶ δέχου τὸ πνεῦμα, πιστεύων ὅτι Καίσαρα φέρεις, καὶ τὴν Καίσαρος Τύχην.' οὕτως ἐπέπειστο τὴν Τύχην αὐτῷ συμπλεῖν, συναποδημεῖν . . . ἢ ἔργον ἦν γαλήνην μὲν ἐπιτάξαι θαλάττῃ, θέρος δε χειμῶνι, τάχος δὲ τοῖς βραδυτάτοις, ἀλκὴν δὲ τοῖς ἀθυμοτάτοις, τὸ δὲ τούτων ἀπιστότερον, φυγὴν Πομπηΐῳ καὶ Πτολεμαίῳ ξενοκτονίαν, ἵνα καὶ Πομπήϊος πέσῃ καὶ Καῖσαρ μὴ μιανθῇ" (*De fort. Rom.* 319C–D). The resemblance between this passage and *Pharsalia* 5.406 ff. is startling (especially the almost verbatim echoes of 577–593).

his soldiers, he speaks, as Cicero does, not of the gods, but of Fortune: "involvat populos una fortuna ruina" (Fortune envelops the world in one disaster) (*ibid.* 89). He appreciates the full irony of Cicero's claim that Fortune is begging him to use her: "precatur / uti se Fortuna velis" (68–69). But he does not have the strength of character necessary to resist Fortune or to resist the gods.

Caesar and Pompey, then, share something in common with Aeneas. They permit their lives to be controlled by a force external to themselves, and their decisions are not made upon the basis of any absolute considerations of right or wrong. What makes Pompey such a figure of pathos is, to a large extent, his awareness that Fortune is unjust and amoral—a thought that never enters Caesar's mind. But Pompey's unwillingness to resist Fortune aligns him with Caesar and Aeneas, not to mention many of the *Pharsalia*'s minor characters. They are all slaves of history.

We must now turn to an examination of the difference between Fortune and Fate, *Fortuna* and *Fatum*, in the *Pharsalia*. This is a much-discussed subject, but so important that a new look is well worthwhile.

III. *Fortuna* and *Fatum*

The definitive study of the role played by *Fortuna* and *Fatum* in Lucan is still that of W.-H. Friedrich.[42] His most important point is that Lucan seems to make little or no distinction between *Fortuna* and the gods on the one hand and *Fatum* on the other; they all approximate roughly to the idea conveyed by our word Fate. Rather than go over again the ground Friedrich has covered so thoroughly, we will begin where he left off—assuming that Fortune and Fate are much the same, but with one slight reservation: they are not completely identical.

In affirming the identity, or even the virtual identity, of *Fortuna* and *Fatum*, we encounter a semantic problem, the classic illustration of which is supplied by Servius in his comment on *Aeneid* 8.334:

Fortuna omnipotens et ineluctabile Fatum . . . He is speaking in Stoic terms. For the Stoics attributed birth and death to the fates, and

42. W.-H. Friedrich, "Cato, Caesar und Fortuna"; cf. note 36 above and E. Malcovati, *M. Annaeo Lucano*, Milan, 1940, 51–59.

everything in between to fortune (*fortunae*); for all aspects of human life are uncertain. Consequently Vergil combines them, to illustrate the dogma in its most definitive form. Nothing is more the opposite of fate than chance (*casus*): but Vergil is talking in Stoic terms.

Of course, Servius is right when he points out that there is no such thing as chance in the purest of Stoic terms. Chrysippus had observed that what men call chance is really an *aitia adēlos*, a cause for which there is no apparent explanation.[43] Thus he would argue that we merely attribute to chance those things our intellects cannot grapple with, but that this does not prove that they lie outside the causal network. Rather, we do not understand what their place is within the network. Something as utterly spontaneous as chance has no place within Stoic physics.

It is interesting to note, however, that Servius, in his concluding slash against Stoic doctrine, substitutes *casus* for *Fortuna*. He wants to emphasize that by *Fortuna* one should understand "chance." [44] This strongly suggests that Servius feels there is some ambiguity in the word *Fortuna* which might weaken his argument, and which, therefore, he would rather evade.

Indeed there is. *Fortuna,* as we have already seen, frequently implies not just chance, but some sort of *controlled* chance, administered, however whimsically and erratically, by a supernatural agency. It comes, then, more readily to the lips of the Stoic than to those of the Epicurean. In short, *Fortuna* occupies an uncomfortably ill-defined stage, half way between *casus* and *fatum*. But whereas *casus* and *fatum* are both fairly impersonal, *Fortuna* is not. And this is one reason to avoid translating it as History. Like *Tyche,* Fortune's Greek counterpart, *Fortuna* is personal enough to be regarded as a goddess. As distinct from *Tyche,* however,

---

43. Plutarch *De Stoicorum Repugnantiis* 1045B = *SVF* 2.973; cf. *SVF* 2.965–972 and 974. J. Brisset says much the same when she observes (57) that Fortune "n'est que l'apparence inintelligible du Destin."

44. Cicero (*Nat.D.* 2.56) seems to share, for a moment, the same feeling that Fortune = chance: "nulla igitur in caelo nec fortuna nec temeritas nec erratio nec vanitas inest contraque omnis ordo veritas ratio constantia." But Cicero here is reacting very strongly to Lucretius. The notion of *Fortuna* is common among Stoic writers, particularly Seneca and Lucan. For more on the Stoic notion of causation in Seneca, see J. Gould, "Reason in Seneca," *JHP* 3 (1965), 13–25, especially 16; see Seneca, *Prov.* 1.3, and M. Pohlenz, *Freedom in Greek Life and Thought* (trans. Carl Lofmark) New York, 1966, 128.

whose name is more neutral in its connotations, *Fortuna* is, as noted earlier, quite positively associated with *good* luck. The adjective *fortunatus,* no less than its English derivative, fortunate, is used exclusively of those whom Fortune favors. The Greek, by way of contrast, must specify either εὐτυχής or δυστυχής (even ἀτυχής); some element of the word must tell us whether the luck was good or bad.

However arbitrarily Fortune appears to select her favorites, the very fact that she is thought of as having favorites makes her, even in the most popularized and nonphilosophical sense, a marginally deterministic force. In this she is akin to a Homeric god. An exceptionally blessed or lucky person might even be regarded as the *child* of Fortune (*filius Fortunae*)—though surely not as the child of chance or of fate.[45] Thus it would be easy to see Julius Caesar as the offspring of *Fortuna,* not merely of Venus, and perhaps this is in the forefront of Lucan's mind in the *Pharsalia.*

Finally, *Fortuna* is rarely used to describe a single, discrete happening, as *casus* and *eventus* are. *Fortuna* suggests a series of occurrences forming some kind of pattern, however illogical or amoral. Perhaps, then, there is nothing really contradictory in the fact that the Stoics at Rome used *Fortuna* and *Fatum* together. For Fortune is that hidden factor operating within the causal network, but of whose precise relationship to the nexus no one felt completely sure. In short, there is a clear and very direct relationship between the concept of *Fortuna* and Chrysippus' *aitiai adēloi.*

Plutarch, in the *Quomodo adulescens,* seems to confirm this thesis. The passage quoted (p. 293) typifies his attitude. He treats Fortune and Fate (*Tychē* and *heimarmenē*) as being virtually identical: both terms are used, as indeed the names of the gods are, to explain those events and causes we do not understand. Another passage from the preceding paragraph of the same essay illustrates the point a little more thoroughly: "Not yet [i.e., in the time of Homer] did men call Fortune (Τύχη) by its name. But they were aware that the power of causation (αἰτία) which runs its irregular and unpredictable course was strong and inaccessible to human reasoning. So they tried to express it in terms of the names of the gods" (24A). Chrysippus himself could hardly have put it

45. For the notion of *filius Fortunae,* see Horace *Sat.* 2.6.49.

more succinctly. *Tyche,* or *Fortuna,* is a means of expressing *aitiai adēloi.*

Stoic notions of the differences among Fate, Fortune, Nature, and the gods are, at best, confused. In the *De Providentia,* for example, Seneca tells us that it is easy (and correct) for us to renounce nature (6.8)—despite the fact that one of the fundamental notions of Stoicism is that one should live a life according to nature. Similarly, in *De Providentia* 3.3–3.4, Seneca describes Fortune as the force that puts men to the test; but in 3.14 it is Nature that prepares the obstacles Cato must face. It is, Seneca declares, the function of the good man to offer himself to Fate: "praebere se fato" (*ibid.* 5.8); yet earlier he argues that we should offer ourselves to Fortune: "praebendi fortunae sumus" (*ibid.* 4.12).

There is little doubt that these various terms used by the Stoics to describe the forces governing the universe refer to essentially the same deterministic process. Obviously, then, their meaning overlaps to the point where they become virtually interchangeable. Yet each term does have its own particular color. Fortune, as we have seen in the previous section, underscores the unpredictability of events and of history while at the same time assuming a divine guise. Fate is more commonly used to suggest the definite and distinguishable aspects of the determined world order, the beginning and the end, the impassive and immutable. This distinction can be broadly stated in terms of Servius' comment on *Aeneid* 8.334 (*SVF* 2.972): "Nasci et mori fati stant, media omnia fortunae" (Birth and death are the provinces of fate; all that lies between is the province of fortune). It would be more correct to say that Fate is used to stress the ultimate boundaries of life, and Fortune the process of life on the individual or cosmic scale. The choice of term will depend on which dimension of the deterministic order looms uppermost in an individual's mind at a given moment. This, in fact, seems to be the gist of Seneca's comment in *De Beneficiis* 4.8.3: "sic nunc naturam voca, fatum, fortunam: omnia eiusdem dei nomina sunt varie utentis sua potestate" (You can talk of nature, fate, fortune; all are the names of the same god using his power in different ways).

One important distinction commonly made between Fate and Fortune by Roman writers can be illustrated in two of the passages from *De Providentia* cited above. One should offer oneself to Fate (5.8); one should also offer oneself to Fortune (4.12). But the purpose of offering oneself to Fortune is to struggle against her, in order to be hardened by her: "ut contra illam ab ipsa duremur" (4.12). The notion that one should struggle against Fate, however, is, so far as I can see, absent in Seneca's prose works. To struggle against Fate is to struggle against death; and to struggle against death is to rebel against the only knowledge a man has. As Lucan's Cato observes in 9.582–583, "non me oracula certum / sed mors certa facit" (it is not oracles that make me sure, but the sureness of death).

Stoic determinism, ironically, can yield only one totally positive statement about life: what is born must die. Since death is the only knowledge and the only certainty, it is, paradoxically, the only event in life over which the individual may exercise some control. As Seneca's god observes in the *De Providentia*, "I have, above all, ensured that nothing can control you against your will: the door is open (*patet exitus*)" (6.7). That is why Lucan's Cato addresses his men in 9.379–380 as soldiers who have only one wish, to die free. This goal they can achieve regardless of the vicissitudes of Fortune, of defeat or victory. It is hardly surprising, then, that suicide should be so highly regarded in Roman Stoicism. For freedom can be attained by death if it cannot be achieved in life. The knowledge that death is inevitable frees one of the obligation to be the slave of history.

Hypothetically, then, the wise man need have no concern for Fortune, since Fortune represents those tribulations that will confront him between birth and death. Seneca tells us:

boni viri laborant, impendunt, impenduntur et volentes quidem; non trahuntur a fortuna, sequuntur illam et aequant gradus. si scissent, antecessissent. [*Prov.* 5.4]

(Good men toil, expend and are expended willingly. They are not dragged by Fortune, they follow her and match her step for step. If they had had the knowledge, they would have preceded her.)

To follow Fortune willingly, however, requires the total indifference to anything other than one's own spiritual welfare that

Lucan's Cato finds unacceptable. It is, of course, true that Seneca, in *De Constantia Sapientis* 5.6–6.8 praises as an example of the perfect man the philosopher Stilbo who drags himself out of the ruins of his city unharmed, declaring that he lost nothing that was his. The collapse of everything around him is a matter of indifference. He simply comments to the destroyer of his city, Demetrius Poliorcetes, "vicit fortuna tua fortunam meam (your fortune has defeated my fortune) (6.6). Lucan's Cato has no use for this narrow, apolitical virtue Seneca toys with from time to time. He would more readily agree with Sophocles than with Zeno: a man who compromises with tyranny becomes a slave.

Lucan perceives more clearly than Seneca, I think, that there is but a hairline distinction between nonresistance to a historical process of which one disapproves and actually condoning it. That is why it is interesting to compare the passage from *De Providentia*, cited above, with Cato's opening remarks in *Pharsalia* 2:

> Summum, Brute, nefas civilia bella fatemur;
> sed quo fata trahunt, virtus secura sequetur.   [2.286–287]

> (I admit, Brutus, that civil war is a most unholy thing; But virtue will follow unconcerned wherever the fates drag her.)

We have already noted in Section II of Chapter 7 that this statement is at variance with Senecan usage, that the use of *trahunt* suggests disapproval of what fate has in store. But it is worth adding that Cato's choice of *fata* rather than *fortuna* in this context may be more than gratuitous substitution of terms. In the first place, Cato, like Lucan, sees the civil war as something evil—an evil for which the gods must bear the blame. He does not share the Senecan view that the gods are merely putting him and Rome to the test, and that the gods and providence are benevolent. Second, Cato sees the war as the inevitable death of the republic, comparable to the great *conflagratio* in which the universe will be destroyed. Thus his use of *fata* is particularly appropriate in this context, since his avowed intent is to commit himself to death, so that he may join his doom with that of the state. Since fate has pronounced the sentence on Rome, he has pronounced sentence upon himself, much as he does in Seneca, *Ep.* 104.32. Finally, for

Cato to say, at this point, that he is following Fortune would bring him uncomfortably close to Caesar, who declares in 1.226–227: "Te, Fortuna, sequor . . . credidimus fatis, utendum est iudice bello (Fortune, I follow you . . . we have put our trust in fate, and war must be the judge).[46] The evolution of events, Fortune, history, call it what you will, is Caesar's god. His actions and his notion of justice are wholly relative to events. But the wise man's conduct needs a more solid basis than that provided by a series of nonevident causes. As Lucan points out:

> servat multos Fortuna nocentis
> et tantum miseris irasci numina possunt.   [3.448–449]

(Fortune preserves many who are wicked, and supernatural powers are capable of limiting their anger to the downtrodden.)

To Seneca's Stilbo, these larger issues of justice transcending the bounds of the wise man's personal *virtus* may be indifferent. But to Cato they are not. He follows Fate not because he approves, but because death is inevitable. As far as his relationship to Fortune is concerned, he is quite eclectic. He feels it best for him to side with Pompey in 2.319–323 so that Pompey, if favored by Fortune, cannot conclude that he has won a victory for himself. But when his *virtus* would be compromised by an association with Caesar's victory, he has an obligation to do battle with Fortune. The fact that tyranny is inevitable does not mean that he must succumb to the tyrant as he must succumb to death, since death may be his means of avoiding tyranny.

Cato's actions, then, are based on his understanding of the limits of existence, birth and death, the world order as encapsulated by the word Fate. Caesar, however, views life from a different perspective; his preoccupation is with the purely temporal, that which lies between birth and death, that dimension of existence that is the province of Fortune. While Caesar views Fortune as an ally, whose favors he avidly solicits, Cato sees her as a force that will, at best, inflict upon him hardships to test his mettle. The only

46. I revert to the MSS. for the reading of 227. Housman's substitution of *satis his* for *fatis* is an unnecessary emendation which yields a weak line in terms of meter, syntax, and sense. For more on the notion that the Stoic follows fate willingly see Rist, 127–128.

favor he asks of her in the *Pharsalia* is that she may allow Juba to treat him as Ptolemy treated Pompey if it is his fate to fall into someone else's power (9.212–214).

In Cato we see what Seneca called the greatest gladiatorial contest of them all: *virtus* and *Fortuna* battling it out to the bitter end.[47] Cato epitomizes the struggle of man to rise above the nexus of events to become master of his own life. He elevates himself above the benefactions of Fortune, so that he may be something more than an instrument of destiny. In this sense he resists the tyranny of the predetermined world order as well as the tyranny of Caesar and Caesarism. Herein lies the crucial paradox of Cato's being. By resisting not only human fears of death, but Fortune as well, Cato can conquer even in apparent defeat. What happens at Utica is not the suicide forced upon him by adversity. On the contrary, it is the defeat of an attempt to force him to live against his will, his victory over both Caesar and Fortune.[48] As Horace observes in *Odes* 2.1, the civil war is the game of Fortune, the *ludus Fortunae*, which tamed everything on earth except the fierce soul of Cato.

In conclusion, let us turn again to what is, perhaps, the most famous line of the *Pharsalia:* "victrix causa deis placuit sed victa Catoni" (1.128) (The conquering cause pleased the gods, but the conquered cause pleased Cato). This ingenious *sententia* reties many of the threads we have been attempting to distinguish. Fortune's favorite, Caesar, descended from the line of Venus, won the day, under the battle cry of *Venus Victrix*. This was, indeed, as Lucan's Roman readers knew, the *victrix causa*. The republican cause, whose battle cry was *Hercules Invictus*, lost. This now became the *victa causa*. But, in the terms of Lucan's epic, these divine elements survive only in the most oblique allusions. The poet has rearranged the approving forces: on the one side stand the gods, on the other, subsuming the place of Hercules, stands Cato. Herein lies the real sting of Lucan's words. Indeed the gods approve the winning cause; but winning was morally worse: "vincere

47. *Prov.* 2.9: "ecce par deo dignum: vir fortis cum fortuna mala compositus, utique si et provocavit."

48. Cf. Seneca *Constant.* 8.3, who observes that when virtue battles Fortune, Fortune never emerges victorious: "quotiens cum virtute congressa est numquam par recessit."

peius erat." Divine approval has amounted to nothing more than acquiescence in the amoral, even criminal, verdict of history. By resisting Fortune, Cato has replaced the gods as the measure of human conduct. He will become, Lucan tells us in 9.601–604, a god "by whose name Rome will not be ashamed to swear." In this he stands in sharp contrast not only to the deified Caesars but to the Olympians and even to the very physical principles of the universe itself. For he alone adheres to the knowledge and practice of right conduct, of *virtus*. The gods remain silent, and in their silence lies proof of their unworthiness and impotence.

CHAPTER 9

The Scope and Title
of the Epic

I. Preliminary Considerations

When we turn from examination of what Lucan wrote to speculation as to what he might have written we walk on very treacherous ground. Indeed, it can be argued that such speculation is
both presumptuous and futile, for, to a large extent, it is. Lucan's
attitude to history and politics were surely intensified and perhaps
radically altered by his experiences in late 64 and early 65. There is
evidence of this within the books we have. Book 7, as we have seen,
shows the poet in a gloomy and satirical mood, despairing of all
possibility of restoring freedom to Rome.[1] Yet book 10 shows him
in a mood of greater confidence.[2] Caesar suddenly becomes more
vulnerable, and Caesarism less monolithic. How far this modification in Lucan's view might have affected his epic is impossible to
say. Had the Pisonian conspiracy succeeded and Lucan lived, the
entire *Pharsalia* might have been radically rewritten. And it is this
possibility of total revision that makes mockery of all theories
about the scope of the epic.

On the other hand, it is a rare reader who does not wonder how
the poet would have concluded the *Pharsalia*. Thus it is not surprising that scholars have advanced numerous theories about the
planned scope of the epic. Unfortunately for our understanding of
Lucan, some influential critics have based their interpretation of
the ten books we have on their speculations about the ending
Lucan envisaged. Their proposed continuations of the *Pharsalia*
are so extensive that the portion Lucan actually wrote constitutes
less than half the total. I offer my own thoughts on the possible

1. Above, Chapter 1, Section IV.   2. 10.332–546.

scope of the *Pharsalia* in the belief that such theories must be in-validated if we are to restore a reasonable critical perspective on Lucan.

II. Before or After Philippi?

Scholarly opinion is divided as to the most likely terminal point for the *Pharsalia*. The most popular endings are the death of Cato, the death of Caesar, the battle of Philippi and the battle of Actium (or shortly thereafter). It has also been suggested that the epic is complete as it stands. The most improbable of these suggestions are the two extremes: that the *Pharsalia* is complete and that it is far from complete.

The key arguments of the notion that the *Pharsalia* is complete as it is are (a) that Lucan's narrative concludes at almost the same point at which Caesar breaks off his *Civil Wars,* and (b) that it is unthinkable the epic could continue after the death of one of the leaders, i.e., Pompey. This hypothesis, advanced by Haffter and Schrempp, has been vigorously attacked by Buchheit and Marti.[3] The chief virtue of Haffter's theory is that it draws attention to Lucan's use of material derived from Caesar. But even if the *Pharsalia* were intended as a counterpoise to Caesar's *Civil Wars,* as I suspect it is, Caesar does not break off in mid-sentence as Lucan does in *Pharsalia* 10. More important, Caesar concludes where he does so that he can represent the wars after Pompey's death as foreign rather than civil and thus celebrate triumphs for his victories in Alexandria, Africa, Pontus, and Spain. Lucan would hardly want to concede this view. As we noted in Chapter 3, Lucan carefully points out that in Africa, for example, the Africans were involved in the war for private reasons.[4] Far from suggesting that the republicans were fighting for Juba, the poet will not even concede in so many words that Juba was fighting for them.

The argument that Lucan could not possibly continue the tale

3. H. Haffter, "Dem schwanken Zünglein lauschend wachte Cäsar dort," *MH* 14 (1957), 118–126 and O. Schrempp, "Propheziehung und Rückschau in Lucans *Bellum Civile,"* Diss. Winterthur, 1964. For the refutation see V. Buchheit, "Lucans *Pharsalia* und die Frage der Nichtvollendung," *RhM* 104 (1961), 362–365; B. Marti, "La Structure," 3–38, especially 17–18 and W. Rutz, "Lucan 1943–1963," 262–271.
4. See above Chapter 3, Section VI.

of civil war after Pompey's death is refuted by the simple fact that
he does continue, and that the focus shifts away from Pompey to
Cato and Caesar in books 9 and 10. The last two books of the epic
are clearly looking forward to future conflicts.

The Actium theory needs more lengthy treatment. Its chief pro-
ponent is R. T. Bruère, though has drawn a number of scholars
with him, notably Paul Jal and Lynette Thompson.[5] The propo-
nents of this conclusion all share a more or less similar perspective.
They argue that Lucan is not irreconcilably opposed to the principate of Nero, that he did not intend his remarks about the desolation of Italy and the Roman world after the battle of Pharsalia
to be taken seriously. Lynette Thompson suggests that the flattery
of Nero in 1.33–66 and the references to Domitius Ahenobarbus
show that Lucan really was sincere when he claimed that the civil
wars were worthwhile because they led, ultimately, to the principate of Nero.[6]

As we saw in Chapter 1, however, the evidence for a pro-
Neronian *Pharsalia* is so slim that it is altogether unconvincing.[7]
There is far too much that cannot be accommodated to such a
thesis. But if one postulates a pro-Neronian *Pharsalia,* one obviously has to find an ending that will support such an idea, and
Actium seems the most logical choice. (It brings a definitive end
to civil war and the final triumph of Caesarism, thus preparing
the way for the principate of Nero.) But the difficulties accompanying the continuation of the epic to Actium are simply staggering. In the first place, the sheer massiveness of the resultant
opus is more suggestive of a history than an epic; even as history
it would probably have been longer than Livy. Livy covered the
twenty-one years of civil war in twenty-five books. Lucan spends
ten books on the first twenty months. His narrative of the affairs
of 49–48 B.C. is almost twice as long, page for page, as Julius
Caesar's account of the same period. It is hard to imagine that
Lucan would have covered the remaining events in less than fifty
additional books. The end product would then have been as long

5. R. T. Bruère, "Scope of Lucan's Historical Epic"; P. Jal, *La Guerre
civile,* 54; Dilke, *Lucan,* 9–10, inclines toward a similar view. L. Thompson,
"Lucan's Apotheosis," accepts Bruère's arguments.

6. L. Thompson, 147–153.   7. See Chapter 1, Sections IV and V.

as the sum total of all other extant Latin heroic epic to the time of Claudian, including Vergil, Silius, Statius, and Valerius. Even the wordy Nonnus and the prolific Antimachus rested their pens and the world after a mere forty-eight books.

It can, of course, be argued that Lucan need not have dwelt so heavily upon events subsequent to the material in book 10, that he would have been highly selective in his choice of episodes. But none of the pro-Actium theories of recent years has made any attempt to suggest which events might have been contemplated for such a selection, aside from Lynette Thompson's hint that the wars in Sicily would probably not have been included.[8] And this meshes uncomfortably with other arguments offered in defense of Actium, that the corpse who prophesies to Sextus Pompey clearly hints at a later incident in Sicily involving Sextus Pompey.[9] But what would Lucan have omitted? The assassination of Caesar, the Philippi campaign, the Perusine wars? Since most of the arguments in favor of Actium grasp tenaciously at every mention of an incident subsequent to Caesar's death, it is only fair to point out that Lucan makes specific mention of campaigns at Mutina, Philippi, the Perusine Wars, and the Slave Wars (i.e., the struggle between Octavian and Sextus Pompey), in addition to Actium. Finally, Bruère justifies his preference for Actium partially on the grounds that Lucan was preparing an *immensum opus*—which Bruère clearly takes to mean a work of truly gigantic proportions.

A general abbreviation of events would not be easy to envisage, unless we concede that Lucan was proposing to write a very unbalanced work with a tremendously detailed account of the Pharsalia campaign and its protagonists, and a much more sketchy treatment of subsequent history. Further, of all the characters who play any major role in the ten books we have, only Sextus Pompey survives Philippi. Mark Antony is, of course, mentioned and Octavian's name appears, but no attempt is made to develop them as potential protagonists. It is hard to imagine what role Lucan might have contemplated for Sextus Pompey in subsequent books, since he describes him as the "cowardly offspring of Pompey," "an unworthy offshoot of a great parent," one of the "degenerate

8. L. Thompson, 153.   9. See Chapter 4, Section III.

minds" whom fear drives to consult Erichtho, and a man who will end his career as a Sicilian pirate.[10] He is hardly promising material as a successor to Pompey and Cato.

To continue even beyond the battle of Munda, Lucan would have to develop characters who have been, at best, adumbrated in our ten books. Even Brutus merits sparse treatment in the epic up to this point, a vengeful shadow hovering in the background. Lucan would have to develop a whole slate of new characters to take us beyond Caesar's death—and surely he would not be able to rest content with mere thumbnail sketches of Antony and Octavian, if he expected them to counterpoise Pompey and Caesar.

If Sextus Pompey is unprepossessing, perhaps even repulsive, Mark Antony has even less to offer from a republican point of view. The ruin he brought upon Brutus and Cassius, his share in Octavian's proscriptions, and his affair with Cleopatra were hardly calculated to win the sympathies of even the most impassioned hater of the Caesars. So much of the ten books is centered on the ideological issue involved in the civil wars, the struggle between liberty and Caesarism, that it is difficult to see what Lucan would have found to replace it in the struggle for power between Antony and Octavian. In terms of moral or ideological significance, Antony's cause has, so far as I can see, nothing to be said for it. It would demand a tour de force of poetic genius to avoid making Octavian the hero of Actium.

But Actium not only brought peace to the Roman world; it brought the triumph of Caesarism. As Nigidius Figulus notes in 1.670, when peace comes it brings a tyrant with it: "cum domino pax ista venit." And Lucan leaves us in no doubt as to his personal attitude to the purchase of peace at the price of freedom:

> post proelia natis
> si dominum, Fortuna, dabas, et bella dedisses. [7.645–646]

(Fortune, if you were going to give a tyrant to us who were born after the battle, you should have given us a chance to fight.)

There are, of course, references to the wars subsequent to Caesar's death from the very beginning of the *Pharsalia*, most

10. 6.589; 420, 417; 422.

notably the catalogue in 1.38–45. Yet curiously enough, this catalogue does not bolster the arguments of those who would extend the epic beyond Caesar's death. Rather, it administers them the *coup de grace:*

> diros Pharsalia campos
> inpleat et Poeni saturentur sanguine manes,
> ultima funesta concurrant proelia Munda,
> *his,* Caesar, Perusina fames Mutinaeque labores
> *accedant fatis* et quas premit aspera classes
> Leucas et ardenti servilia bella sub Aetna,
> multum Roma tamen debet civilibus armis.

(Let Pharsalia fill its terrible fields, let the ghosts of Carthage be drenched in Roman blood, and let the battle-lines clash for the last time at deadly Munda. *Let there be added,* Caesar, *to what the fates demand,* the famine at Perusia, the struggle at Mutina, savage Actium which crushes fleets, and the slave wars waged beneath seething Aetna. Despite all this, Rome owes much to civil strife.)

The manner in which these subsequent struggles are mentioned is important. Everything after Mutina is dismissed as an afterthought: "his . . . accedant fatis." Compare the descriptions of Pharsalia, Thapsus, and Munda with those of the Perusine War, Mutina, and Actium, not to mention the wars of Sextus Pompey: "Perusina fames" (the Perusine famine), the *labores* at Mutina, "aspera Leucas" (savage Actium), the "servilia bella" (slave wars) of Sextus Pompey. The terms in which they are described suggest that Lucan is intentionally minimizing their importance. He does not even bother to list them in chronological order. Although Thapsus and Munda follow in correct historical order after Pharsalia, Lucan places Perusia first, Mutina second, Actium third, and the wars with Sextus Pompey last, even though these encounters occurred in 41, 43, 31, and 36 respectively. Further, not only is Actium not the last battle on the list, but it is bracketed with the slave wars as an afterthought to an afterthought. At least Pharsalia and Mutina are encompassed by the "his . . . accedant fatis." This should show conclusively that these battles are the addenda to Lucan's theme, not its substance.

In all of this catalogue, there is not the slightest mention of the battle of Philippi, which surely deserves as much notice as Mutina or Perusia—if Lucan planned to include it. If this section is intended to be a résumé of the events to be included in the epic, then, not only is it carelessly ordered, but it contains a gaping hole. Was Lucan not intending to tell of Philippi, but planning to bypass it on the way to Actium? Surely not. More probably its exclusion demonstrates that neither Philippi nor Actium was to have any place in his narrative.

There is one more issue to consider in relation to this passage in book 1. It may be argued that, despite Lucan's down-playing of events subsequent to Caesar's death, he still classifies them generically as *civilia arma*, civil conflicts. But it is worth noting that famine, toil, and slave wars are, at best, mild terms for such conflicts. Even the "servilia bella" of Sextus Pompey, are not of the same order of significance as civil wars in the opinion of ancient writers, even though they constitute a subcategory of civil war.[11] In calling the wars against Sextus Pompey slave wars, Lucan is demeaning them in much the same way he demeans Sextus himself in 6.422, by calling him a Sicilian pirate. This degrading of one phase of Octavian's struggle for supremacy has an interesting parallel elsewhere in the *Pharsalia*, when Pompey addresses his troops in 2.552–554. Pompey expresses the wish that Crassus were alive to deal with Caesar as he had dealt with Spartacus. The reason Pompey assumes such a rhetorical posture and takes no credit for his own part in the defeat of Spartacus is surely that he wishes to infer that the conflict with Caesar is a slave war, not a real and full-fledged civil war. It is, consequently, a little beneath his dignity to have to fight Caesar.

Of course, this is boastful rhetoric for the benefit of his troops.

11. Such distinctions are not mere hair-splitting. After all, civil wars are the only wars within the general classification of internal wars which actually pit citizen against citizen, social equal against social equal. Florus 2.14.8 talks of "civilibus, externis, servilibus, terrestribus ac navalibus bellis." Subdivisions become even more complex with Isidore of Seville who distinguishes "servilia bella" from "piratica bella" (*Etymologiae* 18.5); cf. Ampelius *Liber Memorialis* 41; Orosius 5.22.6. For a full discussion of these and other passages see Jal, *La Guerre civile*, 19–42. What emerges from the testimony of ancient authorities in general is that piratic and servile wars are *minus quam civilia;* see also Horace *Epod.* 4.17–19.

But it does illustrate an important point, namely that Pompey is trying to pass off the fight with Caesar as something *less than a civil war*. Similarly Lucan's allusions to the wars after Caesar's death treat them as something less than civil war: a famine, a struggle, a harsh encounter with oppresses fleets, and a slave war. But the announced theme in 1.1 is: "Bella per Emathios plus quam civilia campos" (wars more than civil waged upon the Emathian plains). The scholiast in the *Commenta Bernensia* paraphrases this line as: "bella canimus gesta per Emathios campos" (we sing of the wars waged on the Emathian plains). He adds that these wars are "plus quam civilia a qualitate," because they involved father-in-law and son-in-law.[12] They are more than civil because they involve men who are related to each other. Paul Jal provides full corroboration for what the scholiast says. In his comprehensive list of ancient references to *bella plus quam civilia,* every passage he quotes points in this one direction: the authors are trying to express the *kind* of struggle involved, not its *duration*.[13]

Oedipus in Seneca's *Phoenissae,* for instance, cries:

> non satis est adhuc
> civile bellum: frater in fratrem ruat,
> nec hoc sat est . . .   [354–356]

(Civil war is no longer enough: let brother rush against brother, nor is this enough . . .)

The war, then, must be more terrible than mere civil war. The very fact that Lucan's epic will tell the tale of *cognatas acies,* of battle lines in which the opponents are related, makes his a tale of *bella plus quam civilia* with no less certainty than the *fraternas acies* of Statius' *Thebaid* make it too something more than an ordinary civil war.[14] Lucan's Perusia, Mutina, Actium, and slave wars do not quite match up to this, however bloody, terrible, and significant they really were in history.

12. "A qualitate, ut (pote) inter generum et socerum gesta, ubi et fili cum parentibus et fratres dimicavere cum fratribus." Similarly the scholiast of the *Adnotationes:* "inter generum et socerum gerebantur."

13. Jal, *La Guerre civile,* 35–37. Florus refers to the war as a "plus quam bellum" (2.13.4).

14. *Pharsalia* 1.4; *Theb.* 1.1.

Many of the difficulties of continuing the epic to Actium apply also to a continuation to Philippi, particularly Lucan's failure to mention Philippi at all in his catalogue in book 1. More important still, in the *Pharsalia*, as elsewhere in Latin poetry, Philippi and Pharsalia are treated as if they were fought upon the very same battlefield. This is the case in 1.680 and 694 and more dramatically, in the very last word of book 7, where Lucan refers to Pharsalia as Philippi at the very end of his description of the battle of Pharsalia itself.[15]

Similar identifications of the sites of Pharsalia and Philippi are made in 6.582; 7.591–593 and 9.271 ff. and, among other writers, in Vergil, *Georgics* 1.490 and Statius, *Silvae* 2.7.65–66. The Statius passage is particularly interesting because it is describing the content of Lucan's epic:

> albos ossibus Italis Philippos
> et Pharsalica bella detonabis . . .
>
> (You will sing of Philippi white with the bones of Italy, and of the Pharsalian wars . . .)

This identification of the two battlefields is, of course, historically incorrect. But to insist that poets confused them out of historical ignorance, as Graves and Dilke do, is preposterous.[16]

Since Lucan has told us, in no uncertain terms, that Pharsalia was the deathblow of the republic, his resources would have been strained to the full to avoid making Philippi a total anticlimax.[17] For Philippi, of all the battles of the civil wars, was the most like Pharsalia. It can, of course, provide a more impressive list of republican casualties, but it does little more than confirm the verdict of the earlier and more decisive battle. In 1.692–694, Lucan acknowledges the repetitive nature of the phase of wars after Caesar's death:

15. 7.872; see Chapter 2, Section II.   16. Graves, 45; Dilke, *Lucan*, 33.
17. For Philippi as the ending, see O. Due, "Essay on Lucan." Due, however, has since changed his mind and now endorses the generally held theory, that Cato's death would have been the end of the epic (*FH* 15.41 f.); also P. Grenade, 44.

consurgunt partes iterum, totumque per orbem
rursus eo. nova da mihi cernere litora ponti
telluremque novam: vidi iam, Phoebe, Philippos.

(Once again the factions rise, and I go round the whole world
again. Give me new shores to see and a new land. Phoebus, I
have already seen Philippi.)

These words are spoken by a frenzied, visionary woman and refer
to the fact that the civil wars will follow a certain pattern not once,
but twice. Bruère quite rightly sees in them "dark glimpses of
Philippi and of Actium." [18] But they surely do not, as Bruère
thinks, prove that Lucan intended to recount the wars after
Caesar's death. Rather, they point to the opposite. The reader, no
less than the "frenzied woman" has no wish to go round the world
again, and "vidi iam, Phoebe, Philippos" would be his cry too if
the poet were to pursue the story of Brutus' defeat.

Given Lucan's own acknowledgement of the repetitiveness of
the Philippi campaign, he is scarcely going to inflict it upon his
reader. His stock of hyperbole has been spent on Pharsalia. He can
replenish it only by turning to something different. Here is one of
the most crucial artistic problems raised by a continuation of the
epic to Philippi or beyond: the repetition of motifs already used.
Even Graves, who is surely one of the most hostile of twentieth-
century critics toward Lucan, concedes that Lucan presents us with
a montage of scenes that is "cunningly varied."

Each of the *Pharsalia's* battles has its own unique quality: the
sea fight at Massilia is not only a rare example of a naval engagement in Latin epic, but it pits Greeks against Romans and, ironically, shows the enthusiasm the Greeks have for ideals the Romans
are supposed to cherish. The episode of Vulteius is characterized
by the motif of *militiae pietas*. The conflict in Spain between
Caesar's army and that of Afranius and Petreius demonstrates the
peculiar horror of brother fighting brother, the agony of men who
are at one moment friends, and at each other's throats the next.[19]

18. Bruère, 227.
19. 3.509–762 (Massilia); 4.452–580 (Vulteius); 4.1–401 (Afranius and
Petreius).

Dyrrhachium is the Pompeian victory that could have turned the tide of wra; Pharsalia the battle where liberty and the republic are lost.[20] There would also have been a unique quality to the battle of Thapsus, no doubt, fought as it was so close to the site of Scipio's victory over Hannibal at Zama. There the ghosts of Carthage, who are constantly depicted as thirsty for vengeance in the form of Roman blood, would have drunk their fill.

But beyond Thapsus and Cato's death at Utica, the problems become more complex. Although Munda is the final catastrophe, "the disaster which Spain will lament," it would, perhaps, be somewhat anticlimactic after Thapsus.[21] Lucan has not developed Cnaeus Pompey or Titus Labienus into characters of any importance, and they would scarcely be figures to rival the shock of the African campaign, marked by the dramatic deaths of Juba, Petreius, Metellus Scipio, and Cato.

There is another objection to Philippi worth mentioning: If Pharsalia was to mark the beginning of slavery until time unknown, what was Philippi to signify? Its hero, Brutus, is neither the symbol of what remained of the old republic, nor is he the incarnation of its spirit in quite as powerful a sense as Cato and Pompey are. He is, rather, the exemplar of tyrannicide, the avenger of liberty lost. His contribution to the struggle between Caesarism and liberty was his murder of Julius Caesar, not his death at Philippi.

If we go beyond Philippi, we have another visit to Egypt, a second *amour* with Cleopatra, and another sea battle, in addition to the manifold problems mentioned earlier. To suggest that Lucan would have ventured forth on such a course is to do him scant credit for poetic sensibility.

III. The Ides of March or the Death of Cato?

Three other possibilities remain as terminal points of the epic: The death of Cato, the battle of Munda, and the Ides of March. Munda is, perhaps, the most problematic of the three, for reasons already discussed. In addition, the Spanish wars constitute a special action, separated from the earlier campaigns by Caesar's triumphal procession at Rome—a sort of mopping-up operation, over-

20. 7.397–459 and 632–646.   21. 6.306.

shadowed by the African war before it and the assassination of Caesar afterwards. Further, not only do they involve a return to Spain, but also the awkward repetition of a key motif, which might be very damaging to the overall effect of the epic. The author of the *Spanish War* describes, in section 39, the death of Cnaeus Pompey, who after withdrawing wounded from the town of Carteia, was captured and killed in a cave where he had taken refuge. He was decapitated, and his head was presented to Caesar at Hispalis.

Lucan makes no mention of Cnaeus Pompey's decapitation in his description of Magnus' death or in 9, when Caesar is presented with the head of Magnus, and for good reason. For to remind the reader that another Pompey died in this way would detract from the power of both scenes and undercut the symbolism of the felling of the great oak. Although we can argue that a return to Spain would not be unparalleled in Lucan, since, after all, Africa is visited twice in the ten books we have, the death of Cnaeus would be awkward indeed, and it is hard to see how Lucan could have avoided it, even if he had stopped short at the battle of Munda itself. Not only would the reiteration of the motif of a decapitated Pompey cheapen the effect of books 8 and 9, but it would revive the memory of Pompey to the detriment of the effect produced by Cato's death at Utica.

If Lucan intended to include Munda in his narrative, he might as well also include Caesar's assassination. Berthe Marti has recently proposed that the death of Caesar was, in fact, the probable end of the *Pharsalia*—an end Lucan could have achieved in sixteen books.[22] The unusual number of books she postulates is awkward, but by no means out of the question. There is nothing sacrosanct about the twelve-book epic in Latin since there are, after all, only two surviving twelve-book epics from the Roman world: the *Aeneid* and the *Thebaid*. On the other hand, there is only one surviving Roman heroic epic *longer* than twelve books, Silius' *Punica*, which has seventeen. Even if we add Ovid's *Metamorphoses*, with its fifteen books, there is no really convincing

22. B. Marti, "La Structure," 3–38; also E. Malcovati, *Lucano*, Brescia, 1947, 58, and F. Marx, "M. Annaeus Lucanus," *RE* 1.2233. On the sixteen books, see Marti, "La Structure," 3–16, 28–38.

parallel. Silius, after all, may well have been imitating Ennius by writing of the Carthaginian Wars in seventeen books, and Ovid's fifteen suggests that the ancients may have constructed their epics in multiples of three rather than in tetrads. Most telling, however, Lucan's biographer, Vacca, refers to the publication of "tres libros quales videmus," suggesting that Lucan published three books— probably the first three, as we shall argue below—before Nero's ban. If this is correct, then probably Lucan thought of 1 through 3 as a relatively self-contained unit. He is unlikely to have published them as a whole if he was composing in tetrads.

Obviously some of the problems which pertain to Munda apply also to an ending encompassing Caesar's death. There would still be a second Pompeian head, for example. At first glance, the attractiveness of Caesar's death as a finishing point for the *Pharsalia* is undeniable; it would give point to the constantly menacing presence of Brutus in the later books.[23] Yet difficulties abound. When Brutus struck down Caesar, he killed the man, but he did not kill Caesarism. The tyrant perished, but the tyranny arose again. If we are to give serious consideration to Caesar's death as a possible ending, it is important to ask what the final motif would be and how it would be treated. If the *Pharsalia* ended with Brutus' claims that freedom had been restored by the slaying of the tyrant, it would be ridden by the pathos and irony of history. The reader would know the transitory nature of Brutus' success, no less than he knows it in Shakespeare's *Julius Caesar*. For Lucan's Brutus, like Shakespeare's, might hope that he could "come by Caesar's spirit," but would succeed only in dismembering Caesar without killing the spirit, which reappears in all its vigor in the person of Octavius.

If the epic were to end, as the *Aeneid* does, with the striking of the fatal blow, some part of the historical irony would be shorn away. It might then seem to be the vindication of *libertas*, if only for a delusive instant. But such an ending would create the illusion that Caesarism too had been struck down, which is neither his-

---

23. For Brutus' vengeance, see 2.284; 5.206 ff.; 6.792 ff.; 9.17; 10.342. References to Caesar's death (other than those above) are 1.529 and 691; 2.546 ff.; 6.588, 802, 810; 7.451, 612–615; 782; 8.610; 10.528 ff. There is also a possible hint at 1.81. I am using B. Marti's calculations ("La Structure," 21, note 1).

torically correct nor consistent with Lucan's emphasis on the continuing struggle between Caesarism and *libertas*. If any of the aftermath of the assassination is included, however, we are on the road to Philippi. Caesar's death is conclusive in terms neither of the establishment of Caesarism nor of the final moments of briefly resuscitated liberty.

Berthe Marti argues that "the *telos* of the *Pharsalia* . . . is not . . . whether or not freedom is still possible. It is to describe fratricidal wars and the legalization of crime. This can only be finally established by Caesar's triumph and his rule or rather tyranny." [24] If this is the case, we can only wonder why she would have the epic go as far as the *assassination* of Caesar. For Caesar's death reminds the reader that it is possible to bring to an end the rule of crime, if only briefly. Or, alternatively, she should more logically argue in favor of a continuation to Philippi. For to reuse the argument she levels against conclusion with Cato's death, the murder of Caesar "is only one of the last, but not the last phase of the *ius datum sceleri.*" [25] The death of Caesar is not the end of anything in historical or dramatic terms. On the contrary, it is the beginning of the cycle all over again. If Lucan had sought the ultimate development of the legalization of crime, the conflict between Brutus and the new Caesarian faction under Antony and Octavian would have been more suited to his purposes. The proscriptions of the triumvirs would provide an even more hideous example of the *ius datum sceleri* than any of the events after Thapsus and Utica.

Berthe Marti argues that if the epic ended with Cato's death "the reader would be left with the feeling of unfinished business, the 'knot' being only partially untied." [26] This argument could be more effectively turned to argue against an ending with the death of Caesar. For Caesar's death, as we will see shortly, does far less to untie the "knot" than does Cato's suicide.

If Lucan had chosen to end the *Pharsalia* with Cato's death, many motifs within the epic would be brought to a very satisfactory resolution.[27] The legalization of crime, which Berthe Marti

24. B. Marti, "La Structure," 43.   25. *Ibid.*   26. *Ibid.*
27. The majority of scholars hold that Cato's death was the intended end of the *Pharsalia:* R. Pichon; W. Wünsch; H. Flume; O. Schönberger, "Zur

stresses, has already been achieved. Caesar is now dictator. More important, I think, are the themes of cosmic, national, and individual self-destruction, and the notion that the civil wars will act as an expiatory offering to Rome's past enemies. The African wars provide an ideal backdrop and historical setting for the final acts of self-immolation. As noted in Chapter 3, the clashing of Roman armies, each led, at least technically, by a Scipio, brings the civil war motif to an almost mythic symmetry. Two Scipios fight on opposing sides at Thapsus, near the site where Carthage stood and in the vicinity of the great victories of their ancestors; and the republican Scipio is also an adoptive son of the Metelli, one of whose number had fought Jugurtha to a standstill.[28] Further, Caesar's victory at Thapsus turns, as even the Caesarian account concedes, into a wholesale massacre.[29] The ghosts of Africa are indeed saturated with Roman blood. Thapsus is, as Silius Italicus seems to concede, a counterpoise to Zama.[30]

Obviously the whole of the civil war is a process whereby the people of Rome turn the sword of conquest into their own guts: "in sua victrici conversum viscera dextra" (1.3), but the African wars give the metaphor of national suicide a very literal significance. Metellus Scipio kills himself, and his blood serves as an appeasement to the ghosts of Carthage; Petreius and Juba seek death at one another's hands; finally, Cato takes his own life at Utica.[31] But Cato's suicide stands apart from the rest for a number

---

Komposition des Lucan," *Hermes* 85 (1957), 251–254, and "Zu Lucan, ein Nachtrag"; E. Burck, "Vom Menschenbild," 149; W. Rutz, "Studien," 3–59; W. Menz; P. Wuilleumier and H. Le Bonniec, 3; G. Pfligersdorffer, 353 and 359; W. Rutz, "Lucan 1943–1963," 262–266; cf. the remarks in *FH* 15.39–50, particularly those of Grimal, Due, and von Albrecht.

28. See above, Chapter 3.   29. *BAfr.* 85.

30. *Pun.* 3.261; see Chapter 3, Section VII.

31. There is some divergence in our sources in regard to Scipio's death. Appian *BCiv.* 2.100 tells us that he behaved courageously until overpowered during a storm at sea; he then stabbed himself and leaped overboard. Seneca *Ep.* 24.9–10, tells us that Scipio, as he sought to leave Africa after Thapsus and was driven back onto a headland by a storm, killed himself. His last words were, purportedly, "imperator . . . se bene habet." The Caesarian *African War,* however, makes no mention of his suicide. It merely tells us that Scipio's fleet was driven ashore at Hippo Regius, where his vessels were surrounded and sunk (96). But the Caesarian account tends to play down the role of the republican suicides as in the brief description of Juba and Petreius

of reasons. First, Lucan has gone to great pains to show us the close relationship between Cato and the ideal of *libertas* both on a personal and political level.[32] Second, he sees Cato's death not as a loss of life, but as a loss *to* life: "nec sancto caruisset vita Catone" (nor would life have been deprived of Cato [if Pompey had won at Dyrrhachium]) (6.311).[33] Finally, Lucan portrays Cato as unconquered despite apparent defeat.

To see how Lucan might have developed the motifs pertaining to Cato's death, let us consider some passages in Seneca, whose view of Cato closely resembles that of Lucan. First, a passage from *De Providentia:*

"Iam Petreius et Iuba concucurrerunt iacentque alter alterius manu caesi. fortis et egregia fati conventio, sed quae non deceat magnitudinem nostram; tam turpe est Catoni mortem ab ullo petere quam vitam." [2.10]

("Already Petreius and Juba have fought and lie dead, cut down by one another's hands. It was a brave and memorable pact with destiny, but not the sort of thing which suits my greatness; for it is as shameful for Cato to seek death from anyone as it is to seek life.")

The speaker here is, of course, Cato himself. Not only does this excerpt stress the potential difference between his suicide and that of Petreius and Juba, but it reminds us of Cato's refusal to accept clemency from Caesar. Plutarch informs us that Caesar was annoyed when he heard that Cato had killed himself, saying, "Cato, I begrudge you death, for you begrudged me the chance to save you." [34] No doubt Caesar's *clementia* was aimed, in part, at neutralizing his vanquished opposition. The psychological effect on

in 94. The account of Cato's death in 88 is full and proper, however; but his cause and his plight are made to appear hopeless. Contrast, for example, the Caesarian statement that Cato attempted to have the slaves set free to defend Utica (88.1) with Plutarch's statement in *Cat. Min.* 60.2 that Cato rejected the notion of any total manumission, but argued that any slaves whose masters set them free of their own accord could be accepted. The Caesarian account implies that Cato committed suicide when his motion to free the slaves was turn down and everything seemed hopeless.

32. See above, Chapter 7.
33. Cf. Seneca's comment that Cato's failure to win the consulship was a loss to the consulship (*Helv.* 13.5).
34. Plutarch *Cat. Min.* 72; cf. Appian *BCiv.* 2.99.

those who accepted his clemency can be seen in the case of Brutus. Plutarch notes (*Caesar* 62) that Brutus felt that "the honors and favors which Caesar had shown him had blunted any spontaneous attempt on his own part to rise and strike for the abolition of monarchy." By refusing Caesar's clemency, Cato became a symbol not only of republican defiance but of uncompromised *virtus*. And surely this is why Cato's suicide irked Caesar so much. When Cicero wrote an encomium of Cato, Caesar became angry, interpreting this as an attack on himself. He felt compelled to write an *Anti-Cato,* in a futile attempt to dispense with the shadow of his dead opponent.[35] Cato dead proved more politically potent than Cato living.

The Cato we see in the *De Providentia* is very conscious of the necessity to be master of his own life and death. He will neither live, as Brutus does, nor die in the fashion of Juba and Petreius. Just as Cato's suicide is special, so too is the sword with which he kills himself. It was, Seneca notes, "civili bello purum et innoxium" (unsoiled by civil war and innocent) (*Prov.* 2.10). What Seneca means here becomes clearer from a comparison with *Ep.* 24.7: "et stricto gladio, quem usque in illum diem ab omni caede purum servaverat . . ." (and, when he had drawn the sword which he had kept clean of all slaughter until that day . . .). Yet even the pure, sacrificial sword is not enough to bring death to Cato. He must die twice, he must wound his wounds: "vulnerat vulnera sua" (*Tranqu. Animi* 16.4).[36] Cato's death is not merely a double personal death. For when he falls upon his sword, he ends not only his own life, but that of the republic: "incumbens gladio simul de se actum esse ac de re publica palam facere" (*Tranqu. Animi* 16.1). The wound with which he dies is the final, bravest wound, through which liberty yields up her soul: "Catonis illud ultimum ac fortissimum vulnus, per quod libertas emisit animum" (*Ep.* 95.72). If Lucan had chosen this kind of treatment of Cato's death, then the motif of the conquering right hand

35. For the *Anti-Catos* see Suetonius *Jul.* 56; Appian *BCiv.* 2.99. For some idea of the kind of charges these contained, see Plutarch *Cat. Min.* 11.4; 54.2 and *Caes.* 54.

36. This "wounding of the wounds" is common to all the major accounts of Cato's death, even the Caesarian *African War* (88); cf. Plutarch *Cat. Min.* 70.

turned into its own guts would have received its supreme
paradigm.

In Cato's death, however, there is more a sense of triumph than
defeat. Lucan might well have used something similar to this as
part of Cato's final defiance of Fortune:

"Nihil," inquit, "egisti, fortuna, omnibus conatibus meis obstando.
non pro mea adhuc sed pro patriae libertate pugnavi, nec agebam
tanta pertinacia, ut liber, sed ut inter liberos viverem. nunc quoniam
deploratae sunt res generis humani, Cato deducatur in tutum."

[Seneca, *Ep.* 24.7]

("You have achieved nothing, Fortune," he said, "by opposing all my
efforts. Up to this point I have fought not for my own freedom, but for
that of my country. I behaved so stubbornly not so that I might live
free, but so that I might live among free men. Now, since the state of
human affairs is beyond lamentation, let Cato be removed to safety.")

He has fought Fortune to a standstill.[37] Now is his moment to
triumph. Though he cannot preserve the freedom of the state, he
can preserve his own freedom; paradoxically, in doing so, he keeps
the ideal of freedom alive. In this sense, Cato is the very spirit of
liberty itself. The people of Utica, Plutarch tells us (*Cat. min.* 69–
71) called him "the only free man," "the only unconquered man."
And this is how Cato sees himself (*ibid.* 64):

αὐτὸς δὲ οὐ μόνον ἀήττητος γεγονέναι παρὰ πάντα τὸν βίον, ἀλλὰ καὶ νικᾶν ἐφ'
ὅσον ἐβούλετο καὶ κρατεῖν Καίσαρος τοῖς καλοῖς καὶ δικαίοις· ἐκεῖνον δ' εἶναι τὸν
ἑαλωκότα καὶ νενικημένον. ἃ γὰρ ἠρνεῖτο πράττων κατὰ τῆς πατρίδος πάλαι, νῦν
ἐξηλέγχθαι καὶ πεφωρᾶσθαι.

(As for himself, he had not only been unconquered throughout the
whole of his life, but he was now victorious in terms of what he desired,
and had defeated Caesar in what is fine and just; Caesar was the one
captured and vanquished; for what he had long denied doing against
his country was now demonstrated and shown up.)

Thus, even in the catastrophe of liberty and the republic in the
African campaign, an element of hope emerges. No longer will the
ashes of Carthage cry out for vengeance. They are satiated. The

37. See Chapters 7 and 8.

disaster is so great that it drives even Hannibal's descendant, Juba, to share the fate of the offspring of Hannibal's conquerors. It is the ghost of freedom, the sacrificial blood of Cato that now cries for vengeance. The dead republic will have the blood of a Caesar. In this new order of things, Brutus is merely the first avenger of the ghost of Roman liberty and of Cato, much as Marius was the first avenger of defeated Africa. Just as Hannibal's ghost had stalked Rome in the declining years of the republic, so Cato's ghost would stalk the Caesars. And the sure knowledge that Brutus' dagger will strike Caesar down leaves the hope, be it ever so frail, that Cato did not die in vain, that the triumph of Caesarism is not complete.

Such an ending would be highly satisfactory dramatically, leaving no "knot" to be untied, save that which only history could untie. For Cato has already scored the moral triumph over Caesar's benefactor, Fortune; the question remains as to whether that moral victory will allow liberty to emerge once more as a political reality. The paradox of triumph in defeat might well have appealed to Lucan at the conclusion of his work as it does throughout the ten books we have. For the essential difference between Cato and Brutus is surely this: Cato was never conquered, Brutus was. Philippi marks the defeat of Brutus' attempt to restore the republic; Cato's suicide marks his defeat of an attempt to destroy freedom as an ideal.

If Lucan intended Cato's death as the ending of the *Pharsalia*, we would see even more clearly the degree to which he sets out to paint a picture of Rome completely different from that of Vergil. In place of the advancement of Rome's destiny by Aeneas' slaying of Turnus, we would find the death of a Roman by his own hand and the slaying of Roman liberty. With Aeneas' victory, the dream of the Roman future assumes an established basis in reality; Italy and Lavinia have been won. With Cato's suicide, the remnants of Roman freedom have been transfigured into a dream.

Of course there are some problems with an ending of the *Pharsalia* during the African campaign of 46. To begin with, the sequence of suicides usually ends with Metellus Scipio rather than with Cato, and in some accounts, most notably the *African War*, Cato's suicide occurs before those of Petreius and Juba.[38] But, as

38. See above, note 31.

we see from Seneca, the order is surely flexible and need be no
particular problem to a poet. A more pressing problem is that of
Munda. Clearly Lucan considers the battle of Munda an integral
part of his scheme.[39] But there are ways of including Munda without actually extending the narrative's scope to encompass a full
account of the Spanish wars. A description of the sailing of the
younger Pompey and Labienus for Spain after the defeat at
Thapsus, with a forecast of the disaster that awaited them, would
be an adequate reminder that more troubles still awaited the
republicans. From this description Lucan could turn to an account
of Utica and Cato's suicide, offsetting the promise of still further
reverses by the moral triumph Cato achieved. It is hard to imagine
that Lucan would have pursued the narrative to Munda at the expense of the dramatic balance of his epic.

In sum, then, it is quite possible that Lucan contemplated an
epic extending no further than the death of Cato. We may, of
course, argue that Lucan, toward the end of his life, became involved in the Pisonian conspiracy, and that he may have found
the temptation to go on to Caesar's murder too tempting to resist,
since he himself had decided to become a kind of latter-day Brutus.
Here we are entering upon incalculables. It is not until 9 that
Lucan emerges from his pessimism about the future of Rome.[40]
He would, I suspect, have had to rewrite much of his material in
1 through 8 if he wished to accommodate it to a note of assured
and ultimate *political* triumph. And, as we have seen, the murder
of Caesar is at best an ambiguous moment in the history of liberty.

If I am right, and the originally planned scope of the epic took
Lucan no further than Cato's death, the remaining subject matter
could have been dealt with in two more books, as Berthe Marti
suggests.[41] We must presume that Lucan moves Caesar from Egypt
to Africa without going into any great detail about his Pontic
campaign. Since Lucan makes no references to this phase of the
wars anyway, and since the Pontic campaign did not involve any
substantial conflict with Roman opposition, it is quite possible

39. See 1.40 and 6.305–306.
40. Particularly 9.601–604, the promise of deification for Cato if Rome is
ever free again (in contrast to the skepticism of book 7) and the apostrophe
to Caesar and poetry in 9.980–986.
41. 9.11–15.

that Lucan would have by-passed the battle of Zela as perfunc-
torily as the commentaries of Caesar and his successors do. "Veni,
vidi, vici" were Caesar's purported words about the battle of Zela.
Lucan need hardly have added much more.

No new characters would have to be developed for the African
campaign, except for Metellus Scipio, who is but cursorily mentioned elsewhere.[42] Afranius, Petreius, Juba, and the other major
protagonists are familiar to the reader from earlier in the epic, all
gathered together now for the final catastrophe of the republican
army.[43] A twelve-book epic would thus be quite plausible, and it
is unnecessary to postulate anything longer.

IV. The Title

Such a twelve-book construction would serve to emphasize that
the battle of Pharsalia occupies the central position not only to
Lucan's theme, but to the overall structure of the epic. Just as
Pompey is the pivotal figure of the work, the symbol of the decadent republic in its final days, so Pharsalia is the republic's *coup
de grace*. It is the battle in which Caesar destroys the New Troy
founded by his ancestor, bringing the cycle of history to its completion. On the grounds of this thematic centrality alone, *Pharsalia*
would not be an unreasonable title for the epic.

There are three reasons for preferring the manuscript title, *De
Bello Civili*, to *Pharsalia*. The first, and by far the most important,
is that no manuscript gives *Pharsalia* as a title; but many have *De

42. There are, in fact, only three direct references to Metellus Scipio in
the *Pharsalia* (2.473; 6.311, and 7.223). None of these amounts to more than
a brief statement of his existence. His name also occurs in two other contexts
which refer to his daughter, Cornelia, Pompey's wife (8.410; 9.277). Similarly,
the battle of Thapsus is never mentioned by name in the *Pharsalia*, only in
terms of its results. All indications are that the *pièce de résistance* of the
African campaign is to be the death of Cato. Scipio may be played down
somewhat by Lucan not only to push Cato into center stage, but because
(a) Scipio, by virtue of Pompey's marriage to his daughter, might emphasize
the Pompeian nature of the enterprise and because (b) Scipio, despite his
heroic death, does not appear to have been an entirely savory character.

43. For Afranius, see 4.1–401 (see Chapter 6, Section I); also Petreius, *ibid.*
Juba is far more frequently mentioned: 4.661–824; also 5.57; 6.309; 8.443;
9.213, 301, 869; 10.146, 475. Pompey refers to him in 8.283–289, but does not
name him. At least all of these have been sent in action before in the *Pharsalia*.

Bello Civili. To the textual critic who insists upon the establishment of readings on the basis of manuscript evidence alone, this makes the whole question of the title an open and shut case. The second reason, best exemplified by R. T. Bruère, is to deny that the epic was closely centered upon the battle of Pharsalia.[44] The third and final reason is a product of the second: if we can postulate an ending far enough removed in time and space from the battle of Pharsalia, we can dislodge Pharsalia from its central position in the teeth of any opposition.

Our previous discussion has already dealt with these last two issues. With Cato's suicide as the ending, Pharsalia is central to Lucan's theme and the fate of the republic. It remains, then, to consider the first of the three objections to the title *Pharsalia*. The only evidence for the title, outside of the headings *De Bello Civili* used in the manuscripts, is a hotly disputed passage in book 9, where Lucan seems to suggest that *Pharsalia* is the title of his work. To this we should add Statius, *Silvae* 2.7, 66, where the epic is referred to as *Pharsalica bella,* and references as early as Dante where the title *Pharsalia* is used. But the crux of the matter lies in 9.980–986:

> o sacer et magnus vatum labor! omnia fato
> eripis et populis donas mortalibus aevum.
> invidia sacrae, Caesar, ne tangere famae;
> nam, siquid Latiis fas est promittere Musis,
> quantum Zmyrnaei durabunt vatis honores,
> venturi me teque legent; Pharsalia nostra
> vivet, et a nullo tenebris damnabimur aevo.

> (O labor of poets, how holy and great you are! You snatch everything from fate and give life to mortal peoples. Caesar, do not be envious of the poet's holy fame. For, if it is permitted for Latin Muses to produce anything which will endure as long as the honors rendered to Homer, people in time to come will read both you and me. Pharsalia, our tale, shall live, and no age shall condemn us to the shadows.)

We have already discussed this passage in some detail.[45] But it would be well to remind ourselves of some of the conclusions

44. "Scope of Lucan's Historical Epic," 217–235.
45. See above, Chapter 6, Section III, especially 219 f.

drawn. Lucan's apostrophe is made as Caesar walks in the midst of the ruins of Troy, where he has arrived after his victory at Pharsalia. It immediately precedes Caesar's arrival in Egypt, where he is presented with the head of Pompey. It is the climactic point in the ten books Lucan wrote, bringing together all the symbolism of the desolation caused by civil war and focusing it upon Caesar. It is the end of an era. The republic exists no longer and will need the services of a poet to remain in man's memory, as Ancient Troy needed Homer. Homer told of the wrath of Achilles and the doom of Troy. Lucan now sings of the doom of Rome and of the achievements of the man who accomplished that doom, Julius Caesar.

Achilles must share his glory with Homer; Caesar must share some of his glory with Lucan. In this sense *Pharsalia* is the joint achievement of both Caesar and Lucan. Pichon (rightly, I believe) took this to mean that Lucan intended *Pharsalia* to be the title of his work.[46] But, more recently, Bruère, following Housman and Postgate, has disagreed, along with most other British and American scholars. Bruère, in fact, even goes so far as to suggest that the "Postgate-Housman explanation" has decided beyond doubt that Lucan did not intend *Pharsalia* as an overall title.[47]

The incautious reader might well be convinced. But Bruère's phrasing is misleading. There is no "Postgate-Housman explanation." There are two utterly disparate and inconclusive assertions, which are neither argued nor explained. Postgate merely offers the following translation of 9.985:

It [sc., *vivet Pharsalia nostra*] does not mean "my tale of Pharsalia shall live," it means "the memory of Pharsalia in which you and I, Caesar, have a share, shall never die."[48]

Of course he is quite right that *nostra* in this context means "our" rather than "my"; and the other element of "our" is Julius Caesar. But surely there is something banal about the idea that Caesar has a share in the memory of the battle of Pharsalia, given Lucan's perspective on that battle and the war in general. It is almost akin to arguing that Achilles has a share in the slaying of Hector. The

46. Pichon, 269.
47. Bruère, "Scope of Lucan's Historical Epic," 218 and 232, note 24.
48. Postgate, *M. Annaei Lucani*, xc.

only possible reason for Postgate's manipulation of an original that clearly says "Our Pharsalia shall live" into "the memory of Pharsalia in which you and I, Caesar, have a share, will never die," is to evade the obvious import of what Lucan is saying. In short, there is no problem with the Latin; there is only a problem in Postgate's unwillingness to accept Lucan's meaning as reasonable.

Housman, who, according to Bruère, "expresses this in more specific terms" merely offers the laconic explanation: "Pharsalia nostra: proelium a te [sc., Caesare] gestum, a me scriptum (a battle waged by Caesar, described by Lucan).[49] This is actually closer to the sense of the Latin. But why must we presume that *Pharsalia* refers to the specific battle and not to the war in general? If the dedication to Caesar were made on the battlefield at Pharsalia, rather than 1800 lines later, this narrower sense would be easier to justify. But since the battle we have learned of Pompey's flight to Lesbos, his death in Egypt, and Cato's march through Libya. There has been much to broaden the implications of Lucan's dedication to Caesar, not least the fact that it occurs at the desolate site of Troy. Besides, the very opening line of Lucan's epic is "Bella per Emathios plus quam civilia campos" (war(s) more than civil waged upon the plains of Thessaly). The battle gives definition to the war. Similarly Statius refers to Lucan's epic as *Pharsalica Bella,* Pharsalian Wars, and obviously thinks of them as including, but not restricted to, the battle of Pharsalia:

> albos ossibus Italis Philippos
> et Pharsalica bella detonabis,
> quod fulmen ducis inter arma divi,
> libertate gravem pia Catonem
> et gratum popularitate Magnum. [*Silvae* 2.7.67–69]

(You will thunder forth Philippi white with Italian bones and the Pharsalian Wars, the thunderbolt that is among the arms of the divine Caesar, Cato burdened with devout liberty, and Pompey, pleasing in his popular appeal.)

The specific reference to the *battle* of Pharsalia comes in the name Philippi.[50] But *Pharsalica bella* is clearly intended to amplify the

49. Housman, *ad loc.*

50. The general confusion over the name and precise location of the battle itself still remains unresolved. For a good summary see Dilke's discussion in

context to include the epic as a whole. Not only will Lucan tell of the battle itself, but of the whole war—including the story of Cato, who was not at the battle of Pharsalia. Seneca, *Ep.* 71.8, may also be using the adjective *Pharsalica* with a broad spectrum of reference: "nihil interest, utrum Pharsalica acie Cato vincatur an vincat?" (Does it make no difference whether Cato conquered or was conquered in the Pharsalian battle-line?). We may, of course, postulate that Seneca is ignoring the fact that Cato was not present at Pharsalia; but it is just as likely that he is using the expression *Pharsalica acie* as *pars pro toto*.[51]

Statius' testimony should not be treated lightly. He is, after all, the closest of all critics in time, place, and profession to Lucan, and is our earliest source of biographical information on Lucan.[52] If any of the ancient critics knew the precise title given to Lucan's epic in the first century A.D., Statius did. Most important, Statius demonstrates that *Pharsalia* is not necessarily to be restricted to one battle, as Housman and Bruère suggest. We could as easily gloss Lucan's words at 9.985 as: "bella a te gesta, a me scripta" (wars waged by you, and written by me).

Scaliger, whom Bruère adduces in support of his argument that *Pharsalia* was not the correct title of the epic, has an interesting point to make: "neque enim recte fecit Lucanus: cui Pharsaliae titulus adeo placuit" (nor was Lucan right to find the title *Pharsalia* so pleasing).[53] Scaliger clearly thought that Lucan was wrong to call his epic *Pharsalia* and goes on to give his reasons, which, in gist, add up to a fundamental disagreement with Lucan

---

his edition of book 7, 41–50, and J. P. Postgate, "The Site of the Battle of Pharsalia," *JRS* 12 (1922), 187–191; F. L. Lucas, "The Battlefield of Pharsalos," *ABSA* 24 (1919–1921), 34–53; M. Rambaud, "Le Soleil de Pharsale," *Historia* 3 (1954–1955), 346–378; R. T. Bruère, "Palaepharsalus, Pharsalus, Pharsalia," *CP* 46 (1951), 111–115. But it is still not reasonable to conclude that Lucan thought the battles of Philippi and Pharsalia occurred in the same place; see my discussion in Chapter 2, Section II and p. 314 above.

51. Plutarch (*Cat. Min.* 55) says that Pompey left Cato behind at Dyrrhachium; none of our other sources (including Caesar and Lucan) mention him at Pharsalia.

52. The suggestion that Vacca wrote in the first century A.D. is wrong. See the Appendix, note 3.

53. *Poetices Libri Septem*, Lyons, 1561, 3.123.

on the historical importance of the battle. But he never suggests that *Pharsalia* was not the title Lucan intended. On the contrary, he is annoyed with Lucan for choosing it.

Here we return to the point where this study began: the question of historical perspectives. Scaliger believed that Lucan was wrong in his understanding of Roman history. This is indeed a legitimate scholarly criticism and has much to support it. But it is a different matter to set out to demonstrate that Lucan was "correct" in his historical perspectives by squeezing the poet into an alien mold, cutting away and dismissing as nonsense those passages where Lucan displays his hostility to Caesarism and his anger at the sufferings of the republic.

The name *Pharsalia* suggests to Lucan throughout the epic the day of doom for the republic, the battle and the war in which Julius Caesar brought an end to the traditional system of government at Rome. Given this, *Pharsalia* is, *pace* Scaliger, a most reasonable title for the epic. Certainly there is no valid reason to assume that Lucan did not intend us to take *Pharsalia* as his title.

As far as the manuscripts are concerned, the fact that none give *Pharsalia* as title must not, I think, be taken as definitive. Not all the manuscripts had *De Bello Civili* as their title either. Arnulf of Orléans, who wrote his commentary on Lucan around the beginning of the thirteenth century (probably not much later than 1225), was obviously using such an untitled manuscript.[54] As far as he is concerned, the title is: "titulus talis: Marci Agnei Lucani liber primus incipit" (The first book of Marcus Agneus Lucanus begins).[55] In fact, it was probably the *lack* of title in early manuscripts that led to the search for a title within the work and the establishment of *Pharsalia* as the canonical title by the time of Dante. Given Lucan's premature death, it is quite possible that his original went to the publisher without a title. Perhaps, as Cazzaniga suggests, *De Bello Civili* was supplied by an editor, but

54. *Arnulfi Aurelianensis Glosule super Lucanum* (Papers and Monographs of the American Academy at Rome, no. 18) ed. Berthe Marti, Rome, 1958, xxxvii. Arnulf was probably not alone in this. Dante, for example, knows the epic as the *Pharsalia* (*De Monarchia* 2.4 and *Convivio* 4.28); this suggests that he extrapolated the title from within the epic.

55. *Loc. cit.* The misspelling, Agneus, is Arnulf's.

not necessarily early in the tradition.[56] Most ancient critics viewed Lucan as anything but a poet, and possibly that editor, like Servius, regarded Lucan as a sort of poetical Sallust, Livy, or Tacitus—a historian using verse as his medium.[57] The subject matter of the *Pharsalia* and the similarity of its scope to Caesar's *Bellum Civile* may well have prompted him to supply a title that reflected the work's historical rather than poetic aspects.

In sum, then, Lucan himself seems to be suggesting that *Pharsalia* is the title of his epic, and this should, in the final analysis, outweigh the uncertainty of the manuscript tradition. *Pharsalia* would agree well with the general importance Lucan attributes to that battle and to the events both before and after it. Most important of all, it serves as a reminder to the reader of Lucan's perspectives on Roman history. These are no mean considerations. For to Lucan, Pharsalia was an unmitigated disaster for Rome, far surpassing Cannae, which, no matter how catastrophic, was at least offset by later recovery and glory. But with Caesar's victory at Pharsalia, the same kind of desolation that Achilles and Pyrrhus had inflicted upon Troy and Rome had inflicted upon Africa came home to Italy. The rift between the two great national gods, Hercules and Venus, was not to be healed, as Vergil had suggested. On the contrary, it was to live on as the perpetual struggle between *libertas* and Caesarism. With the grimmest of black humor Lucan dedicates this vision of disaster to Caesar, and takes Nero as his only Muse.

56. I. Cazzaniga, *Problemi,* 39–40: "si può congetturare che il titulo del *Bellum Civile* potrebbe essere stato dato dall' editore che dopo la morte di Lucano pubblicò i versi." That the title should be given so early seems to me unlikely unless we accept Rostagni's dating of Vacca (see the Appendix). If Cazzaniga is right, it is inexplicable that it did not find its way into our manuscript as the firm, official title.

57. For the adverse criticism of Lucan's poetry, see Chapter 2, particularly Section II.

APPENDIX

Lucan and Nero's Ban

Although the *Pharsalia* is Lucan's sole surviving work, it was by no means his only work. We learn from three ancient sources, Vacca, Statius, and Suetonius, of a considerable body of writing which he produced: the *Iliacon, Catacthonion, Laudes Neronianae, Saturnalia, Epigrammata, Adlocutio ad Pollam,* fourteen *Salticae Fabulae,* ten books of *Silvae,* an unfinished *Medea, Orpheus, Epistles from Campania,* a libelous poem (*carmen famosum*) and *De Incendio Urbis* (On the Fire of the City). This list is not necessarily complete. It is based for the most part on the list in Vacca's *Life of Lucan*—only the *Adlocutio ad Pollam* and the "libelous poem" are not mentioned by Vacca.[1] Vacca himself notes that this is a list of works extant in his own day, implying that there may have been others that did not survive.

Unfortunately we do not know how long after Lucan Vacca lived. In fact, we know virtually nothing about Vacca. Rostagni has argued that Vacca's *Life of Lucan* preceded an edition of the poet published in the first century A.D.[2] If this were true, Vacca would have been a contemporary of Statius, Suetonius, and Tacitus, the other major sources of biographical information on Lucan. But clearly Rostagni is wrong. Vacca's remarks about the works that are extant in his own day implies that he was not writing very soon after Lucan's death. More important, it is odd that a first-century biographer would not list the *Adlocutio ad Pollam* among

1. Vacca *Life* 336.17–22; Statius *Silvae* 2.7; and Suetonius *Lucan* 333.5 are the principal sources for Lucan's bibliography. (Citations from Vacca and Suetonius' *Lucan* are noted by the page and line of Hosius' 1913 edition of Lucan).
2. A. Rostagni, *Svetonio: De Poetis e Biografi Minori,* Turin, 1944, 176–178.

the works extant in his own day. For Statius in *Silvae* 2.7 mentions the *Adlocutio*. Since *Silvae* 2.7 was clearly intended for Lucan's widow, Polla, who was still alive when Statius wrote, and since the most likely date for this poem is A.D. 89, the fiftieth anniversary of Lucan's birth, it is hard to believe the *Adlocutio* was not extant in the latter part of the first century. Unless Polla, and with her the *Adlocutio*, perished in the next decade, an editor contemporary with her must surely have had access to the work.

Perhaps the key to Vacca's date lies in his comment that Lucan gave gladiatorial games during his quaestorship in the manner customary at that time: "more tunc usitato munus gladiatorium." The fact is, however, that it was *not* usual for a quaestor to give gladiatorial games in Nero's reign. According to Tacitus, *Annales* 13.5, shortly after Nero's accession, the obligation to give gladiatorial games, imposed on quaestors-elect by Claudius in A.D. 47, was revoked.[3] The obligation was not reimposed until Domitian's reign (Suetonius, *Dom.* 4). If Lucan actually gave a gladiatorial show he was doing so of his own free will, not in accordance with normal or required practice. A first-century scholar would surely have known this. It is more reasonable to assume that Vacca is writing after the total abolition of gladiatorial games in the sixth consulate of Honorius in A.D. 404 and is pointing out to his reader that Lucan was not being wantonly barbarous by giving such a display, but merely conforming to the usual practice of his times.[4] In short, Vacca is probably no earlier than the fifth century A.D. and thus considerably more distant from Lucan than most of our other ancient sources.

By any gauge of productivity, Lucan was a most prolific poet. Considering that he was not yet twenty-six when he died, his output is staggering, and, according to our sources, he was very proud of it.[5] Unfortunately, almost no fragments of these works have

3. For Lucan's gladiatorial games see Vacca, 336.14–15. For the change in requirements for the giving of gladiatorial games by the quaestor, see the note of J. Jansen, *Suetonii Tranquilli Vita Domitiani*, Groningen, 1919, on *Dom.* 4. Rostagni (p. 177) misconstrues the evidence.

4. For the abolition of gladiatorial games see Prudentius *c. Symm.* 2.1124 and Samuel Dill, *Roman Society in the Last Century of the Western Empire*, (2d rev. ed.) New York, 1960, 56.

5. Suetonius *Lucan* 332.6: "et quantum mihi restat ad Culicem?"

survived, and, in most cases, we have only a general idea of what they were about. From the biographer's point of view, the most serious losses would be the *Silvae,* the *De Incendio Urbis,* and the *Epistulae ex Campania,* together with the "libelous poem" Suetonius mentions. Not only would these have shed some light on Lucan's personal life and political attitudes, but they might have given us the kind of insight into his contemporary mileu that Statius' *Silvae* provide in the reign of Domitian.

There is no way of reconstructing what might have occupied Lucan in the *Silvae.* But with the *De Incendio Urbis* and the *Epistulae ex Campania* there is a possibility of expanding slightly upon what little is known, even though we have only the title and a brief, two-line synopsis of the former and just the title of the latter. Here is the sum total of evidence for the *De Incendio Urbis.* First, Vacca:

Prosa oratione in Octavium Sagittam et pro eo, de incendio urbis, epistolarum ex Campania.

(In prose, speeches for and against Octavius Sagitta, on the fire of the city and (a collection) of epistles from Campania.)

These three items, the Octavius Sagitta orations, the *De Incendio Urbis,* and the *Epistulae ex Campania* are the last three items mentioned by Vacca in his account. No further comment is added. The passage from Statius runs as follows:

> dices culminibus Remi vagantis
> infandos domini nocentis ignes. [*Silvae* 2.7. 60–61]

(You will describe the criminal fires of a guilty master roaming upon the rooftops of the city of Remus.)

Vacca poses a problem immediately. His definitive *prosa oratione* obviously refers to the Octavius Sagitta Orations. But does it also include the *De Incendio Urbis* and the *Epistulae ex Campania?* Heitland and, more recently, Rose and McGann thought so.[6]

6. Heitland, in Haskins, xxiii; K. F. C. Rose, "Problems in the Chronology of Lucan's Career," *TAPA* 97 (1966), 379–396 (hereafter cited as *Rose*); and M. J. McGann, "The Authenticity of Lucan Fr 12 (Morel)," *CQ* 7 N.S. (1957), 126–128 and his "Lucan's *De Incendio Urbis,* prose or verse?" *FRIC* 99 (1971),

Rose and McGann begin by assuming that the *Epistulae* were in prose. Since, then, the first and last items were in prose, it stands to reason that the middle item was also prose. This line of argument would be valid if we could safely assume that the *Epistulae* were in prose. But we cannot, despite Rose's suggestion that they were written in imitation of Seneca's *Epistles to Lucilius*.[7] Verse epistles had been written by Horace and Ovid, and we might add that Lucan's collection, at least as far as the title is concerned, shows less similiarity to Seneca's letters than to Ovid's *Epistulae ex Ponto*.

Rose and McGann do, however, establish one important point of logic: if either the *De Incendio Urbis* or the *Epistulae* can be shown to be prose *or* poetry, the other will be the same.[8] But Vacca simply does not provide enough information to answer the question one way or the other. The crucial and conclusive argument, if it is to be made at all, must be made from Statius, and it is focused on the *De Incendio Urbis*. Only one point of information about Lucan's works can be established so far, namely that Vacca is telling us, in all likelihood, that all of the other works in his catalogue are works of poetry. His *prosa oratione* prefacing the Octavius Sagitta Orations is obviously emphatic, suggesting either that only they, or that they and the *De Incendio Urbis* and the *Epistulae ex Campania,* are the sole surviving prose works of Lucan. This impression is confirmed by the nature of the titles Vacca records. None of them, apart from these last three, is likely to be in prose.

I. The *Genethliacon Lucani*

Statius' poem in honor of Lucan's birthday is one of the most valuable pieces of information we have about Lucan's nonextant work. Not only is it the earliest and fullest biographical sketch of Lucan's career, but it provides a brief synopsis of several works, including the *De Incendio Urbis*. It is also a well-written and very carefully structured poem in its own right. The opening 35 lines praise Lucan's poetic genius and the honor he has bestowed upon

---

63–65; also Rostagni p. 186 and J. H. Mozley, in Vol. 1 of the Loeb Statius, London, 1928, note on *Silvae* 2.7.60–61.

7. *Rose,* 391.   8. *Rose,* 386, note 20, and McGann (above, note 6).

his native Spain. The concluding 29 lines are a kind of apotheosis of the poet and a *consolatio* to his soul. The central, and for our purposes most important, segment of the poem, lines 36–106, gives an account of Lucan's achievements as a poet and is sung by no less a personage than the Muse Calliope, whom Statius depicts as standing above the cradle of the infant Lucan, prophesying the poetic heights he will attain. Her joy is so great upon seeing the child that she abandons her age-long grief for her son Orpheus.

Calliope's first words tell us the reason for her ecstasy: "puer o dicate Musis, / longaevos cito transire vates . . ." (41–42) (O child, dedicated to the Muses, destined to surpass quickly the long-lived bards . . .). His genius, she continues, will bear comparison with that of Homer and Apollonius and surpass that of her own Orpheus:

> non tu flumina nec greges ferarum
> nec plectro Geticas movebis ornos,
> sed septem iuga Martiumque Thybrim
> et doctos equites et eloquente
> cantu purpureum trahes senatum.   [43–47]

(You will not move rivers or flocks of wild beasts or Getic ash-trees with your lyre. But, with your eloquent song, you will draw after you the seven hills of Rome, the Tiber sacred to Mars, the learned knights and the purple-clad senate.)

Calliope's praises are indeed extravagant. She now proceeds to list the works with which Lucan will achieve this Orphean tour de force: the *Iliacon,* the *Catachthonion,* the *Laudes Neronianae,* the *De Incendio Urbis,* the *Adlocutio ad Pollam,* and the *Pharsalia.* At line 73, Calliope refers back to Lucan's achievement: "haec primo iuvenis canes sub aevo" (These works *you will sing* in the first years of youth). *Canes,* you will sing, is the key word here. It definitely suggests that the works she has mentioned are all *poetry.* Line 81 confirms this impression: "nec solum dabo carminum nitorem" (Not only will I give you glory in your poetry).

If, as Rose, McGann, and Heitland (and, less comprehensibly, Mozley in his translation of the *Genethliacon Lucani*) claim, the *De Incendio Urbis* was a prose declamation, probably unpublished, it is strange that Calliope should adduce it as testimony of

Lucan's poetic talent. Furthermore, the *De Incendio Urbis* stands at the precise center of her account: at lines 60–61 of a narrative extending from 40–81. There is nothing to indicate that Calliope was ever the patron of prose declamations, much less unpublished ones, and she would scarcely mention one here if Lucan is to be so great a poet as to eclipse her grief for Orpheus. We can hardly argue that Calliope is trying to bolster a slender bibliography, since she does not mention several of Lucan's other known poetical works. It would, rather, be more reasonable to argue that she is adducing the best—or at least those Statius reckoned to be the best. If the *De Incendio Urbis* was not a poem, there is no logical reason for Calliope to include it here. In addition, the claim advanced by Rose that the *De Incendio Urbis* was unpublished is most difficult to reconcile with Vacca, who states that it was among the works extant in his own day.

Rose also maintains that the *Adlocutio ad Pollam* was prose. Since this work is mentioned by Calliope along with the *De Incendio Urbis,* the same rebuttal must apply. Besides, since Polla was Lucan's wife, the suggestion that the work was in prose says little for Lucan's imagination as a lover and even less for Polla's ability to stir some response from her husband's prolific Muse. In sum, then, there is no reason to assume that the items mentioned by Calliope are not *all* poetry, and every reason to believe they are.

To return to Vacca: it should now be clear that, when the Octavius Sagitta Orations are defined as prose works, they are singled out as the *only* surviving works of Lucan that are not poetical. For if the *De Incendio Urbis* is poetry, there is no possibility of extending the definitive *prosa oratione* to include the *Epistulae ex Campania.* Thus Rose's view that these letters are imitations of Seneca's epistles to Lucilius is without foundation. If Lucan was imitating anyone, Ovid is the more likely candidate since, if our argument is correct, the *Epistulae ex Campania* must have been verse.

II. Content of the *De Incendio Urbis*

Our only evidence as to what Lucan said in the *De Incendio Urbis* is the two-line synopsis in Statius' *Genethliacon Lucani,* 60–61, which, for the sake of convenience, we will repeat here:

dices culminibus Remi vagantis
infandos domini nocentis ignes.

(You will describe the criminal fires of a guilty master roaming
upon the rooftops of the city of Remus.)

Culminibus Remi surely refers to Rome, and leaves no doubt that
Statius is alluding to a poem on the first of Rome, the *De Incendio
Urbis* listed by Vacca. Precisely why Rome is called the city of
Remus is not clear. Several writers, notably Catullus, Propertius,
Horace, and Juvenal, also do so. The usual explanation is that the
substitution of Remus for Romulus is merely *metri causa,* and this
may, of course, be correct. The fact that the fire is described as
criminal (*infandos . . . ignes*) strongly suggests that it was caused
by some wrongful action, and the explanatory genitive *domini
nocentis* makes no sense unless it is indicative of the fire's source.
The blaze was caused, then, by a guilty master, a guilty emperor,
Nero. The import of the lines is clear: either Lucan or Statius
thought Nero was responsible for the burning of Rome, the great
conflagration of July, A.D. 64.[9] Perhaps they both did.[10]

If Statius rather than Lucan is suggesting Nero's culpability, we
must interpret the couplet in some such way: "You will tell of the
fire of Rome—a fire actually caused by the criminal actions of
Nero." The sense is just about plausible, if somewhat forced. But
this would not be the only instance in Calliope's catalogue where
Statius interpolates his own (Calliope's, if you like) comments:

ingratus Nero dulcibus theatris
et noster tibi proferetur Orpheus.   [58–59]

(The thankless Nero and my Orpheus will be produced by you
in the pleasant theater.)

9. For a recent assessment of the evidence on the fire, see J. Beaujeu, *L'Incendie de Rome en 64 et les chrétiens,* Collection Latomus 49, Brussels, 1960,
and the reviews of this study by Piganiol, *REL* 38 (1960), 449–450; van Son,
Mnemosyne 15 (1962), 211–212; Marrou, *REA* 67 (1965), 580; Townend, *JRS*
51 (1961), 244–245; Balsdon, *CR* 11 (1961), 301; and Hübner, *Gymnasium* 68
(1961), 479–481. In general it seems unlikely that Nero actually set fire to the
city.

10. *Silvae* 2.7.100, 104, and 116–119 make it quite plain that Statius does
not regard Nero favorably.

This couplet refers to the *Laudes Neronianae* and the *Orpheus,* both of which were probably early works of Lucan. If the *Laudes* can be dated to A.D. 60, as seems likely, it is most improbable that Lucan would have called Nero *ingratus* at this point in his career.[11] It is clearly Statius' epithet for Nero and refers to the emperor's later treatment of Lucan or to the fact that Nero was not popular with the crowds (if we take *ingratus* as "unpleasing" rather than "ungrateful"). Even more obviously, Calliope's *noster* is clearly her own epithet for her son, Orpheus.

Yet the references to the *Laudes* and *Orpheus,* unlike the references to all the other poems in Calliope's catalogue, make no pretense of being a synopsis of content. Statius gives no hint of what Lucan actually said in the works, other than that their subjects were indeed Nero and Orpheus respectively. Calliope's Orpheus, like Nero, will merely be presented by Lucan: "proferetur tibi." Contrast this oblique and impersonally phrased *proferetur tibi* with the description of the *De Incendio Urbis* which is introduced by *dices,* you will tell (of). A glance at this and other second-person-future forms used by Calliope gives fairly convincing proof that they are used when she wishes to introduce the general outline of what Lucan said in a poem, where she is reporting *content,* not just subject. Compare the summary of the *Pharsalia* at 64–72:

> mox coepta generosior iuventa
> albos ossibus Italis Philippos
> et Pharsalica bella *detonabis:*
> quod fulmen ducis inter arma divi,
> libertate gravem pia Catonem
> et gratum popularitate Magnum;
> tu Pelusiaci scelus Canopi
> *deflebis* pius et Pharo cruenta
> Pompeio *dabis* altius sepulcrum.

(Soon, more noble in your manhood, *you will thunder forth* Philippi white with Italian bones and the Pharsalian Wars: the thunderbolt that was among the weapons of the divine leader,

11. For the date of the *Laudes,* see *Rose,* 386 ff. It is clear from Suetonius' *Lucan* (332.9–11) that Lucan was not only Nero's friend, but a member of his official *cohors amicorum;* see also Vacca *Life* 335.19–21.

Cato, serious in his dedication to most noble liberty, and Pompey, pleasing in his popular appeal. *You will* nobly *weep* over the crime committed by the Egyptians, and *will give* to Pompey a sepulchre more lofty than bloody Pharos.)

Here we have a succinct summary of some of the *Pharsalia*'s high points. Similarly, the description of the *Iliacon* and the *Catachthonion:*

> *ludes* Hectora Thessalosque currus
> et supplex Priami potentis aurum,
> et sedes *reserabis* inferorum.　[55–57]

(*You will toy* with Hector and the chariot of Achilles, and the suppliant gold of powerful Priam, and *you will unlock* the dwellings of the dead.)

Compare also the *Adlocutio ad Pollam:*

> hinc castae titulum decusque Pollae
> iocunda *dabis* adlocutione.　[63–64]

(Then, in a delightful address, *you will tell* the fame and honor of chaste Polla.)

In short, every poem, apart from the *Laudes* and the *Orpheus,* is summarized and introduced by a second-person verb that purports to give a synopsis of the poem's subject matter. The outline of all these seems to be a fair approximation to the known or suspected content of each, and there is no reason to doubt that the same holds true of the *De Incendio Urbis.* It is worth adding that each of the verbs used (*detonabis,* you will thunder forth; *deflebis,* you will weep; *dabis . . . sepulcrum,* you will give a sepulchre; *ludes,* you will toy; *reserabis,* you will unlock; *titulum decusque . . . dabis,* you will give the fame and honor) in some way encapsulates the poet's approach to his material. The synopsis of the *Pharsalia* bears this out clearly. Lucan does thunder forth his theme, he does weep for Pompey, and he does give him a more lofty sepulchre, granting him an apotheosis in book 9.

Dices, you will tell, the verb used to introduce the *De Incendio Urbis,* is very matter-of-fact. It has none of the emotional color of the verb introducing the *Pharsalia.* The implication is that

Lucan is making a simple, factual statement. This suggests not only that Lucan accused Nero of setting fire to Rome but also that Statius agreed with him.

If this is the case, it is not hard to understand the central position which Statius assigns it in his catalogue of Lucan's works. For a poem so damning to the emperor must indeed have been a demarcation point in his career. If modern scholars are right, and Nero was not responsible for the fire, the emperor's fury must have been especially savage. Not only was he being falsely accused of a terrible action, but accused by a poet who was supposed to be his friend and protégé, a man he had personally advanced to poetic honors and high public office.

Precisely what steps Nero took against Lucan after the appearance of the *De Incendio Urbis* we do not know. Around the end of 64, however, Nero placed a ban on Lucan's appearances in the law courts and upon further recitations of his poetry.[12] Conventionally this ban is associated with the appearance of the *Pharsalia*, which either excited Nero's jealousy by its excellence or angered him with its content. While both these factors may have been at work in Nero's reaction to the *Pharsalia*, he could hardly have ignored the *De Incendio Urbis*. Even the mildest of emperors would have found it necessary to take steps against the author of such a work, coming as it did in a moment of severe political embarrassment for the palace. The *De Incendio Urbis*, in and of itself, would have been sufficient reason for Nero to silence Lucan permanently. And that is precisely what the ban did, or at least was intended to do.

The *De Incendio Urbis* can hardly have been published much before the end of July 64. The closer it is dated to the actual fire, the more savage Nero's retaliation is likely to have been. We may, of course, argue that it was published posthumously, but Statius gives us no reason to suspect this, and, as Rose has pointed out,

12. For the ban see Tacitus *Ann.* 15.49: "famam carminum eius premebat Nero prohibueratque ostentare, vanus aemulatione"; Vacca 335–336.24 ff.: "ediderat . . . tres libros quales videmus. quare inimicum sibi fecit imperatorem. quo ambitiosa vanitate, non hominum tantum, sed et artium principatum vindicante, interdictum est etiam causarum actionibus"; Dio 62.29.4: "ὁ δὲ δὴ Λουκανὸς ἐκωλύθη ποιεῖν, ἐπειδὴ ἰσχυρῶς ἐπὶ τῇ ποιήσει ἐπῃνεῖτο." Suetonius does not mention the ban.

Statius' catalogue seems to follow a more or less chronological order.[13] Of all our sources on Lucan, Statius is least likely to have made an error, not only because he was also a poet and almost Lucan's contemporary, but because the *Genethliacon* was obviously intended especially for Polla, Lucan's widow.

III. Lucan the Politician

If my thesis is correct thus far, why do none of our sources connect the *De Incendio Urbis* with Nero's ban?

Of the ancient sources that deal with Lucan in any substantial way, Tacitus and Suetonius are hostile toward the poet, Statius and Vacca relatively favorable. Tacitus mentions none of Lucan's works at all. Yet if he gives him scant credit as a poet, he gives him even less as a political figure. When he mentions Lucan's role in the Pisonian conspiracy, he sets the poet's name side by side with that of Plautius Lateranus and contrasts Lateranus' genuine idealism with the *propriae causae* of personal animosity that drove Lucan.[14] Tacitus is eager to play down the possibility that Lucan joined Piso through any genuine feelings for the restoration of the republic. It was, no doubt, the debacle following the detection of the conspiracy that encouraged Tacitus to think of Lucan in this way. The rumor that Lucan had incriminated his mother, Acilia,

13. For a discussion of the chronological listing of Lucan's works in *Silvae* 2.7, see *Rose*, 386 ff. Rose's arguments are convincing on all counts but one: when he suggests that Statius thought of the *Pharsalia* "as being composed, or of parts being published in the last few months of Lucan's life." All we may safely infer from 2.7.62–66 and 102–104 is that Lucan was still working on the *Pharsalia* at the time of his death, and that the epic was a product of his maturer years. Thus it is reasonable to conclude that parts were being composed in the last months of Lucan's life. But it is not reasonable to conclude, as Rose does in the sentence immediately following the one quoted above, that "the *De Bello Civili* started to appear after July 64." The sole reason for this assumption is that the *Pharsalia* is mentioned by Statius after the *Adlocutio* and the *De Incendio Urbis*. But Statius is quite justified in mentioning the *Pharsalia* last, even if parts of it were written and published prior to July 64. The epic was, presumably, the high point of Lucan's poetic career, and he was working on it at the time of his death. For Calliope to conclude his biography with a minor poem would surely be anticlimactic. After all Statius is writing a poem too, not a month-by-month account of Lucan's poetic career. Rose's argument is somewhat undercut by his own suggestion that neither the *De Incendio Urbis* nor the *Adlocutio* were published poems.

14. *Ann.* 15.49.

in a vain effort to save his own life, would have made any pretense
of high principle on his part shabby and hypocritical in the eyes
of a judge as harsh as Tacitus. And Tacitus clearly believed that
Lucan did accuse his mother.[15] Whether the rumor is true or not
is, at this stage, irrelevant. That Tacitus thought it was true meant
he could not take Lucan's political ideals seriously.

Suetonius shares Tacitus' unfavorable attitude to Lucan. Although both writers have little good to say about Nero, they are
hardly less damning in their treatment of his poet. They regard
the quarrel between Lucan and Nero as a literary feud. Suetonius
is more extreme in this instance than Tacitus. His whole portrait
of Nero is founded upon his caricature of the emperor as the insane and jealous artist. In his account of Nero's murder of Britannicus, for instance, Suetonius insists that Nero killed the young
prince *no less* because of envy of his superior voice than through
fear of his popular appeal.[16] Although Nero may indeed have been
envious of Britannicus' musical abilities, we should surely hesitate
before believing that this motivated Nero as much as the potential
threat Britannicus posed to his security as emperor.

Similarly, in his *Life of Lucan,* Suetonius sarcastically suggests
that Lucan accused his mother of complicity in the Pisonian plot
in order to regain Nero's affections: "sperans impietatem sibi apud
parricidam principem profuturam." Although Lucan may very
well have accused his mother, the idea that his reasoning was:
"You're a parricide; look, I'm trying to be a parricide too" is absurd. Yet again, Suetonius says that Lucan manifested hostility
toward Nero *to such an extent that (adeo ut)* he quoted a half-line
of Nero's poetry while thunderously relieving himself in a public
latrine.[17]

Writers who, like Suetonius or Tacitus, are ill-disposed toward
Lucan, have a fondness for attributing absurd, personal motives to
both emperor and poet. If there existed only Tacitus' and Suetonius' accounts of Lucan, and no extant work, there would be
no reason for us to suppose that Lucan wrote an epic that is not
only anti-imperial, but that regarded the fall of the republic as a

---

15. *Ibid.,* 56. Cf. Suetonius *Lucan* 333.11–15.   16. Suetonius *Ner.* 33.
17. Suetonius *Lucan* 332–333.

catastrophe of gigantic dimensions—an unmitigated disaster whose consequences surpassed those of Cannae.

The apolitical Lucan, however, is not confined to Tacitus and Suetonius. If critics hostile to Lucan have gone to some pains to belittle his political ideals and significance, so have his friends. While Suetonius revels in the interchange of hostilities between Nero and Lucan—and only the petty examples at that—Vacca very carefully omits or glosses over anything Lucan may have said or done that smacks of political action. And Vacca is very favorably disposed toward Lucan. He makes no suggestion that Lucan did anything to offend Nero, other than excel in poetry. On the contrary, the Lucan we see in Vacca is very much the injured innocent. It was Nero's jealousy that brought about the ban, a jealousy which grew over a period of years. Although Vacca tells us that Lucan joined the Pisonian conspiracy, he describes him as the victim of youthful ardor and Piso's trickery: "deceptus a Pisone." [18] Nothing could be more contradictory to what Suetonius says. To Suetonius, Lucan is virtually the standard-bearer of the plot. Needless to say, Vacca says nothing about the incrimination of Acilia. As far as he is concerned, it was Lucan's brilliance as a poet that antagonized Nero, and nothing else.

Although the picture of Lucan we get from Vacca is at odds in many ways with that given by Suetonius, both friend and foe share one point in common: the rivalry between Nero and Lucan was purely literary. Among modern scholars, Rose echoes a similar judgment. Nero's ban, he tells us, should be viewed "in the context of the increasing tensions, in the second half of Nero's reign, between the Stoic circles, led by Seneca, and the less earnest literary group led by Petronius." [19]

Surely Lucan represented a political as well as a literary threat

18. "hoc factum [i.e., the ban] Caesaris iuvenili aestimans animi calore speransque ultionem a coniuratis in caedem Neronis socius adsumptus est, sed parum fauste. Deceptus est enim a Pisone et consularibus aliisque praetura perfunctis inlustribus viris: dum vindictam expetit in mortem inruit" (Vacca *Life* 336.2–7. Cf. Tacitus *Ann.* 15.49).

19. *Rose,* 384. Tension between Stoic and Epicurean literary cliques is hardly an adequate explanation for the ban on Lucan's recitations *and* appearances as an advocate. Besides, Petronius fared no better than Seneca and other Stoics in the aftermath of the Pisonian plot. Nero's literary purge knew no boundaries of philosophical preference.

to Nero. The *Pharsalia* alone indicates this in its outspoken republicanism and hostility toward the Caesars. But Lucan's epic stops short of a direct, frontal attack on Nero himself. If my arguments about the *De Incendio Urbis* are correct, however, this work did not. It would have constituted a tangible political offense which the emperor could scarcely ignore. Moreover, if Nero merely wished to prevent Lucan from receiving applause and credit for his poetry, the second part of the ban would have been unnecessary. Activity in the law courts was, in Rome, a mark of the up-and-coming politician. The severity of Nero's action suggests that he had detected a degree of political hostility on Lucan's part that made it necessary to silence him completely.

We have already seen that there is much to indicate Lucan's political potential at Rome.[20] And even if he was not the virtual standard-bearer (*paene signifer*) of the Pisonian conspiracy, as Suetonius declares, he enjoys a remarkable prominence in the accounts of it that have survived.[21] This prominence was hardly achieved by accident. Lucan clearly moved in, influenced, and was influenced by the inner councils of the senatorial opposition. Statius goes so far as to compare him to an Orpheus who brought the whole of Rome under his spell, particularly the senate and knights (*Silvae* 2.7, 43–47). And the highly political nature of the *Pharsalia*, with its outspoken hostility to Caesarism, surely adds confirmatory testimony. It is not hard to see how Nero could have seen dangerous political potential in him.

IV. The *Pharsalia* and the Ban

It has been inferred from Vacca that the immediate cause of the ban was the publication of three books of the *Pharsalia*, probably the first three.[22] This is unlikely for a number of reasons.

20. See above, Chapter 1, Section IV.
21. Suetonius *Lucan* 333.6–7: "ad extremum paene signifer Pisonianae coniurationis extitit"; cf. Tacitus *Ann.* 15.49. Vacca studiously plays down Lucan's role in the conspiracy (see note 18 above).
22. Some scholars, believing that the political content of *Pharsalia* 1 through 3 is not strong enough to produce such devastating reaction from Nero, have suggested that the three books were other than 1 through 3. See R. Pichon, 270–271, and V. Ussani, "Controversia Lucanea," *RFIC* 29 (1901), 50–58. Brisset, 181–182, and *Rose*, 384, rightly reject this notion, although Rose's argument that "no-one would publish individual books of a historical

Vacca, as we have seen, has no wish to attribute to Lucan any responsibility in causing the ban. He implies, rather, that Nero's artistic jealousy came to a head when Lucan gave an extempore recitation of his *Orpheus* and published the first three books of the *Pharsalia*. Although the *Pharsalia* is the last work mentioned before the ban, Vacca has mentioned it in the same breath with a work that was probably written as early as 60.[23] Clearly Lucan cannot have been banned as early as 60. The earliest possible date for his quaestorship is December 62, and Nero would hardly have banned him from recitations and appearances in the law courts only to elevate him to a quaestorship.[24] Vacca himself assigns Lucan's quaestorship to the happy days of his relationship with Nero, informing us that the troubles did not begin until after the quaestorship was over.[25] On the basis of Vacca's account, the ban cannot have occurred before the end of 63, the earliest possible date for the conclusion of Lucan's quaestorship. Most probably it occurred around a year later.[26] For Vacca, along with Tacitus and Dio, implies that there was little lapse of time between the ban on Lucan and his entry into the Pisonian conspiracy.[27] And there is nothing to suggest that the conspiracy had

epic out of chronological sequence" is far from conclusive. Given a well-structured outline, Lucan could certainly have done so. Further, Rose's argument that 4 through 6 are less anti-Caesarian than 1 through 3 (387) is not at all convincing.

23. On the dating of the *Orpheus*, see *Rose*, 381 and 391–392; cf. O. Schönberger, "Ein Dichter Römischer Freiheit: M. Annaeus Lucanus," in *Lucan*, ed. Rutz, p. 532.

24. For Lucan's quaestorship and augurate see Vacca *Life* 335.14–16 and Suetonius *Lucan* 332.9–11. Rose argues, on the basis of T. Mommsen, *Römisches Staatsrecht*³, Leipzig, 1887, 1.572–574 and 576, that no one, other than members of the imperial family, was advanced to public office more than a year before the legal minimum age of 25 (*Rose*, 394, note 35). This would mean that December 5, A.D. 62 is the earliest probable date for Lucan to have taken office even if we allow for the possibility that a man might become quaestor in his twenty-fifth year, rather than upon passing his twenty-fifth birthday. Schönberger's date of around 60 ("Ein Dichter Römischer Freiheit," 530) is far too early.

25. "Equidem hactenus tempora habuit secunda" (Vacca *Life* 332.11–12).

26. For reasons treated more fully below, it seems preferable to assign the quaestorship to 63 (i.e., beginning in December 62) and the ban to August 64 or thereabouts. See *Rose*, 394, note 35.

27. Vacca *Life* 336 (cited in note 18 above); Tacitus *Ann.* 15.48–49; Dio 62.29.4.

any formal shape before the beginning of 65. Dio, in fact, dates the ban to 65.[28]

If Lucan's quaestorship is dated to 64, then the ban cannot have occurred until December of that year, if the quaestorship was part of Lucan's happy days. But if we date Lucan's quaestorship to 63, then the ban could have taken place during the later months of 64. In any event, we may, with some confidence, date the ban somewhere between July 64 and January 65. Unless we postulate that *Pharsalia* 1 through 3 were published late in 64, then, they cannot have been the immediate cause of the ban. And the only reason for dating their publication so late is Vacca's mention of them immediately before the ban. Since, as we have noted, Vacca sees the *Pharsalia* as only one in a series of literary events over a few years which fed Nero's envy, there is no need to presume that Vacca believed the ban was a direct and immediate consequence of the appearance of *Pharsalia* 1 through 3. Rather he is informing us that these were the only books of the epic to appear before the ban.

Vacca does not mention the *De Incendio Urbis* as part of the chain of events leading up to the breach between Lucan and Nero. This omission probably arises from Vacca's intent to maintain a consistent picture of an innocent Lucan who fell victim to a jealous emperor. It is quite likely he left out the *De Incendio Urbis* to protect Lucan's name, just as he omits the poet's incrimination of Acilia and sees him as a victim of Piso's treachery. But what Vacca omits stands out all too clearly in the *Life of Lucan* written by Suetonius.

V. The *De Incendio Urbis* and the *Carmen Famosum*

Curiously, the Suetonian *Life of Lucan* makes no specific mention of a ban, despite the fact that our other sources do. But

28. Dio, 62.29.4. Dio has a tendency to compress events somewhat, and, given Tacitus' lack of precision, he may be trying to clarify something he found unclear in his sources. Tacitus is explicit in the matter of the inception of the conspiracy, however: "ineunt deinde consulatum Silius Nerva et Atticus Vestinus, coepta simul et aucta coniuratione" (*Ann.* 15.48); cf. *Rose*, 385 and note 19. Despite Tacitus' claim that the secrecy of the conspiracy was not well kept, it is remarkable how little we know about what happened; see my discussion "Lucan's *De Incendio Urbis, Epistulae ex Campania* and Nero's Ban," *TAPA* 102 (1971), 22–24.

Suetonius does tells us that Nero, on one occasion, summoned a meeting of the senate in the midst of one of Lucan's recitations— an act that, no doubt, would have obliged Lucan to terminate his reading forthwith.[29] Not only would Nero have departed, but probably Lucan would also have had to leave, since he was a member of the senate. After this, Suetonius tells us, there was a period in which Lucan attacked Nero quite openly, both verbally and by means of provocative actions.[30]

What work could Lucan have been reciting on this occasion that led Nero to such an outburst of fury? Hardly the *Medea,* which was incomplete, or the *Catachthonion, Orpheus,* or *Laudes Neronianae,* which seem to have been early and completely innocuous. He wrote ten books of *Silvae,* but there is no evidence that *Silvae* were ever recited publicly. Statius, in his preface to *Silvae* 4, implies that his occasional poems were given to those in whose honor they were written and published afterwards. But he makes no suggestion that they were ever recited.[31] Much the same is true of the *Epigrammata* (if that is what they were). The *Epistulae ex Campania* would not be a very likely choice, since we would infer that they were written to a person or persons while Lucan was in Campania. If Rose is right, the *Saturnalia* and *Salticae Fabulae* were probably rather early works.[32] That leaves us with the *De Incendio Urbis,* the *Adlocutio ad Pollam,* and the *Pharsalia*—unless, of course, the work concerned is among those of which we now have no record.

If Suetonius is being truthful, and Nero's only reason for walking out was a desire to "put a freeze on" Lucan's recitation, the *De Incendio Urbis* is hardly a likely candidate. The chances that the *Adlocutio ad Pollam* was read publicly are also slim. Its very title suggests something informal and personal, and there is no reason to believe that such poems were ever recited publicly. To

29. "Si quidem aegre ferens quod Nero se recitante subito ac nulla nisi refrigerandi sui causa indicto senatu recessisset" (Suetonius *Lucan* 332.11–13).

30. "Neque verbis adversum principem neque factis excitantibus post haec temperavit" (*ibid.,* 332–333).

31. Statius, in his letter to Marcellus prefacing *Silvae* 4 tells Marcellus that he had *given* many of his poems to Domitian prior to publication: "multa ex illis iam domino Caesari dederam, et quanto hoc plus est quam edere?"

32. *Rose,* 393.

judge from Juvenal, the works most likely to be read in public were epic and tragedy. Unless, then, Lucan was reciting a work now lost to memory, the most probable answer to our original query is the *Pharsalia.*

Since the *Pharsalia,* was, doubtless, regarded by Lucan as his most important work, his fury at Nero's departure would be quite comprehensible. But, looking at the epic, we can see that Nero might have had some reason for walking out. After all, he himself was a poet and would have been considerably more sensitive to innuendo than someone like Suetonius, whose attitude to Lucan's poetry is somewhat cavalier. In other words, Nero might have detected some note of sarcasm in the *Pharsalia* that offended him. This could indeed have been the moment when the relationship between poet and emperor soured. What books of the *Pharsalia* were involved, we can only guess. It could have been a reading from any of books 1 through 6, though 1 through 3 are the most obvious candidates, especially if what offended Nero was not clear to Suetonius.

After this, Lucan turned against Nero. Then, says Suetonius, he wrote a *carmen famosum,* a libelous poem in which he brought serious charges against the emperor and his most powerful friends.[33] This is the only work Suetonius mentions before Lucan joined the conspiracy. There is no word of a ban and no suggestion that Nero's reaction to the recitation was the equivalent of a ban. More oddly still, the *carmen famosum* is one of only three works mentioned by Suetonius. The others are the *Laudes Neronianae* and the *Pharsalia.* Further, Suetonius is our only source of information for the *carmen famosum,* and the only other work we know of whose contents suggest an outright and personal attack on Nero is the *De Incendio Urbis.*

What could the *carmen famosum* have been about? If the charges were of a very serious nature, as Suetonius' *gravissime proscidit* suggests, the chances are that the content was either a particularly nasty lampoon on Nero's sexual profligacy or offensive political slander. The possibility of a lampoon on the emperor's sex life is less attractive for several reasons. The most important

33. "Sed et famoso carmine cum ipsum tum potentissimos amicorum gravissime proscidit" (*ibid.,* 5–6).

is that Nero, as even Suetonius admits, in *Nero* 39, was indifferent to most ordinary libelous verse. Even references to the murders of his father, mother, and brother were passed off lightly. If Nero was to be hurt, he had to be really crushed.

Since the *carmen famosum* is associated with events immediately preceding Lucan's involvement in the Pisonian conspiracy, it probably belongs to the latter part of A.D. 64, and there was no subject about which Nero would have been more sensitive at this time than the fire of Rome. In short, there is the possibility that the *carmen famosum* is one and the same with the *De Incendio Urbis*. What more severe charge could Lucan bring against Nero and his friends than that they wilfully burned Rome?

Against this hypothesis we can throw one major objection: that Suetonius gives not the slightest hint as to the specific content of the libel. If Lucan had accused Nero of burning Rome, why does Suetonius not tell us that he did so? There is an obvious response: to suggest any such thing would elevate Lucan from the level of third-rate literary idiocy to which Suetonius consigns him. It would make Lucan cut an altogether more significant political figure than Suetonius wants to portray.

Indeed, Lucan appears in Suetonius as an altogether sorry figure, an arrogant and petulant fool whose poetry is poor and whose behavior is infantile. Suetonius' extreme example of Lucan's hostility to Nero is the notorious tale of the quotation in the latrine; his part in the conspiracy is reduced to an idiotic scampering around, promising Nero's head to all and sundry. To credit Lucan with an open denunciation of Nero and the fire, or to admit that Nero thought him dangerous enough to suppress, would be inconsistent with the picture Suetonius wants to portray. He, no less than Vacca, has his reasons for withholding information.[34] Since

---

34. For an interesting study of the differences between the accounts of Vacca and Suetonius, see G. K. Gresseth, "The Quarrel between Lucan and Nero," *CP* 52 (1957), 24–27. Gresseth rightly concludes that there is good reason for questioning Vacca's reliability as an authority, at least on matters of precise chronology, for it is dangerous to read Vacca as if he were intending to be precise. If we were to do the same with Suetonius, we might be tempted to conclude that the *Pharsalia* was written before Lucan's recall from Greece and before his quaestorship (*Lucan* 332.1–11). But surely this is not what Suetonius means.

he omits all mention of the ban, it is scarcely surprising that he glosses over the work that probably caused it.

Thus, although we cannot prove that the *carmen famosum* of Suetonius was the *De Incendio Urbis*, we should, I think, consider the possibility that they are one and the same. After all, the *De Incendio Urbis* was a *carmen famosum* in the most extreme sense.

VI. Chronology of the *Pharsalia:* A Hypothesis

If we piece together our conclusions into a tentative hypothesis, perhaps the overall picture of what happened in the middle of 64 may emerge a little more clearly. Lucan gave a recitation of some book(s) of the *Pharsalia* at some point in 63 or 64, certainly no later than July 64. Nero, taking umbrage at something in the epic, called a meeting of the senate, forcing Lucan to terminate his recitation. Lucan retaliated with outright hostility which culminated, after the fire of Rome, with the publication of *De Incendio Urbis*. Nero replied, probably with some speed, by banning Lucan from further recitations of his poetry and from taking an active part in the law courts. If this is the case, the ban probably took effect not much later than August 64.

If I am right, then Lucan's quaestorship probably belongs to 63 rather than 64, since it seems unlikely that Nero would have banned him during his quaestorship, and since Vacca states quite positively that everything went well until after the quaestorship. Further, the immediate cause for the ban was not the *Pharsalia,* though it no doubt contributed, but the *De Incendio Urbis.* The most obvious advantage of this approach is that it avoids the problems attendant upon the kind of compressed chronology of Lucan's final months proposed by Rose. If Rose is correct, the years 64–65 would have been very busy indeed for Lucan. During this time he would have composed all ten books of the *Pharsalia,* the *Medea,* the *Epistulae ex Campania,* the *Adlocutio ad Pollam,* and the *De Incendio Urbis,* in addition to holding a quaestorship, complete with gladiatorial games, quarreling with Nero, and joining Piso's plot. This telescoping of Lucan's activities is, to my mind, unreasonable, no matter how highly we rate the poet's strength of will and sheer energy. And it is unnecessary.

The *Pharsalia* probably started to take shape no later than 63, during Lucan's quaestorship. Books 1 through 3 were, perhaps, published before the middle of 64, by which time work on 4 through 6 was already advanced. Books 4 through 6 may, in fact, have been ready for publication before August, but hindered by the ban. The unusually gloomy, yet explosive nature of 7 may well reflect, as we have argued earlier, Lucan's initial reaction to the ban.[35] In 8, Lucan has recovered his poise somewhat. The abnormal length of 9 and the unfinished state of 10 may suggest that Lucan was composing more hurriedly than usual, without taking time to revise, possibly in the hope that the work might be complete at the time of Nero's assassination.[36] Lucan's greater confidence in 9 and 10 probably reflects his entry into the Pisonian conspiracy. Briefly, then, my suggestion is that 1 through 6 were written before the ban in August 64 or thereabouts, and that 7 through 10 were written afterwards. Thus Lucan spent some nine months on 7 through 10; and 9 and 10 needed revision. We can hardly postulate less than a year, more probably two years, for 1 through 6. In other words, Lucan began the *Pharsalia* in late 62 or early 63. What we see adds up to between two and three years' work, if his rate of composition was relatively uniform. This is a remarkably short time in which to write an epic, considering that Vergil spent eleven years on the *Aeneid* and Statius twelve on the *Thebaid,* but certainly within the bounds of possibility.

35. See Chapter 1, Section IV; Chapter 9, Section I.
36. Cf. Rose's comments on 388–389, with which I am essentially in agreement. I do not, however, accept the notion that 9.949 or 9.999 was the intended conclusion of that Book. I rather suspect that Lucan would have whittled down his snake saga somewhat.

Selected Bibliography

Ackermann, R. *Lucans Pharsalia in den Dichtungen Shelleys.* Zwei-brucken, 1896.

Adcock, F. E. *Caesar as a Man of Letters.* Cambridge, 1956.

Afzelius, A. "Die politische Bedeutung des jüngeren Catos." *CM* 4 (1941), 100–203.

Ahl, F. M. "Lucan's *De Incendio Urbis, Epistulae ex Campania* and Nero's Ban." *TAPA* 102 (1971), 1–27.

———. Review of Vessey's *Statius and the Thebaid. PQ* 53.1 (1974), 141–144.

von Albrecht, M. *Silius Italicus.* Amsterdam, 1964.

———. "Der Dichter Lucan und die Epische Tradition." *FH* 15.269–301.

Alexander, W. M. "Cato of Utica in the Works of Seneca Philoso-phus." *TRSC* 3 Ser. 40 (1946), 59–74.

Anderson, A. R. "Hercules and His Successors." *HSCP* 39 (1928), 31–37.

Anderson, W. S. "Hercules Exclusus: Propertius IV, 9." *AJP* 85 (1964), 1–12.

Armstrong, R. D. "Roman Epic." *Arion* 7.3 (1968), 448–453.

von Arnim, J. *Stoicorum Veterum Fragmenta.* 4 vols., Leipzig, 1903.

Arnold, E. V. *Roman Stoicism.* Cambridge, 1911.

Arredondo, F. "Un Episodio de magia negra en Lucano." *Helmantica* 3 (1952), 347–362.

Aumont, J. "Cato en Libye." *REA* 70 (1968), 304–320.

Aymard, J. *Quelques Séries de comparaisons chez Lucain.* Montpellier, 1951.

Babbitt, F. C. *Plutarch's Moralia.* vol. 4. Loeb Classical Library. Lon-don, 1936.

Badian, E. "Alexander the Great and the Unity of Mankind." *Historia* 7 (1958), 425–444.

Bagnani, G. *Arbiter of Elegance.* Toronto, 1954.

Barrow, R. H. *Plutarch and His Times*. Bloomington, 1969.

Basore, J. W. *Seneca, Moral Essays*. 3 vols., London, 1928.

Bassett, E. "Regulus and the Serpent in the *Punica*." *CP* 50 (1955), 1–20.

———. "Hercules and the Hero of the *Punica*." In *The Classical Tradition: Literary and Historical Studies in Honor of Harry Caplan*, ed. L. Wallach, Ithaca, 1966, 258–273.

Bastet, F. L. "Lucain et les Arts." *FH* 15.121–147.

Bayet, J. *Les origines de l' Hercule Romain*. Paris, 1926.

———. "Le Suicide mutuel dans la mentalité des romains." *L' Année Sociologique* (ser. 3) 1951, Paris, 1953, 70–88.

Beaujeu, J. *L' Incendie de Rome en 64 et les Chrétiens*. Collection Latomus 49. Brussels, 1960.

Becher, I. *Das Bild der Kleopatra in der Griechischen und Lateinischen Literatur*. Berlin, 1966.

Bellen, H. "Adventus Dei." *RhM* 106 (1963), 23–30.

Bevan, E. *Stoics and Sceptics*. Oxford, 1913.

Bilinski, B. "De Lucano Troiae periegeta observationes." *Eos* 42 (1947), 90–121.

Booth, A. "Venus on the *Ara Pacis*." *Latomus* 25 (1966), 873–879.

Brisset, J. *Les Idées politiques de Lucain*. Paris, 1964.

Bruère, R. T. "The Scope of Lucan's Historical Epic." *CP* 45 (1950), 217–235.

———. "Palaepharsalus, Pharsalus, Pharsalia." *CP* 46 (1951), 111–115.

Buchheit, V. "Lucans *Pharsalia* und die Frage der Nichtvollendung." *RhM* 104 (1961), 362–365.

Burck, E. "Drei Grundwerte der römischen Lebensorndung (labor, moderatio, pietas)." *Gymnasium* 58 (1951), 174–183.

———. "Vom Menschenbild in Lucans *Pharsalia*," In *Lucan*, ed. Rutz, 149–159 (modified from "Das Menschenbild im römischen Epos." in *Gymnasium* 65 [1958], 139–145).

Butler, H. E., and E. A. Barber. *The Elegies of Propertius*. Oxford, 1933.

Cancik, H. *Untersuchungen zur Lyrischen Kunst des P. Papinius Statius (Spudasmata 13)*. Hildesheim, 1965.

———. "Ein Traum des Pompeius." In *Lucan*, ed. Rutz, 546–552.

Canter, H. "Fortuna in Latin Poetry." *SP* 19 (1922), 64–82.

Caspari, F. "De Ratione quae inter Lucanum et Vergilium Intercedat." Diss. Leipzig, 1908–1909.

Castresana Udaeta, R. *Historia y Política en la Farsalia de Marco Anneo Lucano*. Madrid, 1956.

Cazzaniga, I. *Problemi intorno alla Farsaglia*. Milan, 1955.

——. "L' Episodio dei serpi libici in Lucano e la tradizione dei 'Theriaka' Nicandrei." *Acme* 10 (1957), 27–41.

Charles-Picard, G. *Augustus and Nero*. Trans. Len Ortzen. New York, 1968.

Charlesworth, M. P. "The Fear of the Orient in the Roman Empire." *CHJ* 2 (1926), 1–16.

Commager, S. *The Odes of Horace*. New Haven, 1962.

Conte, G.-B. "Il Proemio della *Pharsalia*." *Maia* 18 (1966) 42–53 (Also in *Lucan*, ed. Rutz, 339–353).

Denniston, J. D. *Euripides' Electra*. Ed. with introduction and commentary. Oxford, 1939.

Dick, B. "The Role of Manticism in Lucan's Epic Technique." Diss. New York (Fordham), 1962.

——. "The Technique of Prophecy in Lucan." *TAPA* 94 (1964), 37–49.

——. "The Role of the Oracle in Lucan's *De Bello Civili*." *Hermes* 93 (1965), 460–466.

——. "Fatum and Fortuna in Lucan's *Bellum Civile*." *CP* 62 (1967), 235–242.

Dilke, O. A. W. *Statius: Achilleid*. Cambridge, 1954.

——. *Lucan, De Bello Civile VII*. Cambridge, 1960.

Dill, S. *Roman Society in the Last Century of the Western Empire*. 2d rev. ed. New York, 1960.

Dubourdieu, H. "Le Passage du Rubicon d'après Suétone, César et Lucain." *IL* 3 (1951), 122–126; 162–165.

Due, O.S. "An Essay on Lucan." *CM* 22 (1962), 68–132.

——. "Lucain et la Philosophie." *FH* 15.203–232.

Duff, J. D., ed. *Lucan*. Loeb Classical Library. London, 1928.

Dutoit, E. "Le Thème de 'la force qui se détruit elle-même' et ses variations chez quelques auteurs latins." *REL* 14 (1936), 365–373.

Dyson, S. "Caepio, Tacitus and Lucan's Grove." *CP* 65 (1970), 36–38.

Earl, D. *The Political Thought of Sallust*. Cambridge, 1961.

Eckhardt, L. "Exkurse und Ekphraseis bei Lucan." Diss. Heidelberg, 1936.

Edmunds, L. "The Religiosity of Alexander." *GRBS* 12 (1971), 379–386.

Eitrem, S. "La magie comme motif litteraire chez les grecs et les romains." *SO* 21 (1941), 39–83.

Ercole, P. "Stazio e Giovenale." *RIGI* 25 (1931), 43–50.

Ericsson, H. "Sulla Felix." *Eranos* 41 (1943), 77–89.

Farnell, L. *Greek Hero Cults and the Ideas of Immortality.* Oxford, 1921.

Fischli, W. *Studien zum Fortleben der Pharsalia des M. Annaeus Lucanus.* Lucerne, 1943.

Floratos, C. ʽΗ Προφήτεια τοῦ *P. Nigidius Figulus.* Athens, 1958.

Flume, H. "Die Einheit der Künsterlischen Personlichkeit Lucans." Diss. Bonn, 1950 (pp. 33–39 are reproduced in *Lucan,* ed. Rutz, pp. 354–359).

Fowler, W. W. *The Religious Experience of the Roman People, from the Earliest Times to the Age of Augustus.* London, 1911.

——. *Roman Ideas of Deity in the Last Century before the Christian Era.* London, 1914.

Fraenkel, E. *Horace.* Oxford, 1957.

Friedländer, P. "Das Gedicht des Statius an den Schlaf." *Antike* 8 (1932), 215–228.

Friedrich, W.-H. "Cato, Caesar und Fortuna bei Lucan." *Hermes* 73 (1938), 391–423.

——. "Caesar und sein Glück." In *Thesaurismata* (Festschrift für Ida Kapp) Munich, 1954, 1–24.

Gagliardi, D. *Lucano Poeta della Libertà.* Naples, 1958.

Galinsky, G. K. "The Hercules-Cacus Episode in *Aeneid* VIII." *AJP* 87 (1966), 18–51.

——. "*Aeneid* V and the *Aeneid.*" *AJP* 89 (1968), 157–185.

——. *Aeneas, Sicily and Rome.* Princeton, 1969.

Getty, R. J. M. *Annaei Lucani De Bello Civili Liber I.* Cambridge, 1940.

——. "The Astrology of P. Nigidius Figulus." *CQ* 35 (1941), 17–22.

——. "Neo-Pythagoreanism and Mathematical Symmetry in Lucan, *De Bello Civili* I." *TAPA* 91 (1960), 310–323.

Gitti, A. "Alessandro Magno e il responso de Ammone." *RSI* 64 (1952), 531–547.

Gould, J. "Reason in Seneca." *JHP* 3 (1965), 13–25.

Graves, R., trans. *Pharsalia, Dramatic Episodes of the Civil Wars.* Baltimore, 1957.

Grenade, P. "Le Mythe de Pompée et les Pompéiens sous les Césars." *REA* 52 (1950), 28–63.

Gresseth, G. K. "The Quarrel between Lucan and Nero." *CP* 52 (1957), 24–27.

Grillone, A. *Il Sogno nell' Epica latina.* Palermo, 1967.

Grimal, P. "L'Episode d'Antée dans la *Pharsale.*" *Latomus* 8 (1949), 55–61.

——. "L'Eloge de Néron au début de la *Pharsale*, est-il ironique?" *REL* 38 (1960), 296–305 (also in *Lucan*, ed. Rutz, 326–338).

——. "Le Poète et l'histoire." *FH* 15.53–117.

Griset, E. "Lucanea." *RSC* 3 (1955), 134–138.

——. "Lucanea VI: L'Invettiva." *RSC* 4 (1956), 28–33.

Guillemin, A. "L'Inspiration virgilienne dans la *Pharsale*." *REL* 29 (1951), 214–227.

Gundolf, F. *Caesar, Geschichte seines Ruhms*. Berlin, 1924 (32–36 in *Lucan*, ed. Rutz, 10–14).

Haffter, M. H. "Dem Schwanken Zünglein lauschend Wachte Cäsar dort." *MH* 14 (1957), 118–126.

Haskins, C. E., ed. *M. Annaei Lucani Pharsalia*. Introduction by W. E. Heitland. London, 1887.

Henderson, B. *The Life and Principate of the Emperor Nero*. London, 1903.

Herington, C. J. "Senecan Tragedy." *Arion* 5.4 (1966), 422–471.

Herrman, L. "Le Prodige du Rubicon." *REA* 37 (1935), 435–437.

Heyke, W. "Zur Rolle der Pietas bei Lucan." Diss. Heidelberg, 1970.

Hohl, E. "Caesar am Rubico." *MH* 80 (1952), 246–249.

Holliday, V. *Pompey in Cicero's Correspondence and Lucan's Civil War*. The Hague/Paris, 1969.

Holmes, T. R. *The Roman Republic and the Founder of the Empire*. 3 vols., Oxford, 1923.

Hosius, C. "Lucan und seine Quellen." *RhM*, N.F. 48 (1893), 380–397.

——. *M. Annaei Lucani Belli Civilis.*³ Leipzig, 1913.

Housman, A. E. *M. Annaei Lucani Belli Civilis Libri Decem*. Oxford, 1927.

Hübner, W. *Dirae im Römischen Epos*. Hildesheim, 1970.

Jal, P. "La Propagande religieuse à Rome." *Ant. Class.* 30 (1961), 395–414.

——. "Bellum civile . . . bellum externum dans la Rome de la fin de la République." *LEC* 30 (1962), 257–267.

——. "Les Dieux et les guerres civiles." *REL* 40 (1962), 170–200.

——. *La Guerre civile à Rome*. Paris, 1963.

Jansen, J. *Suetonii Tranquilli Vita Domitiani*. Groningen, 1919.

Jones, F. L., ed. *P. B. Shelley, Letters*. Oxford, 1964.

König, F. "Mensch und Welt bei Lucan im Spiegel Bildhafter Darstellung." Diss. Kiel, 1957.

Kopp, A. "Staatsdenken und Politisches Handeln bei Seneca und Lucan." Diss. Heidelberg, 1969.

Lacey, W. K. "The Tribunate of Curio." *Historia* 10 (1961), 318–329.

Larsen, J. "Alexander at the Oracle of Ammon." *CP* 27 (1932), 70–75.

Latte, K. *Römische Religionsgeschichte*. Munich, 1960.

Lawall, G. "Jason as Anti-Hero." *YClS* 19 (1966), 119–169.

Le Bonniec, H. "Lucain et la religion." *FH* 15. 161–195.

Levi, M. A. *Nerone e i suoi Tempi*. Milan, 1949.

——. "Il Prologo della 'Pharsalia'." *RFC* N.S. 27 (1949), 71–78.

Lewis, C. S. "Dante's Statius." *Medium Aevum* 25 (1957), 133–139 (also in *Studies in Medieval and Renaissance Literature*. Cambridge, 1966, 94–102).

Liegle, J. "Pietas." *Zeitschrift für Numismatik* 42 (1935), 59–100.

Linn, H.-W. "Studien zur Aemulatio des Lucan." Diss. Hamburg, 1971.

Lintott, A. W. "Lucan and the History of the Civil War." *CQ* 21 (1971), 488–505.

Littlewood, R. A. "The Symbolism of the Apple in Greek and Roman Literature," *HSCP* 72 (1968), 147–181.

Longi, E. "Tre Episodi del Poema di Lucano." *Studi in Onore di Gino Funaioli*. Rome, 1955. Pp. 181–188.

Lucas, F. L. "The Battlefield of Pharsalos." *ABSA* 24 (1919–1921), 34–53.

Lugli, G. "La Roma di Domiziano nei versi di Marziale e di Stazio." *SR* 9 (1961), 1–17.

MacKay, L. A. "The Vocabulary of Fear in Latin Epic Poetry." *TAPA* 92 (1961), 308–316.

McCloskey, P. and Phinney, E. "Ptolemaeus Tyrannus: The Typification of Nero in the *Pharsalia*." *Hermes* 96 (1968), 80–87.

McGann, M. J. "The Authenticity of Lucan Fr. 12 (Morel)." *CQ* 7 N.S. (1957), 126–128.

——. "Lucan's De Incendio Urbis, Prose or Verse?" *RFIC* 99 (1971) 63–65.

Malcovati, E. M. *Annaeo Lucano*. Milan, 1940.

——. *Lucano*. Brescia, 1947.

——. "Lucano e Cicerone." *Athenaeum* 31 N.S. (1953), 288–297.

Marti, B. "The Meaning of the *Pharsalia*." *AJP* 66 (1945), 352–376.

——. Review of H.-P. Syndikus, *AJP* 82 (1961), 327–329.

——. "Cassius Scaeva and Lucan's Inventio." In *The Classical Tradition: Literary and Historical Studies in Honor of Harry Caplan*, ed. L. Wallach, Ithaca, 1966, 239–257.

——. "La Structure de la *Pharsale*." *FH* 15.1–50.

——. *Arnulfi Aurelianensis Glosule super Lucanum*. Papers and Monographs of the American Academy at Rome, no. 18. Rome, 1958.

Martin, G. "Golden Apples and Golden Boughs." In *Studies Presented to David Moore Robinson:* ed. G. Mylonas and D. Raymond, St. Louis, 1953, 2.1191–1197.

Marx, F. "M. Annaeus Lucanus." *RE* 1,2226–2236.

Meissner, R., ed. *Rómveriasaga.* Berlin, 1910.

Menz, W. "Caesar und Pompeius im Epos Lucans." Diss. Berlin, 1952 (49–65 and 168–170 reproduced in *Lucan,* ed. Rutz, 360–379).

Metger, W. "Kampf und Tod in Lucans *Pharsalia.*" Diss. Kiel, 1957 (48–63 in *Lucan,* ed. Rutz, 423–438).

Milosz, C. *The Captive Mind.* New York, 1953.

Mommsen, T. *Römisches Staatsrecht.*³ Leipzig, 1887.

Morford, M. *The Poet Lucan.* Oxford, 1967.

Mozley, J. H. *Statius.* 2 vols. Loeb Classical Library. London, 1928.

Nehrkorn, H. "Die Darstellung und Funktion der Nebencharaktere in Lucans *Bellum Civile.*" Diss. Baltimore, 1960.

Nisard, D. *Etudes sur les poètes latines de la décadence.*² Paris, 1849.

Nock, A. D. "The Proem of Lucan." *CR* 40 (1926), 17–18.

———. *Sallustius: Concerning the Gods and the Universe.* Cambridge, 1926.

Norden, E., ed. *Publius Vergilius Maro, Aeneis, Buch VI.*² Leipzig, 1916.

Ogilvie, R. M. *A Commentary on Livy, Books I–V.* Oxford, 1965.

Opelt, I. "Die Seeschlacht von Massilia bei Lucan." *Hermes* 85 (1957), 435–445.

Paoletti, L. "Lucano Magico e Vergilio." *AeR* 8 (1963), 11–26.

Paratore, E. *Dante e Lucano.* Turin, 1962.

Parke, H. W. and Wormell, D. E. *The Delphic Oracle.*² 2 vols. Oxford, 1956.

Pavan, M. "L' Ideale politico di Lucano." *AIV* 113 (1954–1955), 209–222 (also in *Lucan,* ed. Rutz, 409–422).

Pfligersdorffer, G. "Lucan als Dichter des Geistigen Widerstandes." *Hermes* 87 (1959), 344–377.

Phillips, O. "Lucan's Grove." *CP* 63 (1968), 296–300.

Piacentini, U. *Osservazioni sulla tecnica epica di Lucano.* Berlin, 1963.

Pichon, R. *Les Sources de Lucain.* Paris, 1912.

Pohlenz, M. *Freedom in Greek Life and Thought.* trans. C. Lofmark. New York, 1966.

Pöschl, V. *Die Dichtkunst Virgils.* Innsbruck, 1950.

Postgate, J. P. *M. Annaei Lucani Liber VII.* Cambridge, 1917.

———. "The Site of the Battle of Pharsalia." *JRS* 12 (1922), 187–191.

Pucci, P. "Euripides Heautontimoroumenos." *TAPA* 98 (1967), 365–371.

Putnam, M. C. J. *The Poetry of the Aeneid.* Cambridge, Mass., 1965.

Rambaud, M. *L'Art de la déformation historique dans les commentaires de César.* Paris, 1953.

———. "Le soleil de Pharsale." *Historia* 3 (1954–1955), 346–378.

———. "L'Apologie de Pompée par Lucain au livre VII de la *Pharsale*," *REL* 33 (1955), 258–296.

Ramsay, W. *Manual of Roman Antiquities.*[15] London, 1895.

Ribbeck, O. *Tragicorum Romanorum Fragmenta.* Leipzig, 1887.

Rist, J. M. *Stoic Philosophy.* Cambridge, 1969.

Rose, H. J. *The Roman Questions of Plutarch.* Oxford, 1924.

———. "The Dream of Pompey." *Acta Classica* 1 (1958), 80–84 (also in *Lucan,* ed. Rutz, 477–485).

———. *A Handbook of Latin Literature.* New York, 1960.

Rose, K. F. C. "Problems in the Chronology of Lucan's Career." *TAPA* 97 (1966), 379–396.

Rostagni, A. *Svetonio De Poetis e Biografi Minori.* Turin, 1944.

Rowland, R. W. "The Significance of Massilia in Lucan." *Hermes* 97 (1969), 204–208.

Rutz, W. "Studien zur Kompositionskunst und zur Epischen Technik Lucans." Diss. Kiel, 1950 (3–60 in *Lucan,* ed. Rutz, 160–216).

———. "Amor Mortis bei Lucan." *Hermes* 88 (1960), 462–475.

———. "Die Träume des Pompeius in Lucans *Pharsalia.*" *Hermes* 91 (1963), 334–345 (in *Lucan,* ed. Rutz, 504–524).

———. "Lucan 1943–1963." *Lustrum* 9 (1965), 243–340.

———. "Lucan und die Rhetorik." *FH* 15. 233–257.

———, ed. *Lucan (Wege der Forschung 235).* Darmstadt, 1970.

Sambursky, S. *The Physics of the Stoics.* London, 1959.

Sanford, E. M. "Lucan and his Roman Critics." *CP* 26 (1931), 233–257.

———. "The Eastern Question in Lucan's *Bellum Civile.*" In *Studies in Honor of E. K. Rand,* New York, 1938, 255–264.

Sauter, F. *Der Römische Kaiserkult bei Martial und Statius.* Stuttgart, 1934.

Scaliger, J. C. *Poetices Libri Septem.* Lyons, 1561.

Schetter, W. *Untersuchungen zur Epischen Kunst des Statius (Klass. Phil. Stud., 20).* Wiesbaden, 1960.

Schilling, R. *La religion romaine de Vénus depuis les origines jusqu'au temps d'Auguste.* Bibliothèque des Ecoles françaises d'Athènes et de Rome, N. 178. Paris, 1954.

Schnepf, H. "Untersuchungen zur Darstellungskunst Lucans im 8. Buch der *Pharsalia*." Diss. Heidelberg, 1953 (125–151 in *Lucan*, ed. Rutz, 380–406).

Schönberger, O. "Zur Komposition des Lucan." *Hermes* 85 (1957), 251–254 (in *Lucan*, ed. Rutz, 277–282).

———. "Goethe und Lucan." *Gymnasium* 65 (1958), 450–452.

———. "Zu Lucan, Ein Nachtrag." *Hermes* 86 (1958), 230–239 (in *Lucan*, ed. Rutz, 486–497).

———. "Leitmotivisch Wiederholte Bilder bei Lucan." *RhM* N.F. 105 (1960), 81–90 (in *Lucan*, ed. Rutz, 498–508).

———. "Ein Dichter Römischer Freiheit: M. Annaeus Lucanus." *Das Altertum* 10 (1964), 26–40 (in *Lucan*, ed. Rutz, 525–545).

———. *Untersuchungen zur Wiederholungstechnik Lucans*. Munich, 1968.

Schotes, H.-A. "Stoische Physik, Psychologie und Theologie bei Lucan." Diss. Bonn, 1969.

Schrempp, O. "Propheziehung und Rückschau in Lucans *Bellum Civile*." Diss. Winterthur, 1964.

Scott, K. "Statius' Adulation of Domitian." *AJP* 54 (1933), 247–249.

———. *The Imperial Cult under the Flavians*. Stuttgart, 1936.

Scullard, H. H. *From the Gracchi to Nero*.[2] London, 1963.

Stewart, D. J. "Sallust and Fortuna." *History and Theory* 7 (1968), 298–317.

Summers, W. C. *A Study of the Argonautica of Valerius Flaccus*. Cambridge, 1894.

Syme, R. "Caesar, the Senate and Italy." *PBSR* 14 (1938), 1–31.

———. *The Roman Revolution*. Oxford, 1939.

———. *Tacitus*. 2 vols. Oxford, 1963.

———. *Sallust*. Sather Classical Lectures 34. Berkeley, 1964.

Syndikus, H.-P. "Lucans Gedicht vom Bürgerkrieg." Diss. Munich, 1958.

Tarn, W. *Alexander the Great*. Cambridge, 1948.

Taylor, L. R. *Party Politics in the Age of Caesar*. Berkeley, 1949.

Thierfelder, A. "Der Dichter Lucan." *Archiv für Kulturgeschichte* 25 (1935), 1–20.

Thompson, H. J. "Lucan, Statius and Juvenal in the Early Centuries." *CQ* 22 (1928), 24–27.

Thompson, L. "Lucan's Apotheosis of Nero." *CP* 59 (1964), 147–153.

Thompson, L. and Bruère, R. T. "Lucan's Use of Vergilian Reminiscence." *CP* 63 (1968), 1–21.

Tucker, R. "Lucan and the Baroque: A Revival of Interest." *CW* 62 (1969), 295–297.

——. "Lucan and the French Revolution: The *Bellum Civile* as a Political Mirror" *CP* 66 (1971), 6–16.

Tylor, E. B. *Religion in Primitive Culture*.² London, 1873.

Ulrich, T. *Pietas (Pius) als Politischer Begriff im Römischen Staate bis zum Tode des Kaisers Commodus*. Breslau, 1930.

Ussani, V. "Controversia Lucanea." *RFIC* 29 (1901), 50–58.

Vessey, D. *Statius and the Thebaid*. Cambridge, 1973.

Viansino, G. *L. Annaei Senecae De Providentia—De Constantia Sapientis*. Rome, 1968.

Vitelli, C. "Sulla Composizione e Pubblicazione della *Farsaglia*." *SIFC* 8 (1900), 33–72.

Weinreich, O. *Studien zu Martial*. Stuttgart, 1928.

Weinstock, S. "Victor and *Invictus*." *HThR* 50 (1957), 211–247.

Wernicke, K. "Antaios." *RE* 1. 2339–2343.

Wirszubski, C. *Libertas as a Political Idea at Rome during the Late Republic and Early Empire*. Cambridge, 1950.

Wuilleumier, P. and Le Bonniec, H. *M. Annaeus Lucanus: Bellum Civile, Liber Primus*. Paris, 1962.

Wünsch, W. "Das Bild des Cato von Utica in der Literatur der Neronischen Zeit." Diss. Marburg, 1949.

Zeller, E. *The Stoics, Epicureans and Sceptics*. Trans. O. J. Reichel. London, 1880.

General Index

Index of Passages

LUCAN: AN INTRODUCTION

Designed by R. E. Rosenbaum.
Composed by Vail-Ballou Press, Inc.,
in 11 point linotype Baskerville, 2 points leaded,
with display lines in monotype Baskerville.
Printed letterpress from type by Vail-Ballou Press.
Bound by Vail-Ballou Press
in Columbia book cloth
and stamped in All Purpose foil.

Library of Congress Cataloging in Publication Data
(For library cataloging purposes only)

Ahl, Frederick M
    Lucan: an introduction

    (Cornell studies in classical philology; v. 39)
    Bibliography: p.
    1. Lucanus, Marcus Annaeus. Pharsalia.
2. Rome—History—Civil War, 49–48 B.C.
3. Pharsalus, Battle of, 48 B.C.   I. Series:
Cornell University. Cornell studies in classical
philology; v. 39.
PA6480.A4   873'.01   75-16926
ISBN 0-8014-0837-7